The international cocoa trade

ROBIN DAND

John Wiley & Sons, Inc.

New York • Chichester • Weinheim • Brisbane • Singapore • Toronto

Library of Congress Cataloging in Publication Data:
ISBN 0-471-19055-1

Printed in the United States of America

10 9 8 7 6 5 4 3 2 1

Contents

iii

CONTENTS

Preface

O ver the past few years the cocoa market has had to alter its manner of operation. Continued low prices, fewer companies trading and both the perceived and real element of *del credere* risks have brought about the change. Gone are the days when the trader could dodge in and out of deals with a commodity that just so happened to be cocoa. Nowadays the 'CIF-artists' have largely disappeared and those that remain have had to revert to the fundamentals of their business — knowing the needs of their clients and, above all, knowing the commodity. While citing the trader here the same is true of others directly involved in cocoa, the exporter and, final user of the beans, the factory. In the past exporters could rely on dealers sorting out some of their problems for them, likewise the factories off-loaded much of the risk of delivery on to the dealer. Current trading conditions make this more difficult. Therefore all those in the chain of trade, from the exporter, dealer, broker through to the factory not only have to improve their understanding of the market but also some of the difficulties faced by others in the commodity. It is hoped that this book will help all involved in the international trade of cocoa to achieve this.

The requirement of understanding the cocoa trade is not limited to those in the string of buyers and sellers. There are others outside this chain that now have larger roles in cocoa than in the past, in particular the banks, but also the shipping companies and warehousekeepers. Banks need some knowledge of the commodity and its trade practice to assess the risk when either financing companies that trade cocoa, or their involvement in individual transactions concerning cocoa. The increased use of financial derivatives, the futures and options, underline the importance by those lending money in understanding these highly geared instruments and their valuation as well as the underlying commodity and its attendant risks. Likewise developments in the transport of cocoa, bulk shipments for example, and the rise in services offered by warehousekeepers at destinations require a greater knowledge of the commodity by all involved.

The recent expansion of cocoa production from South-East Asia has raised questions over the quality of cocoa. Such concerns are not new; manufacturers were worried over the quality of West African cocoa when it first appeared and continued to worry about it when it represented over 60% of the world production. Such concerns began discussions in the 1930s over how best to assess the quality of cocoa beans – a discussion that rumbled on before the 1930s and continues today. The results of this earlier work laid the foundations for the quality assessment used today, which has not advanced much beyond what was done in the 1950s. The advent of another region entering the market, together with the chocolate consuming public wanting ever higher standards, has once again brought the discussion to the fore.

Working on this book has underlined the importance of earlier writings on cocoa and previous market situations. For example, it was interesting to see that some techniques in the post-harvest processing of cocoa recently propounded were the practice in the early eighteenth century (in fact the assessment of some aspects of cocoa quality has not changed a great deal since then, either). Looking at the past shows that in real terms the international price of cocoa is now at its lowest, certainly since 1854. Principally because they have complete sets of data from 1960 onwards, analysts tend to compare the current position with that occurring in the mid-1960s when there was also a sharp fall in prices. Actually, the current situation may have more in common with conditions at the turn of the century. That period saw the emergence of West Africa as a major cocoa producing area that resulted in a similar decline in prices from the high in 1907 as that experienced since 1977, the all time high in cocoa prices. Expansion in Asian production during the 1980s, which together with the doubling of production by the Côte d'Ivoire (and the recent collapse of consumption in what was the Soviet Union) exacerbated the fall in cocoa prices; producing a similar shaped curve to that from 1907 onwards. The pessimists will note that prices failed to recover fully until after World War II.

While there are other similarities between the two periods, condi-

PREFACE

tions are not the same. The cocoa market is far more sophisticated than it was even ten years ago and despite the low prices it is still the fifth largest food commodity exported from developing countries and the seventh largest food commodity exported in the world.* Trading techniques have developed in tandem with improvements in communications that allow businesses all over the world access to information that was previously hard to obtain. It is hoped that this work will add to this and help some in understanding more about the commodity. Starting with the history of European and North American development of cocoa, the book covers its agronomics and marketing; the actuals and futures markets and their contracts (the details of which form the appendices), together with the supply and demand of the product, its quality and lastly, its processing. In covering these areas, an attempt has been made to keep an eye on the past for the explanation of much that occurs now.

My thanks go to the administrators of those institutions involved in cocoa who have allowed me to reproduce their contract terms: Frederick Dhotel of the Association Française du Commerce des Cacaos; Robin Dauncey of The Cocoa Association of London Ltd and Hans Scheu of the Cocoa Merchants' Association of America Inc. I am also grateful to the London Commodity Exchange and their counterpart, the New York Coffee, Sugar and Cocoa Exchange for allowing the reproduction of their exchanges' rules and regulations.

My thanks also go to those in the cocoa trade with whom I have discussed matters, often at length, over the past year especially: Trevor Johnston, Gerry Manley, Michael Metcalfe and Steve Wateridge of ED&F Man Ltd, and Kees Beemsterboer and Dr E Meursing of ICM, Amsterdam. My thanks to the Economics section of ICCO for pointing me in the right direction on some statistical information and its interpretation, in particular to Navin Mistry and Alan Brewer.

Lastly, but most importantly, I am grateful to ICCO in allowing me to pursue this work and in particular the staff in the Buffer Stock department who have been very patient during this past year. A special thanks goes to Jürgen Plambeck whose comments and analysis on the draft were greatly appreciated and of immense help.

This book represents the views of the author which are not necessarily those of ICCO. The author or publishers cannot be held liable by anyone or anybody for any losses or costs incurred through any action based on or attributed to this book.

Robin Dand

---

* UNCTAD Commodity Yearbook 1991.

1

▨▨ ▨▨ ▨▨

History and origins

The beginning

European discovery of cocoa

W hen Hernan Cortes first set foot on what was to become Mexico, little did he think of one of the lasting effects of his arrival. Out of favour with his king and the local Spanish governor in the West Indies, his main concern must have been that he needed to show success on this venture. Had he known that he would, in some cases literally, be propagating what was to become one of the largest traded food commodities in the world, his actions may have been more muted. However, arriving at a small village (he renamed La Villa Rica de la Vera Cruz) on Good Friday 1519, he gave orders that the small fleet of ships be unloaded and, sometime later, burnt. He and his band of 600 men now had no option but to find their fortune in the area. Apart from the usual trappings of wealth that Cortes found at the Aztec court of Montezuma, he saw that the drinking of a beverage called xocoatl was highly regarded. The Mexican indians considered that the beans from which the xocoatl was made had religious significance.

Myth had it that the tree was brought to man by the god of air, Quetzalcoatl, after man had been driven from the equivalent of the

Garden of Eden. Having helped man, Quetzalcoatl departed, leaving the 'quachahuatl' tree. The Indians therefore included the tree and its fruit in many of their religious ceremonies. Two other reasons why the Indians considered cocoa so highly were, first the taste, and second because the beans that were used to make the beverage were highly prized, rates of exchange of one hundred beans for one slave were recorded amongst central Americans. In 1586 Thomas Candish recorded that 150 beans were the equivalent to a Real of Plate.[1] The fact that Montezuma had some 900 tonnes of dried beans in a store shows the comparative wealth of the Aztec king.

The drink was prepared from dried beans that had been roasted, the shells removed and remaining nib pulverised into a brown, fatty and, to our modern taste, gritty liquid. This was done on a special concave stone called a metate. The brown liquid would have spices added, such as vanilla or pepper, as well as maize. The maize helped to reduce the cost of the xocoatl in addition to making the resulting brew milder. One method included the use of fermented maize, thereby giving the drink alcoholic properties. The resulting mixture was then made into small cakes and placed in a cool place to solidify. When required a cake would be mixed with water, either hot or cold, and beaten with a wooden instrument known as a molinet so that the drink became foamy. Montezuma reportedly drank fifty cups a day of xocoatl, mixed with honey and spices to reduce the bitterness. Before entering his harem he would be presented with a golden chalice of xocoatl, so the presumed aphrodisiac properties of cocoa are first noted.

The beans or 'cacao nuts' came from the cacao tree, not a native of Mexico but to the northern region of South America. Trade routes to this area of South America from Mexico existed and it is presumably by this means that the cocoa moved northwards to the court of Montezuma. Used since at least 1000 BC, the Maya, who also drank cocoa, had set up plantations by AD 600.

Grown under the shade of others in the forest, the cacao tree grows pods that develop out of its branches and trunk. Within each pod there may be up to forty beans covered in mucilage[2] and attached to the placenta. In optimum conditions a mature tree may easily produce more than 50 pods a year. Although the exact process the Aztecs and others followed when they picked the pods is not truly recorded, it is surmised that either the beans were removed from the pods and piled up for a while, or that the pods were kept for a time before being opened. Placing the beans in a pile is, as shall be explained later, an important stage as it

---

1   A small silver coin, circulating in Mexico until 1897 and equivalent to an eighth of a dollar or $6\frac{1}{2}$d circa 1900.

2   A viscous mass or pulp surrounding the beans in the pod.

2

allows the mucilage to ferment. It is this process that produces the precursors of the chocolate flavour in the beans.[3] However, the Aztecs may have fermented the cocoa in order to remove the mucilage as it becomes liquid[4] and runs off and to kill the beans which would otherwise begin to germinate, thereby spoiling their flavour. Once fermented, they dried the beans in the sun, which meant that they could be stored for future use, a practice they also undertook with potatoes. Drying the beans correctly is important because otherwise the beans become mouldy, thereby destroying the delicate chocolate flavour.

Cortes was not the first Spaniard to witness the drinking of xocoatl, or to bring it to the attention of Europe. In 1502 Columbus took some of these beans back to King Ferdinand of Spain. Perhaps Columbus did not discover the proper way of preparing the beans for a drink, or the beans were spoilt during the arduous homeward voyage, but the king was not impressed with this gift and there was no demand for the drink. This changed when Cortes returned to Spain and wrote to Charles I about a 'divine drink' that banished tiredness. The Spanish court accepted the drink, perhaps in part because of the recent discovery of sugar, which greatly enhanced the drink of chocolate.

In 1631 a recipe, supposedly based on Aztec practices, was published in Madrid[5] that consisted of:

> Take seven hundred cacao nuts, a pound and a half white sugar, two ounces of cinnamon, fifteen grains of Mexican pepper called Chile or pimento, half an ounce of cloves, three little straws or vanillas de Campecho or want thereof, as much aniseed as will equal the weight of a shilling, of archiot[6] a small quantity as big as a filabeard, which may be sufficient only to give colour, add thereto almonds, filabeards and the water of orange flowers.

The use of the sugar in the recipe is likely to be a later addition and not an original part of the recipe.

Spain kept the secret of chocolate for some 90 years after its discovery in Mexico. The religious element continued as monks took over the preparation of the cakes from the beans. Drinking chocolate was the preserve of the king, his court and presumably some inquisitive monks. Certainly the use of cocoa was not appreciated by the British during the

---

3 Some early accounts do not refer to this fermentation stage but it would seem probable that some form of fermentation took place.
4 Later plantation owners in the West Indies were to describe it as the 'sweatings'.
5 de Ledesma Colomenero: 'Curioso tratado de la naturaleza y calidad de chocolate', 1631.
6 The seed of the annato tree, *Bixa orellana*.

first part of its progress into Europe. In 1604 Joseph Acosta described it as '...loathsome to some such as are not acquainted with it...' This was confirmed by John Parkinson, Apothecary who wrote '...but to the Christians at first it seemeth a wash fitter for hogs, yet by use even accepted by also in the want of better.'[7] Words were backed up with deeds according to an account written in 1671 by Ogilby, 'When the *English* commander *Thomas Candish* coming into the Haven *Guatulco* burnt two hundred thousand Tun[8] of Cacao, it prov'd no small loss to all *New Spain*, the Provinces *Guatimala* and *Nicaragua* not producing so much in a whole year'.[9] English ships that captured Spanish merchant men would throw overboard sacks of cocoa beans as they had no idea of their use. So things continued, the preparation of the drink not changing very much except for the inclusion of other spices; oranges, nutmeg, cloves, aniseed, almonds and even rose water, to name a few. Still served cold, it would come in a modified version of a coffee pot with an extra hole in the lid to accommodate a molinet to beat the mixture before serving.

At the beginning of the seventeenth century the secret seeped out to the rest of Europe. In 1606 Antonio Carletti took the drink to Italy. In 1609 the first book on cocoa was published in Mexico, *Libro en el cual se trata del chocolate* (Book of treating chocolate). However the seepage became a stream in 1615 when Louis XIII married Anne of Austria. She brought to the court of her husband the secret of chocolate. Like the Spanish court the French began to take to the new taste and the use of the cocoa beans began to spread. In 1648 Thomas Gage published 'A New Survey of the West Indies' in which he records that chocolate drinking was liked by all on the plantations without the inclusion of sugar or spices. Two years later in 1650 the first use of chocolate in England was noted to have taken place in Oxford. By 1657 chocolate, in the form of a drink or the ingredient to make a drink, was on sale in London. At a price of ten to fifteen shillings per pound, it was reserved for those who had a purse to match the price. 1660 saw the marriage of Spain's Princess Maria Theresa to Louis XIV. The marriage further popularised chocolate drinking in Paris. What was the preserve of the Spanish court now became available to anyone with the money.

---

7   Parkinson J: 'Theatrum botanicum', 1640.
8   Tun here must mean a container or barrel. Two hundred thousand tonnes would be a prodigious level of production in the seventeenth century.
9   Ogilby J: 'America, being the latest and most accurate description of the New World', 1671.

Early production

Spanish propagation

During the course of his voyages Cortes did more than carry the dead dried beans with him. He, and others, took seeds and planted them in the course of their travels. In a little over a century from Java to Jamaica the Spanish introduced cocoa as a crop. In 1525 cocoa was taken to Trinidad, 1560 saw the Celebes and Java with cocoa, and by the end of the century Haiti and Fernando Po had also joined the list. Whether by accident or design all the locations used by the Spanish to grow cocoa were islands, the last of which was Jamaica in about 1640.

The type of cocoa grown in Mexico at that time seems to have originated from an area of southern Mexico to Nicaragua. It came to be called Criollo, meaning 'native'. Although of a quality eminently preferred by consumers in terms of flavour, it is a dainty variety of a delicate species. It is particularly susceptible to disease and drought. Although growers probably knew of other varieties the flavour of these other stronger stock was not preferred. The Criollo cocoa was the pre-eminent variety at the time.

The French influence

From about the middle of the seventeenth century the spread of cocoa as a crop fell more to the French. Martinique and St Lucia both had started plantations that provided most of the cocoa consumed in France by the end of the following century. In 1702 the first exports of cocoa from Surinam took place. Planters there grew the cocoa without the benefit of shade trees. Although the trees grow quickly they require larger amounts of nutrients and water. For Surinam the end came in the 1890s when practically all their crop died. This technique of growing has recently re-emerged in Indonesia, although the growers use a different variety and method of propagation (see Chapter 4).

Trinidad

Many of the plantations of cocoa subsequently started elsewhere in the world were based on seeds grown from Trinidad stock. The introduction of the first cocoa to Trinidad from Mexico laid the foundations of much of the development of the crops for the future, the effect of which we still benefit from today. Initially Criollo cocoa was brought in and became well established until 1727 when the whole area of the West Indies was subjected to a 'blast'.

The 'blast'

The French continued to plant cocoa in new areas. In 1714 they introduced cocoa to Grenada from Martinique. However, the expansion of the
cocoa grown in the Caribbean area suffered a major setback. In 1727 a
'blast' destroyed cocoa grown in the area. Interpretations to the meaning
of the blast include hurricanes, drought or a fungal attack. It should be
remembered that most cocoa cultivated at that time was the Criollo
variety, a type naturally susceptible to all manner of diseases and drought,
and therefore all of the interpretations to the 'blast' are valid. The effect on
the West Indian population was dramatic as cocoa was the sole export. In
Trinidad, where cocoa represented the main export, many of the colonists
and their slaves left the island for the mainland; by 1733 the adult male
population, excluding the indigenous Indians, had dwindled to 162.

The disaster of 1727 in the Caribbean was the forerunner to many
similar occurrences where the Criollo cocoa had been introduced from
Mexico, which, up to the middle of the eighteenth century, included most
of the commercial plantations. It is of interest to note that historians
say one plantation (owned by a planter called Rabelo) survived the
'blast'. Tradition had it that he planted the 'inferior' but hardier Forastero
variety. For cocoa this perhaps serves as an early lesson in the perils of
monoculture.

It is also of interest to know why this information survives. Growers
in Trinidad faced paying tithes on their cocoa. Apparently many evaded
the payment by selling their crop in advance (why the administration
could not cope with this is not known) but Rabelo was unable to sell
his cocoa forward, because the buyers considered it an inferior variety.
Consequently the records show he invariably paid the tithe. The interesting point concerns the forward sale of cocoa. These days forward
sales (selling something now for delivery at some time in the future) is
very common. It does not appear to be greatly favoured in the cocoa trade
much before the twentieth century, but in the early eighteenth century
Trinidadian growers seem to have utilised this form of sale.

Recovery

Either Arogonese Capuchin Fathers or the Dutch re-introduced cocoa into
the devastated plantations in Trinidad in 1756. This was a hardier variety
of cocoa from eastern Venezuela, also a Forastero like Rabelo's. These trees
were crossed with the few existing Criollo trees giving a hybrid, hardier
than the Criollo although with an inferior flavour. This hybrid was named
'Trinitario' and, in one form or another, went on to become the basis of

many plantations that needed to be replanted after the 'blast' or other misfortunes.

The trend of replacing the original Criollo variety with hardier Forastero stock occurred throughout the world with only a few exceptions of 'pure' Criollo remaining. (There were, however, some blended versions using existing Criollo stock, as was the case with Java cocoa in 1888.)

Early consumption

Drinking houses

By the middle of the seventeenth century coffee houses were beginning to be opened in England and, within a few years of their only providing chocolate coffee was also on offer. By the end of the century such drinking houses had become popular places for the gentry to meet, talk business or just gossip. The government was quick to impose an excise duty on cocoa; in 1650 that meant chocolate was soon advertised at half a shilling a pint. To help put this price into perspective a foreman would expect to earn about £20 a year. On top of the cost of the drink the house would also charge an entrance fee of one or two pennies per person. Such venues provided the meeting place for like minded people. It was therefore not surprising that some houses became known for their gaming activities (White's in St James Street); others for business (Lloyds in Lombard Street) and some for political discussion (The Cocoa Tree). The latter category caused some concern for Charles II as in 1676 he attempted to close down the drinking houses. He felt that they were fomenting political dissent, a view that failed to be enacted.

The drinking houses helped to set the trend for those who could afford chocolate. As the chocolate houses faded away or became private clubs they had left their former clients still wanting the taste of chocolate. Partly as a result of this, sales of cocoa to be prepared as a breakfast drink continued to grow during the eighteenth century. The other main reason why sales continued to grow in the United Kingdom as well as in the rest of Europe concerned the unfounded claims that chocolate had therapeutic benefits. Sales of chocolate were promoted at the spa towns for those who were there to 'take the waters'. Against the tide of chocolate consumption at this time some medical practitioners sanctioned caution on drinking chocolate. In 1624 Johan Rauch[10] considered chocolate to inflame the

10   Rauch Johan: 'Disputo medico diotetica de aere et esculent de necnon porta', 1624.

passions; Dr Duncan[11] in 1706 although mostly referring to coffee, grouped chocolate, tea and brandy together and maintained that the blood would become too sharp, too hot, too subtle and too thin with excessive chocolate consumption. However, their advice did little to stop the interest in drinking chocolate.

The improvement of the taste of chocolate took time to develop. The addition of sugar to the early Spanish drinking chocolate was the first major step, the second took a little longer to work out – the idea of using milk rather than water to make the chocolate. Confusion exists in the minds of some historians, failing to distinguish between using milk for drinking chocolate and the development of solid milk chocolate. A recipe exists in *The American Physitian*[12] in which;

> ... *then take half Milk, and half Water,* ... *and then make it boil; and when it boileth, put in your Chocolate and bread together, and let it boil a little afterwards; and then sweeten it with sugar, and sup it hot, without frothing. If you please, or if you will you may froth it in your chocolate-Pot with a Molinet, as they do here.*

This shows the use of milk in drinking chocolate in 1672. Sir Hans Sloane, founder of the British Museum, was thought to have invented the use of milk in drinking chocolate, but in 1672 he was twelve years old. What he may have invented was the use of milk in eating chocolate, although at the time this never became a commercial venture.[13] Definitely a man before his time, as solid milk chocolate only became commercially available 200 years later.

Early European manufacturing

In 1728 Joseph Fry opened a chocolate factory in Bristol. Apprenticed to a doctor (and eventually having his own practice) Joseph Fry no doubt had a suitable background to make medicinal chocolate. Realising that there was more opportunity in his manufacturing interests he gave up his medical practice to concentrate on the industrial side of his enterprise. At the forefront of technology Dr Fry incorporated a 'water engine' invented by Walter Churchman, to grind the beans at the factory at Castle Mills. The

11   Duncan (Dr) D: 'Wholesome advice against the abuse of hot liquors particularly of coffee, chocolate, tea, brandy and strong waters', 1706.
12   Hughes William: 'The American physitian of a treatise of the roots, plants and trees growing in English plantations in America including a discourse on the cacao nut tree', 1672.
13   Shephard C Y: 'General history of the production and consumption of cacao', 1932.

family continued to make use of the innovations of the age as in 1795 the factory moved to new premises where power was by a steam engine, made by James Watt. He also used his medicinal background as he advertised his product as something to improve those of a weak constitution and of suffering from 'sharp humours'.

The second half of the eighteenth century saw the establishment of chocolate manufacturing in Europe. Prior to this the grinding of beans had been mostly by hand either in the drinking houses, or those shops selling tea and coffee, or by the apothecaries preparing chocolate for medicinal purposes. Three companies destined to become major chocolate factories in the United Kingdom; Rowntree, Terry, and Cadbury started as shops. Before Joseph Terry joined the partnership of Messrs Bayldon and Berry (confectioners) he too was an apothecary and introduced chocolate to the company. Others who started at about that time included Lombart in France (1760), von de Lippe in Germany (1765) and Rowntree's in England in 1785.

Early American consumption

From about the middle of the eighteenth century seamen based in Massachusetts began to import cocoa beans from the West Indies to their home ports. This was in preference to carrying the cargo to Europe involving a longer and more hazardous voyage. Their buyers in America were the apothecaries. As in Europe, chocolate was considered to have medicinal properties and the apothecaries were ideally equipped with pestle and mortar to grind the beans. So the American drugstore began its involvement with confectionery.

As in Europe, chocolate consumption continued to increase, not specifically for medicinal purposes, but for itself. In 1780 Dr James Baker financed the first water powered cocoa mill in America, operated by John Hanan and located in Dorchester, Mass. By 1790 half a million pounds (just over 225 metric tonnes) of cocoa were imported into the United States, compared to a consumption of 143 metric tonnes in the United Kingdom in 1825.

Cocoa powder

Two important advances in drinking chocolate were capitalised on in 1828, the first of which came to lay the foundations to eating chocolate. By pressing the ground up cocoa nibs (the cocoa liquor) a significant proportion of the fat or cocoa butter could be removed, leaving a residue that could be powdered to make a lighter, less fatty and therefore more palatable drink. The pressed-out fat (cocoa butter) was not considered important until later when confectioners found it of value in making eating chocolate. The second discovery was that the flavour and colour of the cocoa powder could be altered by adding a small amount of alkali during the processing. The flavour characteristics mellowed and some considered, erroneously, that alkalised cocoa had a stronger flavour. Perhaps the change in the colour to a more appealing darker hue led people to think the product more flavoursome. Many also thought that by alkalising the cocoa it became more miscible in water. This is also untrue, although too much alkali will result in saponification of the fat, which means the fat turns into soap which *is* miscible in water, but of course, ruins the taste of chocolate.

Although these discoveries made in 1828 are now attributed to CJ van Houten of the Netherlands, there is some evidence to show that a process involving the pressing of cocoa liquor was being performed in France during the last half of the eighteenth century.[14] In addition, in 1789 the use of alkali in the preparation of drinking chocolate was recorded,[15] and even may have been based on Aztec practices.[16] However, van Houten was the first to capitalise on the processes and the use of alkali in the production process is still known as 'Dutching', in honour of its early industrial proponent.

Early eating chocolate

The van Houten process of extracting the excess cocoa butter had provided a source of flavoursome vegetable fat that had no obvious role. For a raw commodity that was expensive the loss of some 30% of the weight in the extraction of the excess fat meant that there was a great incentive to find a use for this expensive by-product. The tablets of the roasted and ground beans, mixed with sugar that were used to make drinking chocolate had made interesting but dry and gritty eating; the addition of cocoa butter made a much more pleasant confection. This new product became available commercially from a United Kingdom manufacturer in 1847 when Fry and Son first sold their eating chocolate.

14 Eileen M Chatt gives two references in 'Cocoa cultivation, processing, analysis', 1953. The first is 'Encyclopaedia of Diderot and d'Alembert', 1763 which shows a press removing the cocoa butter and in 1768 F Merli talks of a superior drinking chocolate made from defatted liquor.

15 de Osasunasco Desiderio: 'Observaciones sobre la preparacion y usos de chocolate', 1789 mentioned in International Chocolate Review, 1953 (8) 179.

16 The addition of wood ash to the preparation of xocoatl by the Aztecs had been observed. Wood ash contains a proportion of potash, the alkali potassium carbonate.

This was to combat the chocolate that was entering the United Kingdom from the Continent, notably from the French and Swiss manufacturers. Eating chocolate quickly became popular, both with the public and with the manufacturers as they were now able to dispose of the excess cocoa butter. Within a few years others followed the lead; by 1849 Cadbury was also selling eating chocolate. As the market for eating chocolate expanded the sales of the powder diminished as the public began to move away from the original drinking chocolate. This reversed the existing relative importance of powder over the butter and established their modern roles. Powder had been the important item in the sales of drinking chocolate, it was now less so as consumers preferred the eating chocolate made with cocoa liquor and the once unwanted cocoa butter.

This change also formed two types of manufacturers: those that converted the beans into the cocoa products of cocoa liquor or cocoa butter and powder, and those that actually made chocolate. This distinction, although a little blurred, continues to the present with the two types of factory processes, one making the intermediate and the other the final products.

Wholesomeness

The early 'defatted' cocoa produced under the van Houten method had about two-thirds of the cocoa fat removed and while the more palatable drink found favour in the general public, the argument of cocoa's healthiness continued. There were some who distrusted the use of chemicals in the production of cocoa powder and continued to circumvent the problem of the extra fattiness by the addition of other materials, such as flour or arrowroot, much as the Aztecs had done. It is ironic that the blending of other materials into the cocoa powder led to the first scandal concerning the quality of the cocoa product.

In 1851 the Lancet published an article on the analysis of 50 commercial cocoa powders showing that 90% were adulterated with a variety of fillers including: starch, animal fat, red and yellow ochres, red lead, vermilion, sulphate of lime and chalk. This was the first of a number of articles concerned with the adulteration of food that continued to be published up to 1854. Such adulterations were not confined to chocolate or cocoa confectionery; in 1850 two girls were ill after eating sugar sweets bought in the Petticoat Lane market. On investigation, high levels of arsenic were found in the sweets. In 1855 'Food and its adulteration'[17] was published, summarising the Lancet articles. It is of interest to note that

---

17 Hassall A H: 'Food and its adulteration', 1855.

despite the inclusion of these adulterants, some drinking chocolate was still marketed for medicinal purposes as either 'dietectic' or 'homeopathic'.

The explanations given were those of cost. It must be remembered that cocoa was an expensive item, the high level of tax that was levied on it certainly did not help. In 1851 cocoa beans were 25/- to 47/- a hundred-weight and the importation tax on them ranged from 18/8d for foreign imports to 9/4d on cocoa coming from British possessions. The tax element therefore amounted to between 17% to 43% of the total. Therefore there was pressure on the confectioner to extend the amount he had to sell as best he could. In fact, this continues today in certain parts of the world[18], although hopefully, not with the addition of items that would be injurious to health. Other fillers that were noted during the mid-1850s consisted of: brick dust, red ochre and red lead for colouring; coconut oil, lard, clarified mutton fat, suet and tallow for replacing cocoa butter.

These problems, however, were not only found in the United Kingdom. In 1830 an order by the prefect of police in Paris stated that 'It is expressly forbidden to make use of any mineral substance for colouring liqueurs, bonbons, sugar plums, lozenges or any other kinds of sweetmeats or pastry.'[19] Today the confectioners jealously guard the wholesomeness of their products; they all understand that the slightest allegation made against a product would result in the end of that product line.

Other advances

In 1866 the first of an important line of chocolate consumption was introduced by Fry's when they first sold the Chocolate Cream bar. It was the first of the filled bars of chocolate that contain a non-chocolate centre. Traditionally both the United Kingdom and United States consumption showed a preference for such confectionery, although in recent years the trend in other major chocolate-consuming countries has been away from the solid form of chocolate and towards the filled bar.

By the beginning of the last quarter of the nineteenth century Swiss manufacturers had been in existence for some time. In 1819 Françoise-Louis Cailler set up a chocolate factory, as did Phillip Suchard in 1826 and Rodolphe Sprüngli-Amman in 1845. In 1876 Daniel Peter, working in conjunction with Nestlé, whose creamery was next to his factory,

18 In the winter of 1990 one factory in the Far East was observed to add, according to the operator, about 10% of potato flour to cocoa powder at the milling stage. The manager explained that 'it made the cocoa powder go further'. The second travesty was that the powder was made from prime Trinitario beans that would otherwise fetch a premium on the world market as a fine and flavour cocoa.

19 Normandy A H: 'A commercial handbook of chemical analysis', 1850.

formulated the first commercial milk chocolate recipe. As only a small amount of moisture is permissible in the making of chocolate, it was only the inclusion of Nestle's new 'condensed' milk that enabled Peter to produce a smooth tasting product. Milk chocolate had the advantage that not only was the flavour milder but that less of the expensive cocoa butter was needed in the manufacturing process. Others were quick to follow the lead in making this milder flavoured chocolate that now forms the majority of the cocoa consumption.

Three years later in 1879 Lindt provided the last major manufacturing technique to producing 'modern' chocolate. He discovered that a much smoother textured product could be made if the chocolate was repeatedly rolled from side to side, in a stone vessel by a grinding stone. This process, called 'conching' could continue for up to five days. It gradually reduces the size of the agglomerated particles of cocoa and sugar, and ensures that the butter fully covers the particles. Conching also enhances the chocolate flavour by removing some volatile flavours and acids.

The benevolent employer

One aspect of the chocolate manufacturing industry had been the role of many employers. In the United Kingdom and United States these manufacturers held, and some still do, certain views concerning the well-being of their workforce. During the eighteenth and nineteenth centuries alcoholism was rife amongst the working classes in the United Kingdom. At the same time, especially in the eighteenth century, religious intolerance could affect business opportunities of those who did not follow the main religious practices. One such group on the fringe of the mainstream religion were the Quakers. People who held such views found it difficult to develop within existing businesses, so a trade that ensured a degree of autonomy became an important requirement. Confectionery and cocoa afforded that; together with the benefit to their fellow man by providing an alternative to alcohol. This attitude also spilled over into the management of their workforces. When Cadbury moved out of the centre of Birmingham to a site near the River Bourn in 1879, they took the opportunity to build cottages near to the factory. The company let these houses in Bournville at reduced rates to workers considered to be worthy. Rowntree was also founded by Quakers and, under the guidance of Seebohm Rowntree, the company took great interest in the health and welfare of its workforce, establishing the Welfare Workers Association in 1913. This became the Institute of Personnel Management. Following Cadbury, in the early 1900s they also built a model village for employees, at New Erswick.

Not only were these two companies concerned with their own employees' welfare. By 1901 it was apparent that working conditions in the cocoa estates of São Tomé and Principe were extremely poor and bordered on conditions of slavery. Cadbury issued a warning that if matters did not improve they would stop buying cocoa from the islands. In 1903 William Cadbury began investigating the matter with the approval of Rowntree, Fry and Stollwerk in Germany. The result of the eventual report was that companies in both the UK and USA began buying cocoa from places other than São Tomé and Principe.

The benevolent employer was also at work in the United States. In 1893 Milton Hershey, owner of a company that made caramels, decided to switch his company's attention to making chocolate. By 1900 he had sold his caramel business and concentrated solely on producing chocolate. Within three years of the change of direction the company had outgrown its premises. This afforded Milton Hershey the opportunity to build his own new factory. Not content with just that he also built a town around the factory for the benefit of his employees. The factory was commissioned in 1905 with the town completed within three years and included an amusement park, zoo and golf courses. The residential areas were to be kept free of 'taverns, piggeries, glue, soap, candle, lamp-black factories', following the tone of the other model villages set up by the Quakers on the other side of the Atlantic. During the Depression of the 1930s, Hershey made use of the cheap labour and building costs to expand the town. New schools, office buildings and community centres were built. He contended that no one in the town of Hershey had lost their job because of the Depression.

More recently, both the number of cocoa processors and chocolate manufacturers has contracted. In the 1970s there were 118 of the larger factories in the world involved in cocoa which had reduced to 75 by the beginning of the 1990s. Despite the smaller number, production of chocolate has continued to expand, recently stimulated by the lower prices of the raw products, see Chapter 4.

While the lower prices stimulate demand for chocolate and chocolate flavoured products it has not promoted any great diversification in the use of cocoa. Compared with other edible fats, cocoa butter is expensive and the remaining solids have only their attributes of flavour and colour. Manufacturers of cosmetics use cocoa butter in some of their products and a small amount of cocoa goes to pharmaceutical companies to extract theobromine, a heart stimulant. But both of these alternative uses represent a tiny proportion of the overall demand for cocoa.

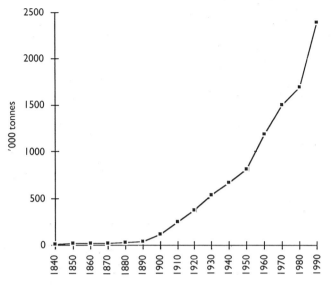

Sources: Gordian, Gill & Duffus and ICCO.

1.1 World production of cocoa.

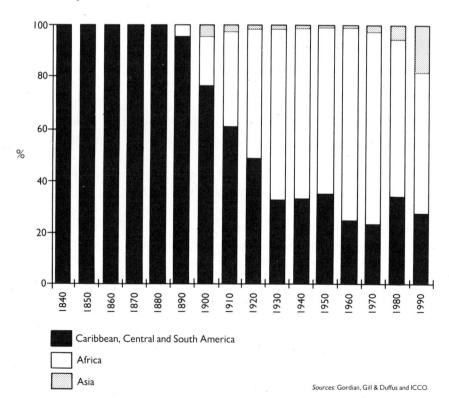

■ Caribbean, Central and South America

□ Africa

▒ Asia

Sources: Gordian, Gill & Duffus and ICCO.

1.2 Evolution of cocoa production by region, as a percentage of world production.

Forastero cocoa and cocoa production since 1840

Over the past 150 years cocoa production is dominated by one fact; its success. This success may be attributed to the Forastero variety of cocoa. In 1840 the world production of cocoa was 14 000 tonnes, by 1880 it had more than doubled to 31 000, in a further 50 years it was more than twenty times as big again at 672 000 tonnes. In 1990 2.4 million tonnes were grown. Figure 1.1 illustrates this evolution that rests on the Forastero cocoa.

Underlying the growth during this period has been a major change in the production pattern. Figure 1.2 shows, in percentage terms, the amount grown in the various geographical regions.

As may be seen, the nineteenth century was dominated by cocoa grown in the Caribbean and Central and Southern Americas. After 1920 African production eclipsed all others.

South American production

Although now overtaken by production in Africa, South America remains an important cocoa growing region, currently producing some 653 000 tonnes; over a quarter of world production. Ecuador and Venezuela now produce a smaller proportion of world cocoa in comparison with their production in the nineteenth century. Their output within South America has also been reduced. Brazil now accounts for over half of the cocoa grown in South America. Production in Brazil is mainly from the state of Bahia. Cocoa was first introduced to this region in 1746 by the French, but it really only started to be grown commercially in the mid-1830s. By 1930 Brazil had become the biggest producer of cocoa in the region, as production decreased in Ecuador and Trinidad. In Ecuador the sudden drop in production from 41 000 tonnes in 1920 to 14 000 tonnes in 1930 was due to two diseases that devastated the crop. The first was monila pod rot that destroyed a large proportion of the cocoa in 1917 and the second, in 1922, was witches' broom disease. Production in Ecuador did not recover to the 1920 levels until the 1960s.

African production

Cocoa may have been introduced to Fernando Po (an island off the coast of Africa, now part of Equatorial Guinea) during the sixteenth century. However, it was only during the nineteenth century that such introductions became widespread. In 1822 growers planted cocoa on the island of Principe and by 1830 cocoa was growing on the nearby island of São

Tomé. Significantly the cocoa was an Amelonado variety of the Forastero stock. As labour for the island plantations was limited, growers introduced workers from the mainland to maintain the cocoa. In 1879, one such worker, Adja, an apprentice to Tetteh Quarshie, successfully brought cocoa from Fernando Po back home to Mampong-Akwapim, inland from Accra on the Gold Coast. Although cocoa had been grown in mainland Africa for some time before 1879, it had not been done on a commercial basis. The introduction of the cocoa, together with some knowledge of its husbandry that was also garnered from the island, formed the springboard of African production. In 1891 the first cocoa from the Gold Coast (now Ghana), 80 pounds in weight, was exported.

Other countries in Africa followed. In 1880 Nigeria introduced cocoa; the 1900s saw production start in the Cameroon and in 1919 the Côte d'Ivoire also began producing cocoa. With the exception of the Cameroon, all West African cocoa was Amelonado. While a German colony, two types of cocoa developed in the Cameroon. In the west, Trinitario varieties were introduced (hybrids of Forastero and Criollo cocoa), while in the east a mixture of Trinitario and Amelonado developed. The alternative source of plant material gave rise to a cocoa with different characteristics (beans with a high fat content that gave a red coloured powder) to that grown elsewhere in West Africa. From Fig. 1.2 it is apparent that the increase in African cocoa production was dramatic. In 1900 the region accounted for 20 000 tonnes, within ten years it had more than quadrupled to 87 000 tonnes and by 1940 it had quadrupled again to 434 000 tonnes. In 1990 it accounted for 1.3 million tonnes, just over half the world production. To be expected, production during this time was not evenly distributed. Three countries dominated; Ghana, Nigeria and Côte d'Ivoire. Current production levels in these countries account for 1.1 million tonnes of cocoa with the Côte d'Ivoire producing 720 000 tonnes.

The importance of Africa as a production centre determines the start of the year in the cocoa trade. In Africa the exports of the new crop of cocoa begin in October and the main crop harvest finishes in April. Consequently the cocoa trade considers the crop year to begin on October 1 and to finish on September 30. References to double years, e.g. 1991/92, refer to the period October-September.

Asian production

One other aspect to the change in geographical distribution is apparent from Fig. 1.2. It is the recent increase of cocoa coming from the Far East, in particular Malaysia and Indonesia. Cocoa was first grown in peninsula Malaysia in 1788 but attracted little interest. Over the past twenty years, the interest has developed, especially in the state of Sabah on the island of Borneo. Although the rate of Malaysian production seems to be slowing in the face of recent continued falling prices, Malaysia is the fifth biggest producer in the world.

Although Criollo cocoa had been introduced to Indonesia in 1560 its production was small and limited to the southern part of the island of Java. In 1888 Forastero type cocoa was introduced by mistake to the Criollo stock that resulted in a hardier variety but still maintained the flavour and colour characteristics of what is known as the 'Java A' bean. Production of this Trinitario cocoa remained small and, until recently, represented most of the cocoa exported. Following the Malaysian example Indonesia has started to produce Forastero type cocoa throughout the islands making up the country. Most notably Sulawesi, Kalimantan and Sumatra have joined Java as production centres.

Prices

Consumption during the past 150 years has broadly kept pace with production, although there have been periods when production and consumption have not operated in tandem. The cocoa industry faces one such period at the moment, caused by supply exceeding demand. This is not new. From 1907 until the end of the 1930s the enormous leap in cocoa supply, caused by African production (see Fig. 1.1), resulted in oversupply of cocoa to the market. Naturally this affected the price. Figure 1.3 shows the evolution of import values of cocoa arriving in the United Kingdom since 1854.[20]

Excluding the period of the Second World War (during which the UK government imposed its own values on imports of cocoa) in real terms the price of cocoa is currently at its lowest in the series; in 1991 it was £668/tonne in 1990 terms.

The 1900s and the 1980s

Modern analysts looking for earlier examples of low prices tend to quote the lows reached during the mid-1960s. This period was the most recent of the low prices and one for which there is plenty of data. Perhaps because of the difficulty in obtaining early prices and other details, like

20 Although the series extends further back than 1854, the clerks compiling the annual government returns seem to have confused coconuts with cocoa (often referred to as Cocoa Nuts), an error only rectified from 1854 onwards.

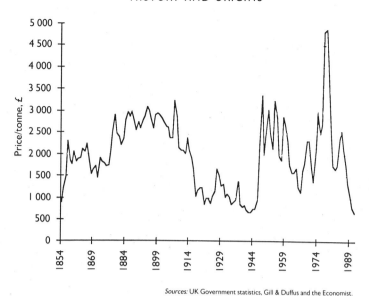

Sources: UK Government statistics, Gill & Duffus and the Economist.

1.3 Evolution of UK average annual cocoa bean import values from 1854 to 1991 in constant 1990 terms.

stock-levels, none seem to note the similarity of current conditions and those during the early part of this century. With Africa starting production at the turn of the century the price of cocoa fell and by the end of the 1930s had dropped by about 80%. Even excluding the short but violent upsurge of prices in 1977, a similar situation occurs today. Prices have fallen by a similar amount, timed at the point when Asia entered into sizeable cocoa production. In both cases a new region growing cocoa occurred at the same time as the fall in prices. In the first, the arrival of West African production was the main cause of the bear market. In the second, the combination of a doubling of production in Côte d'Ivoire together with Asia entering the cocoa market exacerbated conditions. Note the similarity in shape of the graph from 1907 to 1916 with that from 1977 to the present. In both cases cocoa hit an all-time high only to collapse, retrace some of the loss, and then to continue down. At the time of writing we still seem not to have reached the bottom of the current bear market (see Chapter 4).

Two other similarities exist between the two periods. The first concerns a reaction by producers in the face of low prices. In 1937 the Gold Coast farmers withheld cocoa from the market in protest at the low prices. This resulted in the spike of prices during that year (see Fig. 1.3 and Chapter 4). In 1988 the Côte d'Ivoire tried to push prices higher by imposing a lower limit on the price of their exports, below which they would not sell. Both ventures failed to provide sustainable price increases – underlining the trader's adage: 'no one is bigger than the market'.

The second similarity between the two ages concerns the complaints by buyers over the cocoa quality from the new origins. Early in the century buyers despaired over the quality of the African cocoa that they had to use; similar to the comments made by some these days over the quality of the Asian cocoa. In both cases the comments were reflected in the prices paid for the cocoa, the new origins fetching lower prices than the existing cocoa (see Chapter 8). Despite these complaints buyers have less difficulty in finding the quality of cocoa they need during times of easy supply. The problem starts when supplies tighten, and as the Brazilian growers' proverb has it:

> *When there is plenty of cocoa, all cocoa is thought rubbish and when there is only a little cocoa, all rubbish is cocoa.*

2

Agronomics

Classification

The first classification of cocoa was in 1753 when Linæus, mindful of the early Indian traditions, appropriately gave the name *Theobroma cacao* (food of the gods) to the cocoa tree.[1] The genus *Theobroma* has subsequently been divided into 22 species of which *Theobroma cacao* is the most widely distributed in the world. In turn, two sub-species of *T. cacao* have been identified and classed as *T. cacao* spp. *cacao* and *T. cacao* spp. *sphaerocarpum*. The first sub-species may be considered to be the Criollo cocoa and the latter to be all other types of cocoa. This principally includes two types referred to as Amelonado and Trinitario. Figure 2.1 shows the basic family tree of Sterculiaceae with reference to *T. cacao*. Of the other species of *Theobroma* two are worthy of mention. The first is similar to *T. cacao* and is *T. bicolor*. Although its beans make poor quality chocolate, South American growers sometimes adulterate their true cacao produce with beans from this species. Slightly more distantly related is *T. grandiflorum*. Grown in the Brazilian state of

[1] Although this was not its first latin name. Petrus Martyr Anglerius called cocoa *Amygdaloe pecuniarioe*, on account of its use by the Indians as money. 'Blessed money! which exempts its possessors from avarice, since it cannot be hoarded nor hidden underground'. From 'The historie of the West Indies, 1626.

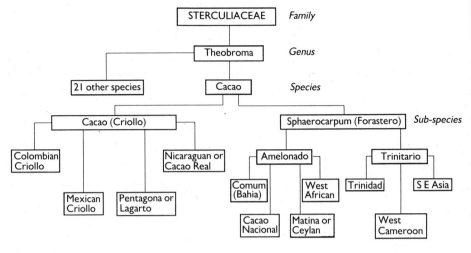

2.1 Family tree of *Theobroma cacao.*

Para its value lies in the pulp or mucilage in the pod, used to prepare a drink.

Criollo

As was seen from Chapter 1, the historical interest lies in the Criollo type beans. Up to the middle of the eighteenth century plantations, somewhat confusingly called nurseries, grew Criollo trees. Giving a delicate chocolate flavour when processed, the insides of the Criollo beans are white or at their darkest, a pale purple. When ripe the pods are soft, coloured red and have an elongated shape and contain up to 30 beans. Botanists still use these, and other characteristics of the pod to identify the variety of cocoa. Nowadays pure Criollo trees are very few and far between, the Forastero type cocoa dominates the world crop.

Forastero

Amelonado

Representing cocoa grown in the majority of West Africa and Brazil, Amelonado type cocoa is now by far the largest and most widespread of the Forastero cocoa. When ripe, the pods are hard and each contains 40 or so beans. The shape of the pods is different to the Criollo, being more rounded and melon shaped – giving the origin of the name Amelonado. When opened, the beans are smaller and much darker than the Criollo,

22

ranging from pale to dark purple. The flavour, all-important, is stronger than the Criollo cocoa.

Trinitarios

The Trinitarios are a cross between the Criollo and Forastero types. Botanists classify the Trinitarios as a Forastero type and consider them as occurring through the agency of man as they do not appear in the wild. While called Trinitario, after the island of Trinidad, Trinitario trees also appear independently of the strain developed in the Caribbean island. Notably this occurred in Venezuela, West Cameroon and Java. As mentioned in Chapter 1 the early planters discovered that the Criollo trees were susceptible to disease and intolerant to drought. The introduction of the Forastero to produce the Trinitario gave a hardier variety with higher yields. Many of the characteristics of the pod and beans were similar to the Forastero parent, 30 or more beans, with the ripe pods being mostly hard. However, it is a characteristic of the Trinitarios that because of the differing parentage they are not as uniform as the Forastero, especially the Amelonado.

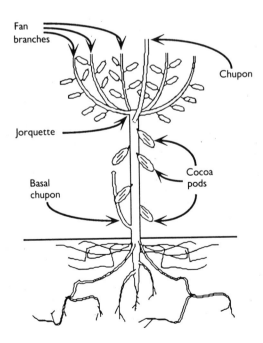

2.2 Schematic representation of a mature cocoa tree.

The cocoa tree

Before looking at some of the environmental factors that affect the growth of cocoa it is of interest to look at the structure of the tree itself, and to note some of the terms that are used. Figure 2.2 shows schematically the structure of a mature cocoa tree.

Growth

Grown from seed, the cocoa tree goes through three stages of development. The early stages involve the initial growth of the seed; first when the cocoa germinates and pushes the cotyledons about an inch above the surface of the soil (botanically known as epigeal germination) and the second when it produces the first leaves. The next stage gives the plant further vertical growth until fan branches appear. The number of these sideway growths can vary depending on the variety, but Amelonado cocoa usually grows five. The growth of the fan branches forms a jorquette. Environmental factors, principally the amount of light, determine if the tree will grow any higher. Further vertical growth depends on chupons; branches that normally develop on the main trunk and that grow up above the fan branches. The chupons may then form a new jorquette with their own fan branches. The height of the tree is typically between eight to ten metres.

Root system

The root system may be divided into two parts: the main tap root and the mass of fine lateral roots growing just below the soil surface. In suitable soils the tap root may grow to a depth of some 1.5 metres and, under normal conditions, is not primarily involved in the take-up of water and nutrients.[2]

Leaves

Leaves on the cocoa tree grow in intermittent bursts, known as flushes. When they first appear they are normally a reddish colour, changing to green when they harden off. Leaf production depends on moisture and nutritional factors, as well as light intensity.

---

2   The nature of its function is more of structural support, although in dry conditions its depth will enable it to absorb water lying deeper underground.

Flowers and pods

The flowering of the cocoa tree is unusual in that it is cauliflorous; the flowers form, not at the leaf nodes but on the trunk and branches of the tree. This results, after successful pollination,[3] in the pods growing directly out of the tree trunk or branches. Although a large number of the small whitish-pink flowers may grow, only a small proportion will continue to produce a cherelle or young pod (described botanically as an indehiscent drupe).[4] Later on the tree will further reduce the number of cherelles by a process known as cherelle wilt. It is difficult to assess the number lost by this natural process because the dead cherelles remain on the tree and their appearance is similar to those killed by disease. Once the loss caused by cherelle wilt has passed, the remaining cherelles will go on to form mature pods.

Climatic requirements

Hot, moist conditions suit the growing of cocoa. Specifically, temperatures between a maximum of 32 °C and a minimum of 18 °C, together with a minimum annual rainfall of 1250 mm to a maximum of 3000 mm. Should the region have a dry season, it should not be prolonged (less than three months) and during this period the rainfall should not be less than 100 mm per month.

Cocoa growing areas

The factors of temperature and rainfall above all others, determine the location of successful propagation of cocoa. Most of the world's cocoa grows within 8° of the equator where the temperature and rainfall within these requirements. The most northerly area of cocoa production is in Hainan, China at about 20° N and the most southerly is 24° S, around São Paulo, Brazil. Both areas are minor cocoa producers. Primarily the temperature determines the altitude at which cocoa will grow. Most cocoa grows below 300 metres above sea level, although some planters cultivate cocoa well above these altitudes, notably 1100 to 1200 metres in Uganda, but again, production is small.

3   Pollination occurs by insects, mostly the flying female midges of Forcipomyia and various crawling thrips and aphids.
4   A mature tree may produce 10 000 flowers during a year, which may result in only 10–50 pods.

Protection from sunlight

In the wild cocoa grows beneath the overhead canopy provided by larger trees. These trees help protect the cocoa and act as a buffer during extreme conditions. The first protection given is against direct sunlight. Certainly young cocoa needs shade. When more mature, after two or three years and once the cocoa tree forms a canopy, the amount of shade may be reduced and in a few cases dispensed with altogether. As with most things to do with cocoa, timing is everything. Removing the shade too soon forms gaps in the canopy and weeds will grow beneath the trees. This will cause extra labour for the grower in maintaining the plantation. Unshaded cocoa may give high yields but in such conditions the trees need high levels of inputs, in the form of nutrients and water. The level of inputs can determine the amount of shade given to the cocoa.

Protection from wind

The second area of protection that the cocoa tree needs is against wind. Even persistent breezes at low speeds will damage cocoa trees. The harm is primarily a mechanical one that affects the leaves. The presence of shade trees helps to cut down the air flow through the plantation, although the need for this type of protection varies considerably from one location to another. Some plantations may have good protection from winds, others may need extra defences, such as hedges surrounding the growing area.

Humidity

The relative humidity of cocoa-growing areas tends to be high especially at night where 100% is not unusual. High humidity presents problems in the post-harvest preparation of cocoa as well as in the spread of fungal diseases. Those locations that have a dry season (most of West Africa, for example) benefit from the reduction of humidity during this period as it provides a natural break in the incidence of black pod rot (*Phytophthora* pod rot) as the fungus prefers high humidity. In addition, less humid conditions allow the grower to dry the beans naturally.

Soil

The ideal soil for growing cocoa depends greatly on the prevailing climatic conditions, particularly the amount and distribution of rainfall. Too much

Table 2.1 Soil orders

Soil order	Primary characteristics	Relevance to cocoa growing
Entisols	Mineral soils virtually lacking horizon development (e.g., fresh alluvium).	World-wide occurrence. Likely to be suitable for cocoa if not too sandy, wet or shallow.
Inceptisols	Mineral soils with only weak horizon development.	World-wide occurrence. Very likely to be suitable for cocoa if not sandy, wet or shallow.
Aridisols	Soils of acid areas that are not deep cracking or humus-rich.	Confined to arid areas. Not suited to cocoa.
Mollisols	Mineral soils with deep humus-rich topsoil, typical of steppe areas.	Unlikely to occur in the humid tropics but basically suitable for cocoa.
Spodosols	Soils showing 'podzolic' translocation of humus, aluminium (and iron).	Not common in humid tropics. Generally not suited to cocoa.
Vertisols	Deeply cracking, self-churning clay soils.	Not suited to cocoa.
Ultisols	Soils showing evidence of vertical clay movement and intense leaching.	Widespread in the humid tropics. Usually adequate for cocoa.
Alfisols	Soils showing evidence of vertical clay movement but no excessive leaching.	Found occasionally in the humid tropics. May be ideal for cocoa.
Oxisols	Extremely weathered tropical soils. Very low capacity for retention of nutrients and moisture.	Not as widespread as once thought. Usually marginal for cocoa.
Histosols	Organic soils – peats.	Generally not suited to tree crops.

rain on a soil with poor drainage may prevent the root system from respiring. Although able to withstand flooding, if these conditions persist the trees will die. Similarly, cocoa is intolerant to drought conditions and therefore a sandy soil that has poor water retention will stress the tree. The depth, type, acidity and amount of organic material in the soil are factors that go towards the suitability of growing cocoa.

Table 2.1 shows a simplified key to soil orders derived from the Department of Agriculture of the United States.[5]

5   Smyth A J: 'Soil classification and the cocoa grower' Cocoa Growers' Bulletin 1980 (30).

Composition

The soil type has to afford water retention as well as allowing adequate drainage. A difficult feat but one which is best served by a composition of 50% sand, large particles that give good drainage; 30 to 40% clay, small particles providing water and nutrient retention properties; with the balance of 10 to 20% made up of intermediate particle-sized silt.[6]

Acidity

Cocoa grows in soils that have widely differing acidities; pH values of 4.0 up to 8.5 have been noted.[7] While the cocoa itself may tolerate these extremes, the level of nutrients will vary at either end of this acidity range. For example, highly acidic soils will have low phosphorous levels available but higher amounts of iron and copper salts that may have deleterious toxic effects.

Methods of production

Those who grow either the Amelonado or Amazonian hybrids have a cocoa that is, relatively speaking, genetically consistent. It may be grown from seed without inordinate variations appearing. In most countries growers may obtain the seeds of these types which presents them with an easy way to start production. Cultivating Trinitario cocoa, or cocoa that gives a wider range of variations, grows better through the use of cuttings or buddings. This vegetative method of production not only requires sufficient quantities of suitable cutting or budding material but also extra labour compared to raising the trees from seed.

Seed production

Producing the seed material requires specialised and careful management. Unwanted crosses may give variable seed material if the grower either fails to impose strict control or use untrained staff. Many leave this task to those agencies/companies that specialise in this aspect of cultivation and that have seed gardens. The grower may then obtain either the seeds or, more usually, the seedlings. These will then spend the second part of their

---

6   Wood G A R and Lass R A (Ed): 'Cocoa', 1985.
7   Smyth A J: 'The selection of soils for cocoa' Soils Bulletin 1966 (5) FAO Rome.

lives in the grower's cocoa nursery in preparation for their final planting in the estate.

Vegetative production

Growing cocoa varieties that have a high incidence of variability generally requires the nursery technique of producing plants from cuttings or by budding. Of the two types of propagation the use of cuttings has the disadvantage of needing more of the required plant material than the budding technique. Growers normally take cuttings from chupons, as those taken from the fan branches develop into 'bushy' shaped trees and require specialised pruning.[8] As chupon growth is not as readily available as fan branches, propagation by cuttings generally gives rise to extra pruning in the plantation. Better use of the chupon wood is by budding. In this method, the grower cultivates sound root stock, which, when about three months old may be used in the budding. This involves cutting and exposing a two-inch length of the bark on the stem of the root stock and introducing a similar sized piece from the bud wood which is bound into place with tape. After a couple of weeks, the top of the root stock stem is cut off and the tape binding the bud patch is removed. Growth from the budding is stimulated a week or so later by the removal of the remaining top part of the root stock stem and by bending the stem away from the bud patch.

Cocoa nursery

The running of a nursery places specific demands on certain resources; in particular an adequate supply of water and protection from the sun and wind. Growers usually locate it close to the main activities of the plantations, the offices or workers' village or fermentary, so that people are on hand to check the nursery. The seedlings normally grow in individual polythene bags that contain topsoil, or where the topsoil is mostly clay, topsoil and sand. The open-ended bags are arranged under some form of canopy that gives good protection from the sun and wind. Growers sometimes use a natural canopy, i.e. shade trees, or construct a framework of poles and cross-pieces and cover them with netting or palm fronds.

Watering

Over-watering the seedlings is one of the main causes of loss in the nurseries. It causes fungal attacks that destroy the young shoots' stems or

---

8   See Chapter 3 (Production strategies – the Indonesian experience) for an example of cuttings made from fan branches.

tap-roots. In order to reduce this type of loss, the bottom of the polythene bags must be perforated to allow excess water to escape. The amount of water given is, naturally, dependent on the prevailing climatic conditions. Assuming that the grower waters the seedlings every two days, during a four month period in the nursery each plant will need between five and a half to seven litres of water. A nursery servicing an estate that needs planting material for, say, ten hectares (24.7 acres) will need between 5700 to 30 000 seedlings, allowing for a 20% mortality and depending on how far apart the trees are finally planted.[9] The water resources for the nursery alone are substantial.

Planting out

It is unusual for growers to keep seedlings in the nursery for longer than six months or for less than three. The most opportune moment for planting out varies on the region and depends much on the climate at the time. Prior to planting out, the seedlings should be 'hardened off' by reducing the shade cover in the nursery. This helps the young trees to withstand the replanting in the estate. Before replanting, growers have to check the seedlings and remove any that are small or weak. It is important that growers only cultivate the most viable plants.

Sowing at stake

Popular in West Africa, sowing at stake involves the farmer planting seeds directly in the ground, thereby by-passing the nursery stage. Its main disadvantage is that the farmer needs more seed material, two or three times the amount required using a nursery. Losses are mainly from poor germination and rodents attacking the young shoots.

The plantation

Thinned forest

That cocoa requires shade has been established. The nature of the shade provided is various. Before planting his estate, the grower must decide whether to cultivate the cocoa under thinned forest or under planted shade trees. In West Africa, the use of thinned forest is very common. Its advantages are that the grower requires little capital expenditure

9   This wide range shows the difference between planting the trees closer together or further apart.

to start operations; no additional shade trees need be bought nor any additional waiting for them to develop. Its drawbacks are that the correct levels of shade may not occur; optimum use of the ground is unlikely, due to the haphazard arrangement and types of the shade trees. In addition some of the remaining forest trees may compete with the cocoa for nutrients, they are unlikely to be leguminous and help to increase the nitrogen levels of the soil, and they may act as host to diseases and pests that attack cocoa. On the other hand, clearing the forest and establishing shade trees is expensive, both in terms of labour as well as in the extra delay from the crop returns.

Shade trees

The establishment of shade trees gives much easier control over the management of the plantation. Regularly spaced trees, both shade and crop, provide easier pruning, pest and weed control and harvesting. One other benefit to the grower is the sale of the timber on the cleared land. The money raised on the timber sales reduces the cost of establishing the plantation; although this is not always possible, a certain infrastructure has to be available for logging to take place, as well as suitable trees that need to be cleared. The grower has also to forgo the benefits to the soil of either leaving the timber on the land or of burning it. Both will return some of the nutrients to the soil.

The shade trees most frequently grown are; *Gliricida sepum*, various species of *Erythrina* and *Leucaena leucocephala*. Although growers use many other shade trees, and their success depends on the local conditions, the objectives for their use remain the same. The aim is to provide the correct level of shade as quickly as possible that the grower may sub-sequently vary it, by pruning or removing from the cocoa stand, as the trees develop. Complete removal of shade trees after the establishment of the cocoa trees may well lead to high yields, although these production levels are difficult to sustain. Conditions that suit this are rare and must include high levels of both nutrients in the soil and available water. Without adequate shade cocoa becomes more susceptible to attack by capsids,[10] and therefore cost the grower more in chemical control. Shading the cocoa both prolongs the economic life of the trees and reduces the amount of nutrients needed, as well as reducing the amount of insecticide the grower may have to use in controlling capsid attacks.

---

10   A generic name for various sap-sucking insects (also referred to as mirids) mainly found in West Africa. Two species, *Distantiella theobroma* and *Sahlbergella singularis* cause the most damage and tend to proliferate where there are breaks in the canopy.

Interplanting

Growers may successfully cultivate cocoa by interplanting it with other crops. Mature coconut provides good shade cover and is often grown in conjunction with cocoa in the South Pacific where the soil is volcanic and has sufficient nutrients. Growers also use bananas and plantains to give extra shade for the young cocoa plants and to provide another cash crop, although these are not usually continued in the mature plantation. The benefit to smallholders in having a number of different crops growing on their land makes for sound economic and environmental sense. Monoculture production, while being efficient, makes the grower vulnerable to the vagaries of price fluctuation of that particular market and the attack of particular pests or diseases. By producing other crops not only is the grower protected from adverse market changes in one crop but is also protected should one crop fail. While there are many different combinations of intercropping, mainly dependent on the soil type, Fig. 2.3 shows a layout that includes four different crops grown on the same land, one of which was cocoa. This was under trial in the South Pacific and shows that, especially for the smallholder, there are possibilities in varying the production.

Cocoa growers in the larger plantations that practise intercropping favour coconut. However, the recent low prices for copra (dried kernels

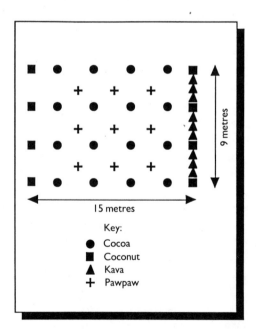

2.3 Plan of trial intercropping of cocoa with three other crops. (Trial undertaken at IRCC station, Vanuatu.)

of the coconut) have meant that at least in one case where cocoa is planted under coconut, the management consider the crop of coconuts as a nuisance. The cost of the collection and processing of the nuts is greater than the value of the resulting copra. Unfortunately the fallen coconuts have to be collected otherwise they germinate where they lie resulting in unwanted shade trees.

Spacing

The aim of all growers is to cultivate as much as possible with the least cost. How far apart the trees are planted becomes central to the eventual yield of the cocoa; if only that, once taken, the decision is irrevocable during the lifetime of the tree. Growers can always change their minds on how much fertiliser or fungicide to apply during a crop year, but they cannot alter the spacing between the trees. The optimum distance between the trees depends greatly on the type of cocoa and the environmental factors of climate and soil. The spacing can vary, from as distant a planting as 5 by 5 metres[11] apart, down to 1.2 by 1.2 metres. Each region has developed its own ideal of spacing. Generally, planting the trees closer together gives higher early yields of cocoa, although this falls away when the cocoa forms a full canopy and the soil becomes depleted. Early high yields are of great interest to the grower as the faster the returns, the better the cash flow.

Cocoa canopy

It is important that the cocoa develops an overhead canopy as soon as possible. This is for two reasons; first, the quicker the trees cover the intervening space by productive photosynthetic material (i.e. cocoa leaves) the faster the tree will develop and produce pods. Second, the less light that can penetrate the canopy to the ground the lower the likelihood of weeds. However, until the trees fully establish the canopy, weeds will grow and compete with the young cocoa plants. The grower has to control them by frequent and regular spraying or cutting down the vegetation surrounding the trees. This will result in stronger and more productive cocoa, especially if fertiliser had been applied to the crop. The resulting cut or dead vegetation should be left on the ground to inhibit the growth of further weeds. Those trees that either die or become diseased and need to be removed should be replaced as soon as possible.

11   Spacing is usually given in two dimensions as some are not equidistant.

Quick replacements will not only improve the yield but cover the gap in the canopy.

Pruning

Initial pruning

Where the plantation has been formed by clearing and replanting, pruning both shade and cocoa trees plays an important role in the maintenance of the crop. In West Africa where growers cultivate most of the cocoa under thinned forest and the overall control is therefore less, the need to prune the trees is limited to the removal of basal chupons. Initially, pruning in the more controlled environment of plantations allows for easy access to the trees for harvesting and control of pests and diseases. The initial task for the grower is to ensure that the first jorquette is at a reasonable height and to remove any low branches and basal chupons. The height of the jorquette depends on the amount of light that penetrates through to the young plants; low levels of shade will give a lower jorquette, as the higher light levels stimulate the plant to branch sooner.

Pruning of established cocoa

Once the trees form the canopy the grower still needs to exert a degree of control, but attention focuses on the fan branches. While the canopy should remain complete, the growth from one tree should not significantly interfere with that of another. This control prevents the undue spread of at least one disease that affects cocoa, that of black pod rot (*Phytophthora* pod rot). Water droplets carry spores of the fungus, transmission of the disease from one tree to another is therefore made easier by the branches from one touching another's and the water running down to the next tree. Another aspect of the control of this particular disease (which probably causes the highest losses of cocoa throughout the world) is that pruning may increase the airflow under the canopy. This will help to prevent the formation of the water droplets by reducing the relative humidity.

Pruning also reduces the damage to pods by rodents; pruned branches make it more difficult for mice and rats to move from one tree to another.

Naturally one of the reasons for pruning is to make the trees more productive. Productive trees are those that have the correct balance between the amount of carbohydrate within the tree and the available nitrogen. The tree holds such reserves of carbohydrate in the wood and therefore the immediate effect of removing a portion of the carbohydrate

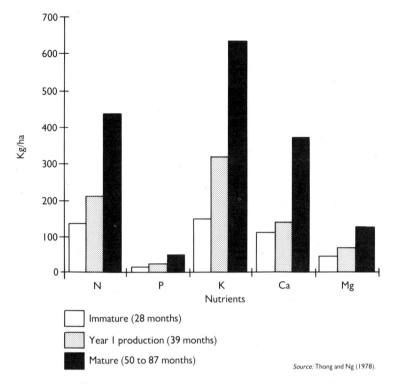

2.4 Estimation of major nutrient requirements of cocoa plants at different stages of development.

is a loss in yield. However, the grower should remove branches that do not support productive leaves as they are a drain on the resources of the tree.

Nutrients

As mentioned above, the level of nutrients required by the cocoa tree largely depends on the amount of shade under which the tree grows. The more shade given to the tree the less nutrients it requires and the more prolonged is its economic life.[12] Not only does the level of shade help determine the amount of nutrients needed but the tree requires different levels of nutrients for each of its stages of development. If planted in poor soil nursery seedlings may need some fertiliser, although the

---

12   The grower must, of course, balance this against a lower yield; although the tree
     may have a longer productive life it may not produce much lurking below in the
     shadows.

grower has to limit the application as the young plants are sensitive to nutrient imbalances. When developing the canopy the trees need considerable quantities of nutrients in order to produce the vegetative matter. Subsequently the nutrients needed by the mature cocoa depend primarily on the crop removed from the trees. Figure 2.4 shows the major nutrient requirements of cocoa's three stages of growth: an immature tree (average age 28 months); first year production (39 months) and a mature stand (50 to 87 months).

As can be seen, the effect of harvesting the pods from the mature cocoa requires approximately twice the level of nutrients as that of the first year's production. Although Fig. 2.4 is compiled from data applicable to Malaysian cocoa it may be seen from Fig. 2.5 that the nutrient composition of the beans from various origins and of differing varieties is approximately the same.

Beans from different sources appear to remove the same quantities of nutrients from the soil. This is not the case when considering the composition of the pod husks. For the same varieties and origins in Fig. 2.5, Fig. 2.6 shows the nutrient composition of the pod husks. This shows that the environment affects the pod husks more than that of the beans;

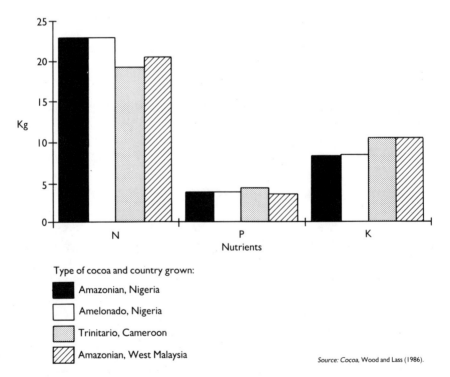

Type of cocoa and country grown:

Amazonian, Nigeria

Amelonado, Nigeria

Trinitario, Cameroon

Amazonian, West Malaysia

Source: Cocoa, Wood and Lass (1986).

2.5 Comparison of the major nutrients in cocoa beans, removed in a crop of 1000 kg dry cocoa beans.

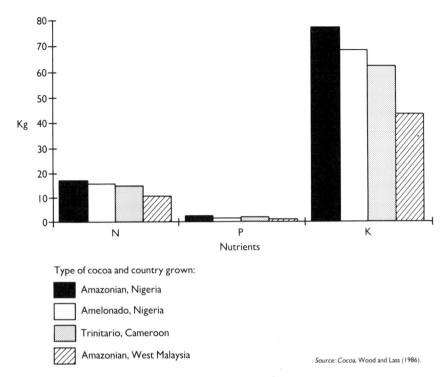

Type of cocoa and country grown:

▮ Amazonian, Nigeria

☐ Amelonado, Nigeria

▨ Trinitario, Cameroon

▨ Amazonian, West Malaysia

Source: Cocoa, Wood and Lass (1986).

2.6 Comparison of the major nutrients in cocoa pod husks, removed in a crop of 1000 kg dry cocoa beans.

with one variety (Amazonia) grown in Nigeria needing nearly twice the nutrients of that grown in Malaysia.

With the exception of rich and very fertile soil (for example that in Papua New Guinea) the grower will need to apply fertilisers at some juncture during the life of the cocoa tree. The soil's composition and the manner in which the grower cultivates the cocoa[13] determines when and what is needed. The greatest demands come from the mature trees after the cocoa has made its major vegetative growth in producing the canopy. At this stage the grower has to undertake regular monitoring of the soil and fertiliser applications.

Although the above concentrates on the major nutrients, the grower has also to pay attention to the minor elements, deficiencies of which may also affect the cocoa. These include zinc, boron, iron and aluminium.

13   Not only does the amount of shade affect the nutrients taken up and therefore possible fertiliser requirements, but if the estate management allows for the pod husks to be returned to the soil this also helps to reduce the fertiliser bills. This is not always possible as in some regions, notably Malaysia, insect pests breed on the pods, see cocoa pod borer, *Conopomorpha cramerella*.

Special care should be taken where the soils are either highly acidic or extremely alkaline.

Diseases and pests

Diseases

Substantial losses occur to the cocoa crop from diseases and pests. Although attempts have been made to quantify the losses, it is extremely difficult to arrive at a global figure. Even if, after much research, analysts agreed on such a number for one particular year, it would not be safe to assume that it would apply for other years. Epidemics of certain diseases or an upsurge in the population of a pest in a major cocoa growing area would undermine the accuracy of the figure. In the 1950s and 1960s losses were estimated as 20–45% of the world crop.[14] Whatever the losses actually are, they are high. Cocoa is a delicate tree susceptible to many pathogens. Indeed, just the sheer number of known diseases and pests that attack cocoa makes one wonder how enough chocolate bars are ever produced and is a testament to the skill and hard work of the cocoa grower.

Just as the first part of this chapter is intended only to outline the procedure for growing cocoa, this second section deals with those problems that either cause, or have the potential to cause, the largest economic losses to cocoa.

Pod rots

There can be nothing more disheartening to the cocoa grower, who, having seen trees studded with healthy looking pods finds them developing black or brown lesions – the sign of one or other of the pod rots. The various pod rots probably account for most of the cocoa losses in the world. Of these, one genus causes the most damage as it occurs in all the cocoa producing areas.

Phytophthora pod rot – black pod rot   Until 1979 it was considered that one species of fungus, *Phytophthora palmivora* caused all losses from black pod rot. However, four species of the same genus were found to produce similar types of loss; *P. palmivora*, the most widely distributed throughout

---

14   Hale S L: 'World production and consumption 1951 to 1953', 1953 and Cramer H H: 'Plant protection and world crop production', 1967.

the world and *P. megakarya*, mostly present in Africa, may account for the greatest economic loss. *P. capsici* is, according to Wood and Lass,[15] not satisfactorily identified, but is considered to occur mainly in Central and South America, whilst the fourth, *P. citrophthora* has been identified in Cameroon and Brazil.

Identifying the cause of pod loss is not as easy as it might seem. For example, the cocoa tree naturally adjusts its production of pods by stopping some developing further than the cherelle stage. Unlike many fruit trees that similarly adjust their production, the small, immature and now blackened and dead pods remain on the tree, displaying many of the symptoms of *Phytophthora* pod rot. Apart from the initial stages, cherelle wilt has all of the appearance of the immature pod suffering from *Phytophthora* pod rot. Therefore growers may consider such losses to be an attack by the pathogen and not a natural adjustment by the trees themselves. However, the major economic loss to the grower from *Phytophthora* pod rot comes from attacks on the pods within two months of their harvest, i.e., about three months after flowering. Infection at this juncture may lead to the total loss of the pod. The first the grower is likely to notice is a dark brown or black spot on the pods that appears a few days after their infection. Within a couple of weeks the whole pod will be black. If the infection took place just before harvesting, the grower can save the beans as in ripe pods the husk detaches from the beans and therefore slows the rate of infection; otherwise the beans will be destroyed.

Water plays an important role in the spreading of the fungus from one pod to another and in the actual infection of the pod itself. Water droplets, containing the zoospores or sporangia of the fungus, running down the branches, dripping from leaves and pods on to uninfected pods are a recognised method of fungal transmission. Once on the fresh pods infection is quick as the zoospores or sporangia develop mycelium that penetrates the pod. High relative humidity in the canopy at best means that the pods remain damp for longer and, at worst, allow the warmer morning air to condense on to the cooler pods thereby providing the medium for the transmission and growth of the fungus. Significantly, one of the usual places for the infection is at the tip of the pod, where water drops naturally collect. The grower can help prevent infection by pruning the trees thereby reducing the shade to allow both greater air flow through, and more sunlight into the canopy. Growers have to remove infected pods from the trees on a regular basis, and keep the diseased pods well away from the rest of the cocoa.

The most widespread chemical control against *Phytophthora* include the copper-based fungicides that growers apply to the developing pods.

15   Ibid Wood G A R and Lass R A, 1985.

Consisting of simple chemicals (for example, a water solution of copper sulphate and calcium hydroxide generally known as Bordeaux mixture) they have the advantages of wide availability and simple application. The empty pod husks left in the field after removal of the beans are also a source of re-infection and therefore should be sprayed. The limiting factor is that of cost. As rain washes off the copper solution, growers spray regularly in order for the application to be effective. This is made worse as the higher incidence of the disease occurs normally during the rainy season. Some systemic fungicides are also available, notably metalaxyl-based chemicals, one of which is marketed by Ciba-Geigy under the name 'Ridomil'. Although the cost of both labour and chemicals loom large in the mind of the grower, the spectre of the damage that *Phytophthora* pod rot may do to a crop at risk should be larger.

Phytophthora canker

While the major economic loss by *Phytophthora* is in its attack on the pods, it can also affect other parts of the tree, in particular the stems. This form of the disease is *Phytophthora* canker and, if severe, may kill the tree or force the grower to cut it down. The main cause of the disease seems to occur through pod infection, the fungus then passing into the tree. Another probable cause is by insects boring into the stem causing physical damage and allowing the fungus to take hold. Criollo type trees suffer the most, the disease causing major losses to the early growers of cocoa. While there have been isolated incidences of losses caused by the canker it is not now considered to be a major loss-causing form of the disease.

Moniliophthora pod rot – Moniliophthora roreri A fungus, originally identified and named as *Monilia roreri*, but now reclassified as *Moniliophthora roreri*, causes substantial losses to cocoa from northern South America up to southern Central America. Peru, Colombia and particularly Ecuador suffer the most by the disease. Fortunately the Andean range has confined it to the north-west region of South America therefore protecting the large production areas of Brazil. However, the recent spread of witches' broom disease into the Bahia cocoa estates does not augur well for the continued absence of this fungus from the rest of South America.

After the infection, a pod looks healthy for at least a month. Brown lesions then appear that develop until the whole pod is covered. The fungus then sporulates, giving a white 'dusting' effect on the pod that led to the common name 'frosty pod rot'. An infected pod gives no beans, a fact that has significantly contributed to the decline, starting earlier this century, of production in Ecuador. A study undertaken in 1926 by J B

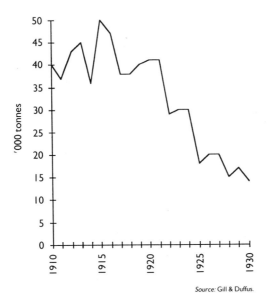

Source: Gill & Duffus.

2.7 Cocoa production in Ecuador, 1910–1930.

Rorer,[16] the man whose name was given to the fungus, showed in one estate the decline in production from 33 tonnes of beans in 1917 to 1.5 tonnes in 1919. Figure 2.7 shows the evolution of production in Ecuador from 1910 to 1930 and illustrates the dramatic decline after 1915, mainly through the attack of *M. roreri*.

At the moment there is no economic chemical answer to preventing the disease. The recommended course of action in managing the spread of the fungus is the careful removal of infected pods from the trees thereby taking away the source of the fungal spores. This containment exercise will have to continue until a disease resistant cultivar is found, as growers have not adopted other forms of farm management.[17]

Witches' broom – *Crinipellis perniciosa*

Witches' broom is a disease that causes cocoa trees to produce branches that bear no fruit and ineffective leaves. Although the deformed growth of the branches gave rise to the common name 'witches' broom', the fungus also attacks the pods and may cause severe losses. The fungus originates in the Amazon basin and has been the cause of production losses in most Latin American countries. It is now present in most of the major cocoa

16   Rorer J B: 'Ecuador cocoa' Tropical Agriculture Trin 1926 (3).
17   For example, forcing the trees to produce pods during the dry season when there is a lower incidence of the spores. This production technique involves hand pollination of the flowers and is therefore labour intensive.

growing areas in South America. Until recently it had not been found in Bahia, the Brazilian state that produces over half of the South American cocoa. Its spread into this region in 1989 is a major long term threat to Brazilian production.

Control of the fungus is limited to pruning and burning the infected branches. Growers should burn the infected material well away from the area of cultivation. This is very labour intensive, and for it to be effective, growers have to ensure that they prune out all infected material from their plantations, and that their effort must be matched by their neighbour's, to prevent re-infection. Chemical control has not been found to be economic as the fungus attacks the actively growing parts of the tree, which, because of their growth, are difficult to protect. The more vigorous plants are more susceptible to frequent and repeated infections and therefore slower growing cultivars, produced under heavy shade, are more adept in with-standing the disease. However, the grower has to strike a balance between the amount of growth and the risk of infection from witches' broom, as well as other diseases that prefer the increased shade. At the end of the nineteenth century cocoa grown in Surinam without shade cover was devastated by the fungus, showing the effect on what must have been fast growing cultivars. As with the other major maladies of cocoa, the long term answer lies in finding disease resistant material.

Very great care should be exercised in the movement of plant material. It seems likely that the introduction of the disease to Bahia was caused by infected plant material being brought into the region and not by any natural vectors. Proper quarantine restrictions should always be enforced.

Cocoa swollen shoot virus

West Africa is blessed with not having witches' broom, but in its place, Ghana and Nigeria in particular, have cocoa swollen shoot virus – the only virus that causes serious losses to cocoa.[18] There is little doubt that Ghana's record production of 566 thousand tonnes in 1964/65 would have occurred much sooner had the virus not been present. First identified in 1936, but probably present since 1907, by the end of the Second World War the virus had infected large areas of Ghana's cocoa growing area, killing many of the trees. The authorities implemented a policy of cutting down diseased trees, and those close to the infection. This met with success – success in restricting the spread of the virus but not in its eradication. This policy of removing the infected trees and, in some cases,

---

18 Other viruses are known to affect cocoa but they have not inflicted the scale of losses that swollen shoot has done.

those surrounding the infection remains, at present, the best way to combat the spread of this debilitating disease. In Ghana during 1959 over one million diseased trees or those near to the infection were cut down every month.

There are a number of different strains of this virus that both vary in symptoms and in the way of transmission from one tree to another. The effect on the tree also varies; the more virulent, which are the most widespread, can kill the tree within three years while other strains merely induce the shoots and roots to swell. Unfortunately for West Africa, Amelonado cocoa is particularly susceptible to the virus. The vector transmitting the virus is one or other of at least a dozen species of mealy-bug. These insects feed on diseased material and then carry the virus to another tree. Attempts to control the mealy-bug population, or of the ants with whom they have a symbiotic relationship, have failed. Work on finding resistant plant material continues.

Dieback

As the name suggests, dieback is characterised by the tips of the branches dying and extending back along the branch towards the jorquette. Observers have noted dieback in all regions of cocoa production and rather than described as a disease, this loss of plant material is more akin to a particular condition of the cocoa tree. The tree may suffer dieback from an external agent or a physiological reaction to its environment. Subsequent fungal attacks on the affected portions of the tree have led to the mistaken identity of the cause of the dieback. Trees stressed by too much or too little water, insufficient nutrients or shade, prolonged wind (e.g. the Harmattan in West Africa) or a combination of such environmental factors may show symptoms of dieback. Attacks by insects on trees may also induce dieback.

Unlike the other diseases mentioned, where the cause of the loss is singular, if perhaps difficult to identify, the first step in combating dieback is to identify the cause. The remedy may well be more of a question of farm management (rectifying a lack of nutrients) or waiting until adverse temporary conditions change (the abating of the Harmattan wind) rather than combating a specific causal pathogen (to date, only one has been found).

The fungus *Oncobasidium theobromae* causes the specific dieback known as vascular streak dieback or VSD. Identified in 1971 it exists in parts of Papua New Guinea, Malaysia, the Philippines and Indonesia. An infected live branch, if split, will show brown streaks which gave the disease its name. The spread of the disease is slow. Growers may control the fungus by pruning out the dead branches on a regular and frequent basis. Trees over five years old can withstand an attack of the fungus by the promotion of vegetative growth, specifically by the application of nitrogen based fertilisers. This method of control has the benefits of not over-stressing the trees by continual pruning, no loss of pod bearing wood and reduced costs (frequent pruning is expensive). The use of fungicides as a preventative measure has not been successful as the fungal growth occurs within the tree.

Ceratocystis wilt – Ceratocystis fimbriata

Losses to cocoa production from this fungus have been estimated to run to millions of trees[19] although no quantifiable figures exist. The fungus occurs throughout the world and therefore all cocoa is at risk from it, although in general, Forastero types are more resistant to it than are the Criollo. Wilting leaves, followed by the death of the infected branch are the initial symptoms. Typically, the dead leaves remain on the tree for some time after the death of the branch. Diseased parts of a tree will usually have been attacked by Xyleborus beetles; one of the main agents involving the spread of the fungus. The Xyleborus beetle bores into the tree allowing the fungus to take hold in the wound. The other cause of the spread of Ceratocystis is through wounds made in pruning the trees (the French name for the disease is 'mal de machete'). By applying a fungicide to the wounds and cleaning the pruning knife, again with a fungicide, after attending to each tree will prevent infection from this source. Other attempts to control the beetle population and/or fungus itself have not worked. Growers should remove diseased branches and trees, although this action, unless carefully done, may cause further liberation of the spores from the infected wood.

Pests

Insects

Although the number of insect types thought to feed on cocoa[20] is above 1500 researchers gathered over 65000 different kinds of insect from cocoa estates in Costa Rica.[21] Fortunately only a relatively small number have any economic effect on cocoa, and in any one area this may well consist of a handful of types.

Damage to cocoa through insects falls into two main categories: those

19   Sanders J L: 'The Xyleborus-Ceratocystis complex of cacao' Cacao 1965 (10).
20   Entwistle P F: 'The pests of cocoa', 1972.
21   Cook L R and Meursing (Dr) E H: 'Chocolate production and use', 1982.

that directly attack the tree and those that transmit or help establish a pathogen.

Those that cause the most direct or primary damage to cocoa are the mirids or capsids. Entwistle[22] identifies ten major genera of mirids that attack cocoa. One or more of them is present in all the main producing areas of the world. They feed on the sap of trees which naturally damages the plant material and may kill saplings; the creation of a wound allows fungi to attack the tree more readily. Their wide dispersion makes them a significant pest to cocoa growers.

The rise of Malaysia as a cocoa producer in recent years has been marred by the cocoa pod borer. Historically known as the cocoa moth, *Conopomorpha cramerella*, the larval stage of this insect has caused large losses to the growers in the Far East. The moth lays its eggs directly on to the pod, usually in a crack or crevice. Within a week, the larvae hatch and bore into the pod, feeding on the pulp and destroying the development of the beans.

Of the second type of insect attack (those causing losses through secondary infections) the mealy-bugs cause the worst damage through transmitting swollen shoot virus in West African cocoa. Although mealy-bugs are in all cocoa producing areas, their feeding on the cocoa trees does little damage in itself. By feeding on the sap, they exude honeydew thereby attracting ants which protect the mealy-bugs from predators. For some species of ant the protection includes building 'tents' of vegetative debris over the feeding mealy-bugs. This makes chemical control of the pests difficult.

As mentioned earlier, the relationship between *Ceratocystis fimbriata* (Ceratocystis wilt) and the *Xyleborus* beetle, particularly *X. ferrugineus*, has caused significant economic losses. The action of the beetle boring into the trunk and branches causes wounds that become infected with the Ceratocystic fungus. The fungus makes further use of the galleries bored by the beetle as it releases its spores through them – the beetles help disperse the spores by ejecting them from the galleries along with the frass etc.

Control of insects The main control of insect pests is chemical and despite the attention being focused on other, potentially less damaging, methods it remains the most effective. All who deal with cocoa, from the growers onwards, should be aware that consuming countries' authorities and confectionery companies monitor chemical residues and tolerances are continually lowered. Questions over the wholesomeness of their products, in the United Kingdom initially asked of the confectionery

22   Ibid Entwistle P F, 1972.

industry in the 1850s, have not been forgotten. Growers should, in conjunction with research stations develop production techniques that reduce the need for chemical controls. In Malaysia, growers practiced 'rampasan', the removal and destruction of all pods from the trees during the low season, to try and break the life cycle of *C. cramerella*. In Vanuatu, to protect a research station's cocoa from rose beetles (*Adoretus versutus*) that flew into the plantation at night, the director planted a physical barrier of broad leafed plants around the edge of the cocoa stand. The purpose of the layer of green leafed protection was to prevent the majority of the insects reaching the cocoa leaves.

Attempts at biological control (the introduction of predators of the pests) have met with limited success, research being far from complete. One example of such control is the introduction of the ant *Anoplolepis longipes* to cocoa grown in Papua New Guinea, which reduced the numbers of mirids and other pests.

Other pests of cocoa

Small mammals and birds can do considerable damage by attacking cocoa pods. Of the mammals: rats, squirrels, monkeys and civets probably account for most of the destruction. Even if the animal only slightly damages the pod, the wound will allow the development of one or other of the fungi. Parrots and woodpeckers also feed on the pods and can extensively damage the crop. Losses from vertebrate pests may account for up to 5–10% of the world crop[23] – making them one of the major causes of damage to cocoa.

Harvesting and post-harvest practice

After all the hard work in cultivating the cocoa, growers may still fail to produce a worthwhile commodity when they harvest and process the beans. These critical stages set the future use of the cocoa, and help determine the eventual return to the growers. There are three main steps in this: the harvesting, the fermentation practice and lastly the drying of the cocoa. All three are important, the harvesting in the selection of the ripe pods for reasons of yield and flavour; the fermentation process to develop the flavour and colour of the beans; and lastly the drying which not only makes the cocoa marketable but, if done correctly, should also improve the flavour of the chocolate.

23   Ibid Entwistle P F, 1972.

A considerable body of work exists on the post-harvest preparation of cocoa. Built up, mainly during the first half of this century, the secret surrounding the formulation and retention of the chocolate flavour in the cocoa bean has intrigued many. The interest lay not only in how the cocoa should be processed but also in understanding the very complex chemical reactions that take place both in the bean and outside it. While the detail of the latter interests the scientist, to the grower the importance lies in producing a marketable commodity.

Harvesting and pod storage

It may seem obvious that growers should only harvest ripe pods, but it has to be stated. This means that the trees need regular and frequent visits during the harvest period (trees do not obligingly ripen all their pods at the same time). Removing the pods becomes an expensive exercise as it can only be done manually (there is no harvesting machine). Checking each tree once a fortnight is a suitable practice.

The workers recognise ripe pods by their colour. Depending on the variety grown, ripe pods range from a yellow-orange (Amelonado) through to a deep dark red russet (Trinitario). If harvested too early the beans within the pods will not only be smaller than they would otherwise, but the important fat content within the bean will be lower. The mucilage surrounding the beans in unripe pods will not contain much sugar, which will also affect the fermentation stage. If left too late, there is an increased chance of the pod becoming infected, or in some cases, of the beans within the pod germinating which makes them unsuitable.

When removing the pods, the harvesters have to exercise care not to damage the tree. Most harvest the pods using a cutlass or knife. If they cut the cushion, where the pod joins the tree, such damage provides a good entry point for fungal pathogens. They have to take care not to damage the flowers or other ripening pods.

The collected Forastero type pods are then placed where they may be kept for a week to ten days. It is difficult to explain the advantages of pod storage to some growers as the difference lies in the flavour character-istics. These are not specified in a sales contract or directly experienced by the grower as there is low chocolate consumption in most cocoa producing countries. However, chocolate made from pod-stored beans is less acid, bitter or astringent and has an enhanced chocolate flavour. It is close to the model requirements of manufacturers, as currently met by Ghana cocoa.

Pod storage also presents difficulties for some growers. Irrespective of origin, there is always pressure on growers to have their produce ready for the market sooner rather than later. This may come from the banks concerned about existing loans, or even middle-men buying cocoa, all too often telling the grower to sell now as the price will fall in two weeks time. In Malaysia the presence of the cocoa pod borer pushes growers to extract the beans as soon as possible, usually immediately after the harvesting of the pods, as any delay may mean additional losses to this pest. Again, irrespective of origin, the threat of theft exists. Beans, nicely packaged in their pods and left unguarded in the plantation present opportunities to the unscrupulous. All in all this may translate into undue haste by growers and their cutting out what may appear to be an unnecessary delay.

Fermentation

Having 'rested' the cocoa, the workers remove the beans from the pods. This they do by breaking the pods open, preferably with a wooden billet but usually with a machete, and pulling the beans and placenta out. The use of a knife may damage some beans and give the opportunity for moulds to infect the cotyledons (a serious fault for cocoa).

Different regions have different practices at this stage. Most smallholders who ferment their cocoa will pile the beans on plantain or banana leaves and cover them with more leaves. This method is common in West Africa, and if used, the pile should not be less than 100 kilos or greater than 2000 kilos. Another smallholder method is putting the beans into baskets and fermenting them there. As plantations have to process substantially more cocoa than individual smallholders they will have built fermentaries to deal with the greater tonnages. Such fermentaries have a series of boxes, usually tiered, in which they place the beans. The stacked arrangement allows workers to move the beans easily from one box to another, so mixing the beans; an essential part of fermentation.

Some origins that have Cocoa Boards, notably those in the South Pacific, including Papua New Guinea, rely on the work of smallholders to grow the cocoa, but control the post-harvest processing by licensing fermentaries. These are constructed along similar lines to those used by plantations. Smallholders sell their cocoa beans to the fermentaries who then process them and sell the fermented and dried beans to the exporters. As a consequence of the inevitable delay in removing the beans from the pod and their fermentation, the beans may suffer from moulds that would otherwise not have taken hold.[24] Moulds occur on the outside of the ferment, and while not actively sought after, do not give undue

24   In particular the free fatty acid content of the cocoa butter may increase as a
      result of mould and lipase action, see Chapters 7 and 8.

cause for alarm, providing the beans are dried within good time. If the mould persists it will definitely adversely affect the cocoa (see Chapter 8).

Whichever method is adopted, Forastero beans should undergo a fermentation of up to 120 hours, Criollo beans less, some two to three days. Because of the different fermentation times, growers, if they have the two types, should keep them apart (also for marketing reasons). Providing growers follow established practice there is little difference in the resulting cocoa; smallholders can produce equally good quality cocoa beans with their methods to that coming out of a big fermentary.

While left in a pile the beans and their pulp undergo a series of changes that have interested a number of observers, mostly earlier this century.[25] The first activity in the ferment concerns the growth of micro-organisms, particularly yeasts that develop on the pulp and mucilage surrounding the beans. Insects and, in particular, *Drosophila melanogaster* the 'vinegar-fly', are probably responsible for the transfer of the micro-organisms to the piles. Initially the pulp consists of nearly 85% water and 11% sugars, and has a pH of 3.5, mainly from the presence of citric acid. The activity of the yeasts helps to turn the sugar into alcohol. As the citric acid reduces, in part washed out by the release of some of the water in the pulp caused by the operation of micro-organisms, bacterial activity increases. This involves two main types of bacteria: lactic and acetic acid bacteria. The lactic acid bacteria are anaerobic and convert sugars into lactic acid while the acetic acid bacteria produce acetic acid from both the alcohol converted by the yeasts and from other organic acids. As oxygen diffuses into the pile, the increase in oxygen reduces the lactic acid bacteria's activity. Turning the pile over, or moving the pile from one fermentation box to another, improves the diffusion of oxygen in the pile and is important in proper fermentation.

The bacterial oxidation is exothermic, warming the pile up to 40–45 °C. Together with the heat, the presence of acetic acid kills the bean. This allows the pulp liquid to enter through the testa into the cotyledons. At this stage the beans appear bloated and marks the beginning of chemical changes within the cotyledon. These changes affect the eventual flavour of the cocoa and, particularly for Forastero cocoa, the colour. While the changes in the colour are not thought to affect the flavour, workers may assess the completion of the fermentation by cutting a few beans in half and inspecting the cotyledons. Forastero beans turn from a purple colour to a dark red-brown, the latter signifying complete fermentation. Criollo beans turn a cinnamon or tan colour, as they have little or none of the pigment contained in Forastero beans.

25 A series of books was published earlier this century on fermentation. The culmination was the 1937 edition by A W Knapp, 'Cacao fermentation'.

Some cocoa growers, notably from the Dominican Republic and parts of Sulawesi, do not ferment the cocoa at all. This gives an inferior quality cocoa with a poor chocolate flavour and is not a recommended practice (see Chapter 8).

Occasionally the beans do not ferment properly, and can result in the mucilage not breaking down as usual; sometimes giving rise to 'slimy' fermentation, called after the consistency of the mucilage. A lack of either sugar in the pulp and/or *Drosophila* to inoculate the beans may give rise to this condition. Adding sugar in some form and attracting the fruit flies may induce proper fermentation.

Drying

At the end of the fermentation process the beans have a moisture content of about 60%. This must be reduced to at least 7.5% by either sun drying or artificially drying the cocoa. Sun drying occurs in those regions that are free from rain during the harvest period which, notably, includes most of West Africa. The connection between good quality product and sun dried beans is clear. While it is not impossible to produce good quality cocoa from artificially dried beans it is certainly more expensive and requires care.

Basically sun drying the cocoa simply means spreading the beans out either on mats or on trays and allowing the sun and wind to take their effect. Every so often the workers should stir the beans to allow a thorough drying. At night or with the threat of rain, the beans should be protected, by either rolling them up in mats, or arranging some sort of cover. There is a danger of the beans drying too quickly if they are spread on concrete, a method adopted by some, and growers should only expose them to the sun for a short period at the beginning of the drying process. Drying may take between five and seven days.

Part of the secret to successful drying is time. Drying the cocoa too quickly stops some of the chemical reactions started in the fermentation and prevents the escape of part of the remaining acids in the bean resulting in acidic and astringent flavours in the cocoa. Very fast drying leaves the cotyledons wet and merely dries the exterior of the bean, initially giving the misleading appearance that the cocoa is dry. Within a few days the moisture will migrate out to the shell, allowing the development of mould, which should be avoided.

Artificially dried cocoa may result in inferior beans, either through contamination with smoke from the drying fires (which, together with internally mouldy cocoa are major quality defects), or by the grower drying the cocoa too quickly. Growers, using drying machinery, should follow a procedure that emulates sun drying conditions.

Recommended guidelines

Acceptance of Malaysian cocoa is not as widespread as it might be because their cocoa does not have the fully developed chocolate flavour found in similar cocoa grown in West Africa. In particular, manufacturers specify the standards set by Ghanaian cocoa for other producers to emulate. The difference between the two explains the lower prices paid by the trade for Malaysian cocoa compared with the West African. In the late 1980s Sime Darby Snd Bhd, a company with Malaysian cocoa plantations, together with Cadbury, the confectionery company, formulated a practice that growers should follow in preparing their beans for the market. This post-harvest practice became known as the Sime-Cadbury Process, and concentrates on three aspects: the time between harvesting the pods and splitting them open, the fermentation regime and the drying process. In 1989 the Cocoa Growers' Bulletin[26] published the research team's findings, from which CAOBISCO[27] issued a statement as to the correct method of post-harvest preparation for bulk Forastero/Amazon/Amelonado cocoas. The statement recommended:

a) Regular harvesting every 2–3 weeks of ripe, not green or over-ripe, pods;

b) Pods are opened 7–10 days after harvesting;

c) Diseased, rotten, discoloured and germinated beans are excluded from ferments;

d) Fermentation for 120 hours, with no more than one turn, in heaps of 100–2000 kilos of wet beans using banana/plantain leaves. If boxes are used they should be shallow (less than 40 cm deep) and well drained;

e) Ideally sun drying to 7.5% moisture, so that the beans crackle when squeezed in the hand. If artificial drying is necessary the condition should mimic sun drying as far as possible using low temperature/ambient air for the initial drying with higher temperatures only for the final stage;

f) The dried cocoa should be put in clean hessian bags stored off the ground and away from walls in dry, well ventilated, smoke free storage;

g) Finally the cocoa should be transported in similar clean, well ventilated conditions away from odorous material.

Is this new? Well, no, not really. Each generation seems to rediscover

26   Cocoa Growers' Bulletin (42).
27   The Association of the Chocolate, Biscuit and Confectionery Industries of the EEC.

methods propounded by others.[28] The following extracts come from a work by a Frenchman, de Chélus, translated and published in English in 1724, discussing first the harvesting, then pod storage and finally breaking the pods open:[29]

> *It will be proper to gather them when all the Shell has changed Colour, and when there is but a small Spot below which shall remain green. They go from Tree to Tree, and from Row to Row, and with forked Sticks or Poles, they cause the ripe Nuts to fall down, taking great care not to touch those that are not so, as well as the Blossoms: They employ the most handy Negroes in this Work, and others follow them with Baskets to gather them, and lay them in Heaps, where they remain four Days without being touch'd.*
>
> *In the Months that they bear most they gather them for a Fortnight together; in the less-fruitful Seasons, they only gather them from Month to Month. If the Kernels were left in Shells more than four Day, they would sprit, or begin to grow, and be quite spoiled: It is therefore necessary to shell them on the fifth Day in the Morning at farthest. To do this, they strike on the middle of the Shells with a Bit of Wood to cleave them, and then pull them open with their Fingers, and take out the Kernels, which they put in Baskets, casting the empty Shells upon the Ground, that they may with the Leaves, being putrified, serve to fatten the Earth, and supply the Place of Dung.*

Note that the use of knives is kept to a minimum. While de Chélus advocates pod storage for only four days, the cocoa harvested is likely to have been the more delicate Criollo stock that may not have needed so great a time.

Next de Chélus describes the fermentation process:

> *They afterwards carry all the Kernels into a House, and lay them on a heap upon a kind of loose Floor cover'd with Leaves of Balize, which are about four Feet long, and twenty Inches broad; then they surround it with Planks cover'd with the same Leaves, making a kind of Granary, which may contain the whole Pile of Kernels, when spread abroad. They cover the whole with like Leaves, and lay some Planks over all: the Kernels thus laid on a heap, and cover'd close on all sides, do not fail to grow warm, by the Fermentation of their insensible Particles; and this is what they call Sweating in those Parts. They uncover the Kernels Morning and Evening, and send the Negroes among them; who with their Feet and Hands, turn*

---

28 The following work was noted in 1966 in the Cocoa Growers' Bulletin, although the article concerned the similarity in cultivating cocoa in the seventeenth century to modern practices, rather than post-harvest practices.

29 de Chélus: 'The natural history of chocolate', Brookes (Dr) R (trans), 1724.

them topsy turvy . . . They continue to do this for five Days, at the end of which they have commonly sweat enough, which is discover'd by their Colour, which grows a great deal deeper, and very ruddy.

The more the Kernels sweat, the more they lose their Weight and Bitterness: but if they have not sweat enough, they are more bitter, and smell sour, and sometimes sprit. To succeed well, therefore, there should be a certain Medium observed, which is only to be learnt by use. If the Kernels have not sweat enough, or they wrap them too soon in the Mat, they are subject to sprit or germe, which makes them bitter, and good for nothing.

The practice describes similar fermentation practices throughout the world. Although de Chélus allows five days (120 hours) to ferment the probable Criollo beans which seems a little extravagant, they normally take a shorter period compared with the Forastero type. However, the colour '. . . and very ruddy' suggests a Forastero variety.

de Chélus goes on, dealing with the drying:

When the Kernels have sweat enough, they lay them out to air, and expose them to the Sun to dry them, in the manner following.

. . . Upon these Mats they put the Kernels about two Inches in height, and move and turn them very often with a proper Piece of Wood for the first two Days. At Night they wrap up the Kernels in the Mats, which they cover with Balize Leaves for fear of Rain, and they do the same in the daytime when it is likely to rain. Those who are afraid of having them stolen, lock them up.

When the Kernels have been once wrapped in a Mat, and begun to dry, care must be taken that they do not grow moist again; they must therefore be well stirr'd from time to time, that they may be thorowly dry'd, which you may know by taking a Handful in your Hand, and shutting it: if it cracks, then it is time to put them into your Store-house and to export them to sale.

Modern observers may be able to say with some precision the changes that take place during the post-harvest practice but this must translate into good husbandry; *plus ça change*, as de Chélus might have said.

3

Production

Evolution of production

The outstanding feature of cocoa production over the past 150 years is its dramatic growth. The first 50 years of this period, from 1840 to 1890, saw production increase by about 200%, from 14 000 tonnes to 41 000 tonnes. This rate of growth was all but matched in the next ten year period to 1900 when production rose to 115 000 tonnes. By 1916 a further 200% rise had taken place, when production reached 351 000 tonnes. While this rate of increase was unsustainable (it took until 1960 to achieve the next 200% rise) cocoa production continued to expand. Figure 3.1 shows the speed of this growth when viewed on a ten yearly basis. Taken over the 150 year period, cocoa production increased by just over 45% every 10 years. The decennial rate of growth went below 20% only once in the period from 1870 to 1990. Figure 3.1 illustrates this, showing the rate of growth superimposed over the world production figures.

As outlined in Chapter 1, the nineteenth century saw advances in confectionery technology that shifted consumption towards eating chocolate and away from the original drinking chocolate. Eating chocolate contains a higher proportion of cocoa than drinking chocolate. Therefore the consumers' movement towards eating chocolate helped stimulate the

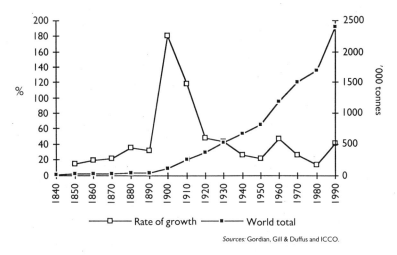

──□── Rate of growth ──■── World total

Sources: Gordian, Gill & Duffus and ICCO.

3.1 Evolution of the world cocoa production and rate of growth.

demand for more cocoa, causing production to increase.

The large 'spike' in the rate of growth from 1890 to 1920 shown in Fig. 3.1 occurred for different reasons. It marks the explosive entrance of cocoa production from mainland Africa. The introduction of cocoa into mainland Africa (see Chapter 1) occurred at the end of the 1870s. In 1890 Africa grew under 5% of the world's cocoa, most of this on the islands of Equatorial Guinea. By 1920 Africa accounted for just under 50% of the world total, with the mainland providing the larger part. African production continued to increase but not at the earlier rate; by 1930 Africa grew 65% of the world's cocoa. The change of production areas from the Americas to Africa also underlined the movement away from Criollo and Trinitario type beans to the Forastero type; causing some concern for the manufacturers (see Chapter 8). Figure 1.2 shows the development of each main geographical area as a percentage of the world crop and highlights the decline of the 'Americas' share of production, which now only forms approximately 30% of the world production.

The Americas

Despite the decline in market share mentioned above, the region's production has expanded. Figure 3.2 shows the evolution of cocoa production by main geographical area in which the Americas total increased from 78 000 tonnes in 1900 to 653 000 tonnes in 1990.

For the countries making up cocoa grown in the region, the evolution of production is far from uniform. Figure 3.3 shows Brazil's expansion of

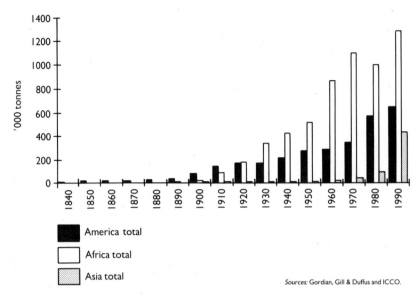

Sources: Gordian, Gill & Duffus and ICCO.

3.2 Evolution of cocoa production.

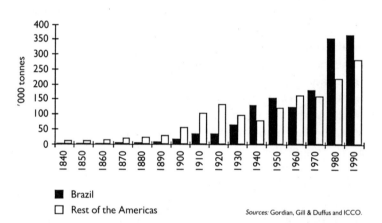

Sources: Gordian, Gill & Duffus and ICCO.

3.3 Evolution of cocoa production from Brazil compared with the rest of the Americas.

production to the current position where it provides 55% of cocoa grown in the region. Latterly, the Brazilian government's cocoa rehabilitation scheme (PROCACAU) promoted the expansion, but growers now face the threat of witches' broom disease and high costs with low returns.

Of the others who have increased production, Ecuador, the Dominican Republic, Colombia and Mexico individually produce more than 40 000 tonnes per year. The remainder each account for less than 20 000 tonnes per year. The most noticeable declines in production have been Venezuela

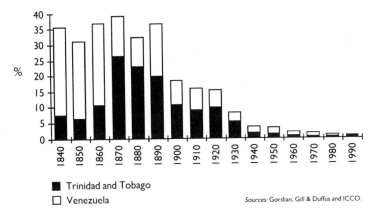

3.4 Evolution of cocoa production of Trinidad and Tobago and Venezuela shown as a percentage of the world total.

and Trinidad and Tobago. Figure 3.4 shows the evolution of these two countries' production, expressed as a percentage of world production. In the 1870s they represented some 40% of world production, although now they provide less than one per cent.

The onset of diseases during the first quarter of this century caused the decline. Trinidad and Tobago notably suffered from witches' broom and in Venezuela a combination of witches' broom, *Moniliophthera roreri*, and *Ceratocystis* wilt. These producers grew predominantly Criollo type cocoa, or cocoa considered to have the qualities of Criollo stock, i.e. cultivars that are more susceptible to diseases.

Africa

Once commercially introduced to mainland Africa, cocoa production swiftly took off, overtaking in terms of importance the traditional sources of supply (see Fig. 3.2). Four countries dominate African cocoa production, and have done so since 1920. Figure 3.5 shows the contribution of the 'big four' African producers as a cumulative percentage of total African production.

Since 1930 Cameroon, Côte d'Ivoire, Ghana and Nigeria produced annually at least 90% of the African total. While this domination of the market has remained stable throughout the past 60 years, there are underlying changes. Ghana's contribution, in terms of volume, has declined in world importance over recent years. In the early 1930s Ghana cocoa accounted for over 40% of the world total – producing more than the Americas and Asia. In 1984/85 Ghana's importance had declined to represent some 9% of world production. Currently it produces 11% of

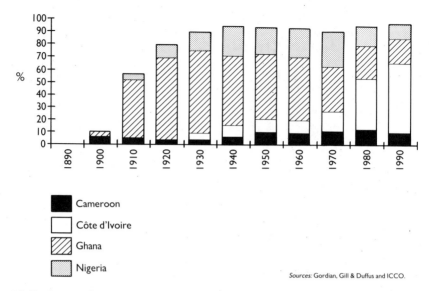

Sources: Gordian, Gill & Duffus and ICCO.

3.5 Evolution of cocoa production in Cameroon, Cote d'Ivoire, Ghana and Nigeria as a percentage of total African production.

the world total, with 272 000 tonnes. Similarly, Nigeria's share of the cocoa production has also diminished, currently growing 12% of the African total. Offsetting these declines within the 'big four' is the production in Côte d'Ivoire.

Since 1950 production in Côte d'Ivoire has all but doubled every 10 years, to reach 849 000 tonnes in 1988/89 – a tonnage equivalent to the total world production in the mid-1950s. While production during that particular year was an exception (the year before it was 674 000 tonnes and in 1989/90 it was 714 000 tonnes) the Côte d'Ivoire's current influence over world production is dominant. At present 30% of the world production comes from the Côte d'Ivoire; the next largest producer, Brazil, grows 15%.

The smallest of the African 'big four' is Cameroon. Growing a different type of cocoa to that of the other three (see Chapter 1) the largest production from Cameroon occurred in 1987/88 when it produced 133 000 tonnes. This has declined slightly to 110 000 tonnes.

Asia

For the sake of ease rather than geographic correctness the term 'Asia' here refers to cocoa produced in any location from Sri Lanka eastwards to the Samoas. Although this describes a segment nearly a quarter of the globe, it provides a useful division in describing cocoa production.

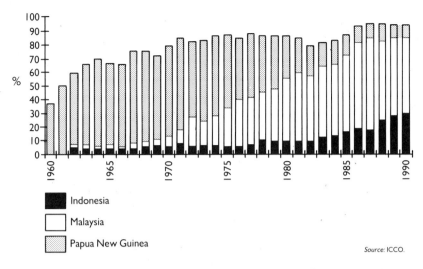

Source: ICCO.

3.6 Evolution of cocoa production in Indonesia, Malaysia and Papua New Guinea as a percentage of total Asian production.

Over the past 30 years Asian cocoa production has risen from representing below 2% of the world total, to 18%, as shown in Fig. 1.2 and 3.2. Similar to African production that of Asia depends primarily on a few countries, in this case Indonesia, Malaysia and Papua New Guinea. Figure 3.6 shows the cumulative production of these three countries as a percentage of the total Asian production. Since 1970 they have represented in excess of 80% of the Asian total, and over 90% during the past 5 years.

Evident from Fig. 3.6 is the reduction of Papua New Guinea's role and the rise in production of both Malaysia and Indonesia. Over the past ten to fifteen years these two countries have expanded their production substantially. While both have been growing cocoa for some considerable

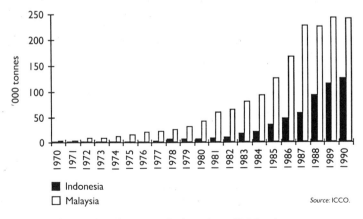

Source: ICCO.

3.7 Evolution of cocoa production in Indonesia and Malaysia.

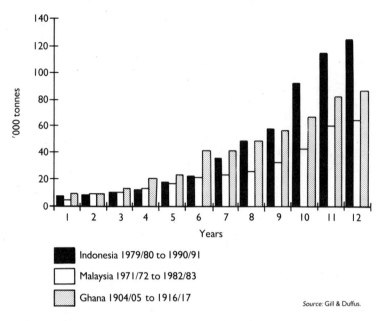

Indonesia 1979/80 to 1990/91

Malaysia 1971/72 to 1982/83

Ghana 1904/05 to 1916/17

Source: Gill & Duffus.

3.8 Malaysian (1971/72–1982/83), Indonesian (1979/80–1990/91) and Ghanaian (1904/05–1916/17) cocoa production.

time[1] until recently neither had sought to increase its market share to any real extent. Figure 3.7 shows the rise in recent production of these two countries.

While Malaysian production seems to have reached a plateau, Indonesian expansion continues. It is of interest to compare the production of the two countries when they initially grew similar tonnages. Figure 3.8 compares the Malaysian production between 1971/72 to 1982/83 with that of Indonesia from 1979/80 to 1990/91. For the first years shown, the growth in both countries appears similar but note that while Malaysia currently produces nearly twice that of Indonesia, it is Indonesia with the higher rate of growth. In future years this may well have considerable importance if Indonesia fulfils its potential as a producer.

On a historical note, Fig. 3.8 also shows the development of production in Ghana during the early 1900s. Despite the lack of modern hybrids and the probable effect of swollen shoot disease, the evolution of Ghanaian cocoa is similar to latter-day Asian countries. The comparison is of interest because this period heralded the last previous occurrence of a new region beginning to grow significant amounts of cocoa; the most recent, of course, being Asia. Nigeria soon followed Ghana's example of

1   Cocoa was introduced to Malaysia in 1788 and 1560 in Indonesia.

growing cocoa, as did the French speaking countries of Cameroon and Côte d'Ivoire. Cocoa production soared and unsurprisingly prices fell. As shown earlier in Fig. 1.3, in 1990 terms, the UK import values collapsed in 1907 from a 60 year high of £3227 per tonne to a low of £795 in 1939.[2] The effect of mainland West Africa entering the market produced a 38 year bear market and reduced the importance of the then traditional cocoa growing regions of Central America and the Caribbean.

While direct comparisons with the situation today may be too simplistic, the effect of new growing regions coming on-stream should not be underestimated. The start of the current bear market began when Malaysia started production in earnest, followed by Indonesia. The current low prices may be set to continue for some time yet.

Apart from the above, the rise of Asia as a third major producing area has had a more profound influence on the cocoa market than if similar production levels had been made in either the Americas or in Africa. This is for two reasons. First it helps to make the supply of cocoa more certain. With only two main geographical areas producing the majority of cocoa a problem with one of them, perhaps because of adverse weather conditions, could mean the disruption of the supply of cocoa, severely if other problems arose in the second major producing area. With a third region producing cocoa this disruption becomes less likely.

Second, the market has had to absorb a different quality-type of cocoa. To some, specially the European chocolate manufacturers, this has been a

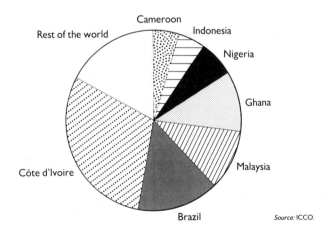

3.9 Cocoa production in 1990/91.

2   Although lower figures were recorded during World War II the UK government controlled prices during this period and so they are therefore not relevant to free market conditions.

question of both re-learning old skills of using a different type of cocoa[3] and of establishing their quality requirements, see Chapters 2 and 8.

From the foregoing it is apparent that a small number of countries dominate cocoa production. In fact, seven countries produce over 80% of the world's cocoa. Figure 3.9 illustrates this distribution.

Recent trends – 1981/82–1990/91

Brazil

Brazilian cocoa production has continued to increase, albeit somewhat erratically, over the past ten years. In 1981/82 production was 311 000 tonnes and the ICCO estimate 368 000 tonnes for 1990/91. During this period it reached the height of 406 000 tonnes (1984/85) and the low of 296 000 tonnes a year earlier. Two main causes for the underlying expansion were the PROCACAU programme that ran from 1976 to 1985 and the effect of high world cocoa prices at the end of the 1970s. The high prices for cocoa at the end of this decade prompted an expansion of the cocoa industry. Allied to this, the PROCACAU programme resulted in 298 000 hectares of either new cocoa farmland or rehabilitated farms. This affected just over 50% of the total cocoa growing area in Brazil. As a high cost producer (see Fig. 3.12) and as cocoa growers operate without direct government intervention or control, production in Brazil is sensitive to the world market price. If prices remain low the growers will use less fertilisers and pesticides (see Fig. 3.17) thereby reducing the yields. Higher cocoa prices will not only prompt the use of more chemicals but if they continue for any length of time the growers will plant more cocoa.

The presence of witches' broom fungus in Bahia, the largest cocoa growing region, is a threat to the long term production. Reports of its incidence in Bahia show, at the moment, low levels of infection. In mid-May 1991 CEPLAC stated that they had found 284 779 infected trees out of 14.6 million checked. This shows an infection incidence of 2% of the number examined, which itself is under 5% of the total number of cocoa trees in Brazil. The long term costs of combating the disease will undoubtedly increase the Brazilian grower's costs of production.

In 1989 ICCO forecast that the 1994/95 production would be in the range of 501 to 538 000 tonnes. In view of the continued threat of witches' broom and current low prices this is optimistic. ICCO now

---

3   This had to be done by the cocoa industry at the beginning of the twentieth century when the Trinitario type cocoa from the Americas was superseded by the African production of Forastero-type flavour.

forecast production in 1991/92 will be 300 000 tonnes; a level that a more recent study[4] considers Brazil may retain for some time.

Cameroon

Production over the past ten years has stagnated at about 120 000 tonnes. At the highest it reached 133 000 tonnes in 1987/88, and the lowest in 1982/83 when it produced 105 000 tonnes. The ICCO estimate for 1990/91 production is 115 000 tonnes and forecast 105 000 tonnes in 1991/92. Falling production is set against the background of the farmers receiving less for their work. In 1989 the price paid to the farmers was reduced from CFA 420 per kilo of beans to CFA 250 per kilo. The following crop year, 1990/91, the authorities reduced the price to CFA 220. The president announced that this price would remain in force for the 1991/92 crop. In constant 1990 terms, this represents half the price farmers received in 1985. The continued low prices are unlikely to promote any expansion of the industry. The tree stock is old (see Fig. 3.15) and there are few reports of cocoa rehabilitation or expansion. In 1991 operational changes in the marketing of Cameroon cocoa may, in the short term, disrupt the export of cocoa, see Chapter 4. Price increases may promote better husbandry which would bring Cameroon's production back towards 150 000 tonnes at the turn of the century.

Côte d'Ivoire

From 1980/81 to 1990/91 cocoa production in the Côte d'Ivoire increased by 95%. In 1988/89, after favourable weather, production reached a record 849 000 tonnes; the ICCO forecast for 1991/92 is 740 000 tonnes. Despite this reduction the underlying trend is upwards. Prices paid to the farmers in earlier years helped lay the foundation for the expansion; although it may have more to do with consistent prices at high levels as against just high prices. Figure 3.10 shows that producer prices in Côte d'Ivoire were relatively flat during the 1980s, albeit about twice the 1990 value. This suggests that fluctuating prices, even reaching very high levels may not stimulate long term growth. From 1984/85 to 1988/89 the authorities guaranteed the farmers a price of CFA 400 per kilo of beans despite tumbling world prices. No doubt new plantings made during this period will increase future production. However, in 1988/89 the government was forced to reduce the farmer price to CFA 250 per kilo. The following crop year the authorities made a further reduction to CFA 200

4   ICCO document ICC/SPEC/16/4.

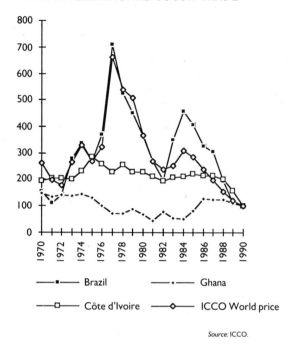

Source: ICCO.

3.10 Evolution of indexed local currency producer prices in selected cocoa exporting countries and the annual average ICCO daily price, all in 1990 terms.

per kilo. The lowering of the farmer price was necessary as the marketing agency, the Caisse de Stabilization, owed some CFA 88 billion (US$350 million). The effect of the lower prices was twofold: a reduction of cocoa entering the country from Ghana as smuggling ceased to be a profitable enterprise, and there were short term difficulties in financing the internal buying of cocoa, as the Caisse was faced with the large amount of debt.

Despite being a low cost producer (see Fig. 3.12) with reasonable yields production in the Côte d'Ivoire may not continue its expansion, although much will depend on the future price paid to the farmers and to the newly planted trees that have not yet matured. As cocoa beans represent 25% to 30% of the total value of exports from the Côte d'Ivoire (25% in 1988), and involves a large number of households (see Fig. 3.15) the crop is very important to the country.

Ghana

During the first half of the 1980s Ghana's cocoa production continued to decline to 159 000 tonnes in 1983/84. This was a continuation of the progressively lower production levels that had taken place since the mid-1960s. In 1964/65 Ghana produced a record 566 000 tonnes. In the mid-1980s the government reassessed the importance of cocoa and undertook a rehabilitation programme on cocoa farms. At the same time the marketing board began paying higher prices to the farmers for their cocoa, see Fig. 3.10. The increased production reflects these changes. The ICCO estimate for 1990/91 is 293 000 tonnes, and forecast 265 000 tonnes in 1991/92. If prices recover in the near future production may rise in subsequent years. Similar to the Côte d'Ivoire, cocoa plays a major role in Ghana's finances as it represents some 45–50% of the total export value, (45% in 1988). Although the yield is low (not helped by a large number of either elderly or very young trees), so are the assumed costs of production.

Nigeria

Nigerian cocoa production continued to decline during the first half of the 1980s, from 181 000 tonnes in 1981/82 to 100 000 tonnes in 1986/87. This marked the end of the Nigerian Cocoa Marketing Board and the privatisation of the cocoa industry. In 1987/88 production shot up to 150 000 tonnes, a level that growers seemed to maintain for the next few years. Analysts estimate a similar tonnage for 1990/91 at 155 000 tonnes. The increase stemmed from the higher prices paid to the farmers by the new exporters. Immediately after privatisation in 1986 many exporters used cocoa as a vehicle for capital flight from the country. Exporters bought cocoa in naira and sold it in hard currency, thereby converting the naira into a sought after hard currency that was often banked overseas. For reasons of supply and demand, the effect was that the growers received a large increase in the price paid for the cocoa. In one extreme case some farmers, at the end of 1988, sold their cocoa for 16 000 naira (US$3020) a tonne. In contrast in 1985/86 the NCB offered farmers 1600 naira per tonne. The situation is now more stable, as fewer active cocoa exporters remain in Nigeria, and they appear not to pay farmers the very high prices that occurred earlier. As a result of these lower prices the ICCO forecast production in 1991/92 at 105 000 tonnes. Unless prices recover, it is unlikely that growers will continue to rehabilitate existing farms or to plant extra land.

Indonesia

In terms of growth during the last ten years Indonesia outstrips all the major producers. In 1981/82 it produced 16 000 tonnes; the ICCO forecast for 1991/92 is 165 000 tonnes. Analysts expect this increase to continue as many of the trees are young and have not reached maturity. A free economy combined with cheap government land grants together with the planting technology and husbandry learnt in the plantations of Malaysia provide the main reasons for this growth. Production costs are low and yields will improve as the trees mature. By the turn of the century Indonesia may produce close to 400 000 tonnes.

Malaysia

Production in Malaysia over the past ten years has also increased substantially, from 62 000 tonnes in 1981/82 to forecasted 240 000 tonnes in 1991/92. The growth steadily increased until 1988/89 after which it plateaued; estimates for 1990/91 appear similar to 1988/89 at about 220 000 tonnes. Low world prices left growers using less fertilisers and pesticides, giving rise to inevitable lower yields. Faced with fighting the pod borer moth, *Conopomorpha cramerella*, achieving low yields and only getting low prices have proved too much for some growers. Helped by government schemes that provide incentives for farmers to grow other crops (for example coffee) growers have taken the opportunity to diversify out of cocoa. Despite this, analysts expect production to increase as there is a large proportion of trees that have not matured. By the year 2000 Malaysia and Indonesia may grow 800 000 tonnes, possibly representing 30% of the world crop.

Factors affecting production

Although seven countries account for most of the world's cocoa production, the dynamics are the same for all. The quantity grown depends on the land area under cultivation, the tree stock characteristics and the yields obtained from such stock. Put a little more prosaically, and in reverse, the effects of the environment on the various types of tree, their age and quantity equals the production potential. Although these three factors determine the level of production they are, in turn, subject to other influences and it is of interest to look at their interaction.

Land area under cocoa

The decision by a farmer to grow cocoa as opposed to other crops may not be easily reduced to provide a universal formula to suit all. What some consider a marginal factor others may find central and influence them towards a different decision. This means the order of the factors shown below are not necessarily in order of importance to all farmers.

Return on investment

High returns for selling cocoa for low inputs will naturally cause more plantings of cocoa to take place. As a tree crop this affects long term production. In the short term higher prices encourage growers to apply more inputs, fertiliser and pesticides etc, thereby increasing the yield of the mature cocoa. However, returns to the farmer in the short term may have little to do with the world market price of cocoa. The farmer's price may be subject to government strictures and set at a particular level; or it may be subject to supply and demand pressures that are an internal feature of the country. For example, a producing country may have an active cocoa processing industry that competes with the exporters for the beans supplied by the farmers. During a time of cocoa shortage in that country, internal prices will soar. Within limits, exporters may or may not choose to trade, if there is a shortage of cocoa they will reduce their sales. But processors cannot treat their factories in such a cavalier fashion, their priority is to keep the factory running and they must pay the going rate for the cocoa. Indeed, the processing (or exceptional demand, see Nigeria above) need not be large or sophisticated for this to occur. Western Samoans are unusual as cocoa producers in that they are also substantial cocoa consumers in terms of the amount consumed per person. 'Koko Samoa' is a rich chocolate drink made out of ground (usually by hand) cocoa beans and drunk in substantial quantities by those living in the Samoan countryside. Cyclone Ofa hit Samoa in 1990 destroying the local cocoa production. This resulted in the price of cocoa for sale in the local Samoan markets in early 1991 to be four times the world market price.

By way of comparison, Fig. 3.10 shows the evolution of some producer prices in constant 1990 indexed terms. An index system avoids difficulties in compiling the non-convertible currencies in the series, although it obscures comparisons between countries. Caution is required in interpreting the data as some countries do not report their internal prices.

The way the internal price in Brazil follows broadly the world price is consistent as free market conditions exist in that country. Both Côte d'Ivoire and Ghana pursue governmental control over prices paid to the farmers, see Chapter 4. Overall, providing the costs of production still make the enterprise profitable, increasing the internal price may give the growers the signal to plant more cocoa and to increase their inputs, thereby exacerbating the current world oversupply.

Government schemes

The role of the government in assisting growers is a leading factor in the grower's decision whether or not to plant cocoa. This assistance can take many forms, from helping to establish a new plantation, through to supporting the growers after the establishment of the stand or indeed, rehabilitating disused farms. The generosity of the assistance also varies, examples of implemented schemes include: cheap government loans or grants to buy the land (Indonesia – up to March 1990); actually giving the land to smallholders for cultivation (formerly Indonesia); providing the smallholder with seedlings, fertilisers, pesticides (Samoa); and rehabilitating unproductive farms (Brazil). Most countries producing cocoa also have extension services to help the smallholders, some more active and better developed than others. A recent example is Indonesia where up to 1990 the government made available loans to help establish plantations. These loans were at substantially lower rates of interest than those available commercially and were repayable in rupiah. The advantage of obtaining sales revenue in a hard currency and repaying the loans in rupiah (a currency that many considered would be devalued during the life of the loan) was hard to resist. As a result many companies that were neither involved in cocoa nor whose core business included cocoa (such as garage and airline businesses) were tempted into growing cocoa.

Alternative crops

Whether a grower chooses to plant cocoa or something else largely depends on what other crops are available to cultivate. Land suitable for cocoa is, fortunately, very able to support other crops, see Chapter 2. The conditions needed to grow cocoa suit the production of other commodities, such as coffee, rubber, palm oil, pepper and copra (coconut). As a last resort, the smallholder may choose to grow food crops and adopt subsistence farming if the return for cash crops is too small.

Changing from growing one commodity to another is not taken lightly. Growers, for the most part, are conservative in their outlook; prepared to withstand low prices for a considerable time before concluding that they need to change crops. As well as those points noted above, the grower considers other factors, not least is the time and labour needed to bring a new commodity crop into production. Uprooting and replanting an existing plantation costs money and the new crop is not likely to give a return for a couple of years. Deciding to change the crop for another is not made easier by the prospect of a reduced cash flow following on the heels of poor returns on the existing crop.

Pests, diseases, drought and floods

The advent of debilitating cocoa diseases or pests will make the decision to change crops easier. The grower may be forced to replant the land with another crop by the combined difficulties of poor yields caused by diseases and/or pests, and the cost in combating them. Not only does the grower have a reduced income from the lower yields but also the added cost of trying to remove the cause of the poor yield. In 1990 some farmers in peninsula Malaysia found the fight against the cocoa pod borer, *Conopomorpha cramerella*, too great in the face of continual low cocoa prices. Aided by a government grant to replant with coffee, they abandoned their cocoa.[5] In some instances such disasters cause the grower to abandon the land totally. Floods and droughts, sometimes severe enough to lead to fires, should be considered in a slightly different light. As such catastrophes are temporary conditions that are, it is hoped, also infrequent, their occurrence will not necessarily force the grower to replant with a different crop.

Yield

The yield, usually measured in terms of tonnes per hectare, is central to the grower's calculation. As it depends on the age, type and planting distribution of the trees, together with the level of inputs needed, the yield shows growers the effectiveness of their work. However, a low cost, low yielding farm may be just as profitable as one with much higher yields but needing a greater level of inputs. Size is no measure of profitability. A smallholder may be content with a yield of 200 kilos per hectare while some estates may blench at yields of anything less than 1200 kilos. The grower must pay the higher expenses with greater efficiency. Those with large capital outlays and expenses need high yields. Figure 3.11 below compares the estimated yields with the costs of production for some of the larger cocoa growing countries. Brazil (500 kilos) and Malaysia (700 kilos) have higher yields, but their costs of production are also more than the others; more than one dollar per kilo for Brazil and between 70 cents to US$1.30 for Malaysia. In 1990 analysts estimated the cost of production for the Côte d'Ivoire at 40 cents per kilo and 45 cents for Nigeria.

5   Public Ledger August 2, 1991. In the following month a report from Brazil said that some coffee growers were replanting their land with eucalyptus as the price of coffee was too low. However, the Malaysian government has also allocated M$12 million (US $432 000) to smallholders who suffer from C. *cramerella* to combat the pest. The four year programme involves destroying existing infected trees. The programme will pay for the replanting and fertiliser.

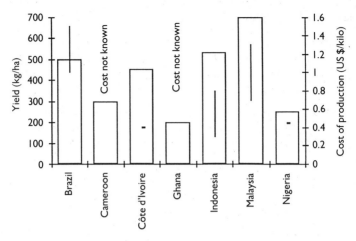

Sources: Ruf and de Milly (ICCO) and ICCO.

3.11 Comparison between estimated yields (bars) and costs of production (lines) for selected countries.

Two strategies in achieving high yields in a new cocoa farm are outlined under 'Production strategies – the Indonesian experience' below.

Tree stock characteristics

The second part of the dynamics of cocoa production primarily concerns the production capability of the trees. The question naturally refers to the planting material. The capability of the cultivars not only includes the number of pods that the trees may produce but also their ability to withstand periods of adverse weather and attacks of pests and diseases. In terms of planting material cocoa production has seen two main changes. The first was the move away from the Criollo stock. This occurred either by chance after disease or drought, as in the Americas, or by happenstance as was the case with the cultivar type that has been the mainstay of African production. Not only did the Amelonado stock have higher yields but it also had a markedly different flavour. A fact that chocolate manufacturers, at the time generally deplored, but came to live with.[6]

Hybrids The second change involved the refinement of the Forastero stock, rather than a move away from the existing cultivar to another. As such, growers introduced the hybrid cultivars in a more controlled manner and achieved by research rather than the seemingly haphazard methods of early cocoa planting.[7] It should be made clear that hybrid

6   See Chapter 8.

7   Note the regeneration of cocoa in Indonesia at the end of the nineteenth century. A fortuitous accident. How many others were not so successful?

means different stock in different places. A successful hybrid used in Africa is extremely unlikely to be similar to one in say, Malaysia. Indeed, there appears to be a trend towards having a number of different hybrids or crosses growing in the same plantation, avoiding a total genetic mono-culture. In cocoa parlance, 'hybrid' although imprecise and meaning dif-ferent genetic crosses to different cultivars, refers to the introduction of a non-traditional strain of cocoa to that area, and crossed with either a type grown in the region, or one from outside the area. They give better yields and are more resistant to the diseases in that area and give cocoa suitable flavour characteristics. Two main agencies develop these hybrids: the plantations of large estates and various research stations throughout the world. Each region and country naturally tends to address its own require-ments, for instance research into growing cocoa resistant to swollen shoot virus is one of the main interests of researchers in Ghana, while in Brazil (and elsewhere) researchers developing cocoa resistant to witches' broom is foremost in their minds.

The growers with larger estates, and therefore more resources, naturally make use of the most up to date genetic material available. The smallholder depends on either the government extension services or, regretfully, seeds from his or his neighbour's trees. Subsequent generations of hybrids, if not bred true, generally lead to less vigorous trees. However,

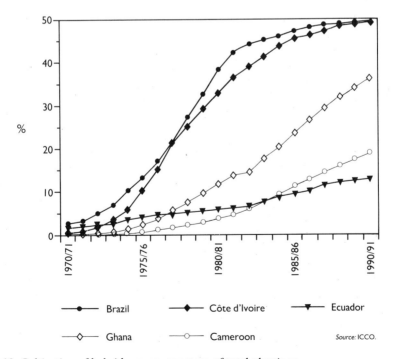

3.12 Cultivation of hybrids, as a percentage of total plantings.

71

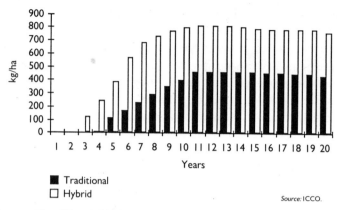

3.13 Age profile of the yields from traditional varieties and those from hybrids.

Fig. 3.12 shows the increase in cultivation of hybrids, albeit somewhat slowly in some cases.

Analysts consider all of Malaysian production to be hybrid, as is the recent increase in Indonesian cocoa production.

Age profile As is evident from Fig. 3.12 the trend is to plant more hybrids and Fig. 3.13 helps to explain why.

Note that the figures making up the graph are averages from a number of countries and some of the yields are estimates. Two aspects of the yield become apparent from Fig. 3.13. First is the greater yield given by the hybrids compared with the traditional varieties. Over a twenty year period the hybrids, as averaged out, are capable of twice the production of the traditional varieties. Second, not only do the hybrids provide a better yield

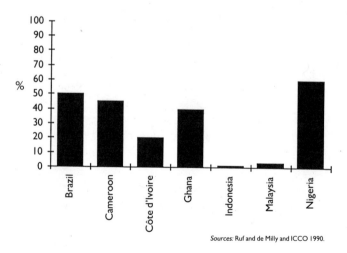

3.14 Percentage of cocoa trees over 30 years old.

when mature but they also provide cocoa sooner than the traditional varieties. They also retain their vigour for longer, although once over thirty years old the trees' productivity will decline markedly. Twenty year old traditional varieties will on average be able to produce 440 kilos of beans while those aged 30 will give 337 kilos.[8]

The age profile of the tree stock is therefore important when assessing potential production. Figure 3.14 shows the percentage of trees older than 30 years in some origins. While the elderly stock still produces pods, younger ones give higher yields. The very low figures for Malaysia and Indonesia underline their production potential as, especially in Indonesia, many of the plantations have not reached full maturity.

Environmental influences

The third major influence affecting the volume of cocoa production (after the planted area and the type and age of the trees) is that of the environment. This includes the effects of man as well as those of nature. Chapter 2 gave details on the influence of individual factors such as the suitability of soil, adequate water, nutrient levels, humidity, wind and temperature. Man's intervention can alter some of these; for instance, applying fertiliser improves the nutrient levels, pruning the shade and cocoa trees affects the relative humidity. The grower may also exert some control over the pests and diseases that would otherwise affect the levels of production. These controls have no natural counterpart and consist of applying pesticides and fungicides etc.

Smallholders and estates

Most of the cocoa production in Africa is by smallholders. Figure 3.15 below shows the number of self-employed farming families involved in growing cocoa in the major African producing countries compared with Malaysia, Indonesia and Brazil. The figures do not include plantation employees. In the Côte d'Ivoire only 5% of the cocoa grown comes from plantations larger than 40 hectares while in Malaysia the figure is 85%, Indonesia 50% and in Brazil it is above 55%.

It should also be noted that most of the cocoa grown in Africa is under thinned forest, which does not give the highest yield, see Chapter 2.

For the smallholder, the extension services become a principal feature in attempts to improve the yield. The extension services can assist, both as

---

8   ICCO document ICCO ECON/SPEC/2.

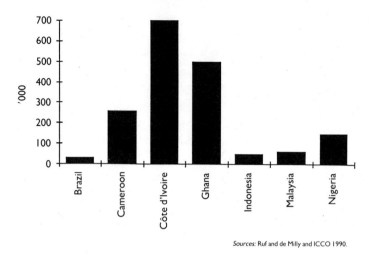

Sources: Ruf and de Milly and ICCO 1990.

3.15 Self-employed families in cocoa farming.

a source of material, fertilisers, pesticides etc, and in giving advice on husbandry. In general, the smallholder achieves lower yields than the estates. For Malaysia in 1990 the average yield for a smallholder was 610 kilos per hectare while the estates averaged 1100 kilos.[9] A number of causes give rise to this difference. First, the land used by smallholders may be marginal and less productive than that used by the estates. Estate owners can afford higher prices for land than smallholders. Second, estates can more easily afford fertilisers and pesticides than the smallholders. Not applying such materials gives lower yields. During the recent prolonged period of low prices this cost cutting came to the fore. Figure 3.16 shows the relationship between cocoa prices and fertiliser use in the Brazilian regions of Bahia and Espírito Santo for the period 1975 to 1985. While not all the cocoa grown in these regions is smallholder, 88% of the cocoa growing land in Bahia, the larger cocoa growing region, is 50 hectares or less giving a preponderance of smallholder activity. Underlining the less efficient use of the land by the smallholders is that in Bahia this 88% of the land grows only 45% of the region's cocoa.

As is evident, the use of fertilisers is sensitive to the price of cocoa, especially when low, and profitability of growing cocoa is marginal.

Third, estates generally have access to the latest information concerning husbandry and, indeed, the varieties grown. Nurseries in estates often conduct their own research and develop different cultivars. One Indonesian estate's nursery in 1990 was preparing 29 different varieties for planting. The smallholder is often in the hands of the extension services,

9   FAMA Malaysia Cocoa Outlook, December 1989.

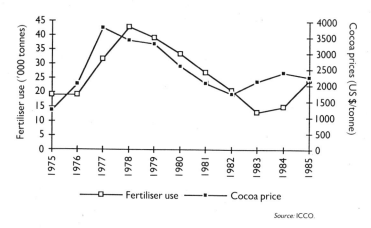

3.16 Cocoa prices and fertiliser use in Bahia and Espirito Santo.

and while not warranting the scale of development that estates have at their disposal, may not have the range of cultivars to choose from.

Setting up

Starting a cocoa farm begins with obtaining the land for cultivating the cocoa. In most cases this is bought with the purpose of setting up a cocoa farm. However, in many parts of the world a seemingly straightforward transaction involving land can have legal repercussions even for the wary. One experienced and worldwide estate owner with cocoa plantations in the South Pacific found individuals instigating claims against the development many years after the establishment of the estate. Based on traditional and local land rights such claims are often difficult to prove one way or the other and are time consuming and expensive. From the costing viewpoint, the servicing of the investment is more important than the outright price paid for the land. Not only will the land price vary from place to place but, as mentioned earlier, growers may obtain the land by different methods. The government may virtually give it away, or provide loans for the capital investment on favourable terms to the borrower. Such schemes reduce the servicing requirement and ease the burden on the grower.

Once the grower buys the land, the cost of operating a cocoa farm falls into two parts: the cost of establishing the cocoa stand and the subsequent costs of its maintenance. Establishing the farm includes clearing the land, planting shade and cocoa trees, pruning, weeding, fertiliser and pesticide applications[10] and constructing the required infrastructure –

10 Until the cocoa farm is established, after which they become a maintenance cost.

roads, irrigation ditches, nursery and processing facilities. These are once only costs which, together with buying the land, the grower may consider as capital costs.

Labour

The largest element of these costs is the labour. This is true for both the establishment costs and those in maintaining the farm. The next major expense is the input costs (fertilisers, pesticides etc). Like labour, they are variable, higher yields need increased inputs. However their use also depends on the nature of the soil and the level of pests and diseases the grower has to fight against. By way of example, in Brazil the input costs were considered to be 25% of the total costs to produce 750 kilos of beans per hectare. Labour made up 62% with the balance consisting of administration and general expenses.[11]

Farm sizes vary greatly, from smallholder plots to expanses owned by multinationals, which makes the idea of labour costs difficult to quantify across the board. Not only do the smallholders, who grow a sizeable proportion of all cocoa, predominantly work the land themselves and do not hire labourers, but wage rates vary around the world. That said the costs, per hectare, for an estate will be markedly higher than those of a nearby smallholding worked by the owner and his or her family. A better measure of labour, one that may be applied throughout the world and is not subject to currency exchange rates or devaluations, is man days per hectare per year.

The amount of labour depends on how the grower cultivates the cocoa. The requirements are different if it is grown under planted shade trees, in thinned forest or interplanted with another crop, for instance coconut. R A Lass in 'Cocoa'[12] gives eight cases of labour used in establishing cocoa farms. An analysis of this data, by the type of production is given in Fig. 3.17.

These figures show the differences between the various methods of cultivation. With one exception, that of growing cocoa under coconut, they are averages and contain a wide variation as farms each have different requirements. They do not give an accurate assessment of the actual labour needs for a particular method of cultivation.

Surprisingly, growers planting cocoa under thinned forest need more labour than planting under shade trees. One possible explanation is that the removal of only a proportion of the trees restricts the movement of

11   'Study of cocoa production in Brazil', ICCO document, 1989.
12   Ibid Wood G A R and Lass R A, 1985.

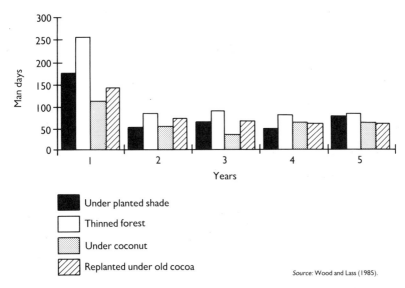

Source: Wood and Lass (1985).

3.17 Labour needed during the first five years to cultivate one hectare of cocoa.

the workers and slows down the work; although planting under an existing crop needs the least amount of work. Measured until the trees are established, planting under coconut requires two-fifths of the man days of that needed under thinned forest. Even replanting under an old cocoa stand has labour requirements comparable to planting under shade trees.

The chart shows that the first year of work is the most intensive. For example, for the five year period under consideration, half of the total labour for cocoa planted under shade trees occurs in the first year. Similar amounts are true for the other methods of growing cocoa, the lowest being replanting under cocoa that needs 38% of the total.

Once the grower establishes the cocoa stand the labour needed to maintain the cocoa stabilises from one year to the next, although with some variations. Between 63 to 84 man days per hectare is the range given by Lass.[13] The lowest was for growing cocoa under coconut, although 67 days was cited in growing cocoa in thinned forest in Africa.

Production strategies – the Indonesian experience[14]

Financial success in setting up a cocoa farm depends on two strategies. The first is to engineer the quick return on the initial investment; i.e.,

13   Ibid Wood G A R and Lass R A, 1985.
14   Hasan I and Chok D K K: 'Efficiency enhancement in a world of excess cocoa', ICCO Advisory Group Meeting, 1988.

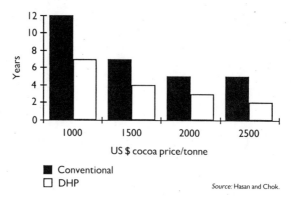

3.18 Comparison between the payback periods of a 'conventional' cocoa farm and that using double hedgerow planting (DHP).

reducing the payback period on the set-up costs. The second involves the economies of scale, increasing the yields thereby cutting the unit costs.

Comparisons between two farms in Indonesia underline the relevance of these needs. The first farm is a conventional cocoa plantation where 1100 to 1600 cocoa trees are planted per hectare, a normal density of planting. In the second farm, up to 5000 budded cocoa fan branches per hectare are planted without shade trees. This second method, known as the 'double hedgerow planting', requires greater inputs and therefore costs more but has the potential of higher and faster returns. Figure 3.18

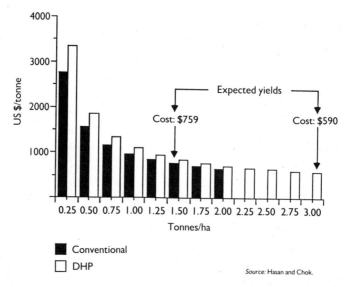

3.19 Comparison between the average cost of production of 'conventionally' grown cocoa and that using double hedgerow planting (DHP).

shows the payback periods of each assuming various levels of cocoa prices. In all cases the more intensive production methods prove to give a substantially faster payback.

The quicker payback period achieved by the double hedgerow planting is worthwhile in itself, but the benefits continue as the costs of production per tonne are also lower than the conventional method. This is not immediately apparent when the costs of the two are compared, as shown in Fig. 3.19. It only becomes clear when one knows that the expected yield for the conventional farm is 1.5 tonnes per hectare and 3.0 tonnes for the double hedgerow planting. With these yields the costs of production are US$590 per tonne for the double hedgerow planting compared with US$759 per tonne by the conventional method; nearly 30% more.

The historical perspective

The prices which cocoa producers throughout the world have received for their product have shown a marked decline during the past few years; and fears have been expressed in some quarters lest production may be developing at too rapid a pace. The problem is not new; indeed it occurs in the case of almost every product in regard to which production is expanding, and especially where the period between planting and the first financial return to the planter is to be measured in years. But cocoa is perhaps of peculiar importance owing to the abnormal rate of expansion of the industry during the past two decades...

The above extract sounds contemporary with this book. In fact it was published in 1930.[15] The current position of high production coupled with large stocks resulting in low prices is evidently not new, although it is true that prices have never been as low as at the beginning of the 1990s. Difficulties faced by the trade in the early 1930s remain the same sixty years on. That prices will recover is not in doubt; as in all commodities the difficulty concerns timing; when will prices rise is the relevant question. Unfortunately for those in 1930 suffering from prices of £44 per tonne[16] (in 1990 terms the price was £1315) the situation deteriorated further, reaching £23 (£857 in 1990 prices) per tonne in 1934. Apart from a

15   'COCOA world production and trade', Empire Marketing Board, 1930.
16   Average annual value of UK imported cocoa.

temporary blip in 1937,[17] it was not until after World War II that prices picked up. While it is hoped that the current low prices will not remain with us for long much depends on adjusting the rate of production increases with developments of demand that have grown at a slower pace and suffered from the severe economic disruptions in Eastern Europe (see Chapter 7).

17   Caused by irate West African farmers refusing to sell their cocoa in the face of low prices and temporarily holding up the supplies. Their action, typical of short term attempts to lift market prices, failed as after the 'hold up' prices fell sharply. The farmers' action, however, forced the British government to appoint a commission to investigate the marketing of cocoa. Their findings laid the foundation for the Marketing Boards of Ghana and Nigeria.

4

The actuals market

Introduction

The two markets

The cocoa trade consists of two markets, known respectively as the actuals and the futures or terminal markets. The actuals market – sometimes also referred to as the physical, or for certain types of sales, the forward market and for others, the spot or cash market – involves the type of business that most people normally think of when talking about trading commodities. All cocoa sold from origin countries is through the actuals market; as is nearly all cocoa bought by manufacturers to make chocolate. The actuals market allows participants to buy and sell specific cocoas on terms that they agree privately between themselves. As explained in Chapter 6, the purpose of the futures market is different. Its function is not to allow participants to purchase particular parcels of cocoa, but to give those trading physical cocoa a way of covering their risks. The connection between the two markets is that the futures price forms the basis of the contract prices in the actuals market. Supply and demand differences that occur in the physical market also feed back to the terminal market that are then reflected in the prices quoted.

History

Both of these markets stem from a certain type of actual or physical business, the spot market. At the start of overseas trade in Europe, merchants undertook ventures in ships they owned, frequently sailing as the master. Those that employed a master instead of going themselves would also have on board a supercargo. While the master was in charge of the running of the ship, the supercargo represented the owner in the trading of goods. Ships would not just visit one or two places overseas and then return home. It was usual for them to visit a number of ports, buying and selling goods. The supercargo's job was to ensure that such trading was profitable. Naturally such ventures took time and were exceedingly risky. Not only was the merchant at home unsure when (or if) the ship would return from the 'marine adventure', he could not be certain of her cargo. The risk of the loss of the ship could be covered by the embryonic marine insurance but the contents of returning holds remained a mystery to the owner until the supercargo jumped ashore. For the owner on board the ship there was little he could do to sell the goods before the ship docked. Being unable to communicate with traders at the next port prevented him selling the cargo before the ship's arrival.

Either way, the merchant was therefore unable to sell his cargo until it had physically arrived at its destination. The merchants sold their cargoes to the apothecaries, manufacturers etc either at auctions or on occasion, privately. For both types of sale, by auction or private deal, the goods were available for immediate delivery. For cocoa it was the start of overseas trade that became known as the cash or spot market. Sales of cocoa by auction in London and Liverpool continued for some time;

> *By Virtue of an Order of the Commissioners for the Care and*
> *Disposal of the Spanish Ships and Cargoes detained, On*
> *TUESDAY, the 8th June, and the following Days, at Ten for*
> *Eleven precisely, At their SALE ROOM, at WEST'S WAREHOUSE,*
> *BILLITER-LANE*
> *14 Serons Cocoa*
> *Being the entire cargo of the Ship San Miguel captured on her*
> *passage from South America, and regularly condemned.*[1]

This was not an unusual method of either sale, or for that time, procurement. Also advertised in the same edition of the Public Ledger were the following;

> *30 Hhds. Cocoa from N.S. del Carmen*
> *473 Tierces Cocoa from Nostra Senora de los Dolores*
> *50 Bales Cocoa from El Dichoso*
> *86 Serons Cocoa from Nova Charlotta from Cumana*

[1]   The Public Ledger and Commercial & General Advertiser, 3 May 1805.

200 Serons Cocoa from Princessa de la Paz
357 Serons Cocoa from St. Andero from Vera Cruz
$6\frac{1}{2}$ Hhds. Cocoa from Sta. Anna from Giuyana[2]

During the seventeenth and eighteenth centuries auctions developed informally. Held in cities that had developed in overseas trade, the proximity of both the wharves containing the overseas goods and the merchant banks became essential. In Europe, London became a major trading centre, with some auctions conducted in local coffee houses in the City. This continued until the opening of the Sale-Rooms in Mincing Lane during 1811 formalised the sale of cocoa and other commodities. Selling specific parcels of cocoa continued in this manner, and not only for beans.

The London Commercial Sale-Rooms
On Tuesday January 8
COCOA BUTTER, 35 tons "Cadbury's"
Guaranteed Genuine
C.M.&C. WOODHOUSE, Brokers[3]

Although the Sale-Rooms were destroyed during the Second World War, the location for trading cocoa and other commodities remained in the London area of Mincing Lane until the 1980s.

The method of buying cocoa on the spot market was sufficient for the small eighteenth and nineteenth century manufacturers of drinking chocolate. Their needs could be fulfilled by this sometimes haphazard method of obtaining cocoa. Once the larger factories began production later in the nineteenth century, the mills needed regular supplies of consistent quality cocoa. This requirement coincided with improved ships and overseas trade. In the same year that François-Louis Cailler set up his chocolate factory in Vevey, Switzerland (1819) the first transatlantic crossing by a ship with an auxiliary steam engine occurred. A ship solely powered by a steam engine crossed the Atlantic in 1838, two years after German and Spanish colonists began to grow cocoa commercially in Bahia, Brazil. No longer subject to the vagaries of the wind, more ships began plying the trade routes. The first steel hulled ship crossed the Atlantic in 1879, the same year that Tetteh Quarshie had cocoa brought into Ghana.

These major improvements to ship design benefited overseas trade. The commerce of overseas goods changed. Regular sailings to estates and plantations meant that it became possible for manufacturers to buy cocoa due to arrive at some defined period in the future. Such business had

---

2 By way of interest: a tierce is a third of a pipe or 42 gallons; a seron is a bale or package and Hhd. (a hogshead) is $52\frac{1}{2}$ imperial gallons. As a rough guide a tierce would contain some 113 kilos of beans and hogshead just over 140 kilos.

3 The Public Ledger, 29 December 1888.

advantages for both the manufacturer and the merchant. The manufacturer knew that his supply was more stable; he could be more certain of the type of cocoa he was to take delivery of and when it was due to arrive. The merchant, now unlikely to be the ship owner, knew what margin he could make on the deal, and would not have to rely on local supply and demand factors affecting the auction prices. This was the start of the forward market.

There was one other factor. Bidding at auction is not a private affair. Everyone else in the room knows what has been sold and at what price. Unless the buyer is clever, the others are likely to know who bought it as well. The merchants, all competing for business, disliked the auction process and sought alternatives.

The wish for privacy of contract coupled with the desire to secure regular supplies meant that the forward contract became more popular. Privacy of contract naturally means that only the parties involved know of the trade. It therefore follows that a crowded meeting place, such as an auction room, is not the best place to conduct business. In fact the term 'actuals market' does not refer to a place, or an assembly of people. It is the business transacted. The actuals market is therefore spread throughout the world and refers to anyone who buys or sells the physical commodity, in this case cocoa. Although concentrated in certain places where cocoa trading traditionally occurs, like London, New York, Amsterdam and Hamburg, it is not true that the market is in these specific places.

As the volume of cocoa business increased, merchants also found it easier to conduct business using standardised contracts of sale detailing the particular contract. With the terms of sale established and understood by both parties, little needed to be discussed at the time of the contract. This left more time free for both parties to continue with the business of trading. With the large increase in world production from Africa taking effect during the early twentieth century, those active in the cocoa trade formed three trade associations to cater for their needs.

Actuals market – trade associations

London, New York and Paris were the bases for these associations. In 1924 the Cocoa Merchants' Association of America (CMAA) came into being. The Cocoa Association of London (CAL) was created in 1928, and Paris during 1935 saw the formation of the Association Française du Commerce des Cacaos (AFCC). Practically all physical cocoa traded in the world is now subject to one or other of their terms and conditions. As well as providing the contracts, all three provide arbitration procedures should the contracting parties find themselves in dispute.

The use of each trade association's contracts

Before leaving the subject of the physical contracts for the next chapter, it should be noted that the exported cocoa's country of origin and its destination determine which trade association's contracts the parties should use. If the export is to the United States, or is to pass through the United States on its way to Canada, then buyers and sellers should contract on CMAA terms. This is because the United States has strict import requirements that are upheld by the Food and Drug Administration (FDA). Cocoa has to pass their inspection[4] and the terms of the contract take this into consideration. Cocoa imported into the other major consuming countries is not subject to such stringent requirements by a third party and so the contracts do not include clauses that cover such eventualities. Exports to other countries are on contracts whose roots are historical rather than pragmatic. Exports from French colonies were mainly to France and made on French contracts. French speaking exporting countries continue to sell cocoa subject to AFCC terms. Similarly, exports from English speaking cocoa exporting countries were primarily to the United Kingdom and used contracts subject to CAL terms. This still continues, even though France and the UK are no longer the main destinations of cocoa traded on AFCC and CAL contracts.

Export marketing

Producing countries' trade structures

Producing countries each adopt different methods of marketing their cocoa. As most end up selling the cocoa on similarly styled contracts, the differences lie in the countries' internal arrangements. Determining which method to apply depends on the individual country's government policy. Central to the government's decision is the degree of control it wishes to exert. Some countries may want considerable control over their exports, others may wish less direct involvement but all retain a watchful eye on proceedings. As examples, at one end of the scale are Brazil and Indonesia where free market conditions apply to the exporters. At the other end is Ghana where a centralised body controls the cocoa industry, including its exports. Varying degrees of governmental control exist between these two examples and broadly speaking, they fall into three types of marketing systems. First are those using the marketing boards, with centralised control over the internal purchasing of cocoa and its subsequent export. Some countries have marketing boards but they have more of an adminis-

---

4   Note that the seller bears the costs if the cocoa fails the inspection.

trative role and, apart from some internal control do not themselves export cocoa. Second, and similar in many respects to the active marketing boards, are the Caisses de Stabilisation. These have a little less control over the export arrangements but do influence all involved in the export of the cocoa, and as the name suggests, include those countries that are French speaking. Third, are the companies working in the free market. Although this implies no control these countries impose restrictions on their exporters in the quality of the cocoa sold and the currency proceeds of the sale.

Most cocoa exports are in bean form, although the tonnage of intermediate cocoa products exported from origin countries has increased over the past forty years. Despite this increase the market share of origin grindings has remained stable at about 30% over the last fifteen years.

Marketing Boards

The British first introduced Marketing Boards to their then colonies during and after World War II. Forty years on many consider them in less favourable light. Ghana is now the only large exporter that retains a Board involved directly with exports, and there is talk of change. However, it is of interest to look at this marketing system.

During October 1937 growers in Ghana stopped delivering cocoa to buyers, mainly in protest against low prices, mentioned at the end of the previous chapter. Some of the farmers wanted to market their cocoa directly, and towards the end of the seven month dispute, they burnt about 400 tonnes of cocoa to mark their disapproval of existing conditions. A truce eventually came about from the intervention of a government commission of inquiry that resulted in the Nowell report.

In the view of the report the marketing of the cocoa was chaotic, involving many middle-men who, according to the report, did not give the growers a fair price for their cocoa. This contradiction (many operators must mean competition) was added to by the report saying that the middle-men also exploited the merchants. The report did not consider that the middle-men provided competition. In addition the report also included the idea that stabilising the price of cocoa to the growers was comparatively easy. It therefore laid the foundations of the Ghana Cocoa Marketing Board, the controlling body in Ghanaian cocoa.

The Board has extensive powers. It decides what price should be paid to the farmers and only it may export the cocoa. Importantly, the Board retains control over the quality of the cocoa bought and subsequently exported. The enforcement of strict quality controls has meant that the cocoa industry considers Ghana cocoa the best of the bulk cocoas.

The internal structure of the Board follows the administrative boundaries. At the village level the farmer registers with a 'primary society.' The primary society responds to a district office, which in turn is responsible to a regional office. The regional office is accountable to the produce buying division of the Board. The Board appoints a produce buying clerk to each of the primary societies, and although the clerk manages the society, he is responsible to its management committee, made up of the farmers. The district office audits the primary societies and provides adequate cash for the buying clerk to pursue his duties. The regional office controls the flow of cocoa needed to fulfil the export contracts while the produce buying division sets the policy and, importantly, the price paid to the farmer. The Cocoa Marketing Company, part of the Cocoa Board, sells the cocoa to overseas buyers. They alone have the power to contract sales from the origin and their terms of the sales are usually cost insurance and freight, with shipping weights.

The quality inspection is thorough. The Cocoa Board has a produce inspection division that enforces the quality standards. The farmers bring their cocoa to the primary society where it is weighed, graded and rebagged. The buying clerk pays the farmer by giving him a cheque, redeemable at a district bank. Importantly, the amount paid depends on the quality of the cocoa. The farmer therefore learns very quickly of any shortcomings and has an interest in providing good quality beans. A review system exists to resolve any disputes over the quality of the cocoa. The rebagged cocoa is sealed and transported to regional warehouses. At these warehouses the inspectors check the quality and weight of the cocoa once more, as they do just before the cocoa is loaded on board the vessel. The strength of the system lies in two areas. First is the immediate feedback to the farmers. It ensures they supply the cocoa at a set standard, if they supply inferior cocoa they get a lower price. Second, the three checks made on the cocoa before shipment substantially reduce the chance of delivering poor quality cocoa to the buyer.

At the beginning of the season the Board sets the farmer prices. During 1989/90 the official main crop price started at 174 400 cedis per tonne and then rose to 224 000 cedis by the beginning of the mid-crop. In addition, farmers received a further 26.5 cedis per kilo of main crop cocoa that they delivered during that crop year. This represented the difference between the projected cocoa price, on which the Board originally based the official purchase price, and the actual revenue received. The Board has set the farmer price for 1991/92 at 251 000 cedis per tonne.

When a country depends so heavily on one commodity it is natural that the government wishes to control it as much as possible. It is true that this system has the greatest government involvement. But it does ask the question whether it is the best for the farmers or indeed for the country. True for all bureaucracies, it is expensive to run. In the early 1980s the

Board had some 100 000 employees. Although that figure is now down to 30 000, some consider that the Board could substantially reduce it further. The heavy government involvement still did not prevent the decline in production from 1965 to the mid-1980s. As the Board was in charge of everything to do with cocoa much of the blame must lie with it for the decline, the main reason for which was the price paid to the farmers. It was significantly below the world market price (see Chapter 3). Nonetheless, production has recently increased and looks to continue at sustainable levels.

In its defence, even though the tonnage declined during the 1970s the quality of the cocoa delivered to the buyers did not. The Board would say that other benefits have accrued to the growers, such as the provision of extension services as well as better infrastructure, for example, they built roads in the cocoa growing regions. The farmers also receive credit through the primary societies, also financed by the Board.

The Board recognises that it needs to improve its efficiency and plans to privatise some of its activities. The World Bank and the Ghanaian government discussed the possibility of privatising the domestic purchasing of cocoa, leaving the Board in charge of export sales of cocoa. The World Bank granted a credit of US $80 million to assist the privatisation programme. During the first quarter of 1992 the Board revealed that companies incorporated in Ghana would be allowed to buy cocoa from the farmers. The Board considers licensing companies that can buy at least 1000 tonnes, and has approved four companies for the 1992/93 crop. A committee will establish a minimum farmer price and fees to be paid to the licenced buyers. Recently the Board has hived off its coffee operation and although small compared to cocoa, the change is significant as it marks a new direction and the beginning of the privatisation process.

Most cocoa exporting countries in the South Pacific have Cocoa Boards that have varying degrees of direct involvement in the export of cocoa. In Papua New Guinea the Cocoa Board administers the internal running of the cocoa economy by licensing fermentaries and exporters. It has the power to export cocoa under its own name but has not done so. Similarly the Solomon Islands has a Board but it exists to help those involved in cocoa rather than directly managing the commodity under its own name. The Vanuatu Commodity Marketing Board markets cocoa to overseas buyers as well as monitoring the country's internal cocoa operation. Western Samoa, traditionally an exporter of fine grade cocoa, disbanded their Cocoa Board at the end of 1990 and now rely on the operation of private exporters. After the devastation of cyclone Ofa and the more recent cyclone Val, the tonnage sold overseas is small and the grade of cocoa is mixed as growers interplanted Forastero type trees with the remaining Trinitario varieties.

Caisses de Stabilisation

Of the larger exporters the Côte d'Ivoire and Cameroon operate this system of marketing their cocoa. In the Côte d'Ivoire the name of the agency operating this is the Caisse de Stabilisation et de Soutien des Prix des Produits Agricoles, refered to as the Caisse. Until 1991 the equivalent in Cameroon was the Office National de Commercialisation des Produits de Base (ONCPB). The Office National du Café et du Cacao (ONCC) now undertakes part of the ONCPB's functions.

The operation of the Caisse system lies in two measures. The first concerns the price of cocoa payable by the commercial buyers and exporters within the country. The Caisse controls this through the Barême, a pricing structure that fixes the farmer price and increases this price by all costs incurred from farm-gate to the point of export. The Caisse sets the Barême at the beginning of each crop year and includes a notional element of profit in the prices it sets at the various stages.

The second measure occurs at the critical point when the government controlled system faces the commercial one; i.e., when the exporter, having bought the cocoa under the Barême system, sells it on to the world market. This too, is controlled by the Caisse, through a system known as 'blockage'. Once bought by the exporter the Caisse 'blocks' the cocoa from shipment. The exporter may only sell the cocoa if it has been 'deblocked'. This depends on the export sale price, the 'deblockage' price, which is effectively the world market price for the various grades of cocoa; and therefore constantly changing. If the Caisse permits the shipper to export the cocoa at a price below that set under the Barême, it undertakes to refund the shipper the difference. Similarly should the export sale price be higher than that specified under the Barême, the shipper will have to refund the difference to the Caisse.

In practice the system depends on middle-men, the traitants. The exporters either employ the traitants to buy the cocoa from the farmers or buy direct themselves. The traitants compete with one another and provide credit facilities and agricultural inputs for the farmers. The source of the financing varies depending on the size of the traitant, the larger ones provide their own funds while the smaller either obtain loans from the exporter or from banks. The use of the banks is widespread, in the past the security of the government backed Barême system helped ensure the returns. In Cameroon the system of buying cocoa was under greater control than that of the Côte d'Ivoire. The ONCPB licensed traitants to operate in certain regions and they also determined the days on which the buying may take place.

Unfortunately in both the Côte d'Ivoire and Cameroon the amount paid to the farmers is the same irrespective of the quality of the cocoa. As a result the quality of the Côte d'Ivoire cocoa is less homogeneous than that of its neighbour, Ghana. For this reason and although the exporters clean, grade and rebag the cocoa at the port, the industry consider that the quality of Côte d'Ivoire and Cameroon cocoa is inferior to Ghana's.

During the past two years the marketing systems of the Côte d'Ivoire and Cameroon have suffered severely from lack of funds. The cause was the price paid to the farmers and others in the domestic chain of buyers and sellers. It was too high. Against falling world prices the Caisses continued to set the Barême prices above their equivalent on the world market. The reserves that the Caisses had built up were depleted in short order, especially as the tonnage in the Côte d'Ivoire had increased, fuelled by the earlier stability and good prices the farmers had received in previous years. In the Côte d'Ivoire these large debts severely disrupted the export of cocoa. The Caisses were unable to refund the amounts owed under the Barême. The banks became unwilling to lend money on the collateral of cocoa sales. Farmers were faced with having to accept much lower prices for their cocoa as the guaranteed producer price was not forthcoming. In July 1991 farmers in the Côte d'Ivoire formed a union, a key aim of which was to ensure that farmers received the full official producer price for their products.

As a result, the Côte d'Ivoire government intends to reduce the domestic marketing costs and to review the marketing policy of the Caisse. The Caisse intends to streamline its activities by reducing its overheads and transferring some of its commercial activities to the private market. It intends to increase its exposure to market forces. Under guidance from the World Bank concerning the restructuring of the Caisse, two-thirds of the 1991/92 crop was sold forward,[5] before the beginning of the season. The Caisse therefore knew what revenue was due and was able to set realistic producer prices. Similar to Ghana, proposals exist to liberalise the domestic marketing system, meaning the end of direct sales made by the Caisse and to abolish export quotas for exporters.

In Cameroon the operation of the Caisse (the ONCPB) collapsed in 1991 under the weight of debt incurred in the same manner as the Côte d'Ivoire's. The government stated that it wished companies to assume an active role in the marketing of cocoa and another government body, the ONCC, has taken a higher profile and assumed some of the tasks previously undertaken by the ONCPB. Principally it controls the quality of the cocoa

---

5 As mentioned earlier, selling forward means selling a product for delivery in the future. Theoretically it can be as far forward as the parties like, but terms for delivery of more than a year in advance are unusual. The period during which the delivery may be made is normally given as a one to three month range, see Chapter 5.

exported, registers the exports and sets a reference price for the export sales that operates in a similar fashion to the Caisse. The President announced that the producer price for the 1991/92 season will be 220 CFA per kilo for grade one and grade two cocoa, 100 CFA for ungraded and 50 CFA for cocoa residue, thereby setting the farmer price. Importantly the farmer does not receive a premium for delivering grade I instead of grade II cocoa which does not help attempts to improve the quality. During 1991/92 poorly fermented and badly dried cocoa was shipped as exporters were indiscriminate in buying from the farmers, a condition familiar in Nigeria. A positive point was that the exporters managed to evacuate the cocoa from the interior more quickly than before, an important factor in such a humid environment as Cameroon (see Chapter 8).

There appears to be a move away from the centralised control of marketing operations, be they Commodity Boards or Caisses. Governments that previously controlled matters through centralised agencies consider such involvement in a new light. Since the mid-1980s many have either disbanded or redefined their roles; reducing their direct involvement in the country's internal processing and trade of cocoa and/or the international marketing of their cocoa. In part this process has brought to prominence the third system, that of the free market.

Free market systems

Four of the seven biggest producers in the world use free enterprise to market their cocoa exports. Although these four, Brazil, Indonesia, Malaysia and Nigeria, collectively produce less cocoa than the other three major producers mentioned above, the relevance of this system to cocoa has increased since 1986. Two reasons account for this. First, the emergence of both Malaysia and Indonesia as significant growers of cocoa added to the ranks of the large free enterprise cocoa producers, notably Brazil. Second, during 1986 the Nigerian government disbanded their Cocoa Board and turned the export of cocoa over to the free market.

Many of the exporters in the four 'free market' countries would not consider that they have any such thing. The term 'free market' sounds like a business practice where all is possible with nothing denied. In fact a complete *laissez faire* attitude towards export business is rare and probably of no lasting benefit to the country of export – whatever the businessmen may say. This is not to deny the exporters their profits but to safeguard the country's reputation in the trading community. In one country where few export regulations exist for cocoa, responsible exporters have formed their own group. One of the proposed functions of the group is to oversee the export procedures of cocoa.

Countries following 'free export marketing' adopt differing types of control. These generally fall into two categories, control of the quality of the cocoa exported and/or of the foreign exchange received. Brazil is the largest exporter of the 'free marketeers' and uses both mechanisms. Before shipment, inspection of the cocoa is usual and certificates showing the quality of the cocoa normally form part of the shipping documents. All export sales pass through the central bank that monitors the sale revenues.

The experience of Nigeria in privatising its cocoa industry is of interest not only to countries that wish to do likewise but also to highlight the importance of retaining export standards on quality. *Laissez faire* trading conditions existed in 1986 after the disbandment of the Nigerian Cocoa Board. As mentioned earlier, currency restrictions in Nigeria at the time meant that businesses that had reserves of naira were unable to convert it to hard currencies. With the privatisation of cocoa entrepreneurs saw an opportunity to buy cocoa from the farmers in naira and to sell it for hard currency to overseas traders. As the buyers made the payments outside Nigeria, many saw an opportunity not only to convert naira into a hard currency but also to move their money overseas. Those involved in this capital flight had no long term interest in cocoa, it was merely the vehicle for the movement of money.

The farmers benefited from the privatisation. Suddenly people were paying them substantially higher prices for their cocoa. Entrepreneurs bought cocoa from the farmers irrespective of its quality. Growers, pressurised into providing cocoa in any condition cut short some of the post-harvest practices. This resulted, for example, in the exporters shipping damp cocoa that arrived at the ports of discharge in terrible condition. The overseas buyers subsequently became extremely wary of Nigerian cocoa and the premium that it once commanded disappeared, not quite overnight, but practically in the time taken to sail from West Africa to Europe. Fortunately the situation improved and exporters became more discriminating in selecting the cocoa for export. Although the Cocoa Association of Nigeria (CAN) has a large register of exporters[6] many are inactive with only a handful of exporters marketing the majority of the crop. As a result of better control, up until 1991/92 the quality of Nigerian cocoa recovered some of its reputation. Unfortunately poor weather during 1991/92 prevented the growers from properly drying their cocoa resulting in substantial quantities of ill-prepared cocoa on the market that has not helped their cause.

In Malaysia the Federal Agricultural Marketing Authority (FAMA) imposes a strict control over the quality of beans exported. Originally its

---

6   The 1991 edition of the World Cocoa Directory lists 280 companies as members of CAN. The International Cocoa Organization annually publishes the World Cocoa Directory.

authority was specifically for peninsula Malaysia, where it was mandatory for all exports. Until 1991 the inspection was at the discretion of exporters based in Sabah and Sarawak (states on the island of Borneo) but it is now also mandatory in these states. The introduction of this scheme was to combat the view, held by many buyers, that the quality of Malaysian cocoa was inferior to West African. In fact there are two aspects to the question of quality: those that are objective and easy to measure and those that involve taste and are consequently harder to assess. The FAMA inspection, along with others conducted worldwide in cocoa, involves primarily the objective tests. While manufacturers retain some reserves over the efficacy of the objective tests – the mixing of different sized beans in a parcel remains as a fault – there has been an improvement in the quality of Malaysian beans. The grading standards help to allay the buyers' worries and work continues in both Malaysia and Indonesia to produce cocoa that is similar to that coming from West Africa (see Chapter 8).

Not only has the volume of production in Indonesia mirrored that of Malaysia but so too have some of the problems. The export of poor quality beans was the major worry to buyers. Many of the exporters, in-experienced in cocoa, were unaware of the buyers' requirements. In 1988 cocoa exporters formed the Indonesian Cocoa Association (INCA). One of their first tasks was to set up quality standards which members undertook to follow. It is similar to the standards set by the Malaysians and involves the objective tests on the beans. The self-regulation provides the framework for buyers to purchase the cocoa with a higher degree of confidence, although much of the trade in cocoa is new to exporters and the quality is very variable. This is especially true for those dealing with the cocoa grown by smallholders. The perantara (middle-men) operating on the island of Sulawesi have seen an enormous increase in cocoa available for export during the past ten years. In 1980 shippers in Ujung Pandang exported 30 tonnes of cocoa. In 1990 they exported 73 470 tonnes and in 1991, 87 668 tonnes were exported. A lack of discrimination over quality has meant that in the past some poorly fermented cocoa was mixed with better prepared beans, leading to inevitable dissatisfaction by the buyers. This condition should improve through the activity of both INCA and the exporters at the port.

Processing at origin

Over recent years some producing countries have considered the merits of processing cocoa beans at origin and exporting the intermediate products of cocoa liquor, butter and powder instead of the beans. As mentioned earlier, 30% of all processing already occurs at origin, and the discussion centres on whether this should increase. Manufacturing the intermediate products of cocoa first results in making cocoa liquor. This requires roasting the beans, removing the shell and grinding the remaining nibs. The liquor is an intermediate product in its own right, but pressing it squeezes out the fat, leaving the cocoa solids. The fat is cocoa butter, the most expensive cocoa product. Grinding the cocoa solids turns the cocoa cake into cocoa powder, the last of the cocoa products, both in terms of processing and in current value.

Processing the cocoa beans at origin seems sensible at first sight, turning a raw material into something with added value must benefit the exporting country. Specifically by attracting a higher priced export as well as providing additional and skilled industrial work and reducing the cost of freight; products weigh less than beans. Unfortunately a deeper analysis shows a number of difficulties that question this assumption.

Most imports of cocoa products are to Western Europe and North America. In 1989/90 these regions accounted for 87.9% of all butter, 80.5% of all cocoa powder and 71.1% of all liquor imports. Therefore these regions represent the location of the potential buyers of the product and also the competition, as these regions also manufacture large amounts of cocoa products themselves.

Looking at the operation of cocoa processors in Europe reveals an industry that prides itself on providing a complete service to the chocolate manufacturers. This includes arranging deliveries of butter and liquor in liquid form. Such processors can arrange such deliveries to manufacturers running on JIT[7] systems. Some chocolate factories now have little space or personnel to cater for butter or liquor arriving in solid form, the only realistic way that origin processors can deliver their product. At worst this limits the number of factories that can take delivery of origin products, and at best means a discount on the price, as the buyer has to perform an extra process in preparing the product.

Not only do the processors look after the precise timing of deliveries but more of them now formulate products individually tailored to particular factories – specific quality requirements that origin manufacturers have found difficult to match. For example, one factory in the Netherlands can deliver over 120 different cocoa powders. These comprise different colours, aromas, fat contents, degrees of alkalisation, and the addition of stabilisers or lecithin. Most powders made in origin countries cannot match these variations, if only for the technical reason that they generally have access to only one type of cocoa bean, the one grown locally. The

7   Just In Time. It refers to a processing system that requires the factory to have the minimum of raw materials; the products arrive just before they are needed. The factory does not tie up money in holding stocks.

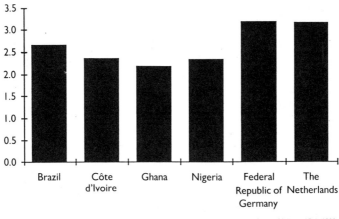

Source: Mehta and Fish, 1990.

4.1 Combined butter and powder ratios for the period 1985–1988.

processors in Europe and North America have a range of beans from different origins to use. This gives them the essential options of blending in beans, especially important in making up the different colours of powders, but also producing various liquors and butter types. Using only one type of bean severely constrains processors in the variation of end-products that they may make.

The restrictions in delivery and of the product itself means that the European/North American processors themselves buy the products made at origin and incorporate them into their own formulations to sell on to the chocolate manufacturers. As the products require additional work, if only to remelt the butter and blend it into others, the price the origin receives is less than that received by processors in consuming countries, see Fig. 4.1.

Health regulations in Europe and North America also present extra difficulties. It is harder to make products with low bacteriological counts in hot damp conditions than in temperate regions. Factories in origin countries have to take much greater care in their production processes, and this increases the cost of production.

As the labour costs in origin countries are much lower than in Europe and North America it makes economic sense to run factories in producing countries that are labour intensive and not capital intensive. For example, in 1990 the average hourly wage costs of manufacturing in western Germany were over US$20, the United States just below US$15. In Malaysia the hourly rate was just under US$1. (If that seems low, Indonesia's average wage is less than half of that.)[8] Unfortunately cocoa processing is

8   The Economist, 4 April 1992.

capital intensive and origin processors have to import much of the costly equipment that needs only a few skilled people to operate; hence the ability of the industrialised countries to compete successfully.

Importers of cocoa products into the EEC from countries that are not signatories to the Lomé convention[9] must pay an *ad valorem* import duty of 11% on liquor, 12% on butter and 9% on powder. In particular this affects exports from Brazil, Ecuador, Malaysia and Indonesia. While there is no import duty on products entering the United States, this fact represents an enormous disincentive to process at origin and export to Europe.

As mentioned in Chapter 3, supply restrictions to only one source of beans may make the origin's internal price of cocoa soar in times of short supply. So having one type of bean not only limits the type of product available but when there is little cocoa on hand, that cocoa becomes expensive and the ensuing products become uncompetitive on the world market. Price movements of origins relative to each other enable European and American users, within the flexibility of their recipes, to buy from the cheapest source. The processors in final consuming countries buy beans with a wide-open eye on their price as well as their quality characteristics.

The cocoa trade measures the price of cocoa products in terms of their multiples to the price of cocoa beans. These are called ratios. Figure 4.1 shows the average combined ratios of cocoa powder and butter from different origins during 1985 to 1988.

The figure shows the European products command a premium of about 25% more than those made in the origin countries. Such a difference questions the viability of manufacturing the products at origin for sale in the traditional markets.

While superficially appearing a profitable enterprise, those considering starting processing operations in origin countries should look carefully at the figures. In particular the banks involved in loans should seek clarification in the overall strategy, especially the disposal of the cocoa powder, the most difficult of the products to sell.

Processing at origin is, like most things, not new.

> *In Jamaica there is a sort of Chocolate made up of only the Paste of the Cacao itself, in rowls or lumps of a pound or two, or three pounds together, the better for keeping good; which the people there account most ordinary, by reason they bestow not so much pains as to grind the smallest particles; and being but grosly made up, they grate it very fine, immediately before they use it for drinks: And this is one of the best masses of Chocolate-Paste that is; and it may be had often here in England, neat and good, of Merchants and Sea-men that travel to those parts, and bring it over: nor is it at all material or*

9 These are the African, Caribbean and Pacific (ACP) countries.

convenient that it be always beaten into such very small parts,
the different Airs it will meet with before it come here, being
thereby the more apt to work upon it: Besides, it doth dissipate
the spirits, which are naturally volatile, and soon vanish
away, leaving the rest much more insipid; and therefore an
indifferent respect must be used in the beating or grinding of
it.[10]

The success of the imported product in 1672 probably lay in one key area, quality of transport. Providing it had not been ground too fine, it kept better than the beans during the voyage. In part this must be due to the sailors not stowing it as they would sacks of beans but treating it more as a foodstuff. So, it is probably safe to say that better handling and shipment of the product gave a better drink than that made from poorly transported beans. The other factors of single-origined beans and costs of manufacture had not reached a significant level of difference; but the lesson to exporters of quality of service should not be lost.

Other participants

Chocolate factories, as a rule do not operate plantations.[11] Those who grow cocoa, again as a rule, do not use it. Therefore as the factories have to buy their cocoa from others, and the sellers would seemingly deliver to the factories, it would seem logical that they would deal direct with each other. In fact this does not happen to any great extent, although it occurs more frequently now than in the recent past.

The reasons why few exporters deal direct with the final users are threefold. The first is that not every time an exporter wishes to sell will he find a manufacturer that wants to buy. Similarly, a manufacturer would not always find an origin prepared to sell on a particular day. As a result a service industry developed that was able to look after the needs of both origin sellers in the tropics and the manufacturers located in North America and Europe. Known as the 'second-hand market', this service element of the business, consisting of dealers and brokers, is as a whole, always prepared to absorb cocoa from the origins and to sell to those who need it. Not only are these intermediaries always on hand and prepared to trade, but without them the price of cocoa would rise and fall violently as one side would be eager to intervene while the other remained withdrawn.

10   Ibid Hughes William, 1672.
11   Only Hershey have an estate (Humming Bird Estate in Belize) but it certainly does not supply all of Hershey's cocoa needs.

The second reason is that buyers can usually find, on any particular day, someone else offering the same cocoa cheaper than the exporters. This occurs because the dealers have a view on the market which usually means a market position. This view means that, for instance, if the trader considers the price of cocoa will increase, capitalising on this would give rise to a long position; i.e., that he had bought more cocoa than he had sold. Another trader may think otherwise, and have sold more than she bought, a short position. As a result of this difference of opinion and of situation, the manufacturers will find competitive sellers able to offer cocoa other than from origin. What applies to the manufacturer is also true for the exporter. Without the second-hand market exporters would probably find less competitive prices for their products.

The third reason is that factories consider their function is to process beans to make cocoa products or chocolate. As a rule they do not wish to involve themselves securing supplies if they can rely on others to do that for them. Their expertise lies in making the product, and therefore consider it the job of the service industry to take on the work of ensuring their supply of the raw material. They feel more comfortable knowing that a body of third party companies exists whose prime function lies in servicing their needs. If a manufacturer buys from a trader who fails to deliver the cocoa, few will trade with that company again. Trust, competitive prices and service is all the second-hand market has to offer both manufacturer and exporter alike.

Brokers

The brokers are companies that introduce buyers and sellers to each other, a service for which they charge a commission. This introduction may take place in one of two ways, either the broker discloses the names of the parties to each other or they remain ignorant of each other's identity. The main effect lies in the contract of sale and the commission rate charged. A straight introduction occurs after both sides agreed all the terms of the sale contract when the broker then discloses the names of the parties to each other. One contract of sale will exist, showing the names of the buyer and the seller, together with the broker and his commission. Known as a pass-name broker this type of transaction is the more unusual of the two. It has the advantage of low commission rates but has the disadvantage of both parties not knowing the identity of their eventual trading partner until striking the deal. Some companies find this an insurmountable obstacle in using pass-name brokers, as the threat exists that the broker introduces a company with whom the client, for a variety of reasons, does not wish to trade. The broker plays no further part in the transaction, the performance of the sales contract remains the responsibility of the two parties involved.

The second type of broker remains a principal to the contract of sale. Under such a transaction, both sides of the trade remain ignorant of each other's name and both have contracts with the broker; the seller a sale contract and the buyer a purchase contract. As a principal of the transaction, the broker charges a higher commission to cover the administrative charges in handling the shipping documents. The clients know throughout the transaction the name of their contractual counterparty, the broker.

One specialist type of broker is the agent. The difference between the two is that the agent always represents one particular party. In the past the cocoa industry supported a number of agents but in line with the decline of prices and the smaller number of participants the role of the agent has also decreased.

As the name implies, brokers and agents never have a market position. They always remain square, for every purchase they have a sale allocated against it. Those prepared to run a market position are the dealers.

Dealers

The larger part of the second-hand market consists of the dealers. These companies trade for their own account. They will consider buying cocoa before selling on to another or equally, sell cocoa for delivery in the future (forward delivery) before having bought it. Such activity oils the market by helping others to trade when they want and not when one party chooses to. Although easing the trade it also generates an element of risk for the dealers. They run a market risk in say, buying at the wrong time and prices then fall; as well as a company risk, buying from a company that fails to deliver the cocoa and defaults on a contract. The dealers may offset some of this risk, but an element always remains and which cannot be avoided. Their readiness in assuming risk benefits the market – providing their activity is successful. Successful traders help to stabilise the market; when prices are low they buy helping to move the market up, and sell when prices are high.[12]

As part of the servicing of clients the second-hand market not only assumes some of the risk but can give added value to the commodity. This is a traditional role for dealers in the North American cocoa trade where dealers operate on 'ex-dock' basis, in which for example, exporters sell cocoa on FOB terms at the port of loading to the dealer who may then

---

12   Hedging the actuals on the terminal market mitigates this action, but it certainly affects the premiums and discounts of individual growths of cocoa.

arrange delivery of the cocoa to the buyer's factory, located say, some distance from the port of discharge. Such a sale requires the dealer to arrange the freight and insurance, to land the cocoa, recondition any damaged bags, see that it passes the FDA inspection and truck the cocoa on to the buyer. In general, European factories do not want that level of service, preferring to buy shipment cocoa and arrange deliveries to the factories themselves.

The level of service offered by the North American dealers not only increases the dealers' administration costs but also requires financing. Such servicing needs the participation of the banks, some of whom recognising the particular needs of commodity houses specialise in providing such facilities. In Europe, some factories buy cocoa on deferred payment terms that requires financing by the seller, although such trading terms are not the norm.

Cocoa processors and chocolate manufacturers

Factories buying cocoa fall into two general groups, cocoa processors and chocolate manufacturers. The cocoa processors manufacture cocoa products, cocoa liquor, butter and powder while the chocolatiers concentrate on producing confectionery. Of the two groups the cocoa processors use the larger quantity of cocoa beans as they produce the semi-finished products which they sell on to the chocolatiers, although an increasing number of processors make couverture for the chocolate manufacturers thereby blurring the division between the two groups. The chocolatiers buy in cocoa beans specifically to make cocoa liquor, essential for the flavouring of the chocolate and usually a formulation that individual companies keep to themselves or only allow a carefully selected processor to manufacture for them.

The recent past

Over the past twenty years the number of dealers, brokers and agents operating in Europe and North America has fallen from 192^1 to 88, of which less than ten are considered as true international traders; the rest local dealers.[13] Too low returns for too high risks is the probable cause of the decline, exacerbated by the vain attempts of some to speculate on a huge scale to recover profitability. This is against a background of a

13   Metcalfe M W: 'Concentration and contraction in the cocoa trade – problems and opportunities', CMAA second international cocoa convention, October, 1991.

bear market since 1983/84 (see Fig. 1.3) and changes in production and marketing (the rise of Asia and the move away from commodity boards). Such changes increased the risk of contractual non-performance for which the dealer is not fully recompensed. In part this led some companies to inordinate and unsustainable speculation. The result is that operators in the market, in all parts of the export chain, are concerned about the viability of other companies.

The contraction in numbers has not been limited to the second-hand· market. The number of chocolate manufacturers also declined during this period, which, including more than 200 takeovers, now results in five companies accounting for just over 40% of the worldwide market.[14] At the beginning of the 1990s, there were 17 cocoa processors, down from 26 in the early 1970s. Some economies of scale must be the main reason for such changes, especially in the face of increased production of cocoa.

Low prices and fewer companies trading, some of whom may be financially weakened, makes the current forward market, if not illiquid at least turbid. Some sellers have found it difficult to trade forward, especially far forward, for lack of buyers. Buyers remain wary of the *del credere* risks with their sellers and find it difficult to hedge the risk on to the terminal market. Until both confidence in the market improves and easier finance becomes available to companies, selling cocoa outright for delivery eighteen months or two years forward will remain difficult.

14   The five, together with their estimated market shares are: Mars (10%); Nestlé (10%); Hershey (8%); Cadbury Schweppes (7%) and Jacobs Suchard (6%).

5

Physical contracts

T he previous chapter commented on the three trade associations, the AFCC, CAL and CMAA, that either issue contract forms or publish the terms for use by the cocoa community. This chapter concentrates on the main terms used in these contracts.

Similarities of the contracts

Although physical sale contracts offer the most flexibility in that the parties may agree any terms they like[1], the terms specified by the associations follow similar lines. Most of the physical sales of cocoa involve the process of shipment. All three associations' contracts reflect that, with only one or two contract types used for sales of cocoa already in the importing countries. While each contract type has its own peculiarities, sales using particular delivery and weight terms according to one association are broadly similar to those made according to the other two.

I   There may be some restrictions imposed by governments in the shipping and payment terms used by exporters. For example, exports from Brazil may only occur on one type of delivery term, free on board, with the payment by letter of credit.

Cocoa beans and not products

For historical reasons, all three associations concentrate on sales of cocoa beans and not on products. As mentioned in earlier chapters, until quite recently countries that exported cocoa beans did not manufacture, in any great quantity, cocoa products for export. Countries that consumed the cocoa not only manufactured the cocoa products but also made the chocolate. Therefore exports of cocoa from origin countries were usually of beans, and not the products. The contracts reflect that proportion. However, the trade pattern may be changing. In terms of bean equivalents, in 1989/90 cocoa products were 61% of the beans exported, compared with 36% in 1980/81. It is worthy of note that the largest cocoa processor in the world is Brazil, a cocoa producer and not a major consumer of chocolate.

Sale by description

All the associations' export contracts sell the cocoa by description. The other option, selling by sample, is unusual and only the CAL has standard terms for such sales. Selling by sample on the other associations' contracts requires the parties to compile their own sale terms. Selling by description is more flexible. It allows parties to agree delivery of the cocoa in the future, the essence of a forward contract. Inherent in this is the need to define the quality of the contracted cocoa. The CAL and AFCC both define cocoa quality terms that parties may, if they wish, choose to include in the contract, while the CMAA leaves all the descriptions of quality to the two parties.

Quality on arrival

All cocoa shipment contracts hold the seller responsible for the quality of the cocoa until the ship discharges at destination.[2] At the unloading the buyer will draw a set of samples, monitored, if required, by the seller's supervisor. Using one of the drawn samples the buyer may check the quality and, if it is below the contracted standard, may institute arbitration proceedings against the seller. This is irrespective of the terms of delivery, including those of free on board, and true of all standard cocoa shipment

---

2   The AFCC has proposed a new FOB contract in which this is not so. The AFCC#2 contract which has FOB shipped weight terms has quality and weight determined on loading. See Appendix I.

contracts. Traders used to strict FOB terms should note this difference.[3] Under strict FOB terms (not those used in the associations' cocoa contracts) sellers complete their duties with the loading of the goods on board the ship. Buyers accept the quality of consignments at the port of loading and not at destination.

Disputes subject to arbitration procedures

Should the cocoa not meet the specifications in the contract then the buyer may institute arbitration procedures against the seller. All three associations maintain, quite correctly, that amicable settlement is preferable to arbitration. Both parties should make every effort to agree such a settlement before the arbitration takes place. If this is not possible each association has its own procedures to be followed by the parties. By far the largest number of arbitrations handled by the associations involve disputes over quality, although arbitrations on quality are less frequent for imports into the United States. The strict quality assessment by the FDA reduces the number of poor quality consignments passing on to the buyer. Other forms of arbitration, i.e., disputes on anything other than the quality of the cocoa, are technical arbitrations and are infrequent.

Weight of the parcel assessed at the place of acceptance

Common to most cocoa bean contracts involving shipment is the idea that the weight of the consignment at the port of discharge affects the invoice value.[4] Similar to the quality assessment mentioned above, the buyer has the parcel weighed, also in the presence of the seller's supervisor, if the seller has nominated one. Weighing the cocoa ex-ship also provides the weight basis for the non-shipment contracts. Sellers delivering cocoa on ex-dock terms use this weight, which is also used in the warehouse warrant weight (known in the United States as the ingoing weight). Sales made on, in or ex-warehouse terms will use the warrant weight as the basis for the invoice value.

Contract terms

Cocoa contracts may be identified by two main terms, those of the delivery and the weight. The use of these two terms (coupled with the

3   See note 2.
4   See note 2.

knowledge of which trade association's terms apply) provide enough for cocoa traders to understand the details of the contract. 'CIF Amsterdam landed weights' is enough for each to calculate their price for the cocoa under discussion. These two main terms therefore deserve attention.

Delivery terms

Most cocoa exports are by sea. Therefore the export sale contracts use the principal marine delivery terms. The most common is that of cost, insurance and freight (CIF) and its variations of cost and freight (C&F), and cost and insurance (C&I). Nearly all the rest of cocoa exports are on free on board (FOB) terms. Although there are two other terms of delivery used in cocoa contracts, those of in or ex-warehouse and ex-dock, exporters rarely use them. Traders, merchants and importers (the second-hand market) contract on these two terms, not exporters.

Marine delivery terms – free on board

The CAL, CMAA and AFCC all provide FOB contract terms. Of the two main export terms, FOB is the simpler although CIF and its variations is the more usual. Despite their simplicity FOB sales usually require the parties to discuss matters in more depth than for CIF terms as the transfer of property and title of the goods require a greater mutual understanding. Under FOB sales the seller's duties are less than for a CIF sale. The seller of FOB cocoa has to deliver the cocoa on board the ship, usually although not necessarily, nominated by the buyer,[5] pay for the loading costs if they do not form part of the freight, clear the cocoa through customs and provide all the necessary documentation to allow the export to take place. Lastly, he must supply the buyer with a clean mate's receipt. In the cocoa trade the seller usually gives a bill of lading instead of a mate's receipt, as FOB cocoa contracts commonly include additional services. The bill of lading is the main document in the export transaction. It is a receipt for the goods on board the ship and gives title to them, as well as providing evidence of the contract of carriage by sea (contract of affreightment).

In a standard FOB contract it is the buyer's duty to contract for the freight by booking the space on board a suitable carrier. Irrespective of whether the buyer or the seller arranges the freight, once the cocoa is on

5   The CAL provide alternative terms for those wishing to sell on FOB terms that allow for either the buyer or the seller to nominate a suitable carrier.

board the ship it becomes the buyer's risk and he is liable for any further costs. This includes the costs of discharging the cocoa at destination.

With the possibility of the seller providing additional services, it is important that both parties understand the exact terms of the particular FOB sale under discussion. Confusion over sale terms increases costs and may lead to disputes that the parties could avoid by clearer understanding of their respective duties at the inception of the contract. Unclear contract terms are the prime sources of dispute.

As mentioned above, under a strict FOB contract the seller has no further interest in the parcel. However, cocoa is not sold according to these terms. Under cocoa contracts the seller is still liable for the quality and weight of the cocoa on arrival at destination.[6]

Marine delivery terms – cost, insurance and freight

Under a CIF sale the seller has five main requirements in fulfilling the contract. Lord Sumner defined these in 1911[7] as:

> 1 *To ship at the port of shipment goods of the description contained in the contract.*
> 2 *To procure a contract of carriage by sea under which the goods will be delivered at the destination contemplated by the contract.*
> 3 *To arrange for an insurance upon the terms current in the trade which will be available for the benefit of the buyer.*
> 4 *To make out an invoice which normally will debit the buyer with the agreed price, or the actual cost, commission charges, freight, and insurance premium, and credit him for the amount of the freight which he will have to pay to the shipowner on delivery of the goods at the port of destination.*
> 5 *To tender these documents to the buyer, so that he may know what freight he has to pay[8] and obtain delivery of the goods, if they arrived or recover for their loss, if they are lost on the voyage.*

---

6   See note 2.
7   Biddle Brothers v E Clemens Horst Co, 1911.
8   The seller pays the freight in a CIF contract, but in this case the buyer was to pay the shipping company, the freight being offset on the invoice. This, too, is not uncommon in cocoa. CIF shipments from Ghana normally include bills of lading that are not stamped 'freight paid' but have the cost of the freight deducted from the invoice. The buyer provides the service of paying the shipping company on behalf of the seller. It is easier for the buyer to pay the freight, usually in US dollars, sterling or Deutchmarks. i.e. a hard currency, than for the Ghana Board to arrange payment.

The buyer's prime duty is to accept delivery of the goods when the seller tenders the documents for payment. Additionally, he is liable for the costs of discharge at destination. Costs for weighing and sampling form part of this charge.

The essence of a CIF contract is the difference between the goods and the documents. The seller discharges the last of his requirements by tendering the shipping documents, not as in the FOB sale, by delivering the cocoa on board the ship. The separation of the documents from the goods they represent provides a very flexible contract and is the heart of much overseas trade.

The buyer takes an important legal step by paying for the documents. It is essential that he only pays for documents that are correct, as paying for them in all but a few cases, means accepting the goods they represent. Note that the buyer may not refuse to pay for the documents if they are correct despite the buyer's concern, perhaps justified, over the quality of the cocoa they represent. Normally when the seller tenders the documents to the buyer for payment the ship is at sea. Only when she discharges can the buyer check the quality of the cocoa and claim against the seller if it is not according to the contract. If the quality of the cocoa is poor the buyer may then have the right to reject it. Outside the United States this is most likely to have been subject to an arbitration. Rejection of parcels in the United States are normally made by the FDA refusing the consignment entry into the country.

It is irrelevant to the performance of the CIF contract if the cocoa arrives in a damaged condition or even if it fails to arrive at all, owing, that is, to the perils of the sea. Including an insurance certificate in the documents presented to the buyer means the cargo owner may claim any losses from the underwriter. The buyer must pay for the shipping documents even if the ship has sunk and both parties are aware of the loss.

Marine delivery terms – cost & freight and cost & insurance

Two variations of CIF sales are cost and freight (C&F) and cost and insurance (C&I). Of the two C&F is the more common. Both the CMAA and CAL issue standard terms or contract forms for C&F delivery, but only the CAL has standard terms for C&I sales. The AFCC does not have contract forms for either C&F or C&I contracts. Cost and freight is the same as a CIF sale but the buyer pays and arranges for the insurance. It may be difficult for an origin seller either to arrange suitable insurance or for him to be competitive with his insurance rates. By changing the sale terms slightly in removing the insurance element from the deal, the seller may secure the business using C&F terms and therefore letting the buyer contract for the insurance. Similarly, if the buyer obtains cheaper freight rates than the seller, trading on C&I terms may secure the deal.

Although the initial export sale may be on one or other of these terms it does not hold that it need remain so if the exporter's buyer wishes to sell the cocoa. Such onward sales of shipment cocoa are very common. If the original purchase was on FOB terms and the buyer intends to sell the parcel it is likely that it will be sold as a CIF consignment. This is made possible by the first buyer paying for the freight and having the bills of lading marked as such and providing the required marine insurance, evidenced by a certificate. Onward sales on FOB terms are unusual.

Non-marine delivery terms – ex-dock

Sales made ex-dock are common in the United States but are rare elsewhere as such ex-dock terms are only available under CMAA contracts. Ex-dock means delivery on the quay at destination; not the quay at the point of loading.[9] It requires that the cocoa be sound, and having passed customs (and the FDA), be available for the buyer to collect. It is not a recommended delivery term for exporters, but is popular with the manufacturers who buy from the second-hand market. Many American manufacturers prefer to take delivery according to this term, leaving the attendant problems of landing the cocoa to the traders. There is a similarity with the FOB contract in that performance of the contract is by physical delivery of the cocoa ex-quay and not by the tendering of documents.

Non-marine delivery terms – in or ex-warehouse

In or ex-warehouse means a sale of goods stored in a warehouse, usually, but not necessarily, at a recognised port of destination. When the buyer takes delivery of cocoa purchased 'in warehouse' or 'in store', he must pay for moving the cocoa from within the shed to the entrance of the warehouse. Sales made 'ex-warehouse' mean that the seller has paid this cost and the buyer's charges begin from the warehouse exit. Ex-warehouse sales are common in the United Kingdom but are rare elsewhere.

The CAL and CMAA have contracts specifically for delivery in or ex-warehouse although all three associations have 'option' contracts based on shipment delivery but that allow for in or ex-warehouse delivery. Traders wanting in or ex-warehouse terms on AFCC contracts adapt the option contracts without too much trouble.

Similar to the ex-dock terms, sellers may deliver only sound cocoa against in or ex-warehouse contracts. The parcel may contain torn and

---

9   Free alongside (FAS) would be a suitable term for such a transaction, although
     there are no particular cocoa contracts for such sales.

slack bags, i.e. where the cocoa is sound but the bags are split. Such bags should be repaired before delivery. The main document of title is no longer the bill of lading, specifically a marine transport document, but the warehouse warrant. Issued by the warehousekeeper it represents title to the goods. Similar to the bill of lading, the warrant may be endorsed over to another third party, either directly, or it may be a 'bearer' warrant, i.e. allowing the holder of the document to take delivery of the goods.

Physical option contracts

First it must be made clear that physical option contracts have no connection with terminal market option contracts. Physical option contracts allow the seller different ways of delivering cocoa to the buyer. The merchants developed such contracts to gain flexibility in both the time and method of making the delivery. In their full form physical option contracts offer the seller three ways of delivering the cocoa, although the basis of the delivery is CIF.

The first is by shipment from origin set to occur during a particular month, the shipment period. If the seller exercises this option the bills of lading must be dated during this shipment month. To all intents this option is indistinguishable from a normal CIF contract. The second option allows the seller to tender shipping documents for cocoa on board a ship due to arrive at the destination during a second period. The second period is normally the month following the shipping period under the first option. Apart from the date of the arrival of the ship displacing the shipment period, this option too, is ostensibly a CIF sale. The third option allows the seller to deliver the cocoa in/ex-store at the port of destination during a third period, which is usually also the month following the shipping period.

Exercising this last option does not comply with the CIF terms of the other two as contract performance is by an in/ex-store delivery. The basis of these contracts is CIF and under the third option the seller incurs the additional costs of landing and storing the cocoa. Under a CIF contract the buyer would pay for these charges. Therefore if the seller exercises the third option the buyer refunds the landing and storage costs to the seller in order that the cost basis of the contract remains CIF. Under CMAA terms the third option allows the seller to deliver on ex-dock terms as well as in warehouse.

Weight terms

Shipment cocoa may either be sold on shipping weight or landed weight terms. Despite these two weight terms all cocoa export sale contracts use the same precept; the amount paid to the seller depends on the weight of the cocoa when it arrives at destination.[10] The difference between the two terms is the application of the 'arrived weight'. The arrived weight involves a calculation based on the sound and full bags discharged from the ship at the port of destination. Broadly speaking, the average weight of one sound and full bag (obtained by dividing the weight of the sound and full bags by their number) multiplied by the number of bags shipped gives the arrived weight, sometimes also referred to as the delivered weight. Note that the arrived weight is not the total weight of the discharged cocoa, unless all the bags are sound and full. It is the assumed weight of the parcel if all the bags had arrived sound and full. That some bags may be torn and/or damaged is immaterial to the calculation, any losses incurred during the 'marine adventure' are recoverable under the insurance.

Shipping weight

A contract made on shipping weight terms is ostensibly simpler in its performance than one on landed weights. The seller's duties end if the contracted cocoa arrives at destination within an agreed franchise limit stipulated in the contract. The seller prepares an invoice based on the traditional weight, the shipping weight, of the parcel. This invoice accompanies the shipping documents to the buyer. Providing all is in order the seller receives payment in full and that is the last he will hear about the consignment. If on the other hand, the buyer finds that the arrived weight is below the contracted weight and that it exceeds the contractual franchise limit, normally 2%, he will raise a loss in weight claim against the seller. In other words if the arrived weight is less than 98% of the contract tonnage the buyer may claim the difference between the two, payable at the contract price. The AFCC#2 contract is the exception to this. Under these terms the weight on loading into the ship is final and is a 'shipped weight' contract.

Landed weight

A landed weight contract is slightly more involved as it needs two invoices. The first is the provisional invoice and is similar to the shipping weight invoice. The difference between them is that the buyer only pays a portion of the full amount, normally 98% or 99%, on presentation of shipping documents. After the arrival of the ship and the weighing of the cocoa, the seller raises a second invoice, a final invoice, using the arrived weight to calculate the balance owed. The balance may be in favour of

10   See note 2.

either party. It means the buyer effectively pays for the cocoa he receives at the port of discharge and is therefore more equitable than a shipping weight contract.

Store weight

Sales made of cocoa lying in a warehouse normally only involve one invoice based on the actual weight of the warehoused cocoa. Usually the final receiver weighs the consignment on its discharge from the ship. This is the weight used on the invoice for stored cocoa. The weighing process involves separating the damaged bags from those that are sound. This is important as only sound cocoa may be sold under the standard contract terms. Any damaged cocoa must be reconditioned (i.e., the damaged portions of the bags removed) before it may be sold.[11] When sold in or ex-store, if the cocoa has not been weighed for six months (AFCC contracts), or a year (CAL contracts) buyers may have the cocoa re-weighed for seller's account.

There is one exception to the actual weight applying to stored cocoa. It is for the now unusual CAL contract, the shipping weight option contract. Under the delivery in/ex-store option the seller may only invoice the parcel based on shipping weights, even though the stored weights may be known. This is because the foundation of the contract is CIF shipping weights and therefore the weight basis has to be respected even if the seller exercises the in/ex-store option. If the parcel's weight exceeds the contractual loss in weight franchise, buyers may claim the loss as if it were a shipment delivery.

Contract forms

The use of the delivery and weight terms is normally sufficient for those involved in the cocoa trade to identify the contract to be used. Table 5.1 below shows the contracts available for those wishing to use either AFCC or CMAA contracts. Both associations issue blank contract forms on which the particular details may be added. The exception to this is the CMAA 1-A contract. This does not exist as contract form but may be invoked if the contract shows the words; 'Subject to terms of standard contract 1-A of the Cocoa Merchants' Association of America, Inc' or such similar phrase. This allows the parties to draw up their own contract form.

Drafting contracts is an intricate business. Parties should exercise great care when amending any contracts as any misunderstanding may

---

11   Such reconditioned cocoa may be described as 'sound and intact', although this term is now infrequently used.

Table 5.1 Summary of AFCC and CMA contracts by their delivery and weight terms

	FOB		C & F		CIF		Ex-dock	In/ex-warehouse	
								Delivery and weight terms	
Trade body and contracts	**S/W**	**L/W**	**S/W**	**L/W**	**S/W**	**L/W**	**W/W**	**S/W**	**W/W**
AFCC 1						●			
AFCC 2	●								
AFCC 3		●							
AFCC 4						●			●
CMA-1A				●		●			
CMA-2A	●		●		●				
CMA-3A									●

S/W – shipping weight, L/W – landed weight, W/W – warehouse warrant weight

well lead to conflicts. Wherever possible it is better to use the standard contract forms or terms rather than meddling with the various clauses.

Short form contracts

Before 20 May 1991 the CAL also issued standard contract forms, ten of them in all. They were the most complete set of forms available, but only obtainable by members of the CAL. Not only did they show the particular details but also, like the contracts issued by the other associations, included most of the other terms applicable to the performance of the contract. Those terms and conditions that were not on the contract form were in the CAL Market Rules, contained in a separate handbook. However, with the advent of computers, members found it difficult to enter the details on to the contract forms using the available technology. It was too difficult to train the computers to fill in the blanks on the forms. Therefore the CAL introduced the short form contract. All sales subject to CAL terms are now on short form contracts. The contract forms, produced on one or other of the party's headed paper, show only the essential particular details of the contract, followed with a similar wording as the CMAA 1-A mentioned above, but pertaining to the CAL. Members may then attach CAL seals on to the two copies of the contract form.

The CAL then rewrote the Market Rules. In May 1991 the CAL disbanded the old contract forms in favour of the short form contracts that referred to the use of new CAL Market Rules, contained in the rules and regulations handbook. This document has all of the terms and conditions

COMPANY'S REGISTERED NAME
ADDRESS

SEAL OF THE
ASSOCIATION

FULL NAME AND ADDRESS OF
SELLER/BUYER

All the terms and conditions contained in the current edition of CAL Market Rules of the Cocoa Association of London Limited shall be deemed to be incorporated in and form part of this contract. Any dispute arising out of the contract shall be referred to arbitration under the arbitration rules of the Cocoa Association of London Limited in force on that date.

SHORT FORM CONTRACT

DATE

CONTRACT NO.

We have this day bought from/sold to you:

QUANTITY	:
DESCRIPTION	:
QUALITY ON ARRIVAL	:
SHIPMENT/ARRIVAL/DELIVERY/LOCATION	:
DESTINATION	:
PRICE	:
TERMS	:
PAYMENT	:
INSURANCE TO BE COVERED BY	:
WEIGHTS	:
SPECIAL CONDITIONS	:

SIGNATURES :

SELLER   BUYER

5.1 An example of a short form contract.

relating to cocoa sales made under CAL terms. This has simplified producing contracts and rationalised their terms and conditions.

Figure 5.1 is an example of a short form contract. It shows the particular details of the sale as well as reference to the Market Rules (see Appendix II). As may be seen on this, the AFCC translation into English and CMAA contracts examples in Appendices I and III, both the seller and the buyer sign the contract form. The contracts are produced in duplicate so that each party may keep a copy, signed by the counterparty.

Using the CAL Market Rules cocoa beans or products may be sold by either shipment or in/ex-store. They also cover sales combining both types of deliveries in 'option' contracts. The contracting parties are free to choose the weight basis of the contract.

Non-members may also use the CAL contract terms. The contract wording should be the same irrespective of whether either party is a member of the CAL or not. The difference is that non-members' contract forms would not have the CAL seal, which is only available to the association's members. A contract not under seal will substantially increase the costs of arbitration in the event of a dispute.

Price fixation contracts

When a contract shows a price of cocoa beans of say, £775 per tonne it is not apparent to outsiders that the parties arrive at this value through the addition of two prices: a terminal market price modified by an amount depending on the growth of the cocoa. Many consider or talk of the first price as 'the price of cocoa' as it forms the basis of the physical cocoa contract's value. It is the terminal market price quoted for the month, usually that nearest to the end of the shipment period in question, and reflects the overall supply and demand of cocoa for that delivery period. This would be sufficient for the contract value if all cocoas were the same. They are not, some attract a higher price than others, depending on supply of the particular origin at the destination in question, its quality and reliability of delivery. As the physical contract will be for a specific growth of cocoa another factor has to modify the terminal market value. This is the origin differential, and is expressed as a premium or discount to the terminal market price. An example might show the terminal market value as £800 and the differential for say, Nigerian cocoa as minus £25. The outright price would be £775 per tonne for Nigerian cocoa for that delivery period.

As there are two parts to the price, traders have developed a form of contract to take advantage of the flexibility this offers – the price fixation contract (PFA). In a PFA contract the two parties agree all the terms except the outright price. In its place is how the parties will determine the outright price. The contract shows the price in two parts: first as the agreed differential value, say $45 discount; and the relevant delivery month on the terminal market, say December 1993 New York. The two parties also agree by when they will agree to fix the December 1993 position and thereby obtain an outright price.

There are three main advantages to PFA contracts. First the trader assumes limited risk until the parties fix the contract price. All forward contracts experience a period of inactivity lasting from the contract's inception through to the beginning of its performance. This period may be extensive, a year or more is not uncommon. Throughout this period the parties to a contract with an outright price are at risk on the difference between the values of the contract and the prevailing market. If one party fails, the other will at the very least, have to contend with additional administrative costs. Sadly on occasion, if the price moves sufficiently against one party they will default on the contract. Fortunately this is uncommon, but it is a risk that traders should be, and are, aware of. This is especially true at the moment with prices at an all time low and with companies in a weakened state. On a price fixation contract the parties limit this risk to the change that may have taken place in the differentials. Neither party assumes the risk for the whole contract value until striking an outright price. This reduces the risk when trading either for distant delivery periods or with a party whose viability is in doubt, a *del credere* risk.

Second, until the parties agree an outright price, neither will have hedged the contract; i.e., the risk will not have been offset on the terminal market. This defers the hedging costs and substantially reduces the risk of large margin payments.

Third, the differential may be locked into the contract while waiting for more favourable terminal market prices. Price fixation contracts are not uncommon and usually have a separate sheet attached to the main contract form outlining both the price basis and when the parties must fix the contract.

The examples quoted above are for cocoa beans but cocoa products use a similar technique, the prices for which are also in two parts. The first part is the same as for beans, the terminal market price. The second, which for beans was a differential, for products is a ratio. This is a multiple to be applied to the terminal market price.

Contract performance

Declarations

All cocoa contracts require sellers to advise buyers of the consignment they intend to deliver. The advice, called the declaration, is essential. Without it the buyer may reject the consignment's shipping or warehouse documents tendered for payment. Exporters normally make this advice when they have all of the required shipping documents in their possession in order that they may compile the declaration on the exact details contained in the documents. The buyer may reject the documents if there is any discrepancy between the declaration or contract terms and the documents presented for payment.

Shipment declarations

Declarations by telex are usual. Although declarations by facsimile machines are popular for those trading under CMAA terms, they are expressly forbidden under AFCC and CAL contracts. While the associations permit declarations made through other media, such as cable or by registered letter, they are rare.

Of the three associations the CAL requires the most detail in the declaration to the buyer. Expressly, paragraph 7.5 of the Market Rules says that a declaration should consist of:

(a) Contract number and date of contract.
(b) Quantity of goods shipped (tonnes, bags and/or packages).
(c) Description of goods shipped.
(d) Name of vessel.
(e) Bill of lading, date and number, container number and container seal number (if shipped in containers).
(f) Port of shipment.
(g) Port of destination.
(h) Marks.
(j) Serial number of original ICCO certificate when applicable.
(k) In the case of charter name of the owner or established authorised agent at the port of destination named in the bill of lading.

Since April 15 1990 sellers need not supply the ICCO certificate mentioned in (j) above. Officially called a certificate of origin, it evidenced payment of the levy on cocoa exported from countries that were signatories to the International Cocoa Agreement. Payment of the levy is currently suspended. Although (k) provides for the ship to be chartered, cocoa exporters rarely do so. Most exporters do not handle sufficient tonnages to justify chartering a vessel.

Other information is often included in the declaration. More than one consignment may be needed to fulfil the contract, especially if the sale was for a large tonnage. Therefore declarations usually say whether or not the shipment completes the contract. If sellers appoint a supervisor to attend the weighing and sampling at destination, they normally advise the buyer in the declaration.

An example of a declaration might be worded as follows:

We hereby declare under usual reserves in partial fulfilment of contract B 5678 dated 14/5/93 the following parcel.
1000 bags 60 MT Superior Bahia temperao 1992/93 crop cocoa beans marked ABC/123/BRAZIL per m.v. FLORENTINA to Amsterdam on B/L 7 dated 20/6/93 at Ihleus.

Supervisors at destination: A.N. Otherveem
Kind regards

Onward sales of cocoa are common. If the exporter's buyer intends to sell the parcel on to another, he will send his own declaration to his buyer on receiving the exporter's declaration. If not, he will advise his warehousekeeper at the port of discharge to expect the parcel. Whichever course of action he intends to follow the shipping documents will be presented to him for payment.

Declarations for stored cocoa

Sellers of cocoa lying in a warehouse also need to declare the parcel to the buyer, although it is different to a shipment sale declaration. The declaration of the tender in or ex-store need not have any of the shipment details; the name of the vessel and the bill of lading details become irrelevant once the cocoa is in store. The only shipment information needed in the declaration of tender is the date of the vessel's final day of landing. This is the date the carrier completed discharging goods at the port where the cocoa lies.

Instead of the shipment details, the advice of tender must include the name of the warehouse and warehousekeeper, together with the warehouse warrant number.[12] In addition, the last day of weighing and the prompt date should appear. The prompt date is the day by which the buyer must pay for the parcel and therefore take delivery. For CAL contracts this is five business days after the declaration of tender, for the AFCC it is four days and three days for CMAA contracts. The buyer may take delivery before the prompt date if he wishes, although he will have to pay for the documents at the earlier time. Sellers must confirm that they have paid the rent up to the prompt date, and insured the cocoa (warehouse, not marine insurance) also up to the same date. For AFCC contracts the insurance has to be covered by sellers up to at least the 15th day inclusive following the date of presentation of documents, usually the prompt date. Note that the seller may only declare sound cocoa to the buyer. Damaged cocoa discharged from the ship must be reconditioned before it can be sold.

Documents

Shipping documents

A CIF sale requires the seller to furnish the buyer with a set of shipping documents representing the declared parcel. Under CIF terms (and

12   See 'Documents'.

irrespective of the cocoa trade) a set comprises at least three main documents; an invoice, freight paid bills of lading and a marine insurance certificate or policy. While all three are necessary for the performance of the contract, for reasons mentioned above the bill of lading is the most important.

Bills of lading come in different forms. All three associations accept conventional or through bills of lading, while a combined transport document[13] is only acceptable for sales under CAL and CMAA contracts. None of the associations accept groupage, freight forwarder's bills of lading or sea waybills. Such documents are not designed for international trade. Charter-party bills of lading are also not permitted as they may not have liner terms. Bills of lading issued under a charter-party must be on liner terms. The cocoa must be 'shipped on board', as evidenced by the bill of lading. For the AFCC contracts this means the bill must show the goods on board the main carrier and not a feeder vessel. 'Received for shipment' bills of lading are not acceptable under any cocoa contract. Claused or stale bills are also not accepted.[14] For CIF or C&F sales the bills of lading must be marked 'freight paid'.

Nowadays most insurance policies exist as open covers, under which sellers issue insurance certificates for the consignments. It is rare to see an insurance policy included with CIF documents. While all three associations stipulate that the insurance be with first class companies, the terms of the marine insurance depend on the association. Sales on AFCC contracts require the insurance be for 102.5% of the shipping invoice value and subject to all risks of the French Marine Cargo Insurance Policy. It must not be subject to any franchise. The certificate should show 'premium paid' and that it 'complies with AFCC conditions'. Sales under CAL terms must be according to the Institute Commodity Trades Clauses (A) and be for 100% of the shipping invoice amount. War and Strikes clauses must also be on Commodity Trades clauses (A). CMAA contracts require Institute Cargo Clauses (A) and the relevant War and Strikes clauses. Similar to the CAL, the sum insured should be 100% of the invoice amount. Insurance certificates for contracts under CAL or CMAA terms should also not be subject to a deductible franchise. Sellers on FOB and C&F contracts need not provide this document.

Other documents required are those that allow the buyer preferential treatment on the import of the cocoa. For cocoa entering the EEC this

---

13   A combined transport document allows the carrying of cargo by different modes of transport.

14   A bill of lading becomes stale once the cargo arrives at the port of destination. Under letters of credit subject to 'The uniform customs & practices for documentary credits', 1994 unless otherwise stated the bill is stale if over three weeks old.

includes an EUR-1 certificate for cocoa coming from countries that are signatories to the Lomé convention. CAL and AFCC contracts therefore specify that the seller must provide it. As mentioned above, since April 15 1990 documents representing shipments from or to countries which are members of the International Cocoa Agreement need not include an ICC-certificate. However, the AFCC and CAL contracts still contain provision for their inclusion should they be required again in the future.

Other documents are optional and include certificates of weight, quality and/or grading, and origin. One document that is also optional, but is recommended for sellers to include is a fumigation and/or phytosanitary certificate. Fumigating the cocoa before shipment reduces the likelihood of it arriving at destination infested with insects. If the cocoa arrives infested, usually the seller is liable for the costs of fumigation. This applies for all cocoa contracts.

All documents must be consistent with one another. Any discrepancy gives the buyer cause for concern. A different weight shown on one document compared with the others gives enough justification to the buyer for delaying payment. The buyer is within his rights not to pay for the documents until the discrepancy is amended.

Documents for stored cocoa

There are two main documents for the sale of cocoa lying in a warehouse. The first is the invoice. This should be based on the actual net weight of the parcel, as it was weighed on discharge of the ship, or on intake into the warehouse; i.e., the warrant weight. The buyer pays the full amount of the invoice. Under AFCC terms, if more than six months has passed since the cocoa was last weighed then the buyer may either have an allowance of 0.5%, or the parcel may be re-weighed and the new weights applied.[15] CAL contracts allow the seller to re-weigh the cocoa and apply the new weights if more than twelve months have passed since it was last weighed.

The second document is the warehouse warrant or delivery order.[16] The warrant is similar to the bill of lading in that first, it gives either the bearer or an assigned party title to the goods. Second, it is a receipt for the goods in store.

15   This is a short explanation. Appendix I shows the text of the AFCC#4 contract, see section III – Weighing.

16   Delivery orders have a number of meanings. Shipping companies may issue them in lieu of bills of lading, wharfingers may issue dock receipts that are sometimes also called delivery orders and warehousekeepers may also issue them instead of warrants. Trading companies used to issue their own delivery orders for stored goods. This last form of delivery orders now is not acceptable under cocoa contracts. The meaning here is a document issued by the warehousekeeper.

In Europe the existence of the EUR-1 certificate will have to be shown to the buyer, although normally the warehousekeeper or customs authority at the port holds this document. Under AFCC and CAL terms the ICC certificate, if necessary, must be supplied. Likewise sellers need not supply any weight, quality or the other certificates that may have accompanied the shipping documents. It is also not necessary to supply a fumigation and/or phytosanitary certificate.

Payment

Ensuring that the buyer pays is one of the seller's main worries. Fortunately for the seller one type of payment, common in many international trades, is unusual in cocoa; that of deferred payment. Credit is not the norm in the cocoa trade. Most contracts are 'cash against documents', i.e. the buyer pays when presented with correct shipping or storage documents. This substantially reduces the risk of the buyer defaulting while holding the seller's documents. Securing payment then centres on how the seller presents documents to the buyer. There are four ways the seller may do this, although he himself may only choose one from three, the fourth option has to be agreed with the buyer at the time of the contract. This option, payment by letter of credit, is popular with many exporters and, in the past, Eastern bloc importers. Some countries require letters of credit on all exports, for instance Brazil.

Letters of credit

Letters of credit provide the securest way of the overseas seller ensuring that he receives payment and that the buyer has the documents he needs. If the parties intend to present documents through a letter of credit, they should agree to do so at the time of the contract. There are two reasons for this. First, the buyer pays the cost of opening the credit, not the seller. The amount is significant and is a factor that modifies the contract price. Second, the buyer has to instruct a bank to open the credit before the shipment period. The buyer cannot be expected to undertake it if it is not a requirement of the contract.

In the terminology involving documentary credits, the buyer is the 'applicant' when he requests the bank to open the credit. This bank, now called the 'issuing bank', is usually one that is near the applicant. The applicant includes the list of shipping documents required by him. The issuing bank then contacts a bank in the seller's country, giving them the details of the credit. This second bank, known as the 'advising' or 'confirming' bank, depending on the type of credit, informs the seller (the beneficiary) that the credit is open. The seller may then inspect the credit, and should pay particular attention to the list of documents the buyer requires. He should do so when the credit becomes available as any amendment may only be made by the applicant and delays only affect the beneficiary. The beneficiary will only receive payment if the documents comply precisely with the terms of the credit. The beneficiary presents the shipping documents to the advising/confirming bank, who in turn, forwards them on to the issuing bank. The issuing bank presents them to the buyer for payment.

There are a number of different types of letters of credit. In cocoa the most frequent is an irrevocable credit. This is a powerful documentary instrument as, unlike a revocable credit, once opened the applicant alone may not rescind it. Knowing this, contracting parties should avoid using revocable credits as it allows either party to change the documentary requirements at will – even cancelling the credit. Sellers may ask the buyers to open another type of credit, one that is confirmed. A confirmed irrevocable credit requires the advising bank to pay the beneficiary on presentation of shipping documents; the bank therefore confirms the

Table 5.2 Checklist for presenting documents under a letter of credit

Credit details
 1. Has the credit expired?
 2. Will the credit limit be exceeded?
 3. Will the documents be presented in time?

Documents
 4. Are the documents consistent, especially the weight, marks, description, number of bags and values?
 5. Do the documents describe the cocoa precisely as in the credit?
 6. Are all the documents called for under the credit present?
 7. Are they all correctly signed?

Bills of lading
 8. Is the B/L dated within the shipping period?
 9. Is the cocoa 'shipped on board'?
10. Are the shipment details correct?
11. Is the B/L clean? (i.e. contains no clauses)
12. Is it liner B/L?
13. Is it marked 'Freight paid', where applicable (CIF and C&F sales)?
14. Is it correctly endorsed?

Insurance certificates
15. Is the certificate valid and does it have the correct clauses?
16. Is the correct amount insured?
17. Is it correctly endorsed?

credit. Many buyers in the cocoa trade do not favour these credits as they prefer to sight the documents themselves before instructing payment.

Most letters of credit are subject to the 'Uniform Customs and Practice for Documentary Credits' (1994). Parties involved in this type of presentation and payment should obtain copies of the publication from the International Chamber of Commerce. In particular, sellers should complete a check-list before presenting documents under a letter of credit, and indeed before tendering any documents to a buyer. Table 5.2 gives a list that, if followed, would show the more common errors banks find with shipping documents presented under credits.

Documentary collection

Letters of credit give a sound basis for conducting business with a new trading partner. However, once both parties gain more confidence in one another and their countries remain economically and politically stable, they should consider another method of securing payment. One way is by documentary collection. Again making use of banks, it confers a degree of security, not as great as the letter of credit, but normally adequate to protect the seller in the event of a default. The advantages compared to letters of credit are that the costs are lower[17] and the seller receives the payment more quickly. The banks only need a perfunctory inspection of the documents, therefore reducing the time taken in processing them compared with a letter of credit.

In the parlance of those dealing with documentary collections, the seller becomes known as the 'principal'. The principal forwards the documents to his bank, known as the 'remitting bank', enclosing the shipping documents with a collection order. The collection order instructs the remitting bank to whom the documents should be presented and what action they should take in the event of the buyer not paying. The remitting bank then forwards the documents with suitable instructions to a bank near the buyer. This second bank, the 'collecting bank', then presents the documents to the buyer for payment. If the buyer fails to pay, the collecting bank may act on behalf of the seller in eliciting the return of the shipping documents, according to the instructions contained in the collection order.

Most of the international sales conducted in cocoa use documentary collections. They provide a less expensive way of ensuring payment than a letter of credit, and have the advantage that both buyers and sellers are familiar with their requirements. Those involved in documentary collec-

17 Although the seller pays the costs of presenting the documents under a collection, remember the seller may also pay for the letter of credit by having to accept a lower price for the cocoa.

tions should familiarise themselves with the 'Uniform Rules for Collections' (1979), published by the International Chamber of Commerce. Most banks apply the Rules in conducting collections.

Presentation by hand

For sales made to companies situated close to the seller neither of the above two methods apply. Much easier and commonly used in the second-hand market is for the seller to present the documents to the buyer himself. On inspection of the documents the buyer hands the seller a cheque. The cheque must be drawn on an account that gives the seller value the day it is cashed. As the decline of trade within the second-hand market continues, this method of presentation has also dropped in usage.

Open account

The open account, or free release, is the last method of payment available to the seller. Providing all goes according to plan, it gives the fastest and cheapest way for the seller to receive payment. Also it may be the most disastrous as it gives the least security. The free release involves the seller sending the documents directly to the buyer requesting payment. There is no security of payment. Most business relationships with overseas companies do not reach the stage of trust that allows this conduct. Sellers should exercise the utmost caution in presenting documents in this manner and restrict it to those companies with whom they have only the best of relationships.

A variation of sending documents direct to the buyer is the telex release which is frequently used in the second-hand market. The seller sends the documents to a warehousekeeper at the port of destination who is usually known and respected by both parties. The warehousekeeper then advises the buyer that he holds the documents at the buyer's disposal against payment to the seller. The buyer requests his bank to advise the warehousekeeper when payment is effected, giving the buyer full access to the documents. Strictly this method of presenting documents requires the prior consent of the buyer, but buyers rarely refuse such a request from a seller in the second-hand market.

Fortunately those trading cocoa today can rely on the experiences of others. The lessons learnt earlier are available in the terms and conditions of the particular contracts issued by the trade associations. Ignoring their work by not using these particular contracts causes more work for both buyer and seller, and increases the prospects of dispute. Knowing when to trade and with whom at what price is important, but understanding the contract terms and their prudent application gives the basis for long term success.

CHAPTER

6

■ ■ ■

Terminal markets

Introduction

A s the trade in cocoa increased at the end of the nineteenth century, so did the attendant risks. Trading forward helped reduce the risk to the manufacturers of running out of the type of beans they needed, but it did not help them to buy the essential raw material economically. For example, chocolate manufacturers could either buy the cocoa in say, January for delivery in say, June, or wait the six months and then attempt to buy the cocoa on the spot market. The risk to the manufacturer in delaying any action until he needed the beans lay in two parts. First was that the type of cocoa wanted would not be available in six months' time. Second, the spot price in June could be higher than the forward price the factory could have had six months earlier. Buying forward may help safeguard the supply of raw material to the factory, the first risk, but it in no way ensures a good price.

The grain markets in Chicago are often cited as first providing the protection against price movements. Prices for grain fluctuated to an extent that made any long term commercial venture difficult to sustain. Farmers, traders and millers alike were unable to manage prudently their affairs when grain prices behaved as if on a roller-coaster. During the 1860s those involved in the trade developed a way of managing the price risk. It concerned a separate contract for the material, a futures contract.

While not first to use futures,[1] the grain traders popularised the method of protecting against price movements. The price of the grain on the terminal or futures market mirrored those quoted on the physical forward market. (Note the difference between the term 'forwards' and 'futures'. Forwards refer to contracts in physicals or actuals for delivery in some prospective period. Futures is a synonym for trades on the terminal market.) This provided a way to safeguard the prices obtained for physical purchases and sales. Known as hedging, dealers trade the same tonnage on the terminal market simultaneously as that done in physicals; buying the futures if they sold the physical, or selling the futures if they bought the actuals. An adverse price movement on the physicals is balanced by a profit on the terminal transaction and vice versa.

Differences between the futures and physical markets

There are a number of differences between the physical and futures market. The first is that futures market describes a forum of people. Unlike the forward market that is dispersed throughout the world, there are three places where cocoa futures may be traded: London, New York and Kuala Lumpur. This does not mean that people living elsewhere cannot trade on the terminals, but that whatever anyone does has to pass through one of these markets. Of the three markets, London and New York are by far the largest as the other two now seem inactive as their market liquidity has reached zero or is close to it. The success or viability of a market depends on the volume of business transacted under its auspices (see 'liquidity').

Second, as the business passes through one of the exchanges the volume, delivery and price become public knowledge. Others on the exchange will know these features although they may not know who is behind the trade. The identity of the broker placing the business on the market is also common knowledge, as is the broker accepting the deal, but the anonymity of the players (people who use the terminal markets) that may be behind the trade remains. In some instances others in the market may correctly guess the player, although at best it will still only be an informed assumption. In physical trades all aspects of the sale remain the private knowledge of the parties involved; the buyer, seller and, if used, the broker of physical cocoa. One or other may choose to leak details of the sale but that is their, and their counterparty's affair.

Third, and most importantly, a futures contract is a standard contract,

---

1   Japan legalised futures trading for rice in 1730 at the Osaka Rice Exchange and during 1826 a futures contract for nutmeg existed in England.

as opposed to a particular contract, i.e., those used in the physical market. Buyers and sellers of futures have limited choice on the terms of the sale, unlike on the forwards, where they can agree practically any terms. Futures markets set the weight for each contract, the lot size, the grade of the cocoa acceptable to the exchange and lastly, where and when the seller may deliver the cocoa. They differ only in price.

The use of standardised contracts has distinct advantages. It allows contracts to become interchangeable, players may buy and sell cocoa on similar terms, providing an easy way of squaring positions. But it is not enough on its own. Trader A may have bought from B on a standard contract, but later B may not wish to sell to A when A wants to square his position. In order to alleviate this problem of illiquidity every terminal market has a central body through which all the trades pass. This body, known as the clearing, is the counterparty to every trade made by members of the exchange. This greatly increases the liquidity of the market. Although A bought from B, his position is with the clearing and not with B. To square his position A does not have to sell to B, his original trading partner, he can sell to any member on the exchange to undo his position with the clearing. As shown later, the liquidity of a market is vital. The inability to unwind a terminal market position for lack of trading partners is the death-knell of a market.

Restrictions on the weight, delivery and quality of cocoa traded may seem strange and unappetising to those who want to buy cocoa to use in a factory. Buyers are limited to buying cocoa in clips of ten tonnes (the lot size), with delivery restricted to five particular months of the year, and the cocoa delivered could come from any number of different origins and be stored in a place inconvenient to the factory. As said earlier, it is not the intention of the futures market to provide an alternative means of supplying physical cocoa. Only a small percentage of the futures trades culminate in delivery of the cocoa. Although a contract on the futures market is a promise to deliver or accept cocoa subject to the requirements laid down by the exchange, players will square their positions before the delivery period. By standardising the contracts players may use the exchange for hedging their physical deals that contain specific and particular details.

The possibility to deliver or take up cocoa ensures that prices on the terminal markets and prices for actuals move broadly in parallel. The fact that delivery of real cocoa may take place under a futures contract links the exchange to the world of physical cocoa. Players that have a futures position, either long[2] or short[3], will have to take up or deliver cocoa when

2   A 'long' is a trader who has bought the commodity and has not sold it.
3   A 'short' is a trader who has sold the commodity and has not entered into a
     purchase contract.

it is due. This cocoa will have had to originate from a physical purchase. The price of cocoa lying in store for delivery on to the terminal market must therefore be the same as that for delivery against a physical contract.[4] The price of cocoa at the time of delivery links the physical to the futures market. This essential connection provides the world of physical cocoa with a reference point when talking about the price of cocoa. In the previous chapter, the price of physical cocoa was described as consisting of two parts, the futures price and the differential. The terminal market provided the larger part of the price, while the differential depended on the origin, quality and destination of the particular cocoa. That the larger part of the price of physical cocoa depends on the terminal market shows the relevance of futures to physicals. If the differential was larger than that provided by the futures it would mean that the terminal market did not adequately reflect the world cocoa market and would not provide a satisfactory hedging medium.

The cocoa exchanges in London, the London Commodity Exchange (LCE), and New York, the Coffee, Sugar & Cocoa Exchange (CSCE), represent all cocoa terminal market transactions in the world. Part of their success lies in the similarity of the contracts and in the time difference between London and New York, allowing business to continue in the United States when London finishes. Similarities of contract help arbitrage business between the two markets. While exact details of futures contracts vary between the two exchanges (not least of which is that the LCE contract is in sterling while the CSCE contracts are traded in US dollars), there are two fundamental similarities.

The first is the lot size. Futures contracts on both exchanges are in ten tonne lots. This has not always been the case, but since 1981 all cocoa futures lots on both exchanges have standardised on the metric system. Players may only trade in multiples of ten tonnes – the lot is indivisible.

The second is the delivery periods. Both exchanges have contracts for delivery during March, May, July, September and December. Contracts for the delivery of cocoa during any other month have to be specially called. This is a rare event. A player with say, a short position of five lots March 1993 cocoa must deliver the five lots of cocoa to the market during March 1993 if he has not squared out his position. A simple example of offsetting the risk on the price, or hedging the commodity, may best explain the principles. It is not the only risk that traders may offset using the terminal market but it is the main one. Other risks are identified and some techniques used to combat them are shown later.

---

4   There may be some differences owing to the specific requirements of terminal
    cocoa, in warehousing, weighing and quality assessment.

An example of a simple hedge

Suppose a chocolate manufacturer wished to ensure that the factory would have a supply of cocoa in six months time. It is now January and so he buys 100 tonnes of physical cocoa for delivery in June at £825 per tonne. By trading with a reputable dealer, he is reasonably sure that the delivery will take place. But if he expected prices for cocoa to fall he would hedge the purchase to prevent major losses that may occur should the decline in price take place during the intervening six months. Therefore at the time of arranging the purchase he would simultaneously sell 10 lots (each lot is ten tonnes) of cocoa on the futures market for delivery in July. (On the futures market it is not possible to trade for delivery in June, the nearest delivery month after June is July.) The price he sold the ten lots for was £815 per tonne. The manufacturer may be described as long of the physical, i.e., the amount of actuals he has bought is greater than what he has sold[5]; and short of the futures, i.e., he has sold more futures than he has bought.

	Physical	Futures (July)
January	Bought 100 t @ £825/t	Sold 10 lots @ £815/t

As the price on the futures market mirror those in the physical market, a subsequent fall in the price of cocoa will show a profit on the futures and a corresponding loss on the forward deal; a rise in the price will show the opposite. Until the seller delivers the physical cocoa and the manufacturer takes action on the terminal market, such profits and losses remain hypothetical, he has not realised the profit and loss.

In this example the manufacturer has, in the parlance of the market, 'sold the terminal short'. He has sold something that, at the inception of the contract, he does not possess. This is neither unusual nor illegal. Those that have a position on either the futures or the forward market have until the time of delivery to supply the cocoa (usual practice with forward contracts) or to square the sale contract with a purchase (common with futures).

During June the trader presents documents to the manufacturer for payment against the purchase of physical cocoa. At that time the price of this type of cocoa for immediate delivery is £790 per tonne. Had the manufacturer waited he could have purchased the cocoa £35 cheaper.

---

5 Some may argue that as a manufacturer he needed the cocoa anyway and therefore is not long of the physicals. If he failed to buy it he would certainly be short.

However, the price on the terminal market has also fallen to £780 thereby counteracting the effect on the physical purchase. Before the futures market delivery month, July, the buyer would undo his futures position by buying 10 lots of cocoa. His position in futures would then be square, i.e., neither long nor short, one that would allow him to realise the profit on the market. This offsets the assumed loss of buying the cocoa at a higher price.

	Physical	Futures (July)
January	Bought 100 t @ £825/t	Sold 10 lots @ £815/t
June	Could have bought 100 t @ £790/t	Buys 10 lots @ £780/t
	Assumed loss £3500	Profit £3500

For the manufacturer the cost of arranging such insurance, hedging, was small, as trading on the futures exchange is highly geared. Players do not have to pay initially the whole amount of the contract value and enjoy lower costs.

Some may wonder why the buyer (especially if he had been a dealer rather than a manufacturer) in the above case did not arrange another physical sale, simultaneously with the first and on the same terms as the purchase, instead of placing the business on the terminal market. In other words hedge the purchase with a physical contract sale. The answer lies at the time of delivery. It may be extremely difficult to buy back the hedge contract from the counterparty – to square the position. At the time of delivery it might not suit the counterparty to the hedge contract to square it out. It is a very illiquid market, with the buyer forced to trade with a single counterparty who can charge a heavy premium to square the hedge contract.

Organisation of futures markets

Members

Terminal markets are specific places where transactions in futures occur and although the contracts are available to all, not everyone may trade directly on the exchanges. The exchange limits trading to its floor members, 30 to 40 companies or individuals that have a seat. Those who are not authorised floor members have to trade through someone who does have a seat, effectively acting through a broker. There are two other types of membership, those of associate and local floor membership. Associate members may not trade on the floor of the exchange but do have access to information systems. Locals are individuals and not companies, introduced to increase the liquidity of the markets by their jobbing activities, i.e., taking a position and squaring it within a short period. In the United States they play a more active role than in the United Kingdom markets. The LCE, consisting of 13 commodities, only permits 50 locals. A local may only trade for his own account, another local or for an authorised floor member. They may not represent a client.

The market

In London the floor members sit in a ring, the outside of which is surrounded by telephone booths that provide the link between the floor traders and their offices. Orders to buy or sell come from the desk traders in their respective offices. The floor traders then execute the orders by open outcry. At first sight, an active market appears totally disorganised with a group of youngsters shouting and waving their hands. A more careful appraisal shows the shouting is the open outcry and the hand waving is the signals backing up the bids or offers. The exchange requires its members to follow a strict etiquette, without which there could be no market. The market rules help prevent members' misbehaviour or trading impropriety.

The New York markets favour a pit arrangement. In this there are no seats, the floor members mill around within 'the pit' and they receive their orders via 'runners' who attend telephones located outside the pit. Its advantages are that it allows many more floor members to trade and is cheaper to run.

The exchanges are corporate bodies that receive money from two sources: first, from an annual levy charged on members and second, they charge a fee per lot, on the trades conducted under their auspices.

Opening and closing

Trading on the markets takes place during set hours. In London the market opens at 0932, closes for lunch at 1230, reopens after lunch at 1400 and concludes at 1645. Ensuring the orderly opening and closing of the market is important. Before the opening in London overnight news concerning the New York market may have triggered a number of orders that must be filled in a methodical way. The closing is also important as many valuations and price fix agreements depend on the final call. In London the call chairman, an employee of the exchange, controls both the opening and closing periods by having the bids and offers passed through him.

The CSCE opens for cocoa trading at 0930 and closes at 1415, New York time. When New York opens, London has had the benefit of trading during the morning session. Thus news from London affects the opening of the CSCE which also requires a controlled opening. With a pit arrangement, ensuring a disciplined opening and closing takes a different course to that in London. The exchange calls the opening, one delivery month at a time, starting with the current delivery month. A warning is sounded five minutes before the close of the market, allowing a controlled closure which can be monitored by the exchange staff.

Clearing

Common to all trading, for every buyer of a futures contract there is a seller. However, it is not the prime intention of players of futures to take delivery of the commodity, the positions have to be squared out before the delivery period. As mentioned earlier, if A bought physical cocoa from B in order to cancel out the delivery A would have to sell the same quantity and on the same terms back to B. In a futures market this would not only be laborious, the market would seize up. Perhaps B wanted to deliver cocoa to A and therefore had no intention of squaring out his position. In addition A's financial position with B may be extended beyond the financial director's limits. The risk of trading with the company and extending the liability may cause the withdrawal of companies trading, reducing the size of the market. The answer to both problems lies in the provision of a third party, the clearing organisation.

Although A may buy from B on the exchange, the counterparty to the deal is the clearing organisation. Contractually, B sells to the clearing house who then sells it on to A, although this is not evident at the inception of the contract, on the exchange floor. The clearing organisation underwrites the trading between members on the floor of the exchange. Not only does this remove the immediate concerns over the financial standing of members at the time of trading but it also allows parties to square out their positions with members that were not concerned with the opening of the position.

It is a prerequisite that members must be acceptable to the clearing organisation, and that confidence in the clearing mechanism remains. Members must therefore be acceptable to the clearing before they may trade. In London the International Commodity Clearing House Ltd (ICCH) fills the role. The ICCH is a profit making enterprise jointly owned by a number of banks. In the CSCE the clearing is by the CSC Clearing Corporation run by members of the exchange.

Margins

As a counterparty to the thousands of outstanding trades made by large and small companies, the clearing structures are central to the smooth running of the markets. The clearing organisations require companies trading on the exchanges to back up their financial standing with cash. This takes two forms. The first is an initial deposit for each lot traded, some 5 to 10% of the value of the contract depending on the current market value of the cocoa and the risk involved. The second is the variation margin that applies to outstanding trades. The clearing organisations value existing trades against the current market. If this results in a loss the clearing organisations will call the relevant members for money to cover the shortfall. Normally the clearing organisations conduct this valuation daily but if the market conditions are extremely volatile, the clearing may call for margins more frequently.

Just as the clearing calls the members for money against their trading losses, the members' clients will also face margin calls from their member brokers. Before trading through a member, every client must have a trading or customer agreement with the member. The margin payment forms an important clause in the agreement. Although clauses vary from customer to customer it is a requirement that members monitor their clients' London accounts daily.[6] Failure by a client to meet their financial obligations allows the member to square out the client's position at the latest after a period of five working days.[7]

Margins play a central role to the physical trader using the futures market as a hedging medium. A trader's unrealised profit on his physical forward contracts may become meaningless with the margin calls made on his hedged futures position. Forward contracts are not subject to margins[8], so traders with inherently profitable physical contracts may only realise the money when the relevant shipping documents become available. In the meantime they may face paying the margins on their hedges. The financing of such costs, especially on large terminal positions, may stretch the company's resources to the extent that its liquidity is in jeopardy.[9]

6 'The professional dealing handbook'. The Securities and Futures Authority, Item 5–28, 1991.

7 Ibid The Securities and Futures Authority, 1991.

8 The exception to this is the AFCC price fixation contract, in which margins may be called, see Appendix I.

9 There is a form of hedging that offers protection against the financing of margins. Players determine the tonnage they should hedge by following a formula that includes the current level of interest rates and the amount of time until the delivery month. Effectively the player hedges a smaller tonnage than contracted on the actuals. The money saved by hedging the smaller tonnage helps to finance margin calls.

Tendering

Squaring out positions result in either a profit or loss payable by the clearing to the member. However, should a member retain a position through to the delivery month the clearing organisation has to take up cocoa from the shorts and deliver it to those who are long – the tendering of the commodity.

The rules for tendering cocoa on the LCE and CSCE are different. Those tendering cocoa on to the exchanges must pay particular attention to the market rules. Making assumptions about the process is dangerous practice, even those used to the process occasionally find themselves in error. Although the lot sizes are the same, both ten tonnes, the quality requirements stipulated to warrant proper delivery are not. Locations of storage are also different; one only allows storage in certain places in the United States while the other states locations in Europe.[10] Storage practices themselves differ between the two markets.

Despite these differences the process of tendering is similar. The short on the futures market must have stored the cocoa according to the market rules. It must be stored by an approved warehousekeeper in a shed licensed by the exchange. Cocoa tendered on the LCE must be warehoused in either the United Kingdom or in Amsterdam, Antwerp, Bremen, Hamburg or Rotterdam. Tenders made on the CSCE must be for cocoa stored in either the Port of New York District, the Delaware River Port District or the Port of Hampton Roads.[11]

For the London market a sample of at least two kilos taken from at least 30% of the bags comprising the lot must be drawn and sent to the exchange for grading. The CSCE requires a five kilo sample drawn by two licensed master samplers from 25% of the bags.[12] The warehousekeeper must at the same time forward the lotting account. This document shows the details of the cocoa making up the lot and should be made within two days of drawing the sample. The exchange has panels of graders who analyse the samples provided and determine whether the cocoa may be tendered on the market. It may be that the graders consider the cocoa to be below the standard set by the exchange, in which case they will stipulate a quality allowance against the cocoa. The exchange then issues a certificate of quality (known as a certificate of grade in the New York market) showing the allowance, if any. If the quality is too bad they will issue a 'non-tenderable' certificate of quality. As it says, the short on

10   Currently one futures market, that for the Euro-differential coffee contract, allows coffee stored in the United States to be tendered against London contracts.

11   See Appendix IV.

12   This is simplified as there are different requirements if the lot comprises bags with different main marks.

the exchange may not tender cocoa which has an 'NT' certificate. The exchange returns both the grading certificate and the lotting account to the member with the short position.

In New York, cocoa on the terminal has to be regraded every tender-month. In London the grading certificate remains valid for six months, allowing players to re-tender the cocoa on the next delivery month without having it regraded. One further difference between the two markets is that the CSCE allows players to tender cocoa before having it graded; the lots may be graded with the allowances payable after the delivery.

Active traders follow the grading results published by the two exchanges. In particular the London market grading, as the LCE has more cocoa tendered on it than the CSCE, and the results are final indicators of the potential tonnage to come on to the market. The gradings provide two pieces of information. Firstly, the potential number of lots the shorts may tender on to the market – players with short positions may only tender cocoa passed by the grading panel. Knowing the potential number of lots that could be tendered may give insights into the intentions of some of the more active players. Secondly, the grading information also includes the origin of the cocoa. Those especially interested in a specific origin may see an opportunity in buying the nearest month in obtaining supplies of that particular cocoa.

Once the cocoa has passed the grading panel the seller may tender the cocoa to the clearing organisation. In London this may occur between 0930 and 1600 on any market day during the delivery month. The tender advice includes details of the lot, together with a valid certificate of quality and the lotting account. The ICCH then allocates the tenders to those members who have a long position.

The 'longs' must therefore be prepared to accept any of the lots tendered to them, irrespective of their origin or location. They know that a short may tender any origin cocoa, providing they stored it correctly and that it passed the grading panel. As the futures contract is a standard contract, any one lot must be equated to any other. For an agricultural product this presents three main areas that give rise to differences, those of weight, origin and quality.

Although the contract is for ten tonnes it is rare for a lot of cocoa to weigh exactly that amount. The market rules provide a weight franchise; 1.5% on the LCE and 1% for CSCE lots.[13] In London, any excess or deficit over or under ten tonnes 'shall be settled at the official quotation of the

---

13   See 'Market Rules', Appendices IV and V. Under CSCE terms deliveries made of lots that weigh between 1 to 5% more or less than ten tonnes are considered to be 'partial defaults' of the contracts; anything greater than 5% then the whole contract is in default.

morning of the date of tender...'.[14] The rules recognise that given time, the weight of cocoa changes. For the LCE, players may not tender cocoa if the seller, the short, has not weighed the parcel within 36 months. Before tendering such cocoa the seller must reweigh it. For every six month period after the date of weighing (whether it was weighed on intake into the warehouse or reweighed) the invoice is reduced by a quarter of one percent. In New York, if the short has not weighed the cocoa within 13 days of the date of delivery, a quarter of one percent may be deducted for every 30 day period since it was weighed.

The second allowance is for the origin of the cocoa. Naturally some growths of cocoa are considered to be at a premium to others and therefore the rules must take note of this. On this subject the two markets differ in their approach. The CSCE divides all cocoas into three categories, A, B or C. Categories A and B are at a premium to the market while C is at par. The LCE has five groups, numbered 1 to 5 with only those in group 1 considered at contract price and the others at varying levels of discount to the market. Appendices IV and V show the allowances.

The third allowance concerns the quality of the cocoa, established by the respective grading panels. (For the details of the assessment of quality, see Chapter 8.) While the two panels use different criteria in assessing the quality of cocoa, both reject cocoa that smells hammy or smoky. The CSCE allows sellers of parcels consisting of small beans to tender them at an allowance. (A parcel of small beans contains more shell than one made up of larger beans, therefore larger beans provide more nib[15], a favourable characteristic and the reason for its measurement.) Graders reject cocoa that would fail the FDA inspection, i.e., certain quality aspects other than determining the bean size. Parcels falling outside these standards are not tenderable. In London the grading panel reverse the relative importance placed by the New York market of bean size compared with the other quality criteria. The London contract is less forgiving on bean size and allows sellers to tender parcels with higher levels of defects, all at an allowance if above the standard set by the exchange. These standards vary depending on the growth. While the LCE do not publish the scales of allowances applied by graders, in New York they form part of the market rules.

There is a further adjustment needed to ensure an equitable tender. The period of rent is unlikely to end when the short delivers the lot to the long, via the clearing. As the tenderer will have had to pay the rent up to the end of this period, the member taking up the cocoa has to refund the rent due from the date of delivery to the end of the rent period.

14   LCE contract rules, see Appendix V.
15   Larger beans also tend to give a higher yield of fat, again a favourable
     characteristic.

All of the above allowances present intricate invoicing. In London the ICCH prepares both the invoice to the member taking up the cocoa and an account sale for the benefit of the short. Fourteen days (ten business days for CSCE contracts) after the date the short made the declaration the lot is deliverable to the buyer. Similar to the physical market, the seller presents warehouse warrants to the buyer, again via the clearing. The warrants give the buyer title to the cocoa.

The board

The board is a summary of the prices offered and bid for the various trading months. The name 'board' derives from a time when a clerk in the exchange wrote the prices on a blackboard. Although such practice has long gone, the name describing the summary of prices survives. Some boards will show just single letters instead of the delivery months, and are common for all commodity markets in the world. Those delivery months used in cocoa trading are:

H March
K May
N July
U September
X November – only traded on the Kuala Lumpur market
Z December

Both the LCE and CSCE allow trading for positions two years ahead, so often the summary includes the last digit of the year to indicate which year applies. Positions for say, the more distant year's December are

Table 6.1 Example of the London FOX cocoa board

Month	Last	Buyer	Seller	High	Low	Sales
Mar	719	718	720	727	718	2231
May	745	745	746	752	745	1582
Jul	772	770	771	777	772	164
Sep	796	796	797	802	795	501
Dec	828	828	830	835	828	100
Mar	860	856	860	865	860	2102
May	880	873	878	883	880	65
Jul	897	890	896	900	897	12
Sep	912	908	910	912	906	1504
Dec	936	932	937	936	935	1545

Total sales 9806

sometimes called 'far Dec' or, by some traditionalists, 'red Dec'. The summary shows two prices for each month, one the selling price of the lowest seller and the other the price of the best buyer or highest bidder. The difference, the spread, is usually small, allowing prospective buyers and sellers to negotiate a price. Large spreads may indicate an illiquid market or a lack of interest by the players for that particular month. The most distant months may not elicit much interest from the players, but as the months become nearer activity increases.

Such a summary will usually show the last price traded for each month, the highest and lowest prices paid during the day for each month and the volume. Table 6.1 shows an example taken at the morning close in London.

Players

Companies and individuals trading futures fall into two categories, those that have an interest in the commodity and those that do not. In this context interest means an involvement with the commodity outside the futures market – there are many who have no interest in cocoa but who avidly follow the rise and fall of its price. Companies or individuals uninvolved in cocoa but who have positions on the terminal market do so for speculative reasons. It is their intention to buy and sell futures solely to make a profit on the transaction. While on occasion those who have an interest in the commodity may also speculate, their main concern is to use the market for avoiding risks entered into elsewhere.

Interested parties

The players that need to hedge risks in the physical market are usually companies. These companies may be divided into traders or merchants, and those involved with processed goods, either chocolate or the semi-finished products of butter, powder or liquor. The traders and merchants predominantly deal in cocoa beans. While the market would also suit those producing cocoa, very few growers use the terminal market to hedge their crops. It was thought that with the advent of the market in Kuala Lumpur, growers in the region would have started to make use of futures. This has not happened, not helped by the lack of liquidity on that market, which has made trading on it very difficult.

Players that extensively use the terminal market may find it more economic to become members of the exchange, instead of dealing through a broker. While there may be economies of scale in becoming a member,

THE INTERNATIONAL COCOA TRADE

there are two advantages in remaining outside the exchange. The first is anonymity. Trading through a broker protects the name of the instigator of the deal; all the outside world sees is the broker trading on the floor of the exchange and not the name of the company he represents. Many companies prefer to hide behind the brokers to protect their trading position, some to the extent of using more than one broker to complete a deal. Such manoeuvres help to confuse the market into thinking there are several players executing their own deals instead of one player simultaneously using different brokers. Secondly, members of the exchange must comply with strict codes of conduct that need in-house personnel to monitor the trades. Many think this too time consuming and expensive and therefore elect to trade through brokers. In London the Securities and Futures Authority (SFA) regulate the activities in the terminal exchanges, while the Commodity Futures Trading Commission (CFTC) govern the exchanges in the United States.

Speculators

Speculators may be individuals or corporations. Either may choose to use futures at times when returns on other investments are low. For both companies and individuals the attraction is to generate large returns with little capital outlay, albeit at a high risk. The larger speculators are commodity funds, often controlled by computer program trading. Such investment funds have developed over the past ten years and now have large resources and are substantial players in the market. Generally, the markets in the United States have a larger number of smaller investors; in the London markets commission houses[16] consider accounts for small investors uneconomic.

Most speculators use certain trading techniques that those with an interest in cocoa use sparingly. The majority of speculators chart the evolution of prices to show trends of price rises and falls. Many of these techniques are sophisticated but essentially rely on the commodity's past performances to indicate trends. Such trading methods have the advantage that speculators need know very little about the commodity and that they may follow a number of different markets simultaneously. Those with an interest in cocoa rely more on the fundamentals of cocoa, the changing supply and demand, crop forecasts etc. They may, perhaps, use charts to

16 Note that players with an interest use 'brokers' while speculators use 'commission houses' or 'commodity-trading advisers' (CTA). Technically there is little difference between the two, except that the commission house or CTA will specialise in servicing the private accounts while the broker will look after the trade accounts.

indicate when it would be advantageous to enter the market but not let it dictate the direction of their trading strategy.

Speculators in commodities have a bad name. Outsiders often consider them as parasites, living off others' hard work. This is incorrect, if anything the relationship is symbiotic. Speculators are as essential to a market as are those who have an interest in the commodity. It is the speculators who provide the liquidity to an exchange and allow those with an interest in the commodity to offset their risks. Their involvement provides counterparties at times when others, for whatever reasons, are unwilling to trade. Also, successful speculators help stabilise the market. When prices are high they sell, helping to push prices down; when prices are low they buy, supporting the price. (A feature that is often lost on many that deprecate the role of speculators and wish the market stable.) While some speculators make a great deal of money, there are many who do not. Their losses and gains reduce the risks of those who have an interest in cocoa.

Liquidity

In a market with regular high turnover it is always possible for players to establish or unwind a position without substantially influencing prices by their actions. In extreme cases on markets with a low turnover players may be 'locked in' or 'locked out' of positions; a disaster, especially for those who hold short positions. Liquidity is the measure of the amount of activity taking place on the market. A successful market is one in which the liquidity is high. If the market consists of only a small number of players whose views on the price of the commodity coincide, the market may die as trading becomes difficult. If everyone wishes to sell and there are no buyers there can be little hope of satisfaction on either side of the deal. An active market needs a number of players who have different intentions. In a liquid market those wishing to square their position may find a counterparty, in an illiquid market this may not be possible.

The most common method of measuring liquidity is by a market's open interest, published every day by the exchanges. The calculation involves the distinction between the members' own accounts and the clients. The open interest is the sum of the client business (gross number of lots long plus gross number of lots short, divided by two) and the net trade house business. Markets with high or increasing open interest levels are liquid; players often use the open interest figure to gain insights into the market's direction.

Figure 6.1 shows a comparison between the volumes traded on the LCE and CSCE.

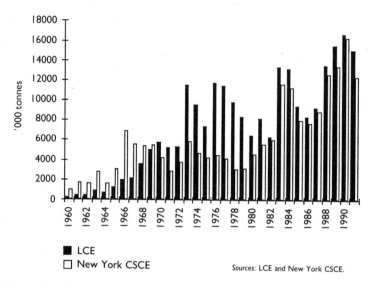

6.1 Comparison between volumes of cocoa futures traded on the London and New York markets.

From the figure three points emerge. The first is the overall growth of volume traded on the two exchanges over the past twenty years, stimulated by the increase in production during the 1970s. The second is the advances made by the CSCE over the last ten years. During the 1970s the volume of business traded on the CSCE was roughly half that on the London terminal. Now both exchanges are neck and neck. The third point underlines the nature of the exchanges, and is the overall tonnage traded on the exchanges compared with annual world production. For example, during 1990 the tonnage traded on both exchanges represented 13 times the total world crop for that year. The fact that players square out their positions before the delivery month explains this; those short of the commodity rarely tender cocoa against their positions.

Another measurement of liquidity, although containing less infor-mation, is the open position. This is a sum of the gross positions of the longs and the gross positions of the shorts, divided by two. This figure does not indicate by how far those with an interest in cocoa have squared their position. When applied to the whole market it shows the overall long and, by definition, the overall short position.

Trading techniques

Introduction

Before looking at some techniques used in trading on the terminal market, some further concepts and terms should be clarified. Supply and demand control the price of cocoa. From the example of the board given in Table 6.1 it may be seen that the more forward months have higher prices than those nearby. This is the usual state of affairs, the market is described as being in a 'contango'. The reverse, when the nearer months are at a premium to those further forward is a 'backwardation'. It should be noted that the differences between the various months do not form a straight gradient, or remain constant.

One determining factor on the price of the forward months compared with the nearby months is the carry cost. This is the cost of buying cocoa for nearby delivery, keeping it and then redelivering it back to the market at some future month. By far the largest portion of such a cost is the loss of interest on the capital used in buying the cocoa. While the remaining costs for such an operation include the warehouse rent and insurance of the cocoa for the period in question, as well as any regrading[17] and reweighing, they are small when compared with the loss of interest. A change in interest rates will affect the carry, and a player with access to money below the market interest rates has a definite advantage. Changes in interest rates will affect the differences in prices between the trading months and traders may use this to their advantage by 'straddling' the months.

From the board shown in Table 6.1 the price difference between buying July (N) and selling May (K) is £26. Now it may be that a player has no particular view whether the overall price of cocoa will rise or fall, let us say there is market talk of shortages during the next few months which will force up nearby prices. The player is not interested in this, it may or may not be true, but he considers that the price difference between the two months will increase. He feels that interest rates will shortly rise. This is likely to increase the difference between the months as the interest rates are the largest factor in calculating carrying costs. He will therefore 'open the straddle' by simultaneously buying the July position and selling the May. So, at the beginning his position would be:

May (K)		July (N)	
Sell @	£745/t	Buy @	£771/t

---

[17] There is always the risk that some of the cocoa will fail the regrading, giving the short the expense of selling off the lot at a substantial discount.

As he suspected, sterling interest rates rise, thereby widening the price difference between the months. As it also happens, but quite irrelevantly, the price of cocoa falls to where May trades at £713 and July at £741. He now squares his position, giving the following:

May (K)		July (N)	
Sell @	£745	Buy @	£771
Buy @	£713	Sell @	£741
Profit	£32	Loss	£30

Overall profit is £2 per tonne. With a market fall of £30, to some a profit of merely £2 seems little. However the player achieved this with little risk at a time of obvious price volatility. Although each 'leg' was for different months one was bought and the other sold. It did not matter whether the price rose or fell, the profit depended on the movement of the price difference between the months.

Hedging

The straight hedge

In the example towards the beginning of the chapter and in the ensuing discussion it would appear that only one type of risk exists for those trading physical cocoa. The risk that the underlying price of cocoa, represented by the futures market, moves adversely against the physicals. Protection against this risk is called 'straight hedging'. The example given was a 'short hedge', so-called as the player's first action was to sell ten lots on the terminal. Had he been selling the physical commodity instead of buying it, his initial action on the futures market would have been to buy, therefore making it a 'long hedge'.

Basis trading

While straight hedging protects against the risk concerning the underlying price of cocoa, the price of physical cocoa consists of two parts. Those with an interest in cocoa also face an adverse price movement on the remaining part, the differential. For the sake of simplicity the earlier example assumed that the differential of £10 premium to the terminal remained the same throughout the six months. Although generally more stable than the futures price, the movement of the differentials does present a risk to those dealing with physicals.

In most instances the risk of the differential moving is small when compared with that of the underlying price of cocoa. Sometimes this is not so. But a small adverse movement of price on very large tonnages will provide substantial losses. Supplies of a particular origin may become extremely tight, for a variety of reasons, so creating a premium for that cocoa. How badly those affected need the cocoa for outstanding contracts will determine the level of the premium.

Unlike straight hedging there is no direct way of protecting against the movement of the differentials. There are, however, techniques that players may use to offset such movements and which may make additional profit for their companies. The technique is similar to that shown above with the straddle except instead of making use of the movement of prices between different trading months, players use the movement of prices between the physicals and the futures.

For example; suppose in February a trader bought fifty tonnes of physical cocoa for forward delivery in August at $910/t and sold five lots of September cocoa at $925/t therefore making the differential $15 below the futures price. His position would be:

Physicals	Futures (U)	Difference
Bought 50 t @ $910/t	Sold 5 lots @ $925/t	−$15

Say the market then fell, but during the time supplies of that origin tightened slightly, narrowing the differential to ten dollars below the terminal. When the trader squared out his terminal market position, the full picture showed:

Physicals	Futures (U)	Difference t
Bought 50 t @ $910/t	Sold 5 lots @ $925/t	−$15
Could have bought 50 t @ $858/t	Bought 5 lots @ $868/t	−$10
Loss $52/t	Profit $57/t	$5

So the trader established protection against the main risk of a falling market and because the differential moved favourably, he made an extra $5 per tonne. Had the differential widened, he would have lost. From this it is apparent that some basic rules exist in how to approach differential trading, see Table 6.2.

Although the opening gambit seems clear cut, it may be at odds with

Table 6.2 Differential hedging – the tactics

Physicals that are	Differentials will	Initial action
Discount to the terminal	Narrow	Buy physicals, sell futures
	Widen	Sell physicals, buy futures
Premium to the terminal	Narrow	Sell physicals, buy futures
	Widen	Buy physicals, sell futures

the overall hedging strategy. In the above example the hedge worked out very well. Suppose the differential had widened, the trader would then have had to judge whether to keep the hedge on in the face of losing against the differential. It is likely that he would have retained it, the risk in the fall in the price of the futures would be greater than the change in the differential. The timing for squaring out the hedge also becomes critical. Opportunities for taking off the hedge before its full time may exist, presenting the player with more decisions.

It presents opportunities as well; some with reduced levels of risk. For example suppose in July a trader bought 100 tonnes of physical cocoa for delivery in November at $928 per tonne, which he hedged at $955. His position would be:

Physicals	Futures (Z)	Difference per t
Bought 100 t @ $928/t	Sold 10 lots @ $955/t	−$27

After a while, reports emerge that the crop for that cocoa appear to be below expectation and the differential narrows. The trader feels this is a good opportunity and seeks to sell the cocoa. One buyer seems keen but thinks that the world crop will be good and therefore the price of cocoa will fall before November. He therefore does not wish to commit himself before the effect of this percolates through to the market. The trader offers to sell the cocoa on a price fixation contract (see Chapter 5). This will allow the buyer to fix the price when he wants. Both parties agree to the sale on the basis of $15 below December terminal market. From this point on the trader has made his money, irrespective of market movement, or of the differential, as the sale locks in the profit.

Suppose, for the sake of a happy ending, that both are correct. The world crop is better than expected and so too is the harvest of the particular cocoa sold, so the differential widens to $20 below the terminal. The buyer decides to fix the contract on the basis of $895. Both parties then arrange their hedges, the trader to square his and the buyer to initiate his own. The full picture is therefore:

Physicals	Futures (Z)	Difference/t
Bought 100 t @ $928/t	Sold 10 lots @ $955/t	−$27
Sold 100 t @ Z-$15 (Price fix contract)		
Contract fixed at buyer's discretion @ $880/t	Bought 10 lots @ $895/t	−$15
Loss $48	Profit $60	$12

Note that the trader did not hedge the PFA contract at its inception, but only when the outright price is available.

Over the past few years manufacturers in particular, have brought to prominence a variation of the PFA contract and the terminal market. The trading technique stems from the wish to trade outright prices on far forward contracts. In the past buyers and sellers considered that the *del credere* risk was small and were content to trade forward with many different companies. Nowadays the trading environment concentrate their minds on the long term viability of their clients. For example, some buyers think that their counterparties may default on deliveries cocoa bought one year or more forward. Using PFA contracts they can still buy the cocoa they want and limit the possible loss should the seller not deliver the cocoa; however it does not provide an outright priced contract. In this case, the buyer may overcome this by using the PFA contract and simultaneously buying an equivalent tonnage on the terminal market, thereby using the futures as the pricing of the physical trade. This is more expensive to operate than an outright physical trade but it does allow, in this case the buyer effectively to purchase the cocoa outright − providing the far forward positions are liquid on the terminal.

Arbitrage

Applying the correct exchange rate to the price of cocoa for a particular delivery month on the London terminal market does not give the US dollar price of the same month trading on the New York market. There is a difference. As mentioned earlier, the structure of the origin allowances that apply to the London market are not the same as those on the New York exchange. In addition, players with long positions will always deliver the cheapest tenderable cocoa on to the markets. What is cheap to deliver on the CSCE may not be so for the LCE. Players make use of this difference between prices of the same delivery months on the two exchanges. Arbitrage trading requires buying on one exchange and selling on the other. As London trades in sterling and New York in dollars, players must also cover the foreign exchange requirement as well. This is not a game for the fainthearted.

The rules outlined above for differential trading on physicals apply to arbitrage, substituting CSCE for 'physicals' and LCE for 'futures' or 'terminal'. (Table 6.2 provides the basic formula for success.) That is the technical side of the trading, knowing whether the differences will widen or narrow is quite a different matter.

Exchange for physicals or against actuals

There may be instances when a player has a futures position and would prefer to exchange it for physicals. Not all exchanges permit this type of trade but it is not uncommon in cocoa on either the LCE or CSCE. The two exchanges use different descriptions for essentially the same transaction, the LCE calls them 'exchange for physicals' (EFP), while the CSCE uses 'against actuals' (AA).

In an EFP or AA transaction both players must be involved in a trade

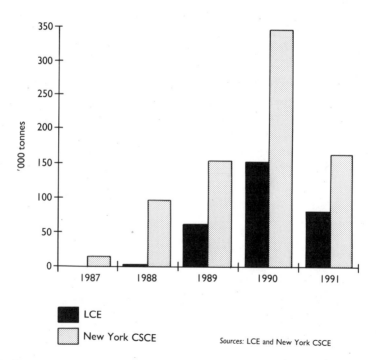

6.2 Comparison between volumes of traded options in London and New York.

on physicals that they conduct privately and not through the floor of the futures exchange. Players may trade EFPs outside the exchange hours, although if this was the case they must register it at the opening of the market on the next business day. Traders of physicals may use EFPs and AAs to open or square their hedges. It provides a flexible way for them to trade the actuals and to use the hedging medium of the two exchanges.

Options

From Fig. 6.2, it is clear that while nowhere near as popular as futures, players' interest in options is growing. The higher volume on the CSCE probably reflects the greater knowledge and confidence in New York for the type of trading needed with this contract. While both markets have had options for longer than the period shown in the figure, the current version of options, traded options, has only existed since 1986. Before 1986 players were able to trade traditional options, a simpler but less flexible form of contract to the current version.

Options – the terms

Options are intricate contracts that require a new vocabulary to explain them. Essentially an option contract gives the party that takes it the right to buy or sell the commodity, but without the obligation to do so that exists with a normal futures contract. The party that provides the option contract is the grantor and his counterparty is the taker. If the grantor gives the taker the right to buy the commodity the option is a call option, if the right was to sell the commodity it is a put option.[18] The price the taker pays to the grantor for the option is the premium. The price basis of the option is the strike price and is derived from the underlying, the commodity futures price. The grantor's obligation to the taker is not open ended. The taker has to decide within an agreed period, up to the expiry date whether to exercise the option, abandon it, or in the case of traded options, to trade out of it.

If the taker exercises the option it becomes a futures contract, based on the underlying with the strike price as the price of the contract. If a taker exercises a put option it becomes a futures sale contract, a call option becomes a purchase contract. If the taker bought a put option and

---

18   A third type of option was available with traditional options, that of the double, which allowed the taker to convert the option to either a call or a put. These are not available in traded options.

the futures market subsequently rose in price, he may decide to abandon it. In this event the taker merely fails to advise the grantor of his interest in exercising the option at the expiry date. Perhaps there is some time left until the expiry date. In that case the option may still have some value, and the original taker may try to sell it on to another to at least recoup some of the loss. This last feature is the main difference between the traditional option and the traded option. Players were not able to trade out of their traditional option contracts.

From the grantor's point of view, he wants the price of the cocoa to move in the opposite direction to that wanted by the taker, or if it goes against him, not to exceed the premium. All he gains from the transaction is the premium. The taker, of course, wants the price to move in a favourable direction and to at least a level where he may recoup the cost of the premium he paid. Following the scenario above, as the contract is now out-of-the-money the premium for the option has reduced, so the original taker will not recover the amount he originally paid when he sells the option. From this it is apparent that the premium holds the key to the trading of options, it is the measure of the risk and of the profit of the contract, and it moves.

The premium

There are three main factors that affect the premium. The first is the intrinsic value of the option. Basically, if the option is a futures contract at the strike price is it profitable? If the answer is yes, it is in-the-money, those that are not are out-of-the-money. The further the price of the underlying moves from the strike price, the deeper the contract is in or out-of-the-money. An option that is in-the-money commands a higher premium than one that is not; the deeper in-the-money, the higher the premium.

The second is the time left until the option expires. If the time until the expiry is short there is less opportunity for more favourable price movements. The longer the time until the expiry the greater the chance for larger price movements. Therefore the amount of time left until the expiry affects the premium. Related to this, the third factor is the volatility of the market. If prices on the futures are subject to considerable rises and falls the risk that the value of the option may increase has to be considered. Grantors have their own ways of calculating this risk, usually based on the past performance of the market.

Changes in the option premium do not necessarily match price movements in the underlying contract. Unless the options are deep in-the-money, the change in the premium will not match the price movement of the underlying futures. Deep in-the-money options have a high delta value, approaching 1.0. Options that are at-the-money (i.e. the strike price is the current value of the futures market price) have a delta value of 0.5. Those that are deep out-of-the-money have a delta value nearing zero. The delta value is a method of risk assessment of the option; players also use it in hedging strategies.

The strike price

Unlike futures, takers of traded options have a choice over the strike price for a particular month at the inception of the deal. The exchange sets prices at specific levels and options are available only at these prices. Currently, the LCE offers cocoa options at prices in multiples of £50 per tonne. The CSCE follows a more complex system. First the exchange makes a difference between options available for the two nearby months compared with the other delivery periods, known as the 'deferred months'. Second, the intervals between the 'prescribed levels' (i.e., available strike prices) increase as the value of the cocoa also increases. Currently, the situation is as follows:

Period	Prices from ($)	Prices to ($)	Intervals of ($)
Nearby months	50	1500	50
	1500	3600	100
	3600		200
	upwards		
Deferred months	100	3600	100
	3600		200
	upwards		

Similar to futures, players may trade options on the floor of the exchanges. Members of the exchange with positions in options are subject to clearing operations and valuations. Members may be trading for their own account or on behalf of clients, who in turn, will have their trading positions similarly valued by their broker member and may be called for margins.

Hedging using options

While options offer a flexible trading instrument that players may use in hedging strategies, most choose the futures market to protect their positions in physicals and not options. This is because the cost of the option premium makes hedging with futures cheaper. However, if there is uncertainty of delivery or performance of outright priced physical contracts, options may provide a better hedging medium than futures.

An example of their use includes situations where counterparties become less financially secure, endangering existing physical contract performance. Suppose in July a buyer bought 100 tonnes of physical cocoa at an outright price of £815 per tonne for delivery in November. At the time of the contract he was confident that his seller would deliver the cocoa and so he sold ten lots of December futures to hedge his position. In September the buyer heard that the seller had experienced severe losses, and while still trading, the buyer was unsure that the seller would be able to deliver the cocoa in November. If the seller defaulted on the contract the buyer's hedge would turn into a speculative position. On the other hand, if the buyer squared his futures position and the seller delivered the cocoa the physicals become unhedged. Either action may entail the buyer 'lifting a leg', uncovering one side of the trade. The buyer decided to use options as his hedge. He squared his futures and took ten put options at £800, the nearest level to the contract price of £815. The cost to the buyer of the option premium was the price to pay against the risk.[19]

If the price of cocoa falls the buyer may cover his physical position by exercising the put options and converting them into the underlying futures, thereby reinstating his original hedge in futures. If the seller delivers[20] the cocoa the hedges cover the losses made on the physical trade, less the cost of the option premium. If the seller defaults on the contract, squaring out the futures position allows the buyer to realise a profit, lessened, of course, by the option premium.

If prices rise the picture is less rosy for the buyer. In any event the buyer would abandon or trade out of the options. If the seller delivers, the buyer gains on the physical purchase, lessened by the premium paid on the options. Should the seller default, a distinct possibility in a rising market, the buyer has limited the loss on his hedges to the cost of the premium. Had his hedges been of futures he may have realised a much larger loss.

Another use of options using a similar technique mentioned above may be where a buyer is in the happy position of hedging the residual part of a crop. In such a physical contract neither party knows for sure the eventual tonnage of the sale. Known as a 'more or less' contract, the parties agree a basic tonnage of say, 15 000 tonnes, with the possibility of

---

19   This action may not be undertaken quite so lightly as it is written. The cost in transferring the hedge to options may be prohibitive. However, the assumption here is that the buyer wishes to transfer his hedge to options and accepts the cost of this action.

20   It is worth noting that if the price fell it is more likely that the seller would deliver the cocoa than if prices rose.

the eventual figure being say, 2000 tonnes either side of 15 000. As the delivery for up to 4000 tonnes is uncertain, the buyer may hedge this using options.

Traders continue to try and find hedging opportunities using options but to date speculators, or interested parties 'having a punt' make up most of the volume on the market.

Regulatory bodies

Both markets offer some protection to players through their respective regulatory bodies. In London, futures business is overseen by the SFA; for the New York markets the task is undertaken by the Commodities Futures Trading Commission, a body in existence for longer than its equivalent in the UK. Both bodies underline the markets own practices in behaviour and business etiquette.

There are three main areas of malpractice that concern these bodies. The first is the movement of money to overseas accounts without clearance from the proper authorities. Players covering margin calls, opening trading accounts, or transferring profits from one account to another result in large amounts of money transferring from place to place. The temptation for covert activity in this area requires overseeing by an authority. Secondly, some large traders may consider manipulating the market for gain. For example, by trading in reasonable volumes at opportune moments, clients' stops[21] may be triggered, forcing a greater run on the market that allows the broker to square out profitably. Third is protecting the client from broker malpractice. At its most basic level it involves preventing brokers charging clients unreasonable levels of commissions and ensuring the brokers correctly execute the client orders on the market.

Most instances of non-compliance results from poor management practice rather than anything nefarious or underhand. Nonetheless, ensuring that players throughout the market conduct their activities in a proper manner is important to safeguard the market, and members trading futures have to comply with their respective regulations or face prosecution.

Those in the cocoa trade who think that current regulation is too strict or too onerous should consider the penalties imposed in Great

---

21   A 'stop' is an instruction given to the broker to square out the position if the market reaches a certain level that is adverse to the player's position. They are there to protect the player from extensive losses. Knowing at what level to place the stops is a fine art in itself.

Britain during the eighteenth and early nineteenth centuries on cocoa dealers. During George I reign the following applied:

> *The counterfeiting of the stamp, or the knowingly selling of Chocolate as has not been entered, and on which duties have not been paid, means the penalty of £500, and of commitment to the next county gaol for twelve months...*
>
> *Every person who shall keep a shop and have in his custody above 6 lb. Cocoa or Chocolate shall be deemed a dealer in the said commodity...*
>
> *Notice shall be given by those who make Chocolate for private families, and not for sale, three days before it is begun to be made, specifying the quantity, &c., and within three days after it is finished, the person for whom it is made shall enter the whole quantity on oath, and have it duly stamped.*

By George III's reign, the following had been enacted;

> *Houses of manufacturing and sale are to be entered on pain of forfeiting £200 and goods &c....*
>
> *The said houses shall be marked over the doors with the words 'dealer in Cocoa-nuts, Chocolate, &c.' on pain of £200. Any dealer buying these commodities of any person not having his shop so marked shall forfeit £100...*
>
> *No person shall trade in Chocolate without an annual license, for which he shall pay 5s 6d., under penalty of £20.*

Conclusion

The futures markets have benefited all in the cocoa trade. By helping to offset the risk of adverse price movements, deals have been concluded that would not otherwise have been made. Even though most exporters do not use the terminal markets, they have gained from their existence. Coupled with the second-hand trade, primarily based in London and New York, exporters always find buyers unafraid because of price, to purchase their cocoa. Without the futures market such deals would not be possible, the risk of price movements being too great.

7

Consumption and stocks

The uses of cocoa

C ocoa provides one of the most sought after flavours in the world. Nearly all cocoa finds its way into chocolate or chocolate flavoured products of one sort or another, the latter ranging from ice cream to cake mixes. Non-traditional uses for cocoa, i.e., those that do not involve confectionery products or drinks, account for an estimated one or two per cent of cocoa production. Figures for non-traditional use are difficult to extract but the cosmetics industry probably account for most of it. Even though an expensive vegetable fat (the cosmetics industry's interest is in the cocoa butter) the cost plays a secondary role. Selling most cosmetics depends more on marketing than the content of the product.[1]

As an alternative vegetable oil, cocoa butter is too expensive,[2] a fact

---

1 The use of cocoa butter in this way is not new: '. . . there being drawn out of the cacao much butter, which in the Indias I have seen drawn out of it by the Creole women for to oint their faces', Gage, Thomas: 'A new survey of the West Indias', 1648.

2 For example, on January 30 1992, the price of cocoa butter was £2050 per tonne. The next most expensive edible fat was hardened coconut oil at £653 per tonne. The Public Ledger.

that severely limits its applications in other food related products. Another minor use is by pharmaceutical companies who extract theobromine (a heart stimulant) from cocoa, but this accounts for only a small tonnage. chocolate and chocolate flavoured products make up most of the consumption of cocoa.

Measuring consumption

In some respects, assessing a country's cocoa production is easier than working out another country's cocoa consumption. Experts talk about the production of a country or an area in definitive terms, while not being so certain when the subject moves on to consumption. They will say, for instance, 'consumption is increasing' but they do not usually quantify it in the same manner as they would when talking about increases in production. This is because consumption of cocoa may be measured in a number of ways, each of which highlights a different aspect of its demand.

For example, measuring the tonnage of cocoa processed into the intermediate products (cocoa liquor and/or butter and powder) provides a useful guide to the tonnage consumed. Even these figures, known as the grindings or primary consumption, now require careful interpretation. Another measure is the tonnage of cocoa imported into a country, thereby indicating a level of demand; but re-exported cocoa plus the tonnage stored in the importing country can make this a poor measure of a country's true consumption. Figures showing final consumption of chocolate give an idea of a country's importance as buyers of confectionery, but may not show where the chocolate originates. Lastly, final consumption per person may indicate the saturation of a country or region's people in buying chocolate but may not show their importance in manufacturing or in the relative size of market.

Grindings

Once the primary use of the cocoa bean changed from drinking chocolate to chocolate bars, the market of the beans also radically altered. Making bars of chocolate requires much more effort and equipment than grinding up beans for a drink. Without special storage conditions, chocolate bars of the type sold in temperate regions will not keep in hot or tropical areas, otherwise, of course, they melt.[3] Thus the final consumption of cocoa moved away from the countries growing the beans to those that had the

3   Such specialist storage equipment took some time to arrive. Up to 1915 there was a thriving international trade in ice, even to countries in the temperate zones.

manufacturing expertise and markets for the sale of chocolate in its solid form.

Once sales of eating chocolate took off, factories that made drinking chocolate were forced to make a choice. They could either continue as they were, producing cocoa powder for the diminishing market of chocolate drinks and supplying the excess cocoa butter to the newly formed companies that made chocolate bars; or become chocolate manufacturers themselves. Most decided to stay in the business they knew best, that of selling cocoa powder and butter. So the cocoa industry developed two types of factories, those that made chocolate bars and those that increasingly supplied them with the cocoa butter needed to make their final product. Nowadays this has come full circle with many processors also having factories that make the final product (both eating and drinking chocolate.)

The common factor to either manufacturing process was the initial grinding of the beans to make the cocoa liquor. One needed it to make powder and butter and the other wanted the liquor to flavour and colour the chocolate. Assessing the grind provided the consumption figure of cocoa beans. There was no need to measure anything further on in the manufacturing process in order to measure the consumption of beans. This is still the case. Economists and those interested in the cocoa market still refer to the grinding figures as a measurement of demand for cocoa, although more guardedly now than in the past.

The careful talk about grindings in connection with a country's consumption stems not only from what is meant by grindings but also in the interpretation of the figures themselves. While the international trade in cocoa products and chocolate remained small, a country's grindings represented its cocoa consumption. As the international trade in products and chocolate increased, the assumption that a country's grind figure represents its consumption of cocoa no longer held true. Net imports and exports of cocoa products affected countries' consumption figures. In addition, some countries do not report an official figure for their industry's grind; for these a more accurate description would be the absorption or disappearance of cocoa within a country's economy, although this is still referred to as the grinding figure. Hence the cocoa pundits' wariness when talking about a country's grindings and its consumption. Despite this limitation, the grind figures are still important for two reasons. First, it represents a good indication of world consumption of cocoa when taken as a global figure;[4] and second, the amount ground by a country also indicates the level of primary cocoa manufacturing.

4   This is true except when there are periods of either substantial stocking or drawdown of stored cocoa products in the world.

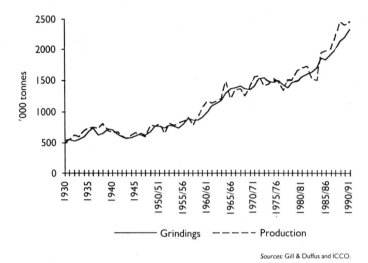

Sources: Gill & Duffus and ICCO.

7.1 Comparison of world cocoa production with grindings since 1930.

Figure 7.1 compares world cocoa production with grindings since 1930.[5] From this two things become apparent, the first being how closely the growth in grindings follows that of production; imbalances between the two existing for only a few years at a time. One reason why speculators traditionally like trading on the cocoa market is the fine balance between the supply and demand of the product. A small imbalance one way or the other presents opportunities as the market price rises and falls, reflecting the change. One of the longest periods of imbalances between production and consumption is the recent period, from 1984/85 to 1990/91, which will be discussed later in the chapter. The second is the growth in world consumption since the 1930s. Taken from 1930 to 1990, grindings increased annually on average by 2.61%. This is despite two periods during which growth faltered. First during the 1940s when grindings in Europe and the United States understandably flattened and more recently from 1965/66 to 1977/78, also during which no sustainable growth took place. Yet the rate of increase recovered and continued to grow. Measured from 1960/61 to 1990/91 the average annual rate of growth rose to 2.8%, and since 1977/78 has been 3.5%. Over the past five years this increased to an average of 4.7%.

Demographically the increase in world grindings over the past 60 years has changed. Figure 7.2 shows how the make up of world grindings

5   Although of small importance in such a coarse scaled graph, the annual figures are crop years (i.e. from the end of September to the beginning of October in the following year) with the exception of the grinding figures from years 1930 to 1945 which are calendar years.

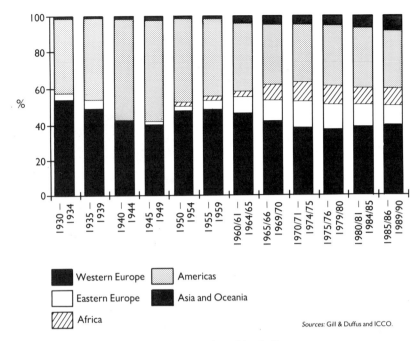

7.2 Regional grindings as a percentage of world grindings.

has evolved by region since the period 1930–34 and illustrates the problem of considering a region's grindings as a measure of its consumption. During the period under review European and American consumption (home of the traditional eaters of chocolate) seem to be at a standstill or decline, while Africa and Asia's population in particular appear to have developed a taste for the confection. Later explanations will show that neither is true.

During 1930–34 the five countries that ground the most cocoa accounted for 78% of the world grindings, some 541.6 thousand tonnes. The United States ground the most, 35% of the world total. The remaining four countries, all European, ground the balance, 43% of the world grind. In the period 1985/86 to 1989/90 the tonnage ground by the top five countries had increased to 1056.3 thousand tonnes. This is a 150% growth on that ground by the top five in 1930–34. Despite this, the tonnage ground by the top five accounted for only 52% of the world total. The United States still ground the most, but only just, at 236 thousand tonnes, hard pressed by Brazil at 230.5 thousand tonnes and the Federal Republic of Germany at 229.5 thousand tonnes. Figure 7.3 illustrates the increase in tonnage ground by the five largest primary consuming countries between the two periods and the change in its composition.

While the Soviet Union ground 14% of the top five countries' total in

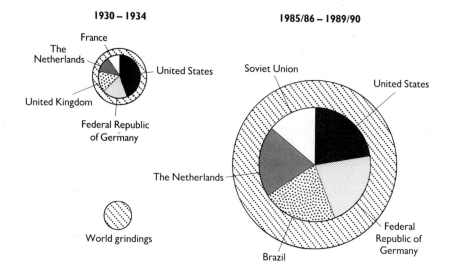

1930 – 1934 1985/86 – 1989/90

Sources: Gill & Duffus and ICCO.

7.3 Comparison of world grindings with those of the five largest cocoa grinding countries for the periods 1930–1934 and 1985/86–1989/90.

1985/86 to 1989/90, it is unlikely that the countries making up the Commonwealth of Independent States (CIS) will continue grindings at this level during the next five year period. ICCO forecasts indicate that their grindings for 1991/92 will be half that shown in Fig. 7.1. Gill & Duffus estimate the figure to be even lower, at 25 000 tonnes.[6] It may take some time for the countries that made up the former Soviet Union to recover to their earlier levels of consumption. The sharp decline in grindings in the former Soviet Union over the past three years (in 1988/89 they ground 201 000 tonnes) has certainly not helped prices to recover.

This may not be true for the other countries in what was described as Eastern Europe. The figures show these countries' grindings have fallen by 21% from 71.7 thousand tonnes in 1988/89 to 56.5 thousand tonnes (the ICCO forecast for 1991/92).[7] However, companies in the United States and Western Europe have invested considerable amounts in the confectionery and processing companies in the former Czechoslovakia, Hungary and Poland since the overthrow of their previous regimes. Returns on this investment already show in the 1991/92 forecasts, indicating a 5% increase on the previous year's grind.

The unification of Germany also affects the ranking of top grinders. The United States will no longer grind more cocoa than any other country.

6   Gill & Duffus Cocoa Market Report No. 343.
7   These figures exclude the former German Democratic Republic's grind, as their figures are included in Germany's.

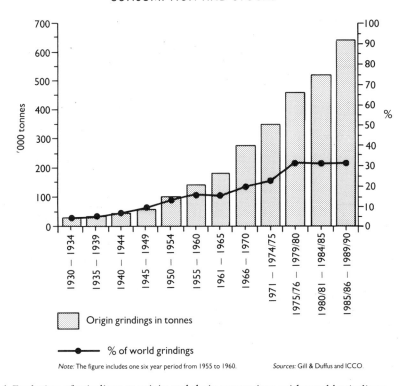

7.4 Evolution of grindings at origin and their comparison with world grindings.

Forecasts for 1991/92 indicate that Germany's grind will be 305 thousand tonnes, against the United States' 295 thousand tonnes and Brazil's 230 thousand tonnes.

The inclusion of Brazil as a leading cocoa processing nation in Fig. 7.3 highlights another change since 1930−34; the increase of grindings made in origin countries. Figure 7.4 shows the evolution in exporting countries' grindings since 1930−34. While the first 20 years of this series show only a small increase, since 1950−54 this sector's grindings grew by more than five and a half times to the last period shown. Despite this continuous growth in outright tonnages their percentage share of the market has not kept pace, rising by only two and a half times over the same period. Figure 7.4 also shows that the origin grind rose to some 30% of the world total during the last half of the 1970s, a level which it maintains. The ICCO forecast for 1991/2 show this to remain at 31.2%.

Cocoa imports

Whether the beans are ground or not, it is of interest to see which regions import cocoa. Figure 7.5 shows imports of cocoa beans and products by

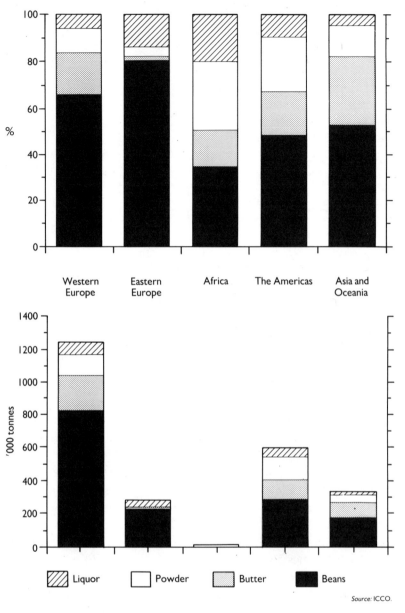

7.5 Import of cocoa beans and products (in bean equivalent) by percentage and tonnage for 1985/86–1989/90.

both percentage and tonnage for the five year period from 1985/86 to 1989/90. The tonnage for the products is in bean equivalents.[8] Three

8   The bean equivalents for products are: butter 1.33, powder 1.18 and liquor 1.25. For example, it would take 1.25 tonnes of beans to make one tonne of cocoa liquor.

regions accounted for 86% of cocoa imports, those of Europe (East[9] and West) and the Americas – although over 80% of the last region was with one country, the United States. Also evident from the chart, the cocoa trade still favours importing cocoa in bean form, making up approximately 60% of cocoa imports.

Compiling cocoa import and export figures requires some care, as inconsistencies develop. For example, it is difficult to reconcile export figures with tonnages imported. These differences come from the different ways, and efficiency, of countries reporting statistical information, together with possible cumulative errors emanating from different methods of calculating bean equivalents for cocoa products. The importance of this last factor becomes more relevant against the background of increased international trade in cocoa products. The interpretation of cocoa import and export figures therefore requires some attention.

Re-exports

Even assuming the import figures were absolutely correct, assessing consumption by the level of imports may lead to false conclusions, firstly by the tonnage of cocoa re-exported. For instance, from Fig. 7.5 Asia and Oceania appear to consume more cocoa than the Eastern European countries, a fact that appears anomalous. The annual tonnage of beans imported into Asia and Oceania over the five year period shown is 176.6 thousand tonnes. Two countries account for 83% of this: Japan with 40.2 thousand tonnes and Singapore with an extraordinary 105.4 thousand tonnes. If this equated to an average annual consumption, the 2.5 million population of Singapore would be the world's biggest chocoholics. However, Singapore is a transshipment port. The re-exported beans reduce the cocoa imported into Singapore by nearly half. In fact the Singaporeans barely eat any chocolate, not featuring in the top thirty consumer countries. They process the beans and export the cocoa products, increasingly as finished chocolate.[10]

During the last half of the 1980s three countries: Singapore, the Netherlands and United States re-exported just under 90% of the world's re-exports. Singapore as a transshipment port accounts for over half of all re-exported cocoa; aided by the recent increased production in neighbouring Malaysia and Indonesia. Imports into Canada usually come through the established cocoa ports of the United States and account for the bulk of the USA's re-exports. Similarly much of Europe's cocoa discharges at

---

9   Including the Soviet Union.

10   Exports of chocolate from Singapore increased by over seven and a half times during the 1980s.

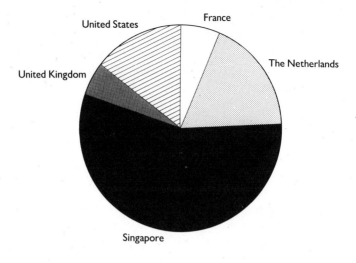

Source: ICCO.

7.6 Average annual tonnage re-exported during 1985/86–1989/90.

Amsterdam, the largest cocoa port in the world,[11] explaining why the re-export tonnage occurs for the Netherlands. Figure 7.6 shows that five countries make up 98% of all cocoa re-exported.

Final consumption

A better way of assessing the demand for cocoa at regional or national level is by final consumption. Final consumption is the sum of the grindings plus net imports of cocoa products, chocolate and chocolate products converted to their bean equivalents. Not surprisingly, from the knowledge that 30% of grindings were by cocoa exporting countries, the ten largest grinding countries differ greatly from the largest final consumers, as shown in Fig. 7.7. It is evident that high grinding figures do not mean correspondingly high final consumption.

Two other points of interest come from Fig. 7.7. The first is that although the United States grinds and finally consumes the most, they import an equivalent tonnage of processed cocoa. Of the other top ten consuming countries only France has such a marked relationship; the French grinding only one third of what they finally consume. This is a recent trend. On average the United States annually ground 78% of their final consumption in the 1965–69 period. Likewise, the figure for France was 71%. During the 1980s this had reduced to 46% for the United States,

11   During 1990/91 the port of Amsterdam handled over 500 000 tonnes of cocoa.

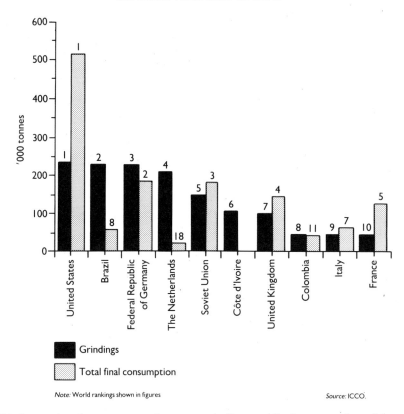

7.7 Comparison between annual average grindings and final consumption of the ten leading primary consuming countries for 1985/86–1989/90.

while for the last half of the 1980s the French grind was 35% of their final consumption figure. Secondly, the reverse is true of the Netherlands, their final consumption is one tenth their grindings. This underlines their role as one of the traditional primary cocoa processors in the world.

The remaining caveat when looking at consumption figures at the beginning of the 1990s is the consumption of cocoa in the CIS. While the average annual final consumption figure for the Soviet Union over the period shown in Fig. 7.7 is 185 thousand tonnes, the figure for 1989/ 90 was 134.2 thousand tonnes. The ICCO estimate for 1990/91 is a further reduction to 93.2 thousand tonnes, half of the average attained during the previous five year period. This would relegate the CIS from third largest final consumer to seventh, after Japan. The timing of the CIS's return to higher consumption is a moot point. That the population, certainly in some States,[12] has the taste for chocolate is clear, but the return to

12 While not final consumption, 75% of confectionery production during 1985 in the Soviet Union was in Russia and the Ukraine. Source: GOSAGROPROM.

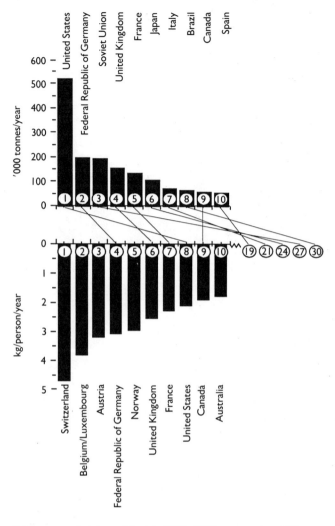

Note: average consumption in beans equivalent during 1985/86 – 1989/90   Source: ICCO.

7.8 Comparison between total final consumption per year and final consumption per person per year of the leading ten countries.

previous levels of consumption depends entirely on how quickly the States generate real wealth to pay for the relative luxury of chocolate.

Final consumption per person

While total final consumption indicates the regional demand for cocoa it by no means shows how much individuals eat within each country. Dividing the population of the country by the total consumption gives the final consumption per person. The lower part of Fig. 7.8 shows the ranking of the top ten countries on such terms. As may be seen, Switzerland and Belgium/Luxemburg jump into first and second places, up from fourteenth and twelfth respectively in total final consumption ranking. The dominance in consumption by the United States ends with this comparison, as they are relegated from first to eighth, at just over two kilos per person per year.

This chart highlights one trend; with the exception of Canada, the top · ten largest consuming countries do not have correspondingly large consumption when measured per person. Those countries shown in the top half of Fig. 7.8 have lower rankings when measured by consumption per person. This may suggest that there is scope for increased consumption in these countries.

There are two caveats to this interpretation. Firstly, the very high figures of 4.67 kilos consumed per Swiss and the 3.81 kilos eaten by Belgian/Luxemburgers may indicate another factor at work. These countries have a well-earned respect for producing high quality chocolate. Visitors may well buy chocolate products to take home. Such purchases would register as sales made within Switzerland or Belgium/Luxemburg, even though the buyer, or the lucky recipient of the gift, eats the chocolate outside these countries. For example, the population of Switzerland is 6.8 million. Each year they are hosts to 40 million visitors.[13]

Secondly, some of the consuming countries have diverse populations and climatic conditions. Affluence and cold climates tend to attract higher chocolate consumption; poor people living in hot regions consume less. When measured overall a country may be eating relatively small amounts of chocolate per person, but this may mask a high consumption in some regions and a low consumption in others. Those regions with high consumption may be at saturation point. Assuming that there is scope for more consumption in such a country may not be correct.

Demand for cocoa may therefore be measured by different criteria, depending on what aspect of consumption is under review. Grindings provide the best way of monitoring global consumption of cocoa. Taken regionally they also indicate the activity in at least primary cocoa manufacturing. Cocoa imports also show this but re-exports and stocks may hide the true figures. Total final consumption shows those regions that consume the final products, even though they may not be involved in all stages of the manufacture of the product. Final consumption per person on a country basis indicates, with some reservations, the capacity of the population to consume more product.

13   Swiss Tourist Board, 1991.

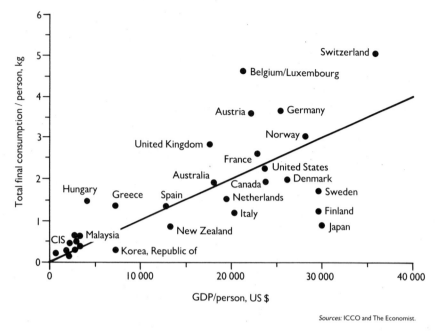

7.9 Total final consumption per person compared with GDP per person, 1991.

Factors affecting consumption

Chocolate

While the demand for cocoa is the main subject this cannot be made without reference to the demand for chocolate; people eat chocolate and not cocoa. It appears there are three main factors that affect consumption of chocolate: the three C's – Cash, Climate and Culture.

First, the money. Those countries with the highest cocoa consumption per person are rich. None of the countries shown in the lower part of Fig. 7.8 have either a GDP or GNP lower than US$17 500 per person. Figure 7.9 shows this with a larger group of countries, and underlines the point that those with a wealthier population tend to consume more. The curve on the figure shows the best fit.

The second factor is the climate. Rich people in some cooler climates eat chocolate. While this generality needs some moderation, the countries shown in Fig. 7.8 tend to support this. Again, the countries with the highest consumption per person either have climates that are temperate throughout the year, or populous regions that have low temperatures at some stage. This helps the handling of the product. However, not all such temperate regions have people that consume chocolate, as the third factor comes into play, that of culture. Chocolate eating is predominantly a

European/North American phenomenon. In Fig. 7.9 above, all the countries that consume one or more kilos per person fall into this category. Those wealthy countries with a different cultural background in similar climatic conditions have not taken to chocolate as much as people in Europe and North America; for example Japan or South Korea.

Two sizeable exceptions to this are Colombia and Mexico. They export very few cocoa beans or products, as they have a reasonably sized domestic market. In 1989/90 Mexico produced 43 000 tonnes of beans, none of which were exported. Cocoa product exports during that year were only just under 8000 tonnes, measured in bean equivalent. Colombia grew 50 000 tonnes but only exported 9400 tonnes of beans and products, as measured in bean equivalents. Both of these countries also import some cocoa products for their consumption.

Price of chocolate

The wealth of the population, or their disposable income is one part of the equation of money and consumption. The second concerns the cost of the product. That the amount of chocolate eaten depends on its price is hardly surprising. The lower the price, the higher the consumption. Figure 7.10 shows this relationship for the United Kingdom market and illustrates how sensitive it is. In order to compare the graphs more easily the sterling scale is inversed, and the prices are in 1990 terms.

While the relationship between the price of chocolate and the consumption is clear in Fig. 7.10, the price of chocolate is not driven by that of cocoa. Figure 7.11 compares the price of the final product with the value of imported cocoa in the United Kingdom market, again the prices

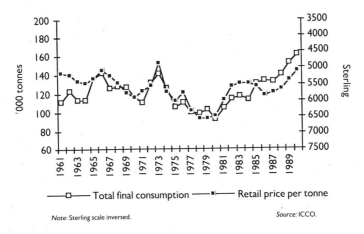

Note: Sterling scale inversed.   Source: ICCO.

7.10 Evolution of UK total final consumption and retail price of chocolate.

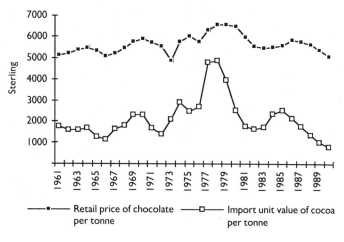

Source: ICCO.

7.11 Evolution of the price of chocolate in the UK and the value of imported cocoa.

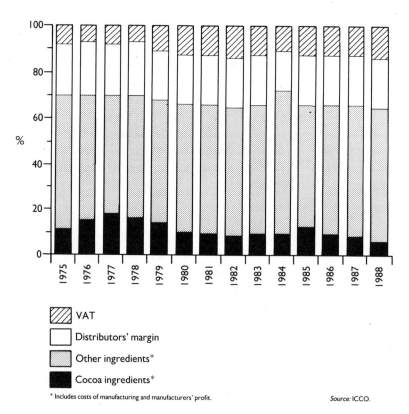

VAT

Distributors' margin

Other ingredients*

Cocoa ingredients*

* Includes costs of manufacturing and manufacturers' profit.

Source: ICCO.

7.12 Evolution of the percentage share of various cost components in the retail price of chocolate in the UK.

shown are in 1990 terms. Clearly while the chocolate price moves in sympathy with the price of cocoa the effect is muted. Over the 30 year period shown, cocoa prices experienced movements of 84%, while the chocolate price changed 26%.

The reason for this apparent anomaly, that the price of the essential ingredient has a small effect on the price of the end-product, becomes clear in Fig. 7.12. This shows that the cost of the essential ingredient represents only a small proportion of the overall retail price of chocolate; during this series the highest proportion of cocoa to the retail price was only 18%.

Cocoa composition of chocolate

Despite the diminishing amount of cocoa ingredients in chocolate (in terms of value) at the end of the 1980s the amount of cocoa used in chocolate increased. There is a relationship between the cost of cocoa and the amount of its use in the final product. Figure 7.13 demonstrates this. It shows the change in the ratio of cocoa in UK chocolate compared with the price of imported cocoa. Note again, for ease of comparison with the change in price, that the scale for the ratio is reversed.

As the price of cocoa rose after 1973, less cocoa went into chocolate as manufacturers tried to keep the price of their product down in order not to reduce sales. They managed to use less cocoa in three ways. Firstly, by promoting confectionery with filled, cheaper centres, i.e., fewer solid

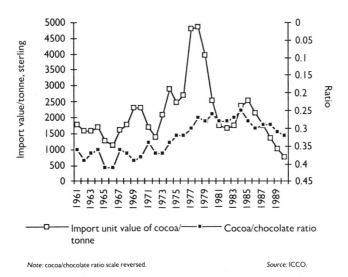

Note: cocoa/chocolate ratio scale reversed.   Source: ICCO.

7.13 Evolution of the UK import value of cocoa and the ratio of cocoa in UK chocolate.

chocolate bars. The second was by using a proportion of other (again cheaper) fats instead of cocoa butter in the chocolate. Thirdly, technology improved to make better use of the existing cocoa. The high prices in the 1970s provided added motivation to the manufacturers to improve their processing, further reducing the amount of cocoa they needed. Even when the price of cocoa fell it took time for the ratio to improve as having altered their recipes the manufacturers were not inclined to use more cocoa. Although the price of cocoa is now at its lowest ever, the ratios have not returned to their previous levels. The change in eating habits (people eating more filled centres, especially cereal centres) and improvements in processing, work against the return to a high proportion of cocoa to chocolate.

The UK market has a different structure to other countries. It uses less cocoa in chocolate confectionery than the other main consumers in the world. This is because of the high volume of filled bars sold in the UK compared with other markets and the use of vegetable fats in the chocolate. Figure 7.14 shows the ratio of cocoa in chocolate in three other major consuming countries. In 1990 only Japan returned to the ratio used in 1961 of 0.52. For the countries under consideration less cocoa is in their chocolate confectionery in 1990 than in 1961, although the ratio increased in the latter part of the 1980s.

The effect of substitutes

The use of cocoa substitutes has a long history in confectionery and drinks, although fortunately the authorities now exert more control over their use than during the nineteenth century (see Chapter 1). Substitution takes place primarily for economic reasons. Confectioners, like all manu-

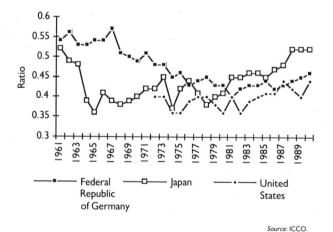

Source: ICCO.

7.14 Evolution of the ratio of cocoa in chocolate for three selected countries.

facturers, continually seek cheaper methods of producing their products. Apart from improvements in the processing that may extend the use of particular expensive products, the other way of reducing costs is by substituting some, or all, of the expensive material with something cheaper. For chocolate production this means finding a cheaper fat to replace cocoa butter. When cocoa powder prices nearly reached those of cocoa butter in the mid-1970s, research quickened to find substitutes to the powder. Since the collapse of powder prices occurred swiftly, interest in powder substitutes dwindled and attention reverted to cocoa butter.

In 1961 Unilever developed Coberine, a patented fat that was compatible with, and had similar characteristics to cocoa butter, except that it did not have any chocolate flavour.[14] Coberine's main advantage was that it was cheaper than cocoa butter. Other cocoa butter equivalents (CBEs) followed but confectioners found that government legislation, outside the United Kingdom, Denmark and Ireland, restricted the use of such fats to making 'chocolate flavoured' products, i.e., that could not be sold as chocolate. In the three countries that allowed the use of CBEs, further legislation restricted its use to 5% of the total weight of the chocolate component.

In 1984 the EEC faced a proposal to extend the use of CBEs to other Community member states. This proposal was withdrawn in 1986 as cocoa producing countries feared a further fall in the price of cocoa should other manufacturers reduce the amount of cocoa used to make chocolate. However, indications show that many of the large manufacturers would favour a more liberal approach and the withdrawal of the 1984 legislation may be only temporary with the further integration of the EEC into a single market. Once all EEC manufacturers are allowed to use CBEs, the question will be whether the United States would follow suit.

Another type of cocoa butter substitute exists, known as cocoa butter replacers (CBRs). These differ from CBEs in that they cannot be easily used with significant amounts of cocoa butter or cocoa powder with a high fat content. They therefore replace all or most of the cocoa butter content. Manufacturers primarily use CBRs as couverture for baked products like cakes or 'chocolate flavoured' bars that have a fat with a higher melting point; these are suited for sale in hot countries.

There are no figures on cocoa substitutes, so the question remains unanswered on what is the effect on the cocoa economy of using substitutes in chocolate. Naturally replacing part of the cocoa component by a substitute reduces the amount of cocoa in the product; so for a given amount of chocolate, cocoa substitution reduces the cocoa consumption.

14   This last factor is not a hinderance as manufacturers reduce the flavour content in most cocoa butter, certainly that for milk chocolate. Chocolate manufacturers deodorise between 70 to 90% of all cocoa butter, see Chapter 9.

However, the claim by some that the use of substitutes in chocolate products directly reduces the overall cocoa consumption may be too simplistic. Consumers buy more chocolate if it is cheaper. Without the CBEs the chocolate may not sell as well, especially for those countries that have less wealthy populations. It is better to sell something with 95% cocoa content (or less) than nothing made totally from cocoa. While on balance the use of substitutes probably does reduce the amount of cocoa consumed, it is not such a straightforward relationship.

To help counteract any decrease in cocoa products used, producing countries may switch attention to the level of tax applied to chocolate. For instance the withdrawal of VAT on chocolate would probably stimulate the UK market, see Fig. 7.12 for the VAT component on chocolate. The use of CBRs in products may also increase demand for cocoa. Although not classified as chocolate, CBR products do contain cocoa powder, and banning their production would result in lower cocoa powder consumption, and deny those in hot countries an affordable product.

During 1992 one chocolate manufacturer began introducing products that contained a low calorie cocoa butter substitute called Caprenin developed by Procter & Gamble. The manufacturers claim that the fat has half the calories contained in cocoa butter which results in one filled chocolate bar product having 25% fewer calories than the equivalent made with cocoa butter. Whether such products will have an appreciable effect on cocoa consumption remains unanswered. At first glance it appears that cocoa consumption would fall if consumers favoured such products. For similar reasons mentioned above concerning the price, this may be too simplistic. Lower calorie bars may increase cocoa consumption by attracting the health conscious to eat such confectionery that contains cocoa solids which they would not otherwise do.

Some substitution is not driven by economics, but by technical reasons. For example, if cocoa butter were used to make the chocolate covering for an ice cream, the covering would flake off as it would set too hard. A softer vegetable fat is more suitable for this purpose.

For other technical reasons, manufacturers sometimes also use fats other than cocoa butter in making chocolate, although for these the term additive is probably more correct. An example of this type is the use of butter oil[15] to prevent bloom appearing on chocolate.[16]

---

15   Butter oil is dairy butter that has no curd or water.
16   Old chocolate or chocolate subjected to heat may develop a white powdery look. This is especially true of dark chocolate or an enrobed chocolate with a fatty centre, like coconut. In this case the bloom is the fat crystallising out on the surface.

Table 7.1 Elasticities of demand on price and income for major cocoa consumers

Country	Price		Income	
	Short term	Long term	Short term	Long term
Belgium/Luxembourg	−0.23	−	0.80	−
Brazil	−0.23	−0.44	0.38	0.71
Canada	−0.18	−0.28	0.21	0.33
France	−0.10	−	0.80	−
Germany	−0.15	−	0.50	−
Japan	−0.30	−	0.60	−
Netherlands	−0.53	−	−	−
Spain	−0.18	−0.95	−	−
Switzerland	−0.06	−0.18	0.44	−
United Kingdom	−0.26	−	1.36	−
United States	−0.20	−0.30	0.44	0.67

Source: ICCO.

Elasticity of prices and income

From all of the above, the price of chocolate does affect the level of consumption. While the discussion ranged over other aspects of demand, it is clear from Fig. 7.10 that consumers eat more chocolate when prices are low.[17] As cocoa represents a small part of the price composition of chocolate, a reduction in the price of cocoa has a correspondingly small effect on the price of chocolate. Economists can assess the effect of price changes on demand, the 'elasticity of demand'. They can also derive the effect of consumption on changes in consumers' income, the 'elasticity of income'. Table 7.1 compares the income and price elasticities of demand with some major cocoa consuming countries. There are two ranges, the effect on the short term, and that on the long term. The Table shows that cocoa is inelastic in both price and income in the short term. Despite this, changes of income have a larger effect on consumption than changes in price. For example, a 10% decrease in the price of cocoa in the United States in the short term will result in a 2% rise in consumption; while a 10% increase of income would double the effect, giving a 4.4% increase in consumption.

17 Even though the explanations were based on the United Kingdom market, they equally apply to other consuming countries. During 1989 and 1990 France and the United States had the lowest prices for chocolate since 1983/84 and the retail price of chocolate in the Federal Republic of Germany and Japan was the lowest on record.

While the Table shows elasticities for a selection of countries, most of whom are major consumers, in global terms a 10% change in price moves consumption in the opposite direction by 0.87%. Similarly, when taken on a global scale, the effect of a 10% rise in income will increase consumption by 6.35%.[18]

Stocks

During the 1980s the level and structure of cocoa stocks have played a major role in the world cocoa economy. Stocks have always exercised the minds of those in cocoa, but two factors drew attention to them in particular during this period. First was the size of the stock levels. After a period of continual oversupply the tonnage of cocoa held in store was the highest on record. Second was the activity of one type of stock holding that had not been used before in cocoa, that of the Buffer Stock of the International Cocoa Organization.

Assessing stock levels

Obtaining verifiable global stock figures is notoriously difficult. If it were to be done, all cocoa held everywhere would have to be checked, whether in go-downs in Ghana, quay-sheds in Korea or ships' holds in Hamburg – and in a single day. Naturally this is not possible, so economists developed a statistical method of assessing stock. Such a method involves establishing stock levels for one particular year and then adding or subtracting successive annual surpluses or deficits. The simple formula for the stocks at the end of the year is previous year's stocks plus net production minus grindings. The net production is the gross crop minus one per cent for loss in weight.

Such a method contains a number of inexactitudes of which compilers of such series are only too aware. For example, the base year data may be wrong and subsequent annual stock levels may contain cumulative errors. Usually analysts select base years when prices are high. High prices indicate low stocks thereby reducing the first error mentioned.[19] The net production figure depends on the accuracy of figures in origin countries,

18   Source: ICCO, 1991.
19   It is of interest to note that even when the price of cocoa reached an all time high in 1976/77, more than double the previous year's average price, the end of season stocks still amounted to 250 thousand tonnes, 17.6% of the annual grindings for that year.

and the appropriateness of the one per cent deduction for loss in weight, may also be incorrect.[20] Conversion factors for calculating bean equivalents from cocoa product imports and exports may also give rise to errors.[21]

The traditional timing for establishing stock levels is at the end of the African cocoa crop year, the end of September. This is because stock levels for those using African cocoa are deemed to be at their lowest at this point, the main cocoa season ending in May and the new crop not yet coming into store. While this still holds true its significance is less than when economists first proposed the timing of stock assessment. Producing countries now tend to sell for delivery throughout the year, storing cocoa at origin after the end of the season thereby spreading out their own deliveries – and have done so for a while. During 1974–77 the average percentage of cocoa exported during July–September was 17% of the annual total. For 1987–90 the same quarter provided 18% of the annual figure. The similarity in the proportion shipped in the two periods is despite the very different supply situations. The mid-1970s saw cocoa shortages while it was in abundance during the end of the 1980s. It is true that stocks are at their lowest at the end of the third quarter, but exporters still ship substantial tonnages during this period. This obscures the cut-off point as old crop cocoa is delivered at the beginning of the new crop season. Another obscurant includes those who use non-African cocoa that have different seasons, providing another source of error for analysts.

Visible stocks

Analysts divide stocks into two: those that are 'visible' and those that are 'invisible'. Visible stocks are those that have open accounting systems and whose levels are a matter of public, albeit specialist, information. At the end of 1990/91, visible stocks consisted of three main items: the Buffer Stock of the ICCO; the United States warehouse stocks and the tonnage tendered on the LCE. In September 1991 these stood at 242 000

20 One study, based on Buffer Stock data, confirms that exporting countries have different losses in weight. For the growths of cocoa contained in the Buffer Stock the average losses in weight applied to cocoa exported may result in losses of between 0.6–0.8%.

21 The conversion used for cocoa liquor is 1.25, i.e. 1.25 tonnes of beans will give one tonne of cocoa. There is little dispute over the correctness of this ratio. The problem lies more with the appropriate conversion factor to use for powder and butter. The standard method is to place equal importance on the powder import/ export figure as to that for butter, thereby arriving at 1.18 and 1.33 respectively. However this may not be correct as most consumption of cocoa involves the added use of butter with the powder of incidental interest. Saying that the two have equal importance may not be correct.

THE INTERNATIONAL COCOA TRADE

tonnes, 175 000 tonnes and 40 730 tonnes respectively. Sometimes this list may be augmented by other stocks, such as the tonnage held by some origins. At the end of the 1980s Côte d'Ivoire and Ghana had stocks held in port areas that were of common knowledge. Stocks held in another official capacity but which are not reported on include that held by the Swiss processors under OFIDA.[22] One such stock, recently abandoned, was that held by the cocoa processors in what was West Berlin. The objective of both of them was to allow the manufacturers to continue processing in the event of the disruption of supplies.

Invisible stocks

The invisible stocks are those not subject to public scrutiny. They are those holdings that belong to companies and are not involved with any public body. The exception to this is the 'visible' holdings in official United States warehouses which may well contain private companies' stocks over and above that destined for the New York CSCE. While some of the 'invisible' cocoa may have been taken up from the terminal markets, and therefore coming from a 'visible' stock, publicly unaccounted stock is primarily the aftermath of physical trading. As outlined in Chapter 5, one of the characteristics of actuals business is that it is private transaction and not of common knowledge. It is therefore extremely difficult to quantify this important part of the stock figure. Analysts break it down into three main categories: cocoa held by factories in North America; and working stocks held in Europe and those in origin countries.

Historically North American factories hold more cocoa, relative to their processing capacity, than their European counterparts. At the beginning of the 1990s analysts estimated the cocoa held by North American processors was five weeks of their capacity, for European factories the equivalent was four weeks. Distance is the key. Major European cocoa processors are close to the port areas and therefore have a nearby source of warehoused stock. Secondly, sailings from Africa take less time to Europe than to the United States, again the source of supply is closer and therefore they need to hold less.

Both groups of users hold less stock now than they did ten years ago. Better stock management and high interest rates, coupled with few disruptions of supply have helped to reduce stocks. This has combined with a change in buying strategies, factories contract less for forward delivery than in the past, although for different reasons. In a falling market, the situation throughout most of the 1980s, there is little incentive to

---

22   Office Fiduciaire des Importateurs Suisses de Denrées Alimentaires.

buy forward today when the cocoa you want tomorrow will be cheaper tomorrow.

While the North American trade's stock forms part of the 'visible' holdings, no official reports exist of tonnages held by the European trade. At the end of the 1980s, cocoa held by this sector reached very high levels with two companies alternately holding unprecedented stocks of cocoa. Eventually in 1990 such unwieldy trading caused both companies either to trim their activities or to stop trading cocoa altogether. The rest of the trade continues to feel the reverberations of their, and others, activities. In particular, the banks have become very wary of lending money to cocoa trading operations.

Origin working stocks not only include the cocoa that the local processors need for their factories but also cocoa that is 'in the pipeline'. This is cocoa on its way to fulfil physical sales; it may be up country, in the port area ready for shipment, or actually afloat on its way to its destination. By taking the cut-off point at the end of the crop year cocoa in the pipeline is less than it would otherwise be during the crop season, but is still a considerable tonnage.

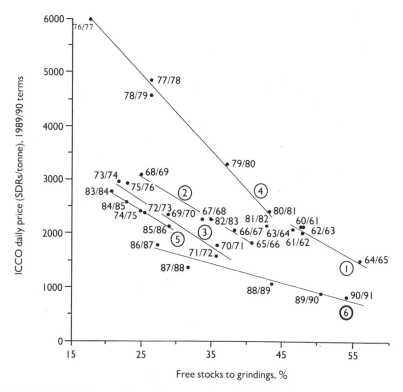

7.15 Stock/grindings ratios and cocoa prices; 1960/61–1990/91.

Relationship of prices and stocks

Tightening supplies of a commodity will result in a rise in prices. Increased stocks indicate no shortages and therefore the prices fall accordingly. This simple supply/demand law applies to cocoa. Figure 7.15 shows this relationship for the period 1960/61 to 1990/91. As consumption increased substantially during the period under review, the outright stock figure becomes meaningless and has to be related to consumption, so the pertinent measurement of stocks is as a ratio of the annual grindings figures. Free stocks mean the stocks available to the market during this period, i.e., excluding the Buffer Stock.

Figure 7.15 not only shows the expected supply/demand curve but that for short periods of time a more direct relationship applies, shown on the graph as a series of short lines. For a few years at a time the annual stock ratio/prices follow or lie close to a straight line. Then, a change occurs and the relationship no longer applies and a new curve begins. The timing of these shifts tends to be in years when there is a significant change in the annual surplus or deficit of cocoa, or when a change in market sentiment takes place. For example, from 1960/61 to 1964/65 each year produced a surplus, i.e. production was higher than grindings; this produced a straight line relationship (see line 1). In 1965/66 this became a deficit, which continued until 1968/69 (see line 2).

What becomes clear is that over the years the angle of these lines has flattened and, with the exception of the 1976/77 to 1981/82 curve, have shifted down the graph. The cause of this is the same as those reasons mentioned earlier, i.e., primarily more efficient stock management and the change in manufacturers buying policies. Clearly, with over six months supply of cocoa lying in warehouse in 1990/91, the processors have no immediate incentive to cover forward. With the forecast deficit for 1991/92 the existing curve in line 6 may come to an end, although the existing high stock levels will cushion any change. The relationship may provide help in forecasting prices. One model of the cocoa market, used by ICCO, shows that a 10% decline in the stock/grindings ratio from one crop year to the next gives a 15% increase between the two June prices. Even if reality proves to be different to the model, at least a 10% decline in stock at these levels would be welcomed by most in the cocoa trade.

The International Cocoa Organization and the Buffer Stock

Forming a large part of the visible holdings during the 1980s the Buffer Stock has exercised the minds of those in the cocoa trade. The presence of

100 000 and then 250 000 tonnes of cocoa lying in North European ports, but effectively removed from the market, has provoked the debate. It is therefore of interest to have a brief history of the Organization controlling the stock.

The first agreement

The International Cocoa Organization (ICCO) was established in 1973 to administer the provisions of the International Cocoa Agreement (ICCA), 1972. Under the auspices of the United Nations Conference on Trade and Development (UNCTAD) in Geneva, representatives of the governments of the majority of cocoa producing and cocoa consuming countries concluded negotiations on October 21, 1972. The principal objective of the ICCA was to stabilise a usually volatile cocoa market on the basis of an agreed price range. This range initially involved a 'minimum' price of 23 US cents/lb and a 'maximum' price of 32 US cents/lb, which were subsequently revised to 29.5 US cents/lb and 38.5 US cents/lb respectively. The price-defence instruments of the ICCA comprised an export-quota scheme and a Buffer Stock with a maximum capacity of 250 000 tonnes of cocoa beans designed to absorb production in excess of quotas. Provision was made in the ICCA for a levy on exports and imports of cocoa by member countries to finance the operations of the Buffer Stock. With the exception of the United States, all the major exporters and importers of cocoa were signatories to the ICCA, which came into provisional effect on 30 June and was formally implemented as from October 31, 1973. The agreement was in force for three years, and throughout that period free market forces alone kept cocoa prices above the agreement range. As a consequence, in the absence of any cocoa in the Buffer Stock, the price defence mechanism of the ICCA could not be activated.

The second agreement

The successor agreement, the 1975 ICCA, came into force provisionally on October 1, 1976. Membership was essentially the same as under the 1972 agreement. Apart from a higher price range to be defended (39−55 cents/lb, subsequently increased to 65−81 US cents/lb), the 1975 agreement was very similar to the previous one. Price regulatory action was not taken throughout the four year life of the agreement as world cocoa prices stayed above the agreed price range and the Buffer Stock had still not accumulated any cocoa. In the meantime sizeable funds were accumulated through the levy system, and by the end of the 1975 agreement, in 1989, these funds had reached around US$230 million.

The third agreement

The third pact, the International Cocoa Agreement, 1980, was concluded on November 19, 1980. It was significantly different from its two predecessors in that the quota system was abandoned and the price defence mechanism was based directly on a buffer stock. The level of prices to be defended was raised and the width of the price band was increased. The revised price range was structured differently from the previous ones and included a 'minimum' price of 100 cents/lb, a 'lower intervention' price of 110 cents/lb, an 'upper intervention' price of 150 cents/lb and a 'maximum' price of 160 cents /lb. The agreement entered into force only provisionally on August 1, 1981. Along with the United States and Malaysia, which had stayed out of the two preceding agreements, the following exporting countries which had been members of the two preceding agreements decided not to participate: Côte d'Ivoire (by now the world's largest cocoa exporter), Gabon, Saint Lucia, Togo and Zaire. Among the importing countries, Australia, Austria, Canada, New Zealand and the Philippines decided not to join. The agreement was extended twice, until September 30 1986.

By 1982, the Buffer Stock had purchased 100 000 tonnes of cocoa in defence of the agreement's price range and its finances were depleted. Consequently, further Buffer Stock buying could not be undertaken despite the need to continue the defence of cocoa prices in 1982. However, in 1983 and 1984 the appreciation of the US dollar in terms of all other major currencies created a peculiar situation. World cocoa prices, although still nominally within the price range of the ICCA which had been set in 1980 dollar terms, exceeded the 1980 equivalent of the 'maximum' price of the agreement in most other currencies. Yet Buffer Stock sales could not be made in order to lower prices because the agreement prices in nominal dollar terms were still within the agreed range. During 1984 the cocoa market experienced a relative shortage.[23] It is probable that the market, knowing that if cocoa prices moved higher another 100 000 tonnes of cocoa would become available, defended the Upper Intervention Price. Figure 7.16 shows the evolution of prices during the first three agreements with the Buffer Stock intervention shown as the shaded area.

The fourth agreement

The 1986 agreement, which provisionally came into force on January 20, 1987, succeeded the 1980 agreement. Côte d'Ivoire, Gabon and Togo

---

23 The end of season stocks in 1983/4 were 20.7% of the grindings – the lowest since 1976/77.

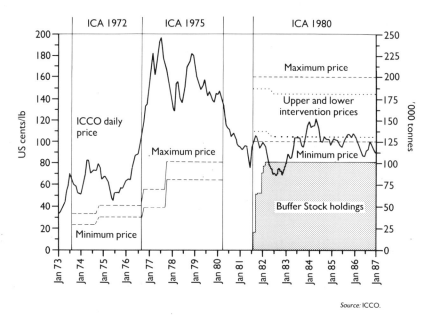

7.16 Monthly averages of ICCO daily price, the price bands of the International Cocoa Agreements, 1972, 1975 and 1980 and the Buffer Stock intervention.

rejoined, but the United States and Malaysia, by now a major exporter, remained outside the agreement. Although this agreement is currently in force, renegotiations for a successor began in 1992.

The 1986 ICCA provided a Buffer Stock mechanism as the main instrument for achieving its price objectives. Unlike its predecessor it prescribed an additional supplementary price defence mechanism, that of a Withholding Scheme. Under this measure, up to a total of 120 000 tonnes could be required to be withheld by exporting countries when certain conditions are met. These relate to the exhaustion of either the physical or financial capacity of the Buffer Stock and to the level of cocoa prices.

A novelty of the 1986 agreement was the denomination of the price range in a basket of currencies instead of the US dollar. For this purpose, the ICCA used the International Monetary Fund's (IMF) unit of account, the Special Drawing Rights (SDRs). The intention was to remove currency fluctuations from cocoa prices, a significant distortion experienced under the 1980 agreement. The price range specified in the 1986 agreement included: a 'lower intervention' price of SDR 1600 per tonne (equivalent to US$0.85/lb at the exchange rate prevailing in July 1986); a 'may-buy' price of SDR 1655 per tonne (US$0.88/lb); a 'median' price of SDR 1935 per tonne (US$1.03/lb); a 'may-sell' price of SDR 2215 per tonne (US$1.18/lb) and an 'upper-intervention' price of SDR 2270 per tonne

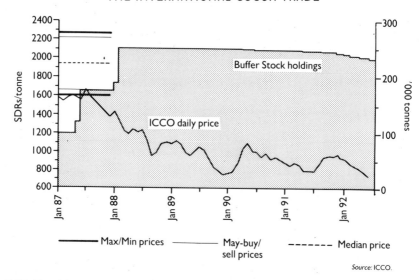

7.17 Monthly averages of ICCO daily price, the price bands of the International Cocoa Agreement, 1986 and the Buffer Stock intervention.

(US$1.21/lb). The agreement provided the revision of the price range either by negotiation or through automatic price adjustment.

Between the entry into force of the 1986 agreement in January 1987 and 25 February 1988, the Buffer Stock Manager bought a further 150 000 tonnes of cocoa, thus exhausting the Stock's prescribed initial capacity of 250 000 tonnes. Soon afterwards, financial constraints deriving from difficulties experienced by a number of member countries in keeping up with Buffer Stock levy payments and disagreements on the interpretation of the agreement's price revision provisions led to the suspension of all price stabilisation measures.

At its 39th regular session in March 1990, the International Cocoa Council decided to extend the 1986 ICCA, but without its market intervention provisions. The extension was for two years, up to October 1 1992, recently further extended to the end of September 1993. During this period the Buffer Stock is frozen and its activities restricted to selling stock that had deteriorated to more than 10% defective beans. The Council also gave the Buffer Stock Manager the authorisation to sell such quantities of cocoa as may be necessary to finance the maintenance of the Buffer Stock should there be financial difficulties in meeting costs during this period. In addition, the Council suspended the Buffer Stock levy as from April 15, 1990. Figure 7.17 shows the evolution of the price of cocoa and the price bands for the 1986 ICA, against the backdrop of the Buffer Stock holdings.[24]

24   Since this was written the Council decided in June 1993 that the Buffer Stock

The effect of the Buffer Stock on cocoa prices is complex and throughout the holding operation has depended on the prevailing market conditions. At the time of purchase the Stock supported the market, but the change from a bull to bear market at the beginning of the 1980s dampened its effect. Increased production pushed prices down, exacerbated by manufacturers who reduced their forward cover and held less stock themselves. At other times, particularly in 1983/84, the Stock helped stabilise the price by preventing its rise to a point where the Manager would have had to sell. After seven consecutive years of production exceeding consumption the Buffer Stock represents a relatively small part of the tonnage held in store.[25] For the moment this, plus the freezing of its intervention and lack of funds, has reduced the impact of the Stock on prices.

Conclusions

Analysts do not expect consumption to continue growing at the annual rate of 4–5%. At the beginning of the 1990s the cocoa market may have entered a new phase after the substantial increases in production during the 1980s. As said by Sir Alec Cairncross:

> *A trend is a trend is a trend,*
> *but the question is will it bend?*
> *Will it alter its course,*
> *through some unforeseen force*
> *and come to a premature end?*

The abundant supply of cocoa that caused the decline in cocoa prices during the last decade, which in turn stimulated demand, may now be ending. Tighter supplies of cocoa will push prices upwards, but this is expected to be a slow recovery in view of the size of stocks. Analysts consider that the higher prices will reduce the growth in consumption to an average rate of 2.4% a year until the year 2000. This growth will primarily take place in the traditional markets, helped by the return of the CIS and the former East European countries as consumers. Although analysts need to exercise some caution:

> *. . . and although consumption has increased, it is unlikely to*
> *continue to increase at the rate which characterized the*
> *immediate post-war period. Meanwhile the low level of prices*
> *is in itself acting as a check on new production. In the absence*

should be sold. The sales were to be in equal monthly instalments over a period not longer than four and a half years. This process started in October 1993.

25   At the end of 1990/91 the Buffer Stock represented 16% of total world stocks.

of fresh developments in cultivation, it is reasonable to expect
that the surplus of stock should be liquidated, and a gradual
recovery in prices follow.

This was written in 1932 and the war referred to here is World
War I[26] ... the recovery in prices did not occur until after 1945.

26   'COCOA', Reports of the imperial economic committee, twenty second report,
HMSO, 1932.

Quality assessment of cocoa beans

I t is only natural that the manufacturers who finally use cocoa dictate the quality requirements of the beans. After all, they have to work up the raw product into goods to sell to an ever more discriminating public. However, defining what they want has been difficult for two main reasons. The first has to do with part of the glory of chocolate, its variation. Everyone who eats chocolate has their own preferences, happily caused by chocolatiers using their own proprietary recipes – which they jealously guard. Even if the manufacturers revealed their secrets, the different formulations and requirements would make it difficult to define an all-embracing quality model; the characteristics needed by one factory will not suit all others. Secondly, the critical characteristic for the chocolatier has to do with flavour, to date predominantly a subjective matter and difficult to quantify. Apart from some characteristics of the bean that analysts may measure (for example the size and fat content of the beans) defining the quality of cocoa depends more on its negative aspects. By saying what is not wanted instead of stipulating the positive points in flavour (except in vague terms, such as 'a fully developed chocolate flavour') manufacturers have protected their individual trade secrets and ensured that variations in the flavour of the bean remain for each to exploit in their own products. Interestingly this has not changed over the years. The following was written in the early eighteenth century:[1]

1   Ibid de Chélus: Brookes (Dr) R (trans), 1724.

> *The best Cacao-Nuts have very brown firm Shells, and when the*
> *Kernel is taken out, it ought to be plump, well nourish'd, and*
> *sleek; of the Colour of a Hazel-Nut on the outside, but more*
> *inclining to Red within; its Taste a little bitter and astringent,*
> *not at all sour or mouldy*. In a word, without Smell, and not*
> *worm-eaten, . . .*
>
> **It gets this Taste either by being laid in a moist Place or by*
> *being wet by Sea-Water in the Passage.*

All in all not a bad definition, although perhaps de Chélus had started a trend, common in cocoa, of forgetting earlier work. Going back a further 50 years to 1672 we have the following advice in choosing cocoa beans:[2]

> *Indeed, there is great care to be taken in the choice of them,*
> *especially of such as are brought into England, that you chuse*
> *them that are well cured, well tasted, not musty, mouldy, or*
> *much venny[3] within when they are broken; and such as seem*
> *fat and oyly are best: Also pick forth all those which are*
> *corrupt, before you make use of the rest.*

This definition commented on an essential feature of modern cocoa quality, the fat content of the beans, and for that reason is slightly advanced of Dr Brookes' translation,[4] although some powder manufacturers would approve of the red colour he was looking for in the bean. In general, modern manufacturers would not disagree on the qualitative assessments made by these early writers.

While the needs of the chocolate makers are important, they are not the only final users of cocoa beans. The butter pressers, processing beans to make cocoa butter and powder in fact use more beans than the chocolate manufacturers.[5] Their interest in the quality of cocoa is different to the chocolatiers, lying more in objective characteristics of the bean, notably its size and fat content. Laboratory analysts can, of course, measure

---

2 Ibid Hughes, William, 1672.
3 The OED defines 'venny' in the figurative context as 'a sharp retort, a pungent remark'. The words 'sharp' and 'pungent' probably apply here.
4 Some may argue that beans with a high fat content may not make the best drinking chocolate of the type drunk in the seventeenth and eighteenth centuries, and that beans selected for their 'oily' content may not make as good a drink as that made with lower fat content. This is slightly pedantic. What is amazing is that so little has changed in the assessment of quality.
5 Although over recent years the distinction between processor and chocolatier is less clear as more processors make couverture for some of the chocolate factories, the difference here is those quality assessments that a butter presser considers when buying cocoa.

these objective attributes, but it takes time and equipment to assess the cocoa directly. Such facilities are not always available to those who are interested in cocoa, i.e., the rest of the trade. They (the growers, exporters, merchants and brokers) need some way of assessing the cocoa that is quick, as objective as possible, and, for the sake of the chocolatiers, assesses the cocoa in terms of its negative attributes. Over the past 50 years the cocoa trade has developed such an analysis, called the cut-test which will be described later in this chapter.

Faults occurring in cocoa

Smoky beans

Cocoa is delicate. Strong smelling products kept next to or introduced to the beans will taint the cocoa. (This is a characteristic that chocolatiers use to their advantage when making flavoured chocolate, usually a citrus or mint flavour.) This attribute presents difficulties for those origins which have to rely on artificial means to dry their cocoa. It requires drying the cocoa using an oven (usually fired by burning wood) which, unless done carefully, results in the beans picking up the strong smoke flavour.

Once contaminated the cocoa must not be blended into another parcel in an attempt to dilute the fault down to acceptable levels. It does not work. The slightest smell, caused by one or two beans amongst many hundreds is enough to ruin a batch of processing. Much better, and true for all faults in cocoa, is for the grower or exporter to sell the smoke tainted beans as such.

Liquor tasting panels will readily discover the taint if it exists, but the cut-test analyst usually need only smell beans warmed by hand to detect this, one of the worst of the off-flavours. Cameroonian farmers forced to dry their main crop of cocoa artificially, maintain that if they wash smoke-contaminated beans immediately after faulty drying a subsequent clean redrying will present smoke-free cocoa. While this action may remove the taint from the shell and thereby allow the beans to pass a rough organoleptic test, it remains unclear if the unwanted flavour stays in the nib-fat thereby perhaps only becoming discernible in the intermediate or final product.

Mould

Manufacturers consider mouldy cocoa as the second of the worst faults in cocoa beans. Even small amounts of fungal infection on the inside of the bean limit its use. Chocolate made from beans with more than 3% mould, as measured in a cut-test, will contain mouldy 'off-flavours'.

Fungi can attack the beans at all stages of their development, although the beans are most susceptible while they are wet. High levels of water content provide a good growing medium for moulds. The longer the grower delays the fermentation or the subsequent drying of the beans the greater the risk of mould developing in the cocoa.[6]

The risk of mould infection increases if the cocoa shell has an opening, providing an entrance for the mould spores. Such an opening may occur in a number of ways. Firstly, if the bean germinates, the radicle will force an opening through the testa thereby providing access for the mould. As the fermentation process normally kills the bean, this should not happen to any great extent, but helps explain why many grading standards consider germination a fault.[7] Secondly, it is not unusual for beans infested by an insect to be mouldy. The mould spores have an easier entrance through the damage caused by the insect boring its way into the bean from the outside. Lastly, in removing the beans from the pods, growers often use a machete to break them open. The knife will frequently cut one or two beans, again giving moulds an easy opportunity to grow inside them.

The beans may become infected before fermentation but the heat generated by the microbiological action is usually enough to kill off any such moulds. However, mould in the beans at the edge of the fermentation pile may survive as the temperature at the periphery of the pile is lower than in the middle. In particular the Aspergilli moulds burgeon between 37 °C and 45 °C.

Although the fermentation process reduces the water content of the beans there is still a considerable amount of moisture to be lost by the

6   Unfermented cocoa is less likely to develop mould. Not only is it dried sooner as it does not have to go through the fermentation process but the internal structure of the beans remains solid, giving the mould less opportunity to grow. The cotyledons of fermented cocoa are not solid but have internal ridges and valleys that provide the moulds with an opportunity to develop. In addition the shell of unfermented cocoa is more acidic than that of fermented beans, the lower pH making it more difficult for the mould to develop. That said, as unfermented beans have a higher water content at the beginning of the drying process there is generally a larger number of spores on the outside of the bean than for fermented cocoa.

7   Germinated beans do not retain their radicle, a loss of some 0.8% of the nib weight. This may have some significance for the yield of cocoa butter but also geminated beans have a different flavour characteristic to ungerminated beans; they give rise to bitter flavoured products. Recent tests in Malaysia have confirmed this, although the industry were aware of this in the 1950s (Chatt E M: 'Cocoa cultivation, processing, analysis', 1953), and even in the eighteenth century, see 'Off-flavours'.

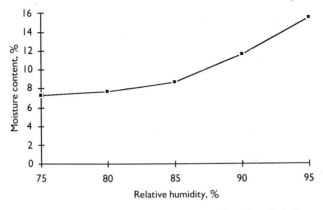

Source: Cocoa, Wood and Lass.

8.1 The effect of the relative humidity on the moisture content of cocoa.

beans before they are considered dry enough to sell. Both fermentation and drying reduce the weight of the beans by some 65%. Naturally most of the water loss occurs during the drying. While sun drying is the best method of reducing the water content in cocoa and for the continued development of flavour it also allows moulds to attack the beans. It is common for sun dried cocoa to have moulds on the exterior. None of the quality standards specify this as a fault, although it is easy for the moulds to transfer into the middle of the bean if conditions allow.[8]

Moisture content in mould control

Water is the main factor in controlling moulds. Keeping the moisture levels of cocoa below 8% will hinder the development of mould. This is not easy. Cocoa is hygroscopic, it will take up water in damp conditions but fortunately, also gives it up in dry air. Figure 8.1 shows how sensitive the moisture content of the bean is to the relative humidity of the atmosphere. While all the cocoa growing areas have equatorial weather, i.e., hot and damp, some have higher relative humidities than others which helps to explain why cocoa from some regions with a high relative humidity, (for example Cameroon) have high percentages of mouldy cocoa.

Figure 8.2 shows the speed at which cocoa absorbs water in different relative humidities. The critical level of 8% moisture within the bean is

8   Washing the beans removes the exterior mould but it also reduces the shell which may make it easier for subsequent internal mould to develop. In addition, washing the beans increases the time the beans are wet, improving the chance for mould to develop.

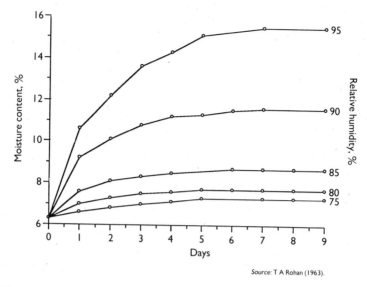

Source: T A Rohan (1963).

8.2 Changes in the moisture content of cocoa beans at various relative humidities.

met within two days exposure to an atmosphere with a relative humidity of 85%, not uncommon in the tropics.[9]

Unless the grower, warehousekeeper and shipper take careful precautions over the handling and storage of the beans, the cocoa will deteriorate. This is not a new predicament, and no doubt will continue. Although William Hughes wrote the following in 1672, apart from the elegance of the language, it might have been written today.

> *The truth is how well soever they seem to be cured when they are in the place they grow and how carefully soever stowed in the ship; yet by transportation, the Air of different places hath such an operation upon them, that many are corrupted and spoiled before they arrive here; and so they are often, by reason of moisture, soon afterwards, if they are not carefully look'd unto and dryed and used in time.*[10]

9   This has been known for some time. In 1928 J L Scott understood the importance of reducing the water content to the critical 8% level or less to prevent the development of mould (Scott J L: 'Preliminary observations on the moisture content and hygroscopicity of cacao beans', Department of Agriculture Gold Coast, Yearbook, 1928). In 1937 A W Knapp said in 'Cacao fermentation', 'A store with an average daily relative humidity of over 82% is unsafe for the prolonged storage of cacao. Whilst in the tropics exposure of the beans to relative humidities of over 82% will cause mould, in England it does not; probably because the air temperature being much lower, the actual percentage of moisture in the air is less'.

10   Ibid Hughes, William, 1672.

It is also a pity that those involved in the first shipments of cocoa by containers in the 1970s were unaware of his warning and, 300 years later, had to relearn about the delicacy of handling cocoa.[11]

White spot

Cocoa beans sometimes exhibit a condition known as white spot. The inside of the cotyledons show small light coloured dots that analysts may confuse with mould. The spots are not mould, but are concentrations of theobromine. None of the grading specifications consider white spot as a fault, but its possible confusion with mould requires its mention. The condition occurs in West African cocoa in years where the Harmattan, a dry wind coming from the desert area in the north during the harvest season, is severe. First noted in 1925, one explanation is that the wind kills the beans when the pod is on the tree. This allows the theobromine to dissolve in the liquid contents in the bean before fermentation, which on later drying is deposited on the cotyledons.

Unfermented cocoa

Unfermented Forastero cocoa has a poor chocolate flavour. Further, cocoa powder made from such beans has an unappetising grey colour. For these reasons, the cocoa trade considers a parcel of cocoa containing a large amount of unfermented beans to be of less use than those which are better fermented. Buyers assess the degree of fermentation by the number of beans that have slaty-grey coloured nibs compared with those that are the more usual and preferred brown colour.

Insect infestation

As mentioned earlier, insects can infest dried cocoa beans, especially at origin. Notable are the warehouse moths, *Ephestia cautella* and *Ephestia elutella*. Both of these moths cause the most damage to stored cocoa. Both moths are similar to one another, except that as its common name suggests the tropical warehouse moth, *E. cautella*, thrives in the cocoa growing regions. Distinguishing between the two moths requires a detailed

11   The early shipments of containerised cocoa were in unventilated containers. The result was that the cocoa arrived with extensive water damage caused by condensation. Cocoa loaded in temperatures of around 30 °C will give up moisture, which if not removed through ventilation will condense and damage the cocoa. A hundred tonnes of cocoa losing 1 % moisture gives off one tonne of water.

inspection, something that the moths themselves appear to do quite easily; in three months under ideal conditions a pair of *E. cautella* can produce 125 000 offspring. *E. elutella* prefers a more temperate climate and is the usual cause of infestation at cocoa destinations; although its cousin will travel with the cocoa it rarely survives the winter months.

Once the moths are airborne the damage has been done to the cocoa beans as during this time they are only interested in reproduction. The pernicious feeding stage lasts for up to eight weeks before the caterpillars pupate. The moth comes out of the chrysalis after about a week, if the temperature is high enough. If lower temperatures prevail, the moth can delay its emergence until more favourable conditions occur. Table 8.1 shows the bionomics of the two moths.

Infestation by beetles and mites also takes place but is less common. There are four main culprits: the coffee weevil (*Araeocerus fasciculatus*), the tobacco beetle (*Lasioderma serricorne*), the flour beetle (*Tribolium castaneum*) and the khapra beetle (*Trogoderma granarium*). In the north European ports at the end of the 1980s stored cocoa beans were infested by spider beetles: the Australian spider beetle (*Ptinus tectus*); the Golden Spider beetle (*Niptus hololeucus*) and the White Mark Spider Beetle (*Ptinus fur*). These are tiny animals that tend to feed on the exterior mould on the beans as well as the fabric of the bags and are more associated with flour mills than with cocoa.

Even if the insects do not damage the cocoa (or even if they help to improve the cocoa by eating the exterior mould) their presence is a fault. The FDA is most particular on this and states that:

> 2.a. *The product contains:*
> *(1) One live insect in each of two or more immediate containers; . . . or three live or dead insects in one immediate container;*
>   *plus*
> *(2) Similar live or dead insect infestation present on, or in the immediate proximity of, the lot . . .*
>   *or*
> *b. The product contains one or more live insects in each of three or more immediate containers.*
>   *or*
> *d. The product is in cloth or burlap bags and two or more live or dead insects are present on at least five of the containers. NOTE: Some live insects must be present . . .*

As cocoa beans need further processing before people consume them the insects have to be alive in order for the FDA to count them in their inspection.

Table 8.1 Bionomics of *E. elutella* and *E. cautella*

	Temperature, °C			Humidity, %RH		Time (days) for life cycle at temp/RH optima on good food	Maximum rate of increase per lunar month*
	Minimum for population increase	Optimum for development	Maximum for development	Minimum for population increase	Optimum for development		
E. elutella	10 to 12	25	30	20	70	40	15
E. cautella	17	30	37	20	75	28	60

*Rate of increase of a population with all life stages present, in 28 days.

Rodent infestation

Insects are not the only form of infestation. Rodents can also attack cocoa; although their interest lies more with the bags than the beans. Jute and sisal make good nesting material for the rats and mice. While their activity does not directly damage the cocoa, their presence results in contaminated cocoa. The FDA maintain the following.

1. *Rodent Contamination*
   a. *The storage facility is rodent infested and:*
      (1) Three or more of the bags in the lot are rodent gnawed;
      or
      (2) At least five of the bags in the lot bear either rodent urine stains at least 1/4 inch in diameter, or two or more rodent pellets;
      or
      (3) The food in at least one container in the lot contains rodent-gnawed material, or rodent excreta or urine.
   b. *Whether or not the warehouse is rodent infested,*
      (1) At least three bags bear rodent urine stains of at least 1/4 inch diameter which penetrate to the product even though the product cannot be demonstrated to have been contaminated;
      or
      (2) At least two bags are rodent gnawed and at least five bags bear either rodent urine stains at least 1/4 inch in diameter, with or without penetration to the product, or two or more rodent pellets;
      or
      (3) The food in at least one bag in the lot contains rodent-gnawed material or rodent excreta or rodent urine, and at least five bags bear either rodent urine stains at least 1/4 inch in diameter or two or more rodent pellets.[12]

The FDA inspectors also check the bags for bird excreta, and apply similarly stringent requirements as they do for evidence of rodents.

Overall condition of the parcel

Before looking directly at the cocoa beans, inspectors or supervisors should assess the condition of the consignment. At this stage the parcel

12   For those wondering how the inspectors detect rat urine on the bags, apparently it becomes visible under ultra-violet light.

should consist of only sound cocoa. If the parcel is for export any damaged bags should be replaced by those that are sound. Shippers should never export damaged cocoa. If the parcel is at the port of final destination the warehousekeeper receiving the cargo on behalf of the final buyer should have removed any bags containing damaged beans either for reconditioning or to sell them off through the insurance survey. Damaged cocoa should not form part of this particular inspection, although often this examination is in tandem with the insurance survey.[13] Primarily the inspection should ascertain whether the parcel needs fumigating against insect infestation. Although insects are an 'inherent vice' of cocoa, the parcel should be relatively free of them. Supervisors should always check that nothing has escaped the attention of earlier inspections; on occasion the second scrutiny uncovers some additional damaged or stained bags[14] that need remedial attention. Inspectors should also look for evidence of rodent infestation.

Fumigation

Removing insects requires fumigation. This takes one of two forms: a passive or an active fumigation. Responsible warehousekeepers normally conduct passive fumigation as a matter of course. It involves spraying a mist of fumigant over the bags of cocoa lying in a warehouse. The fumigant, usually pyrethrum, does not penetrate into the bags but will kill any insect that it contacts. If done properly it will enter the cracks and crevices in the roof and walls of the building that, outside the cocoa, are the favoured hiding places of insects. Ideally this 'fogging' should be done in the evening when the air is still and when the insects prefer to fly. The added benefit is that the warehouse may be closed for the night, allowing the fumigant to have full effect. Regular and methodical application of this will prevent any build up of insect infestation, providing the warehousekeeper follows prudent storage practices; i.e., not storing obviously infested parcels in an otherwise clean shed.

Plastic strips containing Dichlorvos have been used in passive fumigation within warehouses. They provide a continuous control of insect activity, particularly of moth, and need little manual attention, although the overall cost is higher than spraying. Some countries have banned their use, notably the Netherlands, while the use of 'DDVP' is currently under review in the United States.

Active fumigation takes place when the passive variety cannot hold

13   This is conducted when the cargo suffers any damage or loss.
14   Contamination of the bags by chemical powders is as important as staining by water.

the upsurge of insect activity. Sudden and rapid 'explosions' of insects can take place and need a stronger remedy. This generally means using either methyl bromide or aluminium phosphide, Phostoxin. Both of these are dangerous materials and should only be used by trained personnel, preferably an outside pest control company. This is especially true for methyl bromide.

While methyl bromide has the advantage over Phostoxin in the ability to penetrate a stack more quickly, it has the disadvantage of leaving a residue of the bromide radical. The methyl radical may also affect the cocoa, by reacting with the cocoa butter, although the interest lies more with the effect that the bromide might have. People, especially those in wealthy countries, are becoming more and more aware of residues in foodstuffs. Cocoa is no exception and chocolate companies spend a lot of effort in ensuring that their product is wholesome. Guidelines over the residue levels exist and some countries' permitted levels are shown in Table 8.2. Included in the Table are the maximum residue limits adopted by the Codex Alimentarius Commission (as at its eighteenth session).[15] Many countries adopt the limits set by the Commission or base their national limits on their findings. It seems likely that in the future lower tolerances will come into force as people demand more and more 'natural' products. Some cocoa growers have seen this as a marketing opportunity and have begun to sell their cocoa as 'organically grown', hoping to attract a premium to offset the loss in production through not using fertilisers or pesticides.[16]

Other forms of removing insect infestation are available but not widely used. One which does not leave any residue involves putting the cocoa under pressurised carbon dioxide, 40 bars for 15 minutes. However, this uses specialised pressure vessels in order to hold the bags of cocoa and is consequently quite expensive. The attraction of not using potentially harmful chemicals may see it gain more attention. Once insects attack a parcel such 'fumigation' will not help if they also migrate to the fabric of the building. The warehousekeeper will therefore have to spray the structure of the building with some fumigant.

Another form of insect control that had a promising start but has now been discontinued involved the use of irradiation. It had the advantage of not only killing any insect activity but also retarding the progress of mould. Irradiation became unpopular for a number of reasons. The first

15   The Codex contains regional or worldwide standards, accepted by governments, concerning both consumers' health and fair practice in the food trade. It is published by the Codex Alimentarius Commission set up under the joint FAO/ WHO Food Standards Programme in 1962.

16   The French Organic Agricultural Society produces the first organic chocolate, marketed in the United Kingdom as Green and Black, with 70% cocoa solids.

Table 8.2 Maximum chemical and toxic material residue levels permitted in cocoa beans (mg/kg)

	BE	CA	CS	FI	DE	GR	HU	NL	PO	SE	SU	GB	US	COD
Aflatoxin B1, B2, C1, C2										0.01	0.01			
Aldrine/Diedrine							0.01	0.02						
Arsenic							0.50		1.00					1.00
Bromides	50.00		1.00	50.00	50.00		50.00	50.00					50.00	
Cadmium							0.50						0.05	
Chlorothalonil														
Copper+	6.00				6.00		3.00	50.00	50.00					30.00
Cyanides		25.00					0.20	6.00					25.00	
DDT/DDE								0.02						
Deltamethrin						0.05						0.05		0.05
Dichlorvos	5.00					5.00	0.10	5.00				5.00		5.00
Fenitrothion	0.10					0.10	0.10	0.10				0.10		0.10
Fentin						0.10	0.10	0.10				0.10		0.10
Hexachlorobenzene					0.20		0.05							
Hexachlorocyclohexane							0.20	0.01						
Lead							2.00		2.00	2.00				2.00
Lindane	1.00					1.00	1.00	1.00				1.00		1.00
Mercury							0.02							
Methacrifos						10.00						10.00		
Phosphides	0.01					0.01	0.01	0.01				0.01	0.10	0.01
Phosphoramidate								1.00					0.02	
Piperonyl butoxide		8.00												
Propylene oxide													300.00	
Pyrethrin		1.00						0.50					1.00	

COUNTRY CODES
BE Belgium CA Canada CS Czechoslovakia FI Finland* DE Germany* GR Greece* HU Hungary* NL The Netherlands*
NO Norway* PO Poland SE Sweden SU USSR GB United Kingdom* US United States COD Codex Alimentarius

* Countries that follow FAO Codex Alimentarius.

was that public opinion against irradiated products in a number of consuming countries prevented its universal acceptance. Secondly, the cost of such control is high as it needs specialised equipment and personnel. Last, and by no means least, the process affects the quality of the product by oxidising the butter in the beans, rendering them unfit for making chocolate.

Sampling

There would be an enormous advantage if all of the beans making up a parcel could be tested. With indisputable accuracy the result from such a test would define the standing of the parcel. Unfortunately this is not possible as the current methods of analysis effectively destroy the tested cocoa, and therefore analysts have to perform their tests on small quantities drawn from the consignment.

How the sample is drawn is critical. It requires as much attention and takes longer than most of the ensuing quality analyses. An assiduous quality analysis is meaningless if the sample on which it was performed does not fairly represent the parcel of cocoa.

The relevant sampling authority may be the producer inspection services at origin countries, or the FDA of the United States, or it may be made under the auspices of one or other of the terminal markets. Supervisors sampling cocoa subject to a standard physical sale need to apply the terms specified in the sale contract. All the procedures have common assumptions: that the cocoa is in bags,[17] that the sampler selects at random a significant percentage of the bags for inspection and that they use a stabbing iron[18] to draw a number of beans from each of the selected bags. The major difference between the methods lies in the number of bags from which the sample comes.

The International Standards Office (ISO) issues a model ordinance and code of practice that most inspectors follow when drawing a sample; the relevant paragraphs state:[19]

17 The International Standards Office provides sampling of cocoa in bulk. While this form of consigning cocoa is currently rare, the importance of transporting cocoa in bulk may grow, requiring different sampling techniques. At the moment some manufacturers transport cocoa in bulk from warehouses to their factories in appropriately designed lorries. Trial shipments of containers with bulk cocoa have recently been made. This results in reduced labour in handling and lower costs in both the freight and in not having to buy the bags themselves.

18 An open hollow tube, which when pushed into a sack allows a quantity of beans to fall inside it and thereby be extracted without having to open the bag.

19 ISO 2292 Cocoa beans – Sampling.

2   Definitions

For the purpose of this International Standard, the following definitions apply:

2.1   consignment: A quantity of beans despatched or transported at one time and covered by a particular contract or shipping document.

2.2   lot: A quantity of merchandise assumed to be of uniform characteristics, taken from the consignment and permitting the quality of the merchandise to be assessed.

Lots should not exceed the sizes specified in 3.2 and each final sample should represent only one lot. . . .

3   General

3.1   Sampling shall be carried out by sampling experts designated or approved by the parties concerned.

3.2   The complete consignment shall be examined in lots of not more than 25 tonnes on despatch and not more than 200 tonnes on arrival.

3.3   The samples shall be representative of the lots defined in 3.2 and, since the composition of the lots is usually to some extent heterogeneous, a bulk sample shall be taken from each lot by drawing a certain number of primary samples and carefully mixing them. The sample for laboratory examination shall be obtained by successive reductions of this bulk sample.

The sampling of beans which are sea-damaged, or otherwise damaged in transit, or in poor condition, as well as loose collected* or rejects, shall be carried out separately from the sampling of sound beans. These products shall not be mixed with sound material, but shall be assessed separately.

3.4   Special care is necessary to ensure that all sampling apparatus is clean, dry and free from foreign odours. Sampling shall be carried out in such a way as to protect the samples of cocoa beans, the sampling instruments and the containers in which the samples are placed, from adventitious contamination such as rain, dust etc.

Matter adhering to the outside of the sampling instrument shall be removed before the instrument is emptied of its contents . . .

5   Method of sampling

. . . A minimum of 300 beans should be taken per tonne or fraction of a tonne.

5.1.1   Bags

Primary samples should be taken from at least one-third of the bags in each lot, the bags being drawn at

---

*   This term is used to designate material which has leaked from its original container but which is not unduly contaminated.

random throughout the lot. They should be taken by
means of an open trier, at random, from the top part,
the centre and the bottom part of bags in good
condition . . .

Some variations to this are, for example, those followed by the Malaysian grading procedure for export cocoa. This is slightly different as part of the process of extracting cocoa involves the checking of the consignment for live infestation mentioned earlier. The procedure here is:

Inspection
10% of all the bags in a lot of Cocoa to be graded are opened
and passed through an insect sieve . . . A sample is drawn as the
beans are passed over the sieve . . .

Sampling
. . . samples are drawn from a further 20% of the bags in the
lot using a probe. Three probes are done for each selected bag,
one at the top, one in the middle and one at the bottom, and
the samples so obtained are added to the samples obtained
from the 10% of the bags earlier inspected, making a 30%
sample in total. All these samples are mixed thoroughly, and
reduced by quartering (i.e. dividing the bulk sample into four
parts and selecting opposite corners to mix and further divide
into four parts) until a sample of about 800 beans is obtained
(i.e. 200 beans in each quarter). A portion of the sampled
beans is sent to the laboratory for further analysis while the
quartered samples are used for determining the bean count
and for the cut-test.

The AFCC and CAL physical cocoa contracts broadly agree as to how the sample should be drawn, although neither specify the actual procedure:

AFCC

Random sealed samples shall be drawn on a "contradictory"
basis [Translator's note: jointly and simultaneously by the
supervisors of the buyer and the seller] on a minimum of 30%
of the sound bags making up the whole of the delivered
quantity . . .[20]

CAL

At least two sealed samples of cocoa beans shall be drawn by
contracting parties from not less than 30 per cent of the sound

---

20   AFCC contract number I, see Appendix I.

bags only weighing not less than 2 kilos nett for each Bill of Lading/Warrant quantity...[21]

CMA

The situation for the CMA is slightly different. The contracts do not state specifically how the inspector should draw the sample, but in the first instance, rely on the services of the FDA, the body responsible for all cocoa entering the United States complying with import and health standards. At the end of the 1980s the FDA said they wished to alter their existing guidelines for drawing samples but have yet to implement any changes. In the FDA's inspection operations manual, the following applies to cocoa beans:[22]

> *Take the square root of the number of bags in the lot to determine the number of subs to collect. Multiply by 3 to determine the number of bags to sample. Each sub will consist 1 pound of beans composited by taking approximately 1/3 lb. from each of 3 bags. Sample a maximum of 75 bags to yield 25 subs.*

Examples perhaps best explain the procedure. If a lot of cocoa was 385 bags, (a 25 tonne delivery from Côte d'Ivoire) the square root gives 20 'subs' (sub-samples), i.e., below the maximum of 25. The number of 'subs' multiplied by 3 gives the number of bags to sample, in this case 60. Each bag has a third of a pound of cocoa drawn from it to form the final sample. If the lot was 1600 bags, the square root, 40, is higher than the maximum number of 'subs'. So the inspectors need only to stab 75 bags to obtain their sample.

Even if the cocoa passes the FDA inspection (or is given a 'green ticket' and the receiver finds the cocoa in accordance with the FDA standards) it may not fulfil the contractual obligations. The receiver then undertakes to draw arbitration samples according to the following CMA guidelines:[23]

> *Four samples of ten pounds each of each disputed lot of cocoa beans are to be drawn and sealed in the presence of a representative of each disputant. This shall be done by each*

---

21 CAL rules and regulations, see Appendix II.

22 'Inspection operations manual', the Food and Drug Administration, September 6, 1977.

23 Guidelines to be observed by master samplers who draw samples for arbitration purposes under the arbitration rules of the Cocoa Merchants' Association of America Inc, August 2, 1982.

*sampler drawing two ten pound samples.... The samples shall
be drawn from a minimum of 20% of the bags and the
sampler must have random access to this percentage. The
samples must be drawn from as many sides of the pile and,
unless otherwise specifically requested, from clean and sound
bags only. Tryer holes must be frayed shut to prevent spillage
of beans.*

The terminal markets pursue different methods for drawing grading
samples. The LCE requirements are:[24]

*... a sealed dock sample of not less than 2 kg in respect of each
parcel. The sample shall have been drawn from not less than
30 per cent of the number of sound bags in the parcel...*

The CSCE stipulate that:[25]

*(d) The minimum number of bags of cocoa to be sampled by
samplers on sampling orders... shall be as follows:*

Chops of	On Original Sampling	On Re-sampling
5 bags or less	Every bag	Every bag
6 to 25 bags	5 bags	5 bags
26 to 50 bags	10 bags	25% of total
51 to 75 bags	15 bags	25% of total bags
76 to 100 bags	20 bags	25% of total bags
101 and more	20% of total bags	25% of total bags

What is essential to the process of drawing a sample is that it represents the consignment. As the analyst only examines relatively few beans
from the drawn sample, the relevance of what is extracted in the first place
becomes even more important. Most samples consist of about two kilos,
i.e. roughly 2000 beans. If the consignment was 200 tonnes from, say
Nigeria, in theory the sample could be made up of less than one bean from
each bag.[26] It may be difficult to justify the quality of a larger parcel on the
basis of such a sample. Only the ISO standards recognise this and specify
the maximum size of the parcel as 200 tonnes. At best, the rest state a
percentage of the bags to be sampled, at worst a limit is put on the
number of bags from which the sample should be drawn, irrespective of
size of the consignment. It is doubtful that a sample taken from 75 bags of
a parcel made up of variable quality that has more than 230 bags will be
meaningful.

24 LCE rules and regulations, see Appendix V.
25 The New York CSCE rules and regulations, see Appendix IV.
26 Exports from Nigeria are in bags that contain 62.5 kilos of cocoa; 3200 bags make
up a 200 tonne parcel.

This is confirmed by a working group of the European Organization of Chocolate, Cake and Biscuit Alliances (CAOBISCO).[27] They have reported there is little statistical difference between a sample taken from 30% of the bags to that drawn from just 25 bags, providing that the quality of the consignment is homogeneous. If the quality is variable within the parcel, a 30% sample will give a better average than the 25 bag method, but the analysis would not show the range or distribution of the variation of quality – an important factor to the chocolate manufacturers. Ascertaining the distribution of the quality is possible by individually checking the 25 samples (drawn separately from the 25 bags). Those involved in checking the quality of cocoa beans will understand the practical difficulty involved; effectively multiplying their work 25 times, although the cost of sampling is less.

If the parcel of cocoa is truly uniform throughout, a sample could be taken from a single bag; further, if the quality is totally homogeneous, then in theory only one bean need be analysed to determine the quality of the parcel. This, of course, is absurd. Variations occur within export parcels for two reasons in particular. In countries where it is smallholders who predominantly grow cocoa, shippers will make up export consignments from farmers who may grow the cocoa in different regions and whose beans naturally contain some differences. Providing the growers prepare the cocoa in a similar fashion, buyers accept such variations as normal, and indeed welcome it. Natural variations between smallholders' cocoas help to blend in differences each may have and to produce a more uniform product. The second reason is less acceptable to the final user. It is when exporters take advantage of the grading and contract standards to blend good quality cocoa with lower grades in order to sell a larger amount of an acceptable quality standard. Such practice dilutes the better quality with lower and may give the final receiver trouble in processing the parcel. This practice is not new, in 1914 the following was noted:[28]

> ... *We have good reason to believe that some merchants buy cacao which they know to be diseased or unfermented or mouldy, and deliberately mix it with good cacao.*

What was true then has even more relevance today, modern processing techniques depend more on the homogeneity of parcels. This, together with many of the butter pressers also manufacturing couverture[29]

27   Reported to the ICCO Expert Working Group on Quality, December 1990.
28   Booth N P and Knapp A W: 'The qualities in cacao desired by manufacturers' (paper given at the third international congress of Tropical Agriculture), June 1914.
29   Basically chocolate, normally milk chocolate with at least 31% cocoa solids.

for the chocolate factories, means that increasingly the pressers also need better quality cocoa. Unfortunately mixing cocoa will continue until the grading and contract standards alter to deter the practice of deliberate adulteration of cocoa. The prospect of manufacturers paying reasonable premiums for unmixed cocoa is unlikely.

The cut-test: procedure, fault definition and standards

Once the analysts have the samples, the most common form of quality test used for cocoa beans is the macrobiological examination called the cut-test.

Practically all cocoa is subjected to the cut-test. It stems from recommendations made in 1938 by the *Office International du Cacao et du Chocolat*, who proposed a system in which points are given or subtracted for the dimensions of the beans, their colour, odour and the absence of imperfect beans.[30]

Most exporting countries' authorities specify standards dependent on the cut-test, as do normal physical cocoa contracts. The FDA of the United States also use this test, amongst others that they perform on cocoa, to see that the parcel is fit to enter their country. The LCE grades cocoa according to this assessment. The cut-test is quick, requiring little equipment or training and is very common in the cocoa trade. Although widely used, interpretation of the results varies from one agency to another, as do specifications in the sale contracts.

The cut-test provides an assessment of the beans from which analysts may infer certain characteristics of the cocoa. Such inferred quality characteristics provide the analyst with only an indication of the quality of beans, as these may differ with subsequent checks designed to measure the characteristics more directly. Despite this, the processors and chocolate manufacturers still use the cut-test to provide an initial indication of the quality of the cocoa.

When butter pressers buy cocoa the cut-tests only show by inference what concerns them in particular, the yield of butter in the cocoa. Apart from the yield, other characteristics of the beans that interest the pressers are the hardness and melting point of the cocoa butter and the colour potential of the beans to make specifically coloured powders. Although the

30 Some of the parts of the original standards still exist. For example, standards adopted in Nigeria and South West Cameroon included that a sample of 300 beans must weigh at least 11 ounces for it not to be considered 'light'. The Nigerian and nearby Cameroonian mid-crop (as opposed to the main crop) distinguished by smaller sized beans is still called a light crop.

processors check these attributes, many of the characteristics depend on the origin type of cocoa. This allows the processors to buy those growths that have the favoured characteristics without specifying the attributes in the contract. Much of their buying strategies depends on their experience with earlier deliveries of cocoa, again despite the variation between parcels that can occur when dealing with an agricultural product. As a result, their purchase contracts are still subject to the quality assessment by cut-test even though they use other analyses to check on the cocoa's characteristics. As their buying strategies largely depend on the results of earlier findings, consistency of the cocoa purchased becomes essential.

Although the chocolate manufacturers account for a smaller tonnage of cocoa beans than the butter pressers they also choose to buy cocoa on the basis of the characteristics of previous parcels. Sales to them also depend on the basic checks of the cut-test, but chocolatiers rely on specific growths retaining the attributes in previous parcels; specifically those characteristics that affect the cocoa liquor. As mentioned above these characteristics are those of flavour and colour. Certainly flavour is a difficult item to specify and, as such, forms no part of the cocoa sale contract. The chocolatier knows that certain growths will usually give him the flavours that he needs for his recipes and he selects accordingly. Like the processors, the factories need supplies of cocoa with consistent quality attributes.

Procedure

In its basic form the analyst cuts 300 beans lengthwise to expose the maximum internal surface of the two cotyledons. The analyst examines the cut beans in a good light and without artificial aid and records (as a percentage) the number of defects. What constitutes a defective bean varies depending on the trade body or grading panel concerned. Broadly speaking, defective beans are those that are either internally mouldy[31] insect damaged, slaty (i.e. the cotyledons are a grey colour indicating unfermented beans), or germinated. In addition to the cut-test a full analysis of this type will include the bean count. In this part of the test, the analyst counts the number of beans for a given weight, usually 300 grams. The result is commonly expressed as the number of beans for 100 grams, providing an idea of the average size of the beans. Buyers prefer parcels with large beans as they will contain more nib weight with a higher fat content, and less shell than those made up of small beans.[32]

31   Note that William Hughes in 1672 also recommended the inspection of the internal parts of the beans.
32   Another fact not lost on early consumers: see the seventeenth and eighteenth century quotes at the beginning of this chapter.

The advantage of the cut-test and bean count is that they require no specialised equipment other than a knife and a set of scales accurate to half a gram over one kilo. With adequate training an intelligent layman can become tolerably expert within a short period. Despite its universal use there are a number of different ways of carrying out the test. The ISO state the following:[33]

> *The Cut test*
> *1. The sample of Cocoa beans shall be thoroughly mixed and then quartered down to leave a heap of slightly more than 300 beans. The first 300 beans shall then be counted off, irrespective of size, shape and condition.*
> *2. The 300 beans shall be cut lengthwise through the middle and examined.*
> *3. Separate counts shall be made of the number of beans which are defective in that they are mouldy, slaty, insect damaged, germinated or flat. Where a bean is defective in more than one respect, only one defect shall be counted, and the defect to be counted shall be the defect which occurs first in the foregoing list of defects. The 'foregoing list of defects' is shown under 'Definition of faults in cocoa beans by the cut test cocoa beans'.*
> *4. The examination for this test shall be carried out in good daylight or equivalent artificial light, and the results for each kind of defect shall be expressed as a percentage of the 300 beans examined.*

Most analysts follow the above method but there are variations, notably that of the FDA. The following procedure was given to a cocoa trade representative by the New York import district office of the FDA in 1982 as the official FDA policy when examining cocoa bean samples:

> *1. Macroscopic examination*
> *Mix the sample thoroughly and count out 100 beans. Crack open each bean and break in to small pieces so as to expose the entire internal area of the beans* Examine the beans in a good light without the aid of a magnifier** . . .*

---

33 ISO document number 1114.

* This may be accomplished with facility by means of a cracking board made from a 15 inch square sheet of $\frac{1}{4}$ inch aluminium, transite, or plywood by drilling 100 $\frac{7}{8}$ inch holes, equally spaced and arranged in 10 rows of 10 holes each. Place the board on a large sheet of paper on a hard surface. Scatter the beans on the board to fill the depressions. Sweep the excess beans off with the hand and ultimately adjust the empty or double filled holes so that each of the 100 holes contain one bean. Crack open each bean by placing on the bean an iron bolt about $\frac{1}{2}$ inch in diameter and about 3 inches long and gently tapping the head of the bolt with a hammer.

** Magnifiers may be used by experienced analysts to confirm the identification of conditions previously ascertained by the unaided eye. Less experienced analysts

Definition of faults in cocoa beans detected by the cut-test

While the bean count indicates the average size of the beans, the cut-test provides indications on two aspects of the parcel's quality: its degree of fermentation and whether the flavour is likely to have been tainted. Although neither of these assessments directly measures the attributes of flavour and yield, they give pointers towards certain flavour characteristics. The ISO define nine categories of defects for cocoa beans. Their definitions are common throughout the cocoa trade, even though not all are used in grading standards. The important ones in ISO 2451 are:

> *3.3.1 mouldy bean: A cocoa bean on the internal parts of which mould is visible to the naked eye.*
> *3.3.2 slaty bean: A cocoa bean which shows a slaty colour over half or more of the surface...*
> *3.3.3 insect-damaged bean: A cocoa bean the internal parts of which contain insects at any stage of development, or have been attacked by insects which have caused damage visible to the naked eye*
> *NOTE – For the purpose of this International Standard the term "insects" includes mites.*
> *3.3.4 germinated bean: A cocoa bean the shell of which has been pierced, slit or broken by the growth of the seed germ.*
> *3.3.5 flat bean: A cocoa bean of which the two cotyledons are so thin that it is not possible to obtain a cotyledon surface by cutting.*

In addition to these, there are six other general requirements, also common to many grading specifications. The first is that the cocoa should not have any abnormal or foreign odours, in particular that of smoke. The cocoa should not be adulterated in any way to alter either its quality or quantity composition, and there should be no foreign matter with the cocoa. The cocoa should be 'reasonably free' of live insects and also of broken beans, pieces of shell etc. Lastly, the moisture content should not be higher that 7.5%.

While defining nine categories of defective beans, the ISO grading standards use only five of them. The ISO group them into three: beans that are mouldy, beans that are slaty and beans that are insect damaged, germinated or flat.

Similarly the FDA define more categories of defective cocoa than they use. Continuing the FDA procedure of the cut-test, given in 1982, is:

> *...and classify into the following categories:*
> *a. Slightly moldy – beans with (1) small, localized areas of*

may use the magnifying instrument initially in order to become familiar with the appearance of the various conditions encountered.

mold, usually in the germ end, (2) localized spot of spores
around the germ or radicle, (3) light feathery mold, and (4)
exterior mold only.
b. Moldy – beans with extensive mold. i.e., exceeding the
amount described above under a. "Slightly Moldy." Do not
class as "moldy", those beans which have a grayish-blue slaty
appearance but contain no mold filaments.
c. Insect infested – beans containing insects, insect tunnels,
insect excreta or webbing. Include a statement on the kind and
approximate number of insects present.
d. Both moldy and insect infested.
e. Rusty – beans with a red-brown encrustation on the outer
surface of the nibs. Occasionally this "rust" is found in the
folds of the cotyledons.
Report results in the following table:

Sub. #	I	2	3	Etc.	Avg.
# of insect-infested beans					
# of moldy beans					
# of beans moldy and insect infested					
Total rejects					
# of slightly moldy beans					
No. of rusty beans					

Although carefully defined, the FDA only use the first two to decide if
the cocoa may enter the United States. Slightly mouldy or 'rusty' beans
remain recorded but unused in the classification.

Bean count

Neither the FDA or ISO consider the bean count in their grading systems.
Only the CAL defines the way to conduct a bean count analysis.

To ascertain bean count, a sample of not less than 300
grammes of whole beans, irrespective of size but not including
flat beans, will be counted to obtain the number of beans per
100 grammes.

Note the exclusion of the flat beans. In the past this was a source of
dispute between parties conducting tests independently from one another.
One would include the flat beans in their count and the other would not,
choosing to classify them in the cut-test. Both thought that they had made
the same test and considered that the other either could not count or that
they were looking for some advantage.

Cut-test standards

Appendix VI shows the application of most grading standards in the world, all dependent on the cut-test. Included in the faults is one category that has not been discussed; violet beans. As mentioned earlier unfermented Forastero beans are a slaty/grey colour. Partially fermented, they turn a purple/violet colour and an excessive number of these may also be considered a fault. The Ecuadorean grading standards include this as a measure of quality to encourage their growers to ferment their cocoa properly.

The word 'defectives' and the term 'defective beans' have a particular meaning and should be used with care. In particular the grading standards of the CAL and AFCC both use this, or its equivalent in French, to mean cocoa that is either internally mouldy and/or insect infested; with the AFCC including flat beans in their definition of 'defective'.

The limitations of the cut-test and ideas on its replacement

It is extraordinary that a product so advanced in its trading techniques and so dependent on its subtle and gentle flavour still depends on quite basic quality assessments. Like many things in cocoa, railing against contemporary quality and its assessment is not new. Here is an extract from the preface of a book published in 1913:[34]

> *What we particularly want to avoid, . . . are the uneven and unsightly rows of cacao samples to be seen on the counter of any broker or dealer when offering such produce for sale. Anyone with a month's experience of the cacao trade will know the sorts of lots I refer to; beans bright, dull, or grey mouldy and reddish; dark beans, black, mouldy and fiery red lying side by side, and far too often mixed in the same tray or heap. Here is a lot with a thin, light, almost straw-coloured shell nearly as pale as cardamoms, there are some Haitians or San Domingo, with a coating of mould over them that would be a credit to a bottle of fine old crusty port. In any case no two bags or trays are alike, and the samples themselves show a most regrettable mixture of colours and qualities that should not be, since such a defect could be so easily avoided, . . .*

Although the trade has moved forward since 1913, the foundation stone of cocoa quality assessment, the cut-test has distinct limitations. These primarily have two shortcomings: the subjective nature of the test and the faults detected do not directly measure the true status of

---

34   Smith Harold H (Ed): 'The fermentation of cacao', 1913.

the cocoa. The fact that the results of the test are in percentages imbues the process with a sense of scientific exactitude that does not bear up under scrutiny. Even at a basic level, although most aspects of the test depend on eyesight in detecting faults there are no criteria given on required eyesight standards for the analysts. Also, the amount and quality of the light under which the cut-test should be conducted are never specified.

It may be that the next 'cut-test' should move from the general domain of cocoa users into the laboratory where the technicians assess the quality of so many other commodities. The probable outcome is that the successor to the current cocoa quality analysis may require a practical combination of laboratory work and assessments made on-site in the warehouse or dockside.

The importance of analysing 300 beans

If one classified cocoa into three grades of defective beans, the first of 0−5%, the second of 6−10% and the third of anything above 10% defectives,[35] what are the chances of an analyst correctly classifying cocoa from cutting only 100 beans? This is a fair question. Most analysts, faced with cutting 300 beans will divide them into three separate tests, each of 100 beans. Three hundred beans laid out on a table top take up too much space. Some, especially if there is a large number of samples to check, may decide that the result from the first 100 beans is good enough to decide on the quality of the cocoa. Although in the process of reviewing their practice, the LCE is one such, the cocoa graders officially assess cocoa quality on 100 beans. Unfortunately there is a good chance that such an analysis will not provide an accurate classification of the sample. Figure 8.3 shows (by the mathematics of statistical sampling) the degree of certainty of correctly classifying cocoa on a 100-bean cut-test, assuming the even distribution of defective beans within the sample.

The figure may disturb those who depend on analysing cocoa quality by a cut-test of 100 beans. For example, if the analyst found six defectives (6% defective) and classified the cocoa as fair fermented (FF) there is only a 55% chance of her being correct. There is a 41% chance of the cocoa being 'good fermented' (GF) and a 4% chance of it being fair average quality (FAQ). Similarly, if 11% defectives resulted from the analysis, there

35   This is not an arbitrary selection. One standard for cocoa, adopted by many, is the 'good fermented' (GF) and 'fair fermented' (FF) classification. GF beans have 5% or fewer defects, while FF classified cocoa has between 6% and 10% defectives. The cocoa trade commonly calls cocoa above 10% defective as 'fair average quality' (FAQ).

210

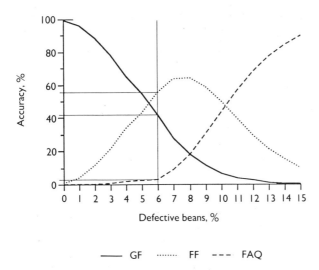

——— GF ········ FF --- FAQ

8.3 Accuracy in classifying the quality of cocoa from cutting 100 beans.

is a 40% chance, in other words a very good chance, that the cocoa is FF and not FAQ, and there is an outside chance that it is actually GF. This has more significance because the grading panels of the LCE designate cocoa as 'non-tenderable' if it is 11% defective or above.

Overall the degree of certainty improves dramatically with the analysis of 200 beans. Good fermented cocoa may be classified with over 90% confidence with up to 4% defectives. Between 7–9% defectives may be considered as FF with over 85% confidence, and anything above 13% defective has over 90% chance of being FAQ. The areas of uncertainty remain at the cross-over points between the grading classifications. A sample showing 11% defectives has less than a two-thirds chance of being correctly graded.

While the confidence improves further with the analysis of another 100 beans, the same degree of doubt hangs over the cross-over points from good to fair fermented and from 10% defectives to fair average quality. Samples containing 6% and 11% defectives have only just over 70% chance of being correct with the analysis of 300 beans, see Fig. 8.4. It is significant though that confidence in correctly classifying other percentages of defectives is high.

The overall result of the above statistical examination is that if the first 100 beans give more than 3% defectives, the analyst must continue. Finding only 3% defectives the analyst has a 90% chance of correctly grading the cocoa as GF. Likewise if she cuts 15% or more she has a similar chance of correctly calling the cocoa FAQ. Any results in between

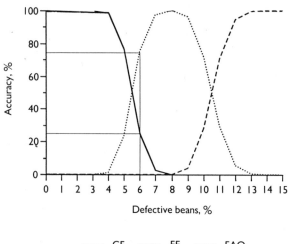

Defective beans, %

—— GF ········ FF ---- FAQ

8.4 Accuracy in classifying the quality of cocoa from cutting 300 beans.

these two figures require additional cutting to provide an acceptable degree of accuracy.

Mould

The main reason for checking the presence of mould in cocoa is that it affects the flavour of the product. Secondly, moulds pose health hazards, principally as some produce mycotoxins, although in recent times levels of pathogenic mycotoxins in cocoa have not transferred to the finished product in significant amounts.[36] While methods exist in measuring mycotoxins[37] the cut-test does not address these two areas directly at all. Moulds become discernible to the palate at concentrations of 10^4 colony-forming units per gram while they are only visible to the naked eye at concentrations of between 10^5 to 10^6. The potential for dangerous mycotoxins to develop may take place at concentrations as low as 10^2.

36   Aflatoxin, caused by some members of the Aspergillus family, and probably the most infamous of all the pathogenic mycotoxins has been found in cocoa beans, albeit at low levels. In 1980, ochratoxin was also found in cocoa beans. In both cases their incidence was reduced substantially by processing. 'Survey of mycotoxins in the United Kingdom', HMSO, 1980.

37   Scott P M: 'Modified method for the determination of mycotoxins in cocoa beans', Journal of the Association of Official Analytical Chemists 1973 (56) 4 and Lenovich L M and Hurst W J: 'Production of aflatoxin in cocoa beans', Journal of the Association of Official Analytical Chemists 1979 (62) 5.

That, at the moment, cocoa beans are not a source of significant pathogenic mycotoxins is no reason for complacency.[38]

The amount of mould detected within a bean is not measured by the cut-test. An analyst has to class a bean as mouldy whether it has only a few mycelial strands visible or if the bean virtually exploded with sporangia when cut. The mouldiness of a parcel with only say, two or three per cent of heavily mouldy beans may be much worse than one with five to six lightly mouldy beans. The cut-test does not allow for variations in concentration, and even if it did, it would be extremely difficult to quantify visually for the differences.

Not only is the amount of mould within a bean not measured, the cut-test will not reveal the type of mould infecting the bean. CA Thorold[39] identified 192 different moulds growing in processed cocoa, many of which may not produce pathogenic mycotoxins, but have varying effects on the flavour, some more detrimental than others. Moulds on the outside of the beans also have differing consequences; for example *Aspergillus fumigatus* attacks the cellulose and pentosans in the shell, especially the weakened tissue opposite the tip of the radicle, and allows the entrance of other moulds to the inside of the bean. *Aspergillus chevalieri* has the ability to develop in beans with a lower moisture content than others in the *Aspergillus* family, and therefore presents a particular threat. In 1931 Ciferri[40] found that one type of mould, *Actinomyces*, was very objectionable in cocoa as it gave a pronounced and disagreeable musty odour.[41] Later work, conducted during the 1930s, concluded that *Actinomyces* was unusual in cocoa, but that three variants of it were isolated and named *Actinomyces cacaoi* I, II and III.

External moulds can present difficulties for workers who handle beans, especially for those emptying bags at a processing plant. The dust etc thrown up by the beans pouring into a hopper may include significant

---

38   In the early 1840s there were 'a few cases' in which sailors and convicts died after drinking chocolate prepared by the government chocolate mills in Deptford. An analysis revealed that the cocoa was milled complete with its shell. The interpretation by Dr Ure was that 'the chocolate had many sharp spiculae of the cocoa bean husks and that hence, when swallowed they were calculated to form mechanically irritating lodgements in the villous coats of the stomach and bowels, whereby they could produce the morbid effects certified by several naval surgeons'. (Supplement to Dr Ure's Dictionary of Arts, Manufactures and Mines, Ure A 1844.) A more plausible explanation is that moulds growing on the outside of the shell caused the illnesses. The problem ceased once the mills only processed the cocoa nibs.

39   Thorold C A: 'Diseases of cocoa', 1975.

40   Ciferri R: 'Studies on cacao' Journal of the Department of Agriculture, Puerto Rico 1931 (15) 223.

41   Actinomyces is present in the earth and is responsible for the 'earthy' smell.

amounts of moulds, which can affect the work-force. Again, *Aspergillus* provides the main danger.

The visual detection of mould may also depend on its stage of development. For example, at the time the mould produces sporangia it is easier to detect than at other stages. The fruiting bodies make it more visible. There is also some evidence that if a sample is thoroughly dry the mould becomes more difficult to see as the mycelia strands on the surface of the cotyledon become desiccated. Despite its dryness and the difficulty in its detection, the mould is still present. Even if the mould were dead, any mycotoxin produced when it was alive would still be contained in the bean.

At the beginning of the 1970s work carried out in the United States tried to isolate a way of determining the level of mould in cocoa by laboratory methods. The initial work involved measuring the increase of methyl ketones in the beans.[42] While the work showed that mouldy beans recorded higher levels of methyl ketones than uninfected beans, no calibration was made to determine the amount of mould. Although further work may lead to a graduated system, this laboratory based detection would not be able to distinguish between different types of mould.

In recent years manufacturers have developed the use of near infrared (NIR) technology for analysing the composition of cocoa products. Although this is a laboratory based system requiring expensive equipment, its advantage is speed. Once calibrated, the laboratory can execute the tests quickly.

A third possibility exists that is currently under development at the Central Science Laboratory in Slough, UK. Initially developed for detecting mould in grain storage it appears to have application for cocoa beans. The technique involves an immunological approach; fungi are used as antigens to induce an immune response in an animal, thereby producing antibodies which will allow both the estimation of amount and identification of the fungus present in the grain or cocoa.[43] The advantage of such a system is that it could be tailored to identify specific moulds, as well as being able to show the amount of fungus present. It could be calibrated to detect mould at concentrations of 100 colony-forming units per gram, well below detectable levels by sight. Best of all, the assay is quick and is intended to be portable. Although not yet available, the intention is to market test kits for use in the field. This test is more in line with the requirements of the manufacturer while being affordable to those in the cocoa chain.

42   Hansen A P and Keeney P G: 'Comparison of carbonyl compounds in moldy and non-moldy cocoa beans' Journal of Food Science 1970 (35) 37–40.

43   Banks J N, Cox Sarah J, Clarke J H, Shamsi R H and Northway Beverley J: 'Towards the immunological detection of field and storage fungi' in press for 'Modern methods in food mycology'.

Insect infestation

Determining the level of insect infestation requires more than the inspection of cut beans. As mentioned above, insects may not be within the beans themselves but may certainly be in the bags. An effective test for infestation should therefore include the emptying of bags and sieving of its contents, along the lines of the Malaysian standard. Such a process would provide a more complete assessment of the levels of infestation.

Bean size

A sieving operation could also double as a way of determining the bean size.[44] By passing the beans through a series of graded meshes the size of the bean could be determined, as is done with grading of nuts. Such a method would have the added benefit of showing whether or not the beans were relatively uniform in size, an important factor for processors at the roasting stage.

If the current weighing of beans continues it may be of benefit to remove the shell first. This would give more meaningful results for two reasons. Firstly, a significant proportion of the moisture content of the bean is in the shell[45], removing it also eliminates most of the differences caused by the varying moisture contents within beans. Secondly, different growths of beans have different shell weights. In removing the shells and weighing the nibs directly, comparison of yields from different origins become possible and commonplace. It is not the size or weight of the bean that matters, it is the amount of nib contained in the bean that concerns the manufacturer.

Degree of fermentation

Unfermented cocoa has a lower value compared with fermented beans. The precursors to the chocolate flavour are not formed and such cocoa has limited uses. The use is restricted principally to cocoa butter; the cocoa cake cannot be used, and a manufacturer cannot make chocolate from such cocoa. That said, setting an approved level of fermentation is

---

44 Proposals for measuring the size of the beans is, like many things in cocoa, not an innovation. The Office International du Cacao et du Chocolat recommended such a system in 1938, and West African cocoa adopted a standard bean size of 22 mm in length and 8 mm thick.

45 Dried beans normally contain not less than 5% moisture of the cotyledons, and 12% in the shells, giving an average value of 6–7%. Theimer O F: 'On the storage of raw cocoa beans in silo compartments', Int Choc Rev 1958 (13) 122–126.

difficult. Different processors like varying degrees of fermentation of the cocoa, principally because certain shades of cocoa powder colour are possible with differently fermented cocoa. Generally, more fermentation is preferable than less, although over fermentation will induce a 'hammy' smell, caused by the production of ammonia in the ferment. Determining the level of fermentation may still depend on a visual assessment of the colour of cut beans, although the current practice of only including the slate coloured beans limits the test. The partially fermented beans, showing purple or violet in the Forastero type, should also be included in the examination. Laboratory methods do exist in determining the amounts of flavonoids[46], as well as anthocyanidines[47], but as of yet do not exist in a useful or practical field kit.

Free fatty acid content

The level of free fatty acids (FFA) in the fat of cocoa beans measures the rancidity of the cocoa. High levels of FFA in cocoa are not acceptable, and in Europe manufacturers may not legally sell cocoa butter containing over 1.75% FFA. The presence of large amounts of FFAs in the fat of cocoa beans tends to indicate other problems with the cocoa; for example either it has been wet for too long and/or it has a high percentage of mould. Fresh cocoa beans should not contain more than 1.0%, and certainly not more than 1.75% of FFA.

Testing for the FFA content remains in the laboratory with no immediate expectation of its release into the general workplace. Despite this, its inclusion into a general test on cocoa beans should be considered as it is a pointer to other faults of cocoa.

Moisture content

The ISO issue a methodology to follow in determining the moisture content of beans[48] that requires laboratory conditions. The technology to do this test on site is now available; this will enable results to be obtained much faster. Such electronic moisture meters allow the inspector to check the moisture content in different parts of the pile; an important factor as often the water will migrate towards the top or to a particular side of a pile of bags containing damp cocoa beans. The fact that the test may be

---

46   The compounds in unfermented beans that make up the final brown colour of cocoa.

47   The pigment responsible for the violet colour in semi-fermented beans.

48   ISO 2291.

done where the cocoa lies is also important as the moisture content of the sample undoubtedly changes from the time of sampling to when the analyst tests it. High moisture readings, i.e., anything above 7.5%, will necessitate the drying of the cocoa.

Organoleptic test

Lastly, the new 'cut-test' should include a controlled organoleptic analysis. The purpose of such a test would be to evaluate the cocoa for other 'off-flavours'. This would embrace the question of smoke damaged beans but should include others, such as the presence of phenols, caused by cocoa stored on wooden pallets previously treated by chlorophenols. A musty smell or flavour may indicate oxidation of the cocoa butter within the beans, another shortcoming. Whether the parcel has a fully developed chocolate flavour should not necessarily form part of the test as what constitutes this varies from one manufacturer to another. What all agree on is that they do not like certain recognised 'off-flavours'.

Factors important to the butter presser

Although the traditional butter pressers are becoming increasingly involved in the manufacture of chocolate or couverture, they still have particular interests in the cocoa bean that others consider to a lesser degree. Quite simply it is how much cocoa product will the beans yield when processed, and what proportion of butter to powder will result. To be expected, not all cocoa beans provide the same return, a fact that the processing industry follows very closely in monitoring the quality of the cocoa received by the factory.

Calculating this return requires more information than provided by the cut-test. The first consideration is how much of the bean the processor is unable to use, effectively a waste product. Two items make up the waste material: the cocoa bean shell[49] and the moisture content. A third may exist for those beans that have a high level of FFA as the processor may have to remove this component from the butter to satisfy government sale regulations, but most beans do not fall into this category. While the bean count gives an indication of the size of the beans and therefore the amount

---

49   The shell does contain a small amount of fat, amounting to some 0.74% of the total fat content of the bean. Its characteristics are different to the nib fat, being softer and containing high levels of FFA. Some do not use it at all, while others will only add it to cocoa butter up to the levels found naturally in the whole bean.

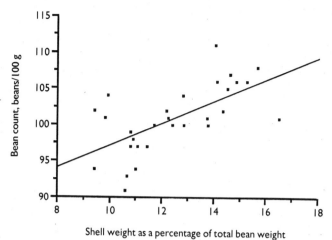

Source: ICM, Amsterdam.

8.5 Relationship between bean count and shell weight for imports into Amsterdam during 1989 from a selection of cocoa exporting ports.

of shell surrounding the nib, it is only an indication. The processors need more exact data, and obtain it by removing and weighing the shell from a sample of beans. This gives a figure, usually expressed as the percentage, by weight, of the shell compared with the whole bean. Figure 8.5 shows the tenuous relationship between the bean count and shell weight of imports into Amsterdam during 1989 from a number of shipment ports. Although a trend is discernible (higher bean counts have more shell) the processor cannot use the bean count exactly to calculate the yield.

If the processors know the percentage of waste, they can arrive at the amount of the bean useful in manufacturing (the dry nib weight) by subtracting the waste from 100. The final piece of information needed to work out the yield is the fat content within the nib. This figure cannot be derived and may only be obtained by laboratory analysis. While each processor will conduct their own analysis of cocoa purchased, Table 8.3 compares the yields from some origin countries with cocoa discharged in Amsterdam during 1988/89.

The first three columns of percentage figures in the Table show the composition of beans. From these three columns, the yields from each origin cocoa is derived in the following manner. By subtracting the nib fat from 100 gives the fourth column, the percentage of dry solids in the nib. The fifth column, '10% powder', requires more explanation. All cocoa powder contains a proportion of cocoa fat, the most common being '10/12'[50], and is assumed to be made in this calculation. As well as 10% of

50   In other words the powder has between 10–12% cocoa butter, although with modern processing techniques it will have just over 10% rather than nearer 12%.

Table 8.3 Intrinsic values of cocoa beans from different origins

%

Country	Waste	Nib weight	Nib fat	Nib solids	10% Powder	Remain butter	Yield
Bahia	19.73	80.27	53.37	46.63	54.22	47.87	81.95
Cameroon	16.45	83.55	53.84	46.16	53.67	48.39	85.27
Côte d'Ivoire	17.36	82.64	54.66	45.34	52.72	49.31	84.32
Ghana	16.75	83.25	55.17	44.83	52.13	49.88	84.92
Indonesia	17.39	82.61	51.20	48.80	56.74	45.44	84.41
Malaysia	20.00	80.00	53.86	46.14	53.66	48.40	81.64
Nigeria	16.69	83.31	53.16	46.84	54.47	47.63	85.06
PNG	22.20	77.80	54.10	45.90	53.37	48.68	79.39

Source: ICM, Amsterdam.

butter, the powder also picks up some 4% of moisture, therefore the final powder weighs 14% more than the dry nib solids. The percentage of powder, reduced by its water content, and deducted from 100 provides the figure for the remaining butter. The yield is the dry nib weight plus the moisture content of the powder.

The resulting figures show that on the basis of these figures cocoa from Cameroon gives the best yield, followed by Nigerian and Ghanaian beans. According to this, with all things being equal, it makes sense to use Cameroon cocoa as it gives the best yields. While this is the case, the calculation of the cocoas' intrinsic value is not yet over as the price for powder is not the same as for butter. Table 8.4 shows the effect of the rankings of the cocoas when annual average prices for the products are included.

Here there is a different picture, with Ghana cocoa now intrinsically worth more than others, followed by Cameroon, Côte d'Ivoire and Nigeria. The promotion from third to first lies in the high fat content of the Ghanaian bean, together with its reasonable nib weight. The last column shows theoretical discounts of other cocoas compared with Ghana, solely based on the differences in yield, taking into account the value of the constituents. This shows that for the powder/butter ratios prevalent in 1989 Ghana cocoa is worth more than the other growths.

The average annual figures given in Table 8.4 suggest that the yields for the different growths remain constant during the year. This is not so – for each origin both the weight of the beans and their fat content vary during the crop year. The important factors determining these appear to be the amount and distribution of rainfall and the temperature during the development of the pod. High temperatures with lower rainfall will produce smaller beans that also have a lower fat content. In addition, as

Table 8.4

Country	%			Sterling values			
	10% Powder	Remain butter	Yield	Butter value	Powder value	Gross value	Discount to Ghana
Bahia	54.22	47.87	81.95	834	304	1138	−66
Cameroon	53.67	48.39	85.27	878	313	1191	−14
Côte d'Ivoire	52.72	49.31	84.32	885	304	1189	−16
Ghana	52.13	49.88	84.92	902	303	1204	0
Indonesia	56.74	45.44	84.41	815	327	1142	−62
Malaysia	53.66	48.40	81.64	841	300	1140	−64
Nigeria	54.47	47.63	85.06	861	317	1178	−26
PNG	53.37	48.68	79.39	822	290	1112	−92

Average annual product values for 1989

Butter	£2171/tonne
Powder	£698/tonne

Source: ICM, Amsterdam and Gill & Duffus.

the trees' reserves become depleted during the course of the harvesting period the beans taken towards the end of the crop also tend to be smaller. If the grower harvests unripe pods, the immature beans are not only smaller but their fat content is also lower.

Naturally the yield and return is not the only reason why some growths of cocoa have a higher market value than others. For the processor the type of butter, its hardness and melting point are important, as well as the colour of the resulting cocoa powder. Remaining questions concerning the consistency of both its quality and delivery contribute towards the desirability of certain growths to others and react on the important supply and demand for the cocoa.

Factors important to the chocolate manufacturer

All of the above is also relevant to the chocolatier. To make good chocolate the beans must be wholesome, the quality must be consistent,[51] there should be a good yield from the beans and the cocoa butter must

51 Not only from parcel to parcel but also within individual consignments. For example, no more than 12% of the beans should be outside the range ± one-third of the average weight. While the chocolate manufacturers state this as an ideal, at the moment it is rare to see a physical cocoa contract including such a term.

have suitable characteristics; i.e., it must be hard. There is one other overriding requirement of the cocoa. Unsurprisingly, it is the flavour of the resulting product which is of prime importance to the manufacturer. Manufacturers check the flavour of a consignment by tasting either the cocoa liquor or the actual chocolate made from the beans. This is usually done by a panel of half a dozen or so expert tasters. They look for a well developed chocolate flavour and the absence of 'off-flavours'. In addition, each manufacturer will look for particular ancillary flavours needed to make their proprietary chocolate. Chocolate manufacturers do not say which of these supplementary flavours they like, preferring to guard their recipes rather than inform their suppliers. In fact, growers have little control over the ancillary flavours, either their cocoa has them or it doesn't; the best they may do is to ensure that the cocoa is not masked by any 'off-flavours'.

Off-flavours

There are four main groups of off-flavours that chocolatiers dislike in cocoa beans. The first can occur with artificially dried cocoa, which may result in the cocoa picking up the smell of the smoke. There is nothing the manufacturer may do to remove this unwanted flavour, blending the chocolate or beans is likely to spoil all of the batch. It is one of the worst of the 'off-flavours'. The second is when the cocoa has high levels of mould; this too, will also result in spoilt chocolate. In guidelines issued by The Cocoa, Chocolate and Confectionery Alliance, beans with above 3% mould (as measured in a cut-test) will give mouldy off-flavours.[52] The third concerns acidic off-flavours. During fermentation the beans and mucilage form two acids: acetic and lactic. Low levels of acetic acid are normal within cocoa but excessive levels of lactic acid will spoil the flavour of the chocolate. Neutralising the acid will neither remove the acidic flavour nor improve the chocolate flavour, which tends to be poor in acidic cocoa. The last group concerns bitterness and astringency. The chocolate flavour involves some bitter taste, but if the beans are poorly fermented this develops into flavours that the manufacturer is unable to remove. Again, just 3% of slaty beans can give such flavours. Another source of astringent flavours comes from germinated beans. This has been known for some time. In 1724 de Chélus wrote;

> If the Kernels {beans} have not sweat {fermented}
> enough, ... they are subject to sprit {sprout} or germe, which
> makes them bitter, and good for nothing.[53]

52 'Cocoa beans chocolate manufacturers' quality requirements', The Cocoa Chocolate and Confectionery Alliance, 1984.

53 Ibid de Chélus: Brooks (Dr) R (trans), 1724.

Wholesomeness

This somewhat old-fashioned word, imprecise as it is, best describes the need for cocoa, along with all other foodstuffs, to be free of any impurities which could injure the health of the consumer. These include the levels of pesticides, insecticides, bacteria and heavy metals. The question of moulds and mycotoxins in cocoa has been already dealt with and so are not repeated here.

As mentioned earlier, over recent years people in chocolate consuming countries have become more health conscious and they, and their governments, pay more attention to the content of the food they eat. Increasing attention is paid to pesticide and insecticide levels, some of which may affect cocoa. This can take two forms; either the type of product used leaves residues that impair the chocolate flavour, or the levels exceed residue limits set by government or international convention. The two main international bodies advising on pesticide levels are FAO/WHO Codex Committee on Pesticide Residues and the FAO/WHO Expert Committee on Pesticide Residues.

All cocoa has colonies of bacteria, attracted by and developed during the fermentation. Cocoa free from bacteria does not exist and, as with mould, the aim must be to keep this down to acceptable levels. While good post-harvest practice reduces the bacteriological count to acceptable levels and the roasting process kills most of the remainder, the truth is that the fewer you start with, the less pathogenic bacteria will survive in the finished product.

Work done on levels of heavy metals in chocolate show that on average they do not present the consumer with any special risk, although some origins tend to have more than others. The cause of higher levels has little to do with pollution or the application of fertilisers but more with the soil itself. For example, those with higher amounts of cadmium come from cocoa grown on volcanic soils, naturally containing an above average quantity of the metal.

Fine and flavour cocoa

There are two main genotypes of cocoa tree: the Criollo and Trinitario cocoa making the fine and flavour category, and the Forastero making up the bulk cocoa. In the past, authors have made the distinction between the two of prime importance, and have waxed lyrical on the superior qualities of the fine and flavour cocoas over the base Forastero beans that make up the 'bulk' cocoas. Most of the chocolate sold is milk chocolate, and

Forastero type beans, with their hard butter (and lower price) are more suited to its manufacture. Some chocolatiers use fine and flavour cocoa to make particular dark chocolate. But as dark or plain chocolate makes up only a small proportion of total chocolate sales the relevance of the mainly Trinitario beans (pure Criollo has all but disappeared) has diminished. This is in line with its production; one estimate puts the amount of fine and flavour cocoa at below 5% of the world crop.[54] In fact it may be much lower as many traditional growers of Trinitario cocoa also produce the Forastero type, and the export figures, on which the estimate was made, do not distinguish between the two. The role of the Trinitario for special high quality chocolate is also under threat; one expert taster working for a large chocolate manufacturer admitted privately that very good dark chocolate, equal to the flavour of that made with fine and flavour cocoa, could be made from selected Forastero beans.

Most growers do not have the choice in selecting the varieties to cultivate, it is dictated to them by what is locally available. Even the advice given by the chocolate manufacturers themselves, presumably the ultimate guardians of cocoa quality, is for prospective growers to check the market carefully; 'If production of significant quantities of fine grades is being considered, the limited extent of the market for such cocoas needs to be borne in mind.'[55] This is sound advice. Fine grade cocoa is more difficult to grow, gives lower yields per hectare, and the returns often do not justify the extra cost in production. The Alliance's advice continues;

> *Within the Forastero populations, particularly within the Amazon hybrids planted widely today, there are appreciable differences in bean weight and it is prudent to avoid planting selections which tend to produce small beans.*

In other words, providing the variety gives a reasonable chocolate flavour[56], growers should concentrate on the yields, both in terms of the bean size and the amount to come off the land, consistent and proper preparation of the cocoa for market, and the all important costs of production.

---

54   'Fine or flavour cocoa', the International Trade Centre – UNCTAD/GATT, Geneva, 1991.

55   Ibid The Cocoa, Chocolate and Confectionery Alliance, 1984.

56   Some Forastero varieties do not, although it is difficult to say whether it is the genotype at fault or the post-harvest processing by the grower. From a compilation made by J N Wintgens, two genetic materials fared badly in this regard, SCA 6 in Costa Rica and UITI in Malaysia ('Environmental and genetic influences on the quality of raw cocoa', 1991).

Achieving quality cocoa

For the grower the best solution is not to rely on the latest method of testing for faults in cocoa, but to follow recognised methods of production, post-harvest practice, storage and shipment. Following such practices will avoid the faults occurring in the first place. This is of more value than knowing the FFA content of the beans to three decimal places. This advice has recently been proposed by CAOBISCO[57] but has its precedence earlier. The following was given in 1914 by the chocolate manufacturers:

> *In general, we believe that if the planter only allows ripe pods to be gathered, ferments for a reasonable period, cures with care, and keeps the beans dry, they will have the right appearance to satisfy the manufacturers, and he will be producing the best that the type of tree on his plantation will produce.*[58]

Some growers may despair knowing that some poorly fermented cocoas from particular regions command a higher price than others that are well fermented and dried. In 1914 NP Booth and AW Knapp[59] coined an illustrative metaphor by comparing the difference to paying more for a badly trained thoroughbred than for a well trained mongrel. What the grower must remember is that the market for well trained mongrels is larger than that for thoroughbreds and thoroughbreds cost more to produce. Well trained thoroughbreds command the biggest premiums, but in cocoa will often not cover the extra cost of production.

Adapting the metaphor slightly highlights another disturbing truth to growers. If all but one in a group of kennel-maids consistently produce well trained dogs that one kennel-maid, selling a badly trained animal, will destroy the premium the others have worked to build up. In the words of Booth and Knapp:

> *In many places the individual who does better work than his fellow-planter does not directly reap his reward in higher prices. This is to be regretted. Indeed, we have been told by planters that it does not pay to take more than a certain amount of trouble in fermenting and curing their cacao, as they obtain the same price anyway, but if all planters worked down to the minimum quality, the price obtained for beans from that district would fall and all would suffer. At present the planter who produces above average is a benefactor to his fellow-planters, and he who produces below the average quality lowers the price of the whole production of that district.*

57 Expert working group on quality, ICCO, 1990.
58 Ibid Booth N P and Knapp A W, 1914.

Consistency remains important, not only to individuals in a particular area but also for the growers from year to year. If manufacturers can rely on a source of beans of a consistent quality (and undisrupted supply) they will have the confidence to build such cocoa into their recipes. With time that becomes a premium in itself, almost irrespective of the actual quality of the cocoa.

The question remains: how much effort should growers put into improving the quality of their product? The answer is the most effort that does not significantly increase the cost of production to bring to the market: cocoa that is of consistent quality, of good bean size, well fermented and free of 'off-flavours', mould and infestation. On the one hand growers sometimes mistakenly think that they save money by skimping on the work on the harvesting and preparation of cocoa. Good harvesting and post-harvest practices do not cost substantially more than poor preparation of the cocoa. On the other hand, anything that costs substantially more is unlikely to gain a worthwhile return. Also, growers should bear in mind that market forces continually work on levelling down the price of different cocoas. Large discounts for some growths promote work by the manufacturers in using the cheaper cocoas in their products. Currently European manufacturers are working hard to use larger proportions of Malaysian and Indonesian cocoa in their recipes. These cocoas, considered as a group, are at a substantial discount to the West African beans, mainly caused by their acidity and poor flavour characteristics compared with the West African beans. The manufacturers are not only actively promoting better post-harvest techniques in these countries but also working on their recipes to try and use more of these Asian beans. The effect will be to depress the differentials for the more expensive beans, so levelling the prices of cocoa.

This was the comment made in 1913 by Harold Smith on the effect of the entry into the market of West African cocoa.[60]

> *The cacao-market has an increasing tendency to minimise the differences in price between the good and ordinary cacaos. Ten years ago the proportional value between the Cameroons and Caracas beans was at 100 to 240 approximately; now it stands at about 100 to 140. Even granted that the quality of Caracas cacao may have deteriorated somewhat, and that of the Cameroon cacao may have improved, the tendency to level down or up all kinds, ... is unmistakable.*

Lastly, some more words from the history books to comfort those origins new to cocoa whose product has, to date, not fully met the favour

59   Ibid Booth N P and Knapp A W, 1914.
60   Ibid Smith Harold H (Ed), 1913.

of manufacturers. In unison, and quite rightly, the cocoa trade hold up the Ghanaian cocoa as the best of the bulk cocoas. This has not always been the case. Again, Harold Smith:[61]

> Great strides have been made of late years in the quality of the beans exported from the Gold Coast, but, in face of the improvements introduced in Grenada cacao since that island came to the front as a leading exporting centre, one can still see that there is much room for improvement in the African beans at times, and I anticipate seeing a steady and continuous levelling-up in its quality as regards evenness colour and general appearance until it can compete in external appearance with San Thomé and leave it behind for flavour, aroma, and freedom from hamminess. But there is much to be done before this is achieved, as was forcibly driven home to my notice the other day when valuing some lots from the Gold Coast, the beans of which were most miserable. Mouldy, greyish, lean, small, illkempt and ill-cured...

In 1939 the situation was quoted as being:[62]

> The quality of the West African product is at best mediocre, and it is only by slow stages that preparation has improved.

That Ghanaian cocoa quality has become the standard others should emulate may comfort those seeking to improve the quality of their own product.

61 Ibid Smith Harold H (Ed), 1913.
62 'Report of the commission on the marketing of West African cocoa', HMSO, 1939.

9

Cocoa bean processing and the manufacture of chocolate

A lthough this is a work on cocoa and not chocolate, a book on cocoa cannot be complete without some description of how manufacturers arrive at the final product. With that in mind and although the emphasis is on cocoa products, this chapter gives an outline of the chocolate making process. Good chocolate requires considerable expertise, equipment and time. In this sense, as in many others, it is dissimilar to coffee, a commodity often compared and confused with cocoa by the public. The casual coffee drinker could prepare a passable cup of coffee if presented with a bag of green coffee beans using no more than normal kitchen utensils – not so for the chocolate lover if similarly confronted with raw cocoa beans.

Figure 9.1 shows, highly simplified, the overall operation in making chocolate. It also shows, in rough proportions, the composition of each of the main stages to make a good milk chocolate, the most favoured form of chocolate.

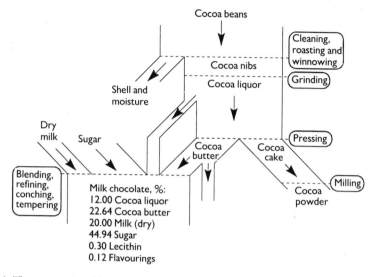

9.1 The processing of cocoa beans to make chocolate, showing the main cocoa products in approximate proportions.

Initial processing

Cleaning

The first stage of any manufacturing process dealing with raw products involves its cleaning. No matter how carefully the grower prepared the beans, or how good the storage or handling, they will contain material that needs removal. This is not only to ensure that the manufacturer uses a wholesome product but also to protect the wear on machinery; pieces of metal or stone can cause extensive abrasion on some of the equipment. Operators slit open the bags and empty them into hoppers through a broad gauged mesh that will remove the largest of any admixture, large stones, branches etc. Recently, warehousekeepers offer this service on behalf of the processors by delivering the cocoa to the factory in bulk from the warehouse. Using this service, processors have the advantage of saving labour and the attendant reduction of health risk, both to the labour and to the finished product; as pouring beans into a hopper tends to throw any bacteria, sporangia etc on the outside of the beans into the air. For this reason factories keep their bean cleaning, roasting and winnowing operations away from the main processing plant to prevent contamination of the final product with undesirable microbiological material on the incoming beans. Irrespective of deliveries made in bulk or in bags, the beans pass through smaller meshed screens removing clusters of beans and any further adulterants. Magnetic separators, brushes and air lifts will remove practically all of the remaining adulterants leaving only the beans.

At this point cocoa processors tend to follow a different path to that adopted by the chocolate manufacturers. This is because the butter pressers want to obtain various cocoa powders and butters that require different processing while the chocolatiers are more interested in the flavour characteristics of the cocoa liquor. Chocolate manufacturers normally follow the next two stages in the order described. Butter pressers may also adopt this, but usually follow a variation on the processing described later.

Roasting

The roasting operation calls for the utmost skill and artistry. Although aided by advances in technology, the roasting operation brings out the flavour of the cocoa and sets the colour of the liquor and powder. All this from a product that is not uniform, either in size, moisture content or ripeness when harvested or fermented. The temperature, time and amount of moisture involved in the roasting process not only depends on the origin of the cocoa but the sort of chocolate or products required from the process and, indeed, the type of roaster used.

The fine and flavour cocoas with their delicate flavours need a light roast; low temperatures, of the range 95–110 °C, for a shorter amount of time as do unfermented cocoas.[1] Low temperature roasting suits beans destined for milk chocolate as do the production of some red-shaded cocoa powders or mild flavoured butter. Fondant chocolate needs cocoa that also has a light roast. Although the bulk Forastero cocoas, such as from Ghana and the Côte d'Ivoire, need higher temperatures it is difficult to state exactly what they should be as there are many variables; the ranges can be from those mentioned up to 149 °C, although a more usual upper temperature seems to be around 120 °C. Cocoa destined for cocoa butter and powder production is easier to press if subjected to a high roast, especially if coming from the NARS (nibs, alkalising, roasting and sterilising) process (see later). Despite all advances[2], the usual way of

---

[1]   While there is no chocolate flavour in such poorly prepared beans the higher temperatures further induce a bitter flavour in the resulting cocoa butter.

[2]   One help to the roasting process includes the assessment of the moisture/equilibrium relative humidity (ERH) of the roasted cocoa. Samples are drawn from the roaster, quickly ground and held at a constant temperature when measured for their ERH. An ERH of 40% or above is considered light, around 30% a medium roast and anything below 20% dark. Again these figures vary from machine to machine.

assessing whether the roast is complete involves the roaster smelling a crushed sample from the oven.

In the roasting a number of changes take place in the cocoa. The bean loses water together with some of the volatile acids within the nib, which darkens and, important for the next stage, the shell loosens from the nib.

Winnowing or cracking and fanning

After roasting the beans are lightly crushed in order to help separate the shell from the nibs. Factories either achieve this by passing the beans through toothed rollers or by using impact rollers that effectively throw the beans against metal plates. Although now separated or cracked, the nibs and shells remain mixed and need the action of the winnowing machine to isolate one from the other. The winnowing machine uses a combination of sieves and air streams to act on the different sizes and densities of the nibs and shells.

This stage is critical for two reasons. The first is the purity of the final product. Making cocoa powder free from shell is not feasible; separation techniques are not perfect and maximum limits of shell content in cocoa powders are set at 1.75%. Most manufacturers can keep this down to about 1.5%. The second is one of profitability; just as the roasting process is critical for flavour and colour the winnowing is for yield. Much of the profit made by the manufacturer's purchasing department may be eroded at this stage. If the machinery is badly set-up or inexpertly controlled a proportion of the nib may be lost, separated together with the shell. The yield of nib should be of the order of 83–84%, including 1–1.75% shell and a moisture content on the nib after roasting of 1.5–3%, depending on the degree of roast. A loss at this stage has a disproportionate effect on the price paid for the beans. For example, suppose the factory purchased cocoa at £700 per tonne which, after winnowing, should give a yield of, say 84%. For some reason the factory only obtains a yield of 80%, i.e., a loss of 4% on the nib weight. A 4% loss on the nib weight translates into a 6% loss on the price of the beans, which in this case amounts to £42 per tonne.[3] A factory wanting a loan to buy a new winnower should perhaps be given a bit more than the time of day by its bankers.

---

3   The arithmetic is: 100/84 = 1.19 and 100/80 = 1.25, the difference between 1.19 and 1.25 is 0.06, or 6%; which on £700 is £42.

Nibs, alkalising, roasting and sterilising (NARS)

Cocoa processors, interested primarily in the yield and making various cocoa powders may modify the above procedure. First, the beans enter a microniser that subjects the cleaned beans to infrared radiant heat for a short time, enough to loosen the shell from the nib without affecting the cotyledons. The beans are then winnowed, which, because the nibs have not become friable in the full roasting process results in a better separation of shell from nib. The lower temperatures also ensure that little of the cocoa butter in the nib is transferred to the shell, therefore improving the final butter yield.

The addition of an alkali, usually a solution of potassium carbonate, to the nibs may occur at this stage. The alkali alters the colour of the nibs during the roasting thereby affecting the colour of the eventual cocoa powders. Up to 3% of the nib weight of anhydrous alkali may be added. Naturally the pH alters, from a usual 5.2 to 5.6 to between 6.8 to 7.5; although for some black powders it can be as high as 8.5, but these have very poor flavours and exist only for their colour attributes. The resulting change in the flavour remains open to debate, some say the flavour of alkalised cocoa is stronger, some say the alkalised powders are less astringent, while others prefer the non-alkalised versions. In the NARS process the addition of the alkali occurs when the nibs first enter the oven. The mixture is then heated at temperatures below 100 °C for some 10 minutes, allowing both the nibs to absorb the alkali and to dry slowly, letting the volatile acids escape, including those in the middle of the nibs. A high heat at this stage will result in these acids being trapped in the nibs and result in a poorer flavour. Once the nibs' moisture content is down to between 2–3%, the second stage of roasting may start, using higher temperatures, up to 130 °C, and for a longer period than the initial roast. The last action of the roasting involves a short spray of water into the oven, done to kill most of the remaining microbiological organisms.

Cocoa liquor or mass

Grinding

The next stage of production involves the controlled milling of the nibs into cocoa liquor, the first of the primary cocoa products. As usually over half the nib weight is fat, the effect of the milling action, together with the heat generated by the grinding, causes the solid nib to become liquid, which will solidify once its temperature drops below its melting point. As would be expected, the milling operation varies according to the type of nibs presented and the product required. For example, the temperature during the milling of delicate aromatic nibs should remain low so that the volatile flavours are not lost; for that reason the modern mills are water cooled. The same is true for liquor destined for milk chocolate; any excess heating at this stage causes harsh flavours. However, by inducing a higher temperature during grinding, millers can use this property to remove some unwanted flavours.

The degree of fineness of particle size is important. If the liquor is destined for cocoa butter and powder production, grinding too finely results in difficulties at the pressing stage and, if too coarse, the pressing will be incomplete as some of the fat will remain in the cell structure. Not only does this affect the butter yield, but the particle size set at the initial grinding determines the eventual particle size for the powders. Subsequent processing of the cake and powder do not reduce the particle size set at the time of grinding but merely break up the agglomerations of powder particles.

The particle size is also important for liquor designated for chocolate. Somewhat perversely it is more economic for cocoa liquor, destined to make coarser chocolate, to be ground finer than that for a more choice final product. A larger proportion of cocoa butter is released by a finer ground liquor, important if no or little additional refining takes place which would otherwise release the remaining cocoa butter. While modern mills can produce liquor containing very small particles (99% through a 325 mesh petroleum sieve), for cocoa powder production a texture of 99.5% through a 200 mesh sieve is sufficient.

Blending

Manufacturers rarely make their products, be they intermediate or final, from one type of beans. At some stage they will need to blend different cocoas. While this may take place at any stage, it is unusual to do so before the roasting, as different nibs or beans require different roasts and compromises rarely bring out the best. Blending at the winnowing stage may present problems in setting the cracking machinery to create evenly sized particles. Heavy shelled beans need more cracking than those with lighter shells; a mixture of both will result in lower yields as the lighter shelled beans will fragment more under the higher pressure needed for the other beans. Blending therefore, can take place at the roasted nib stage. However, this is often delayed until after the grinding as blending nibs can present difficulties in milling, some nibs either grind more easily than others, or should be ground at different temperatures.

Liquor processing

Chocolate manufacturers depend primarily on the cocoa liquor for the flavour of their product and cannot allow any 'off-flavours' to pass through to the product. As factories continue to buy in more cocoa products, care over the quality of the liquor becomes more important. Regrettably, smoky, acidic, hammy or mouldy flavours are not unknown in cocoa liquors, especially those made in origin countries. While there are processes available that can reduce the unwanted flavours, such methods may also lessen the chocolate aroma and cannot be used for liquors that have a high degree of 'off-flavour'. These processes consist of two basic types: either heating the liquor and using water vapour to scrub the unwanted flavour out, or heating the liquor under a vacuum. Determining which system is best depends on the type of cocoa, the unwanted flavour in the liquor and the flavour of the required product.

Alkalising, or 'dutching' the cocoa may take place at this stage, if not earlier with the nibs or later with the powder. It is cheaper and quicker to alkalise the liquor instead of the nibs, although there is an increased risk of inducing saponification of the fat. Saponification creates a 'soapy' flavour which, even in small amounts, is detrimental to the final product.

At this stage the liquor normally contains a small amount of moisture, which if not dispersed homogeneously throughout the liquor will cause sludges to form either in holding tanks or in the pipes of subsequent machinery. While there is some disagreement over the optimum amount of water content in the liquor, an acceptable range is $0.8-1.8\%$, although most factories operate between $1-1.5\%$.

Methods of cocoa butter and powder production

Pressing

Early methods of separating the butter from the remainder of the bean were by boiling the liquor in water and skimming off the fat that floated to the top. After the eighteenth century a more direct method was found which has not altered greatly, other than both a better understanding and control of its operation. As the sub-heading suggests, it involves applying pressure to the liquor thereby squeezing out the fat and leaving the solids behind. Conventional cocoa presses consist of a number of pots, the larger presses have between 12 to 14 of them, into which heated cocoa liquor $(93-102\,^{\circ}\text{C})$[4] is pumped. Once loaded with liquor, which begins to lose

---

4   Higher temperatures produce strongly flavoured butters without better yields.

fat under the pumped pressure, a hydraulic ram collectively squeezes the contents of the pots, so extruding the remaining fat. Modern presses can apply hydraulic pressure of up to 844 kilograms per square centimetre. The ram reverses once the requisite amount of fat has been collected and the remaining cocoa solids, the cocoa cakes, are ejected from each of the pots. The cocoa cake is so called because of its round, flat shape. The extruded fat passes through fine sieves[5] and runs into a collecting pan. In manual systems, by weighing the collected fat the operator can deduce the fat content of the remaining cocoa solids. Automatic machinery dispenses with the need for an operator to control the press as it monitors the activity of the equipment.

The speed of operation depends on the power of the press and the type of cocoa cake required. Cake with a high fat content will take less time to press than cake with a low fat content. A large press can process 1500 kilograms of liquor an hour producing cake with a high butter content; while only managing 500–750 kilograms an hour of low fat content cake.

The manufacturer can vary quite considerably the amount of cocoa butter removed from the liquor. Commercially expressed to within 2%, the normal lower limit of residual fat within the powder is between 10–12%. The press itself sets a maximum limit, as if lightly pressed some machines will not be able to eject the thicker cake. In theory there is no maximum as the manufacturer can always blend in cocoa liquor to the defatted cake/powder to raise the butter content.

Some chemical and physical changes take place during the pressing. Progressively removing more of the fat causes the remaining solids to lose some chocolate flavour and eventually to become harsher flavoured. The original chocolate flavour is not transferred to the butter as it does not return when recombining the cake and butter. When recombined, some 2–4% less fat need be used to create liquor of the same viscosity as the original. This stems from a physical change in the cocoa solids during the pressing. When compressed, the particles making up the cocoa solids become less absorbent. Manufacturers of lower quality chocolate use this attribute to extend their butter requirements as they need use less fat with such processed solids.

---

5   As mentioned earlier, finely milled liquor causes difficulties later, and this is where they are felt. Too small particles (98% through a 400 mesh) block the filters and cause back pressure during the pressing operation. Such finely ground liquors should go into chocolate manufacture and not a butter and powder operation. More efficient pressing occurs with coarser grind, 98–99% through a 200 mesh.

Expeller pressing

Another type of press exists that is used by processors either only interested in the cocoa butter or in making powder with very low fat content. The expeller press involves a tapered screw revolving in an open-ended sleeve. The sleeve has small perforations through which the fat passes as the tapering screw forces the liquor down the sleeve. The combination of the shearing action and increasing pressure results in a powder of 8–9% fat content or lower. High quality nibs (i.e., low shell content) will, after additional grinding of the resulting cocoa solids, produce a powder of particular qualities: low fat and retaining the absorbency lost in powders conventionally pressed.

The usual fare of expellers is not high quality nibs but either nib dust, small beans (whole), shell from badly set winnowers, or even damaged cocoa, i.e., severely mouldy. The interest of the resulting product lies in the fat produced and not the solids, although these may go on to chemical extraction. The butter from expellers requires additional filtering or to be centrifugally separated as it contains solids. Fat coming from mouldy beans will need further refining.

Processing cocoa cake

The cocoa cakes (hard discs of cocoa solids produced by the hydraulic pressing) are the source of cocoa powders. The first action is to break up the cakes into smaller pieces by passing them through rotating toothed rollers. Processors may sell these small lumps as 'kibbled' cake, although it is usual for them to continue the manufacturing to produce cocoa powder. By milling the kibbled cake the solids are broken down to an ever finer size, although never smaller than the size set by the initial liquor-grind. Such milling requires careful control of both temperature and humidity. If the temperature rises and melts the cocoa butter it will clog the machinery, if too low the powder turns a greyish colour. If the air is too dry the powder builds up static electricity and becomes difficult to pack, if too damp the risk of bacteriological and/or fungal growth increases. Air cooled mills ensure the maintenance of optimum conditions.

Cocoa butter

Definitions of cocoa butter vary. The FDA define it as: 'the edible fat obtained from sound cocoa beans (*Theobroma cacao* or closely related species) before or after roasting'; the Codex Alimentarius defines it as:

... the fat produced from one or more of the following: cocoa beans, cocoa nib, cocoa mass, cocoa press cake, expeller press cake or cocoa dust (cocoa fines) by a mechanical process and/or with the aid of permissible solvents. Cocoa butter shall not contain cocoa shell fat or germ fat in excess of the proportion in which they occur in the whole bean.

Some countries restrict it further to the natural fat produced from cocoa nib by conventional hydraulic or expeller pressing.

Pure prime pressed (PPP)

This is the result of the conventionally pressed liquor. No other refining need take place other than filtering out any solids that may have passed through the first sieves. Most of the butter produced is this type.

Expeller butter

If similar beans are used, expeller butter can be chemically the same as PPP butter, although expellers often extract fat from the whole bean which, if raw or lightly roasted, will have a different and milder flavour. Expeller butter from sub-standard beans or winnowed products requires further refining.

Solvent extracted butter

When first introduced this method of extraction resulted in a low grade product as the butter retained some residue of the solvent. Many considered the product unacceptable. Those early difficulties have been overcome by using high grade solvents and the process is common for other accepted commercial fats, although some consider that solvent extracted butter should only come from residues of cocoa nib and not from whole beans or the high shell proportioned products of winnowing. The Codex Alimentarius states that the maximum level in the end-product of extraction solvents[6] is five parts per million.

Much of the solvent extracted butter comes from the solid expeller residues. These 'corns' have the right size, shape and constituency for the solvent extraction process. The resulting fat has some of the properties which suit the production of milk chocolate; mild and bland. Despite the favourable characteristics of flavour, solvent extracted butter normally

6   Hexane (62–82% °C).

only forms between 2–5% of the butter blend for chocolate as it is softer than PPP.

The solvent also extracts other constituents that have to be removed by a further three stages of processing. The first consists of washing the fat, with water and then with alkali, known as lye. This removes gums and free fatty acids. A further washing and then drying the fat under vacuum ends the first stage. The second stage is to bleach the fat using fullers' earth, which is filtered off, leaving the butter to reach the last stage refining, deodorising.

Deodorising

Deodorising cocoa butter results in a mild or bland flavoured product and is not restricted to solvent extracted butter. Processors reduce the flavour of some butters specifically to use with milk chocolate, especially if they prefer a high roast bean for the butter extraction that results in a full-flavoured butter which is unsuitable for milk chocolate. The process involves passing steam through the butter which is under a vacuum. The steam must itself be clean, otherwise it will impart its own flavour into the butter. The steam also must not condense otherwise the water, containing the flavour, will run back into the fat. True of all food processes operators have to maintain a high degree of cleanliness, especially with the deodorising vessel otherwise a build up of flavour volatiles will contaminate the next batch of fat. Subsequent cooling of the butter is important to the process; deodorising takes place at temperatures of 104–110 °C and the butter should cool to 70 °C before storage. As deodorising removes natural antioxidants in natural cocoa butter, such processed butter keeps less well. The storage time for deodorised cocoa is about three to four months, even if in solid form.

Physical characteristics

Although many analysts have published detailed findings on the physical attributes of cocoa butter it is a fat that softens at around 30–32 °C and completely melts at about 35 °C. Some dispute exists over the way to measure the softening and melting points of fats. The Codex Alimentarius determines that the slip point[7] should be between 30–34 °C and that the

---

7   The temperature at which a specially prepared sample of butter will, on heating in a capillary tube of an internal diameter of 1.1–1.3 mm, start to rise in the tube.

clear melting point[8] should be between $31-35\,°C$; although some manufacturers prefer other ways of determining the softening point.

The fact that the melting point and other values are in a range implies that not all butters are the same and that they comprise a mixture of different compounds. Their characteristics are largely dependent on the tree stock and the environment affecting the development of the pod. This has interested a number of analysts who have compared butters with cocoas from different regions. According to one analysis[9] butter made from West African beans had marginally higher melting points than butter from Brazil. While the difference between the fully melted stages were within a degree or two, at $20\,°C$ some 65% of the Brazilian butter was solid, compared with nearly 80% of butter from Côte d'Ivoire. To be expected with an agricultural product, giving generalities can be difficult, but most manufacturers would contend that Brazilian butter is also softer[10] than that made out of West African beans, and that Ghanaian beans provide the most consistent type of butter.

Two other characteristics of cocoa butter are important for the confectioner and both become apparent on the cooling of the fat. First is the useful characteristic of contraction, which allows the moulding of chocolate products and helps to give a 'clean' finish to the product. The rate and amount of contraction depends on the time taken in cooling as well as the final temperature. In one test, butter cooled to $10\,°C$ in 25 minutes contracted by 4.1% of its volume, while if cooled over 100 minutes it contracted by 7.7%.[11]

The second characteristic is that of supercooling. If left undisturbed melted cocoa butter will remain liquid below the melting point. In fact cocoa butter has a very complicated cooling curve as the fat displays four separate crystalline forms, each having its own properties. One form although unstable and known as γ, has a melting point of $17\,°C$ which shows how low the temperature could drop without the butter solidifying.[12] Understanding the different phases is important for chocolate manufacturers as it allows them to temper chocolate so that the butter is stable, known as the β-form, giving the chocolate a permanent colour and gloss.

---

8   The temperature at which the fat clarifies in the capillary tube.
9   Kattenberg H R: 'The quality of cocoa butter' Manufacturing Confectioner, 1981.
10 Measured by the time taken for a weighted cone to penetrate a slab of butter; the apparatus is called a penetrometer.
11 Minifie Bernard W: 'Chocolate, cocoa and confectionery', 1989.
12 The other phases are α, β' and β. The last, β, is stable with a melting point of $34-35°C$ while the others all have lower melting points.

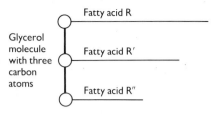

9.2 Triglyceride structure.

Structure of cocoa butter

The molecular structure of cocoa butter provides an insight into the complexity of the fat, its physical properties and also helps to explain the reasoning behind some of the quality assessments of cocoa in general. Chemically, cocoa butter is not a single type of fat, but consists predominantly of one group of fats, the triglycerides. These vary greatly in composition but all have a similar underlying structure: three separate chains of fatty acids each attached (or estered) to one of the three carbon atoms of a former molecule of glycerol. Figure 9.2 shows the basic structure of a triglyceride.

All organic acids belong to the carboxyl group. Commonest amongst the carbon chain molecules[13] containing one carboxyl group are the fatty acids. They form a homologous series[14] of increasing complexity. Cocoa butter has a number of these fatty acids, mostly bound up in the triglycerides. It would be hard enough if each glycerol molecule attracted three of the same fatty acids to its three carbon atoms but, as shown in the above diagram, each carbon atom may have different fatty acids, each of differing length. This provides a mixture with enormous internal variation, the composition of which gives different cocoa butters varying physical properties. For example, if the fatty acids were short chained, the melting point of the butter would be lower; more complex fatty acids can produce higher melting points.

Free fatty acids

Complex organic compounds are subject to chemical changes, some of which mentioned earlier, are used to determine the suitability of the

---

13 Aliphatic compounds, as opposed to the aromatics, which have carbon rings.

14 The general molecular formula is C_nH_{2n+1}. COOH. The simplest is formic acid, H. COOH, followed by acetic acid, CH_3COOH. Two examples of a long chain fatty acids are palmitic acid, $CH_3.(CH_2)_{14}$. COOH, and oleic acid, $CH_3.(CH_2)_7.CH{=}CH.(CH_2)_7.COOH$. The carboxyl group is COOH.

Table 9.1 Typical composition of the main fatty acids in cocoa butter

Fatty acid	Carbon atoms	Double bonds	%
Myristic	14	0	0.1
Palmitic	16	0	25.8
Palmitoleic	16	1	0.3
Stearic	18	0	34.5
Oleic	18	1	35.3
Linoleic	18	2	2.9
Arachidic	20	0	1.1

Source: BW Minifie (1989).

cocoa. One such test is for free fatty acids[15], FFA. High levels of FFA occur in cocoa that is either improperly stored for a long time (i.e., too hot and high moisture) and/or the activity of bacteria or mould in the cocoa. In particular the action of the enzyme lipase, (not only introduced by microbiological activity but also present in the natural raw cocoa) acts to break down the triglyceride into its separate groups of the fatty acids and glycerol thereby 'freeing' the fatty acids. As mentioned earlier, in significant amounts, their presence gives a rancid flavour to the product.

Oxidation

Although natural anti-oxidants (notably lecithin and tocopherols) give limited protection to the fat in the bean[16], oxidation may still occur. This action is similar to that of lipase on the triglycerides but is a little more complex. Instead of splitting off the whole fatty acid, oxygen will attack that part of the fatty acids containing a double bond[17], producing oxidative rancidity in the fat. Not all fatty acids contain double-bonded carbon atoms, but those that do, like oleic acid, see Table 9.1, are called unsaturated.[18] Oxygen will more readily attack the unsaturated acids in the presence of light, some metals[19], moisture and heat. The last two are very important for the storage of cocoa. Not only do low levels of each

15 Chemical analysis usually expresses the acidity as determined by the amount of oleic acid in a sample of butter.
16 These may be destroyed during processing, especially during deodorising which is why such processed butter keeps less well.
17 A double bond is where two atoms, in this case of carbon, share between them four electrons instead of two. It is more reactive than a normal carbon-carbon bond and is usually shown as $C=C$ in chemical formula.
18 As oleic acid has one double bond it is a monounsaturated acid.
19 Pipework in factories should avoid copper content, even in the valves.

inhibit the growth of microbiological activity but they also reduce the level of oxidation. Naturally the fewer double-bonds or unsaturated fatty acids present in the fat, the lower the chance of oxidation taking place. The iodine value, sometimes stipulated in the quality of cocoa butter[20], shows the level of unsaturated fats, hence the possibility of oxidation. Table 9.1 shows a typical composition of cocoa butter, together with the number of carbon atoms and their double bonds.

Saponification

The action of an alkali on a glyceride will produce a soap and glycerol.[21] Similar to the production of free fatty acids in cocoa butter, each of the three 'arms' of fatty acids are broken off, leaving a molecule of glycerol and the remaining fatty acids to react happily with the alkali. Fortunately, as alkali treatment occurs in some cocoa processing, the reaction is relatively slow. Real soap production requires boiling large vats of oils and fats with alkali solutions for hours. Despite this slow reaction, low levels of saponification will affect the chocolate flavour and manufacturers have to guard carefully against its occurrence.

Saponification value

There is a test that provides what is known as the saponification value of the fat. This value indicates the overall molecular weight of the fats, i.e., the complexity of its fatty acids. Fats with short chained acids are termed lauric acids and have high saponification values. One such is coconut oil with a saponification value of around 240. Longer chained acids are non-lauric acids, such as contained in cocoa butter, which according to the Codex Alimentarius, if making chocolate should have a saponification value between 188–198.

Unsaponifiable matter

This is another test using the saponification properties of fats. It shows the amount of material in the fat that is either not saponified by an alkali or that is not volatile. Volatile material is lost as processing the sample

20   The Codex Alimentarius set a range of 33–42 for cocoa butter.
21

$$
\begin{array}{llll}
C_{17}H_{35}.COOCH_2 & & & CH_2OH \\
C_{17}H_{35}.COOCH & + 3NaOH & = 3C_{17}H_{35}.COONa + & CHOH \\
C_{17}H_{35}.COOCH_2 & & & CH_2OH \\
\quad\text{A fat} & \text{An alkali} & \text{A soap} & \text{Glycerol}
\end{array}
$$

requires drying. The unsaponifiable matter comprises a number of different compounds, one group of which is the sterols. The composition of this group helps analysts to differentiate between vegetable and animal fats as vegetable fats have phytosterol while animal fats show cholesterol. While limits for unsaponifiable material may vary, the Codex Alimentarius shows limits of 0.35% for PPP butter and 0.5% for other extracted butters.

Cocoa powders

Types of powders

Large cocoa processors have catalogues containing over 100 different types of cocoa powder available to their buyers. These include powders with different fat contents, various colours, natural or alkalised, the degree of alkalisation and speciality powders that have added stabilisers or lecithin. Such a range implies variety of needs, although requirements for powders may be reduced to three categories: those for wet products, like flavoured desserts or drinks; dry products, like biscuits and cakes and those based on fat systems, like hard chocolate coatings. In addition, each of these may be consumed at different temperatures; a chocolate drink may be served cool or it may come hot. The same type of powder used for each will not give similar flavour characteristics.

Overall fat content

Products with a significant amount of fat need more flavouring. The fat acts as a buffer and for a chocolate flavoured product, a larger amount of cocoa

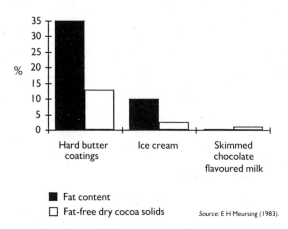

Source: E H Meursing (1983).

9.3 Level of cocoa solids required for different fat-containing cocoa flavour systems.

solids needs to be included than for a similarly flavoured but less fatty product. Figure 9.3 compares the fat content with fat-free dry cocoa solids for three products. It is quite clear that products with progressively more fat need more flavour; the flavoured milk needs only a small amount of cocoa in order for the flavour to emerge.

Fat content of the powders

Generally powders have fat contents of either 10/12%, or higher at 20/22%. Some factories may offer powders with different fat contents, but these two represent the greatest amount sold on the market, which is dominated by the standard 10/12%.

Natural and alkalised powders

Apart from giving different colours, alkalising or 'dutching' the powders can, according to some, affect the flavour. In particular it may reduce the astringent flavour of the cocoa. This is why some use it for those products that do not have any flavour buffer in the form of fat; the fat helps to mask the astringency, and the bitter flavoured Theobromine, in the chocolate product.

Temperature of the product when consumed

In a product with a high fat content the chocolate flavour 'disappears' into the buffer of the fat and is only partially released when the butter melts. If the product is cold, like ice cream, the butter will rarely melt and the chocolate flavour will go unnoticed. Therefore the cocoa used in chocolate ice cream has a low fat content. On the other hand drinking chocolate, served hot can have a much higher fat content. Traditionally manufacturers make powders, sometimes known as 'breakfast cocoa' with a fat content of 22/24% for this purpose. Furthermore, the elements of flavour in cocoa powder are not as volatile as those of say, coffee. This is why hot drinking chocolate can be boiled without any distinct loss of flavour while coffee is spoiled with boiling or prolonged heat.

Chocolate production

Although the last section dealt with cocoa powder, as shown in Fig. 9.3, it is not needed to make chocolate. For this the two important products are

Table 9.2 Composition of chocolate as calculated on the dry matter in the product

	Cocoa butter	Fat-free cocoa solids	Total cocoa solids	Milk fat	Fat-free milk solids	Total fat	Sugars
Chocolate	≥18	≥14	≥35				
Unsweetened chocolate	≥50–58≤						
Couverture chocolate	≥31	≥2.5	≥35				
Sweet (plain) chocolate	≥18	≥12	≥30				
Milk chocolate		≥2.5	≥25	≥3.5	≥10.5	≥25	≤55
Milk couverture chocolate		≥2.5	≥25	≥3.5	≥10.5	≥31	≤55
Milk chocolate with high milk content		≥2.5	≥20	≥5	≥15	≥25	≤55
Skimmed milk chocolate		≥2.5	≥25	≥0.5	≥14	≥25	≤55
Skimmed milk couverture chocolate		≥2.5	≥25	≤0.5	≥14	≥31	≤55
Cream chocolate		≥2.5	≥25	≥7	≥3–14≤	≥25	≤55
Chocolate vermicelli and flakes	≥12	≥14	≥32				
Milk chocolate vermicelli and flakes		≥2.5	≥20	≥3.5	≥10.5	≥12	≤66

Source: Codex Alimentarius

the liquor and butter. The first stage of chocolate production involves the mixing of the main ingredients, the proportions of which depend on the chocolate being made. Table 9.2 shows the minimum requirements for chocolate as set out by the Codex. That requirements are set to such a degree shows the level of interest in the 'food of the gods'.

Following the example of producing a milk chocolate, the liquor, sugar, milk and some of the cocoa butter are mixed together in a blending kettle or continuous mixer. Not all the butter is added at this stage, only an amount of up to 20 to 25% cocoa butter. This ensures production of a rough paste that eases the refining stage of manufacture.

Milk

While there is some discussion over what form the milk should be added to the mixture, it is essential that by the end of the processing virtually all of its water is removed. Fresh milk contains just under 88% water. Most manufacturers therefore use either dehydrated milk powder or at least condensed milk. The freshness of the milk is also important; chocolate prepared from old milk will not keep as well as that made with fresh. This is often a limiting factor for chocolate production in cocoa growing countries where sources of fresh milk are given other, more important priorities.

Sugar

There are many different types of sugar available to the confectioner, but the overriding factors are that it be pure, dry and not contain invert sugar. Invert sugar is an isomer of sugar, that is it has the same chemical composition as sugar but the internal arrangement of atoms is different. Invert sugar in chocolate affects the refining process and the eventual texture of the chocolate as the differently shaped sugar molecules do not readily split as does normal sugar. Before mixing the sugar should be milled to a fine consistency. As this represents a danger (sugar milling can create an explosive dust) some factories add the sugar to the mixture at the refining stage of the process.

Emulsifiers

Chocolate may be considered as a mixture of small particles of cocoa, sugar and milk solids floating around in cocoa butter and the fat from milk. The degree to which this unprepossessingly described mixture will flow into moulds or enrobe what will become filled bars of chocolate depends on the amount of fat present, unless that is, the confectioner can add something to improve the viscosity of chocolate. The addition of an emulsifying agent will do this. Lecithin is the most popular; a dark enrobing chocolate containing 38% of cocoa butter will have similar viscosity if composed of just over 33% butter but with 0.5% Lecithin[22] added.[23] Such a saving on a material as expensive as cocoa butter is important to the confectioner. Lecithin is usually added towards the end of the processing but some chocolate benefits from a portion of the final amount to be added when the main ingredients are mixed.

Cocoa butter equivalents (CBE)

While on the subject of fats (as mentioned in Chapter 7) some countries permit the use of up to 5% of fats other than cocoa butter in chocolate.

---

22   The highest permissible amount under the Codex Alimentarius for most chocolate products.
23   Ibid Minifie Bernard W, 1989.

Currently, the United Kingdom, Ireland and Denmark use CBEs and it would seem likely that their use will extend to other countries within the EEC. These fats have similar properties to cocoa butter except for that of flavour. Their general acceptance, if it occurs, underlines the constant pressure faced by manufacturers in making a wholesome but low cost product.

Refining

Refining consists of running the chocolate paste through a series of carefully controlled rollers. A refining machine may have up to seven rollers (although more usually five) one above the other, each rotating slightly faster and in the opposite direction to the one below. The rollers are not only made of specially hardened steel but are individually cooled by water, providing temperature control. The gap between the rollers is also precisely regulated. The paste is introduced at the bottom of the machine, picked up by the first roller and then transferred to each of the others by their relatively faster rotation. This action both crushes and shears the paste in its movement from one roller to the next. At the top of the refiner, a scraper blade removes the film of chocolate on the last roller.

Once again control is important; not only in the gaps between the rollers (which must be uniform across their length) but also the atmospheric conditions in the refinery. Too humid conditions will cause condensation on the rollers. As the chocolate paste has a large surface area to volume ratio at this stage the chocolate is more likely to pick up moisture, something the confectioner should avoid.

Refining improves the texture of the chocolate. In part this has to do with the particle size of the solids in the fat and the degree of refining depends on the type of chocolate and the confectioner's own recipe. In general, plain or dark chocolate is better with smaller particle sizes (around 0.035 mm) than milk chocolate with some particles up to 0.065 mm diameter. Milk chocolate with particles less than 0.025 mm in size has a slimy texture. Particle size has an effect on the amount of butter needed in the recipe and therefore is of great interest to the chocolate manufacturer. Good chocolate texture and its viscosity depends on covering the solids in chocolate with fat. For a given weight, smaller particles have a greater surface area than larger ones. This means that to achieve the same viscosity, the chocolatier needs to add more cocoa butter to chocolate with smaller particles than he has to for chocolate made up of larger ones.

Conching

Conching describes the final stage of bulk chocolate production. While there are different designed conching machines, their purpose is to add the final touches to the texture and flavour of the product. The original conches consisted of a granite roller working up and down against a granite bed. These, and the chocolate, were held in a bath that had the two longitudinal ends curving upwards so that the chocolate, moved by the roller, would slop back into the bath and not out of its container. The name 'conche' derives from the shape of the original container which looked like a shell, or in French, *conche*.

Although modern machinery and techniques have speeded up the process, conching takes time. Plain chocolate could require up to 96 hours in a longitudinal conch, but milk chocolate can nowadays take as little 10 to 16 hours in more modern equipment. Chocolatiers found working the paste for this length of time gave better dispersal of the solids in the fat, ensuring that they are covered with the butter, which improved the texture of the chocolate. In addition, the chocolate developed a better flavour as some of the unwanted volatile odours and tastes were removed, as was the excess moisture. These last two benefits occurred sooner if the manufacturer first processed the paste 'dry', i.e., not adding the final amount of cocoa butter and emulsifiers until towards the end.

Tempering

As mentioned earlier, cocoa butter can crystallise into different forms. Some of these phases are not stable for long, but will cause discoloration and bloom in the product if the manufacturer allows the chocolate to set without preventing their formation. The answer lies in the controlled cooling of the chocolate while continually stirring, thereby allowing the butter crystals to form correctly and to disperse throughout the mix. Another way includes the addition of a small amount of already tempered chocolate in order to seed the untempered mix with the correct crystals.

All chocolate requires tempering, and although emphasis is placed at this stage, continued temperature control of the product is needed for a while after the chocolate has been either moulded or enrobed to ensure its condition remains good.

The end

From there the chocolate will go into the product designed by the manufacturer, be it a high quality low volume dark chocolate bar, chocolate liqueurs, bon-bons, novelty moulded goods, or a milk chocolate enrobed filled bar that sells in the tens of millions a week. The myriad of different chocolate products available answers the sterile question: which is the best chocolate? Perhaps the true answer is the child's who, if she can be bothered to say it with her mouth full, answers: 'The one that's in my mouth.'

Bibliography

Anglerius P M: 'The Historie of the West Indies'. 1626.

Battley N: 'An introduction to commodity futures and options'. McGraw-Hill, 1989.

Booth N P and Knapp A W: 'The qualities in cocoa desired by manufacturers', Third international congress of tropical agriculture, 1914.

Chatt E M: 'Cocoa cultivation, processing, analysis'.

de Chélus: 'The natural history of chocolate', Brookes (Dr) R (*trans*), 1724.

Ciferri R: 'Studies on cacao' *Journal of the Department of Agriculture*, Puerto Rico 1931 (15).

Cook R L and Meursing E: 'Chocolate production and use'. 1982.

Cox P D and Bell C H: 'A review of the biology of moth pests and stored products', ADAS Slough Laboratory, 1981.

Cramer H H: 'Plant protection and world crop production'. 1967.

Dand R J: 'Cocoa: a shipper's manual'. Geneva ITC UNCTAD/GATT, 1990.

Duncan D (Dr): 'Wholesome advice against the abuse of hot liquors particularly of Coffee, Chocolate, Tea, Brandy and Strong-waters'. 1706.

Entwistle P F: 'Pests of cocoa'. Longman, 1972.

Fish J R and Mehta K B: 'Relative returns to exporting cocoa beans and their derivatives'. ICCO Advisory Group Meeting, Ghana, 1990.

Gage, Thomas: 'A new survey of the West-Indias'. 1648.

Hale S L: 'World production and consumption 1951 to 1953', 1953.

Hansen A P and Keeney P G: 'Comparison of carbonyl compounds in moldy and non-moldy cocoa beans' *Journal of Food Science* 1970 (35) 37–40.

Hasan I and Chok D K K: 'Efficiency enhancement in a world of excess cocoa'. ICCO Advisory Group Meeting, Mexico, 1988.

Hassall A H: 'Food and its adulteration', 1855.

Historicus: 'Cocoa: all about it'. 1896.

Hughes W: 'The American physitian or a treatise of the roots, plants and trees growing in English plantations in America including a discourse on the cacao nut tree', 1672.

Kattenberg H R: 'The quality of cocoa butter' *Manufacturing Confectioner* 1981.

Knapp A W (Ed): 'Cacao fermentation', 1937.

de Ledesma C: 'Curioso tratado de la naturaleza y calidad de chocolate', 1631.

Lenovich L M and Hurst W J: 'Production of aflatoxin in cocoa beans' *Journal of the Association of Official Analytical Chemists* 1979 (62) 5.

Metcalfe M W: 'Concentration and contraction in the cocoa trade – problems and opportunities', CMAA second international cocoa convention, Florida, 1991.

Normandy A H: 'The commercial hand-book of chemical analysis', 1850.

Ogilby J: 'America being the latest and most accurate description of the new world' London, 1671.

de Osasunasco, Desiderio: 'Observaciones sobre la preparacion y usos de chocolate', 1789 mentioned in International Chocolate Review, 1953 (8) 179.

Parkinson J: Theatrum Botanicum 1640.

Rauch J: 'Disputo medico diotetica de aere et esculent de necnon porta' 1624.

Rorer J B: 'Ecuador cocoa' *Tropical Agriculture* 1926 (3).

Ruf F and de Milly H: 'Comparison of cocoa production costs in seven producing countries'. London ICCO 1990.

Sanders J L: 'The Xyleborus-Ceratocystis complex of cacao' *Cacao* 1965 (10).

Scheu J J: 'Fine or flavour cocoa' Geneva ITC UNCTAD/GATT, 1991.

Scott J L: 'Preliminary observations on the moisture content and hygroscopicity of cacao beans'. Department of Agriculture, Gold Coast, Yearbook, 1928.

Scott P M: 'Modified method for the determination of mycotoxins in cocoa beans' *Journal of the Association of Official Analytical Chemists* 1972 (56) 4.

Shephard C Y: 'General history of the production and consumption of cacao'. 1932.

Smith H H (Ed): 'The fermentation of cacao'. 1913.

Smyth A J: 'The selection of soils of cocoa' *Soils Bulletin* 1966 (5), FAO Rome.

Smyth A J: 'Soil classification and the cocoa grower' *Cocoa Growers Bulletin* 1980 (30).

Theimer O F: 'On the storage of raw cocoa beans in silo compartments' *International Chocolate Review* 1958 (13) 122–126.

Thong K C and Ng W L: 'Growth and nutrient composition of monocrop cocoa plants on inland Malaysian soils'. Proc int conf cocoa coconuts, Kuala Lumpur.

Thorlod C A: 'Diseases of cocoa', Clarendon Press, 1975.

Ure A: 'Supplement to Dr Ure's dictionary of arts, manufacturers and mines'. 1844.

Wintgens J N: 'Environmental and genetic influences on the quality of raw cocoa'. 1991.

Wood G A R and Lass R A (Ed): 'Cocoa' Longman. 1985.

Cocoa beans tests 1952/53 Gordian 1953.

Cocoa beans, chocolate manufacturers' quality requirements. The Chocolate and Confectionery Alliance, 1984.

'COCOA world production and trade', Marketing Board, 1930.

Gill & Duffus Market Reports

International Cocoa Organisation quarterly bulletins of cocoa statistics.

The professional dealing handbook. Securities and Futures Authority, 1991.

The Public Ledger, London, 1888.

The Public Ledger and Commercial & General Advertiser, London, 1805.

Report of the Commission on the Marketing of West African Cocoa. HMSO, 1939.

Report of the Imperial Economic Committee, 22nd report COCOA, HMSO, 1932.

'Study of cocoa production in Brazil' ICCO document, 1989.

'Uniform customs and practices for documentary credits'. International Chamber of Commerce, 1983.

'Uniform rules for documentary collections'. International Chamber of Commerce, 1979.

'The world cocoa directory', ICCO, London, 1992.

I

AFCC cocoa contracts

Physical cocoa contracts translated into English* issued by the

Association française du commerce des cacaos† (AFCC)

AFCC# 1

AFCC# 2

AFCC# 3

AFCC# 4

Price fixation addendum

Market Rules

*Note: These translations are without prejudice. At law the original French versions apply. While the author and publishers have tried to ensure accuracy, neither are responsible for any decisions taken nor losses incurred based on these or their interpretation in the text.

† Contract forms are available from:
Association française du commerce des cacaos
2, rue de Viarmes
75001 Paris
France

Tel 42 33 15 00   Tlx 670882   Fax 40 28 47 05

APPENDIX I

ASSOCIATION FRANÇAISE DU COMMERCE DES CACAOS

1st january 1990 — **FORM N 1**

Company/trading name of seller

OFFICIAL CONTRACT FOR TRANSACTIONS
IN COCOA BEANS ON C.I.F. NET LANDED WEIGHT TERMS

Date

N°

Company/trading name of buyer

We confirm the verbal sale which we made with you	1
through	2
by order and on behalf of	3
subject to the Market Rules of the ASSOCIATION FRANÇAISE DU COMMERCE DES	4
CACAOS and the general conditions of this contract, specified on the reverse, which the parties	5
declare they are familiar with and accept.	6

Quantity	(tonnes of 1,000 kg).	7
	With a tolerance of plus or minus 2%, on shipment, of which the weight shown on the bill of lading	8
	shall be proof.	9

Cocoa		10
		11
		12

Quality on arrival	Fair merchantable. Mandatory acceptance of the goods in all cases.	13

Price	Fixed and indivisible.	14
		15
		16
	Cost, insurance and freight, net landed weight, with a tolerance of plus or minus 2% in relation to	17
	the quantity sold.	18

Packing	In new, exportable, woven, non-returnable bags ; actual tare.	19

Port(s) of destination		20
	At buyer's option; to be declared not later than 15 days before the first day of the shipment period,	21
	by minimum quantities of 25 tonnes per port.	22

Shipment period	From origin during	23
	at seller's option.	24

Payment	Net cash for 99% of the amount of the provisional invoice at first presentation and in exchange for	25
	shipping documents complying with the conditions of this sale (cf. clause # 3).	26

Special conditions (1)		27
		28
		29
		30

BUYER'S STAMP AND SIGNATURE   SELLER'S STAMP AND SIGNATURE

(1) Insert "None" if there are no special conditions.

253

A.F.C.C. GENERAL CONDITIONS

1° / SHIPMENT

Shipment shall be effected by through bill(s) of lading specifying the goods with the number of bags, shipping marks and serial numbers.

The date of loading shown on the bill of lading shall be taken as the date of shipment, unless there is proof to the contrary. The bill of lading marked "loaded and/or received on board" shall be taken as proof of shipment.

2° / ADVICE OF SHIPMENT (DECLARATION)

All advices of shipment made by telex or telegram or registered letter shall be deemed to be valid.

They shall specify: the origin of the goods, the name of the vessel, the tonnage involved, the number of bags, the shipping marks and serial numbers, the date and number of the through bill of lading, the destination and, if any, the name of the supervisor appointed by the seller.

The declaration shall specify whether the parcel is in complete or partial fulfilment of the quantity sold. Any significant error may be rectified up to the opening of the hatches.

In the case of a voyage including transshipment(s), the name of the main carrier to the port of final destination shall be forwarded to the buyer by the seller not later than 7 days before the arrival of the vessel in the said port.

A declaration which complies with the terms of this contract shall be irrevocable.

Each declaration shall be for a minimum of 25 tonnes, except for the balance of the quantity sold. In the event of several bills of lading appearing on the same declaration, each bill of lading shall be considered to be a partial declaration. Each partial declaration shall be considered to be the execution of a separate contract.

The seller shall be entitled to declare a shipment against this sale ship lost or not lost, subject to him submitting proof of shipment and providing the buyer with all the shipping documents (cf. clause # 3).

Each seller shall forward the declaration to his buyer promptly (cf. Market Rule # 5).

If the declaration arrives after the opening of the hatches at the port of destination, the buyer shall not be entitled to refuse it but may charge the party responsible for the financial consequences resulting from the delay in the transmission of the declaration.

If the buyer has not received the declaration by midnight on the 14th day following the shipment period, he may refuse a subsequent declaration and, declaring the seller to be in default, may ask for the terms of the close-out of the contract to be fixed by means of arbitration (with any price difference, penalty and interest to be borne by the latter).

However, if each buyer who receives the declaration after the 13th day forwards it promptly to his buyer, the said declaration shall be covered by the contract and cannot be rejected.

3° / DOCUMENTS

(a) **List:**
- provisional invoice;
- complete set of freight-paid clean on board negotiable bills of lading marked "loaded and/or received on board" (letter of guarantee for any missing copies) or delivery order raised by the carrier;
- policy, or insurance certificate marked "premium paid" and "complies with A.F.C.C. conditions" or letter of guarantee;
- certificate of origin or movement, or letter of guarantee in provisional replacement;
- any certificates and documents required under international agreements applying to cocoa transactions between the country of origin and the country of destination.

N.B.: The buyer may demand that all letters of guarantee be bank guarantees.

(b) **Presentation and payment of documents:**

If the documents complying with the conditions of this sale are not presented before the expiry of the free quay rental period, only the additional rental charges and/or bank guarantee charges incurred shall be borne by the seller.

In the case of transshipment stated in the bill of lading, the presentation of documents can be effected only after loading onto the last main carrier.

In the event of non-payment by the buyer for documents complying with the conditions of this sale, the seller may give him formal notice to effect payment within 48 hours.

If payment is not made within that period, the seller may freely dispose of the goods and, declaring the buyer to be in default, may ask for the terms of the close-out of this contract to be fixed by means of arbitration (with any price difference, penalty and interest to be borne by the buyer).

(c) **Charges and taxes:**

All unloading charges, taxes and customs duties incurred or which may be incurred at the port of discharge and/or within the country of final destination shall be borne by the buyer.

4° / SUPERVISION, WEIGHING AND SAMPLING

Supervision, weighing and sampling of each bill of lading or delivery order shall be obligatory and carried out without interruption in the presence of the buyer's and the seller's supervisors at the port of destination specified in the bill of lading, at the buyer's expense, within a maximum of 15 days after the final day of landing of the vessel, failing which the seller may issue the final invoice on the basis of the bill of lading (or delivery order) weight increased by 2%.

This method of invoicing shall not apply if the buyer is not responsible for the delay and if the buyer weighs the parcel without delay as soon as he has access to the goods.

If the valid documents are not presented when the vessel arrives, the above-mentioned period shall commence from the date of their presentation.

(a) **Supervision:** The buyer shall summon the supervisor appointed by the seller, failing which the latter may issue the final invoice on the bill of lading (or delivery order) weight increased by 2%. If no supervisor is appointed by the seller before the arrival of the vessel, as defined by the responsible authority, the weighing and sampling carried out by the buyer's supervisor or by a sworn weigher or duly authorised company shall be binding on the parties.

(b) **Weight:** In the event of losses or damage it shall be for the buyer to safeguard his rights of recovery against the shipping company and the insurers.

In the event of the tolerance of minus 2% being exceeded, the total shortfall shall give rise to compensation calculated on the basis of the difference between the selling price and the market value on the final day of landing of the vessel, if the market value is higher than the selling price. In the event of the tolerance of plus 2% being exceeded, the total excess shall remain for the account of the seller, if the buyer refuses to take delivery of the total excess at the market value on the final day of landing of the vessel.

(c) **Sampling:** Sealed samples shall be randomly drawn in the presence of the buyer's and the seller's supervisors on a minimum of 30% of the sound landed bags at the time of the weighing performed within the stipulated period, failing which the buyer shall lose the right to claim arbitration on quality.

In the event of various shipping marks appearing on the bill of lading, each mark shall be sampled separately. The samples shall weigh a minimum of 2 kg and be packed and sealed in woven bags.

5° / FINAL INVOICING

The net landed weight to be invoiced shall be calculated by multiplying the average weight of the sound and full bags agreed on arrival by the number of bags shown on the bill of lading (or delivery order).

The seller shall issue the final invoice within 30 days from the last day of weighing and attach to it a copy of the supervisor's report. After this period, the invoice may be issued by the buyer.

If the seller has not appointed a supervisor, the buyer shall forward or have forwarded to the seller the document certifying the weight, issued by one of the parties indicated in line 58 above within a period of 15 business days from the last day of weighing, failing which the seller may invoice on the basis of the bill of lading (or delivery order) weight.

The balance shall be paid on receipt of the final invoice if it is in favour of the seller, or when the invoices despatched if it is in favour of the buyer.

The interest owed, due as from the date of the final invoice but at the earliest from the 31st day after the weighing, shall be calculated by the creditor at the official bank rate applying to the currency of this contract, plus 2% per annum.

30 days after this date the rate of interest chargeable shall be increased by half, but not above the maximum legal rate of interest.

6° / INSURANCE

The goods shall be insured by the seller at the contract price plus 2.50% with first-class insurance companies, subject to the following conditions:

– full reimbursement without deduction of franchise;
– including the risks of theft in general and pilferage, and partial or total loss of the goods insured;
– and subject to the all risks conditions of the "Police Française d'Assurance Maritime sur Facultés".
The seller shall insure the goods against risks of war, mines and strikes; his obligations shall be limited, however, to the terms and conditions in force in France at the time of shipment. Any excess over 0.50% of the total amount of premium for risks of war, mines and strikes shall be for the buyer's account and the latter shall be informed of this at the latest at the time of declaration.

In the event of total or partial loss of the goods covered by this contract, or damage leading to subrogation to the insurers, the seller shall not be bound to replace them and the quantities lost shall simply be deducted from the quantity sold.

The buyer shall pay the full value of the goods in exchange for the full set of bills of lading or delivery order, the invoice and the insurance certificate, allowing him direct recourse against the insurers.

7° / SHIPPING COMPANIES

The freight shall be paid by the seller. Unless expressly stated to the contrary by the buyer he shall use first-class shipping companies and load the good on board liner vessels with A1 classification on one of the registers listed in the "Police Française d'Assurance Maritime sur Facultés".

8° / ARBITRATION CLAIMS

(a) **Quality claims:** Any claim for inferior quality shall reach the counter-party and the A.F.C.C. within a maximum period of 21 days after the final day of landing of the vessel. The claim shall be forwarded promptly by telegram or telex along the string of buyers and sellers.

(b) **Technical claims:** Any claim shall reach the counter-party and the A.F.C.C. within a maximum period of one year after the final day of landing of the vessel, or after the last scheduled date for shipment if such has not taken place.

(c) **Arbitration procedure and appeal:** The parties shall refer to the rules of the "Chambre Arbitrale" of the A.F.C.C.

9° / FORCE MAJEURE

The claim for Force Majeure shall be made not later than 8 days after the shipment period, failing which it shall be deemed to be inadmissible. In the event of shipment being prevented or delayed by reasons of unforseeable and insurmountable events resulting from a ban on exports, fire, strike, lock-out, riot, war, revolution or other cases of Force Majeure, the shipment period shall be extended by one month.

If the shipment delay exceeds one month, the buyer shall have the option:
– either of terminating this contract in respect of any quantity not shipped,
– or of continuing to perform this contract by a shipment effected as soon as the original cause of the prevention or delay has ceased to exist, but not later than 5 months after the end of the first month's extension. When this period has elapsed, this contract shall be automatically cancelled for any quantity not shipped.

This above-mentioned option shall be declared in writing by the buyer to the seller as soon as the latter has notified his inability to ship during the extended period, but not later than 7 days from the end of the month following the shipment period stipulated in this contract.

This contract shall be deemed void if the buyer does not declare the above-mentioned option in the manner set out above. In all cases it shall be for the seller to give prompt notice to the buyer and supply proof of Force Majeure.

10° / ARBITRATION CLAUSE

By express agreement, any dispute arising between the seller and the buyer for any reason whatsoever relating to this contract shall be settled by arbitration by the "Chambre Arbitrale" of the A.F.C.C. in accordance with its rules which both parties declare they are familiar with and accept. The arbitration award shall be final and not subject to appeal.

11° / APPLICABLE LAW

This contract and its consequences shall be subject to French law.

APPENDIX I

1st january 1993 — **FORM N° 2**

Company/trading name of seller

OFFICIAL CONTRACT FOR TRANSACTIONS IN COCOA BEANS
ON F.O.B. SHIPPED WEIGHT TERMS

Date

N°

Company/trading name of buyer

We confirm the verbal sale which we made with you	1
through	2
by order and on behalf of	3
subject to the Market Rules of the ASSOCIATION FRANÇAISE DU COMMERCE DES	4
CACAOS and the conditions set out on both sides of this contract, which the parties declare they	5
are familiar with and accept.	6

Quantity (tonnes of 1,000 kg). — 7

With a tolerance of plus or minus 1 %, on shipment, of which the weight shown on the weight certificate shall be proof. — 8

Cocoa — 9

Quality on shipment Fair merchantable. — 10

Price — 11

Packing In new, exportable, woven, non-returnable bags; actual tare. — 12

Shipment period From origin during — 13

Shipment port(s) — 14

At seller's option; to be declared not later than 45 days before the first day of the shipment period, — 15

failing which shipment to be effected from the major cocoa port of the country of origin. — 16

— 17

Freight At buyer's expense. — 18

Marine insurance At buyer's expense. — 19

Payment Net cash for 100 % of the amount of the invoice. — 20

(cf clause # 5) (a) by irrevocable letter of credit, in conformity with the contractual conditions agreed by the parties. — 21

(b) at first presentation in   and in exchange for shipping — 22

documents complying with the conditions of this sale (1). — 23

Special conditions (2) — 24

— 25

— 26

— 27

— 28

BUYER'S STAMP AND SIGNATURE   SELLER'S STAMP AND SIGNATURE

(1) Delete as appropriate, failing which paragraph (b) shall be deemed to be deleted.   (2) Insert « None » if there are no special conditions.

F.O.B. NET SHIPPED WEIGHTS TERMS

1° / FREIGHT

The seller shall bear the costs and risks relating to the goods until such time as they have passed the ship's rail at the port of shipment at origin.

The buyer shall advise the seller of the following:

– the name of the vessel (or her substitute);
– the name of the ship's agent at the port of shipment;
– the estimated time of arrival (E.T.A.) of the vessel at the port of shipment;
– the quantity to be loaded on board;
– the name of his supervisor, if he appoints one.

The buyer shall send this advice to the seller not later than 15 days before the scheduled date of the vessel's arrival at the port of shipment, failing which the seller shall not be obliged to load the goods on the said vessel and may require the buyer to provide, within the required time, an advice regarding a vessel named as substitute. In any event, if an advice has been forwarded promptly along the string of buyers and sellers, it shall be considered to have been received within the required time by the first seller.

If the loading cannot take place by the scheduled date:

– either because of late arrival of the vessel,
– or because of a refusal by the carrier to accept the goods on board (unless the seller is at fault),

the buyer shall reimburse the seller the extra costs incurred by the latter, from the second day following the latest E.T.A. of the vessel notified in writing by the buyer to the seller up to the date of arrival in the port of shipment of the delayed or substituted vessel, provided that the goods have been tallied, in the presence of the buyer's and the seller's supervisors if the buyer has appointed a supervisor.

If the buyer is unable to nominate within the required time a vessel due to load during the shipment period stipulated in this contract, he shall be deemed to be in default.

If the seller cannot make the goods available for loading onto the vessel nominated by the buyer, he shall be deemed to be in default.

In the event of either party to this contract being in default, the other party may ask for the terms of the close-out of this contract to be fixed by means of arbitration (with any price difference, additional costs, penalty and interest to be borne by the party in default).

2° / SHIPMENT

Shipment shall be effected by through bill(s) of lading specifying the goods, with the number of bags, shipping marks, and serial numbers if they exist.

Unless there is proof to the contrary, the bill of lading marked «loaded on board» shall be taken as proof of shipment and its date as the date of shipment.

3° / ADVICE OF SHIPMENT (DECLARATION)

All advices of shipment shall be made by telex or telegram.

They shall specify: the origin of the goods, the name of the vessel, the tonnage involved, the number of bags, the shipping marks, the serial numbers (if they exist), the date and number of the loaded on board bill of lading, the destination and the mode of transport (conventional, container, bolster, etc.).

Any significant error may be rectified up to the opening of the hatches.

Each declaration shall be for a minimum of 25 tonnes, except for the balance of the quantity sold. In the event of several bills of lading appearing on the same declaration, each bill of lading shall be considered to be a partial declaration. Each partial declaration shall be considered to be the execution of a separate contract.

A declaration which complies with the terms of this contract shall be irrevocable.

The seller shall be entitled to declare a shipment against this contract ship lost or not lost, subject to him submitting proof of shipment and providing the buyer with all the shipping documents (cf. clause #4).

Each seller shall forward the declaration to his buyer promptly.

Any costs and consequences which may result from failure to comply with the above obligations shall be borne by the party responsible.

4° / DOCUMENTS

The seller shall provide the buyer with the following documents:

– invoice;
– complete set of clean, negotiable, loaded on board bills of lading marked «Freight payable at destination»;
– certificate of origin or movement;
– weight certificate complying with the conditions of this sale, and confirmation of drawing of samples in the presence of the buyer's and the seller's supervisors, or by the seller's supervisor if one had not been appointed by the buyer;
– quality certificate complying with the conditions of this sale, signed by the seller's supervisor;
– phytosanitary and fumigation certificates issued in accordance with the requirements of the country of export;
– Any certificates or documents required under international agreements and regulations applying to cocoa transactions between the country of origin and the country of destination.

APPENDIX I

5° / PAYMENT

(a) By letter of credit issued by a first-class bank at the buyer's expense:

In any event, the seller's bank shall receive from the issuing bank notification of the opening of the credit before the commencement of the shipment period, failing which the buyer shall be deemed to be in default. The validity of the credit shall extend at least 21 days beyond the shipment period stipulated in this contract.

(b) Payment against documents:

Payment shall be by net cash, without discount, at first presentation of the documents listed above.

In the event of non-payment, by the buyer, for documents complying with the conditions of this sale, the seller may give him formal notice to effect payment within 48 hours.

If payment is not made within that period, the seller may freely dispose of the goods and, declaring the buyer to be in default, may ask for the terms of the close- out of this contract to be fixed by means of arbitration (with any price difference, additional costs, penalty and interest to be borne by the buyer).

6° / SUPERVISION, WEIGHING AND SAMPLING

Supervision, weighing and sampling of each bill of lading shall be obligatory and carried out without interruption in the presence of the buyer's and the seller's supervisors on shipment at the seller's expense with each party bearing the costs of its own supervisor.

The tonnage shown on the weight certificate shall be final, whether the buyer is represented or not at weighing.

(a) Supervision: If no supervisor is appointed by the buyer within the period stipulated in this contract, the loaded goods are deemed to comply with the conditions of this sale.

(b) Sampling: Sealed samples shall be randomly drawn in the presence of the buyer's and the seller's supervisors on a minimum of 30% of the bags to be loaded. In the event of various shipping marks appearing on the bill of lading, each mark shall be sampled separately. The samples shall weigh a minimum of 2 kg and be packed and sealed in woven bags.

7° / FORCE MAJEURE

If shipment is prevented for reasons of unforeseeable and insurmountable events, the shipment period shall be automatically extended by one month.

If, at the end of such extension, shipment is still impossible for the reasons indicated above, the buyer shall have the option:

– either of terminating this contract in respect of any quantity not shipped,

– or of continuing to perform this contract; in this case, the freight booked shall be the first available after the day when the buyer is informed by the seller that shipment is now possible; the shipment period shall be extended, such extension, however, being limited to five months; when this period has elapsed, this contract shall be automatically cancelled for any quantity not shipped.

The above-mentioned option shall be declared in writing by the buyer to the seller as soon as the latter has notified his inability to ship during the extended period, but not later than seven days from the end of the month following the shipment period stipulated in this contract.

This contract shall be deemed void if the buyer does not declare the above-mentioned option in the manner set out above.

In all cases the seller shall give prompt notice to the buyer and supply proof of Force Majeure.

8° / ARBITRATION CLAIMS

(a) Quality claims: Any claim relating to inferior quality shall reach the counter-party and the A.F.C.C. within a maximum period of 21 days after the date of the bill of lading. Notwithstanding article 17 paragraph 1 of the Rules of the «Chambre Arbitrale» of the A.F.C.C., the arbitration shall be made within 50 days from the date of the bill of lading.

(b) Technical claims: Any claim shall reach the counter-party and the A.F.C.C. within a maximum period of one year after the date of the bill of lading, or after the last scheduled date for shipment if such has not taken place.

(c) Arbitration procedure and appeal: The parties shall refer to the rules of the «Chambre Arbitrale» of the A.F.C.C.

9° / ARBITRATION CLAUSE

By express agreement, any dispute arising between the seller and the buyer for any reason whatsoever relating to this contract shall be settled by arbitration by the «Chambre Arbitrale» of the A.F.C.C. in accordance with its rules which both parties declare they are familiar with and accept. The arbitration award shall be final and not subject to appeal.

10° / APPLICABLE LAW

This contract and its consequences shall be subject to French law.

APPENDIX I

ASSOCIATION FRANÇAISE DU COMMERCE DES CACAOS

1st January 1993 — **FORM N° 3**

Company/trading name of seller

OFFICIAL CONTRACT FOR TRANSACTIONS
IN COCOA BEANS ON F.O.B. NET LANDED WEIGHT TERMS

Date

N°

Company/trading name of buyer

We confirm the verbal sale which we made with you	1
through	2
by order and on behalf of	3
subject to the Market Rules of the ASSOCIATION FRANÇAISE DU COMMERCE DES	4
CACAOS and the conditions set out on both sides of this contract, which the parties declare they	5
are familiar with and accept.	6

Quantity
(tonnes of 1,000 kg).   **7**
With a tolerance of plus or minus 2%, on shipment, of which the weight shown on the bill of lading shall be proof.   **8**

Cocoa   **9**

Quality on arrival   Fair merchantable.   **10**

Price   **11**

Packing   In new, exportable, woven, non-returnable bags; actual tare.   **12**

Shipment period   From origin during   **13**

Shipment port(s)   **14**
At seller's option; to be declared not later than 45 days before the first day of the shipment   **15**
period, failing which shipment to be effected from the major cocoa port of the country of   **16**
origin.   **17**

Port(s) of destination   **18**
At buyer's option; to be declared not later than 15 days before the first day of the shipment period,   **19**
by minimum quantities of 25 tonnes per port.   **20**

Freight   At buyer's expense.   **21**

Marine insurance   At buyer's expense.   **22**

Payment   Net cash for 99 % of the amount of the provisional invoice.   **23**
(cf. clause # 5)   (a) by irrevocable letter of credit, in conformity with the contractual conditions agreed by the parties.   **24**
(b) at first presentation in   and in exchange for shipping   **25**
documents complying with the conditions of this sale (1).   **26**

Special conditions (2)   **27**
  28
  29
  30

BUYER'S STAMP AND SIGNATURE   SELLER'S STAMP AND SIGNATURE

(1) delete as appropriate, failing which paragraph (b) shall be deemed to be deleted.   (2) insert "None" if there are no special conditions.

APPENDIX I

F.O.B. NET LANDED WEIGHT TERMS

1° / FREIGHT

Freight shall be booked with first-class shipping companies, and the goods loaded on board vessels with A1 classification on one of the registers listed in the "Police Française d'Assurance Maritime sur Facultés" by the "Syndicat Français de l'Assurance Maritime et Transports" in its most recent edition.

The seller shall bear the costs and risks relating to the goods until such time as they have passed the ship's rail at the port of shipment at origin.

The buyer shall advise the seller of the following:
– the name of the vessel (or her substitute);
– the name of the ship's agent at the port of shipment;
– the estimated time of arrival ("E.T.A.") of the vessel at the port of shipment;
– the quantity to be loaded on board;
– the port of final destination.

The buyer shall send this advice to the seller not later than 15 days before the scheduled date of the vessel's arrival at the port of shipment, failing which the seller shall not be obliged to load the goods on the said vessel and may require the buyer to provide, within the required time, an advice regarding a vessel named as substitute.

In any event, if an advice has been forwarded promptly along the string of buyers and sellers, it shall be considered to have been received within the required time by the first seller.

The duration of the voyage shall be that of regular liners serving the ports of shipment and final destination stipulated in this contract.

If the loading cannot take place by the scheduled date:
– either because of late arrival of the vessel,
– or because of a refusal by the carrier to accept the goods on board (unless the seller is at fault),

the buyer shall reimburse the seller the extra costs incurred by the latter, from the second day following the latest E.T.A. of the vessel notified in writing by the buyer to the seller up to the date of arrival in the port of shipment of the delayed or substituted vessel, provided that the goods have been tallied.

If the buyer is unable to nominate within the required time a vessel due to load during the shipment period stipulated in this contract, he shall be deemed to be in default.

If the seller is unable to make the goods available for loading onto the vessel nominated by the buyer, he shall be deemed to be in default.

In the event of either party to this contract being in default, the other party may ask for the terms of the close-out of this contract to be fixed by means of arbitration (with any price difference, additional costs, penalty and interest to be borne by the party in default).

2° / SHIPMENT

Shipment shall be effected by through bill(s) of lading specifying the goods, with the number of bags, shipping marks, and serial numbers if they exist.

Unless there is proof to the contrary, the bill of lading marked "loaded on board" shall be taken as proof of shipment and its date as the date of shipment.

3° / ADVICE OF SHIPMENT (DECLARATION)

All advices of shipment shall be made by telex or telegram.

They shall specify: the origin of the goods, the name of the vessel, the tonnage involved, the number of bags, the shipping marks, the serial numbers (if they exist), the date and the number of the loaded on board bill of lading, the destination and the mode of transport (conventional, container, bolster, etc.).

Any significant error may be rectified up to the opening of the hatches.

Each declaration shall be for a minimum of 25 tonnes, except for the balance of the quantity sold. In the event of several bills of lading appearing on the same declaration, each bill of lading shall be considered to be a partial declaration. Each partial declaration shall be considered to be the execution of a separate contract.

A declaration which complies with the terms of this contract shall be irrevocable.

The seller shall be entitled to declare a shipment against this contract ship lost or not lost, subject to him submitting proof of shipment and providing the buyer with all the shipping documents (cf. clause #4).

Each seller shall forward the declaration to his buyer promptly.

Any costs and consequences which may result from failure to comply with the above obligations shall be borne by the party responsible.

4° / DOCUMENTS

The seller shall provide the buyer with the following documents:

– provisional invoice;
– complete set of clean, negotiable, loaded on board bills of lading, marked "Freight payable at destination";
– certificate of origin or movement;
– phytosanitary and fumigation certificates issued in accordance with the requirements of the country of export;
– any certificates or documents required under international agreements and regulations applying to cocoa transactions between the country of origin and the country of destination.

5° / PAYMENT

(a) *By letter of credit issued by a first-class bank at the buyer's expense:*

In any event, the seller's bank shall receive from the issuing bank notification of the opening of the credit before the commencement of the shipment period, failing which the buyer shall be deemed to be in default. The validity of the credit shall extend at least 21 days beyond the shipment period stipulated in this contract.

(b) *Payment against documents:*

Payment shall be by net cash, without discount, at first presentation of the documents listed above. In the event of non-payment, by the buyer, for documents complying with the conditions of this sale, the seller may give him formal notice to effect payment within 48 hours. If payment is not made within that period, the seller may freely dispose of the goods and, declaring the buyer to be in default, may ask for the terms of the close-out of this contract to be fixed by means of arbitration (with any price difference, additional costs, penalty and interest to be borne by the buyer).

6° / SUPERVISION, WEIGHING AND SAMPLING

Supervision, weighing and sampling of each bill of lading or delivery order shall be obligatory and carried out without interruption in the presence of the buyer's and the seller's supervisors at the port of destination specified in the bill of lading, at the buyer's expense with each party bearing the costs of its own supervisor, within a maximum of 15 days after the final day of landing of the vessel, failing which the seller may issue the final invoice on the basis of the bill of lading (or delivery order) weight increased by 2%.

This method of invoicing shall not apply if the buyer is not responsible for the delay and if the buyer weighs the parcel without delay as soon as he has access to the goods.

If the valid documents are not presented when the vessel arrives, the above-mentioned period shall commence from the date of their presentation.

(a) **supervision:** The buyer shall summon the supervisor appointed by the seller, failing which the latter may issue the final invoice on the bill of lading (or delivery order) weight increased by 2%. If no supervisor is appointed by the seller before the arrival of the vessel, as defined by the responsible authority, the weighing and sampling carried out by the buyer's supervisor or by a sworn weigher or duly authorised company shall be binding on the parties.

(b) **weight:** Net landed, tolerance plus or minus 2% in relation to the quantity sold.

In the event of the tolerance of minus 2% being exceeded, the total shortfall shall give rise to compensation calculated on the basis of the difference between the selling price and the market value on the final day of landing of the vessel, if the market value is higher than the selling price.

In the event of the tolerance of plus 5% being exceeded, the total excess shall remain for the account of the seller, if the buyer refuses to take delivery of the total excess at the market value on the final day of landing of the vessel.

(c) **sampling:** Sealed samples shall be randomly drawn in the presence of the buyer's and the seller's supervisors on a minimum of 30% of the sound landed bags, at the time of the weighing performed within the stipulated period, failing which the buyer shall lose the right to claim arbitration on quality. In the event of various shipping marks appearing on the bill of lading, each mark shall be sampled separately. The samples shall weigh a minimum of 2 kg and be packed and sealed in woven bags.

7° / FINAL INVOICING

The net landed weight to be invoiced shall be calculated by multiplying the average weight of the sound and full bags agreed on arrival by the number of bags shown on the bill of lading (or delivery order).

The seller shall issue the final invoice within 30 days from the last day of weighing and attach to it a copy of the supervisor's report. After this period, the invoice may be issued by the buyer.

If the seller has not appointed a supervisor, the buyer shall forward or have forwarded to the seller the document certifying the weight, issued by one of the parties indicated in lines 65–66 above within a period of 15 business days from the last day of weighing, failing which the seller may issue the invoice on the basis of the bill of lading (or delivery order) weight.

The balance shall be paid on receipt of the final invoice if it is in favour of the seller, or when the invoice is despatched if it is in favour of the buyer.

The interest owed, due as from the date of the final invoice but at the earliest from the 31st day after the weighing, shall be calculated by the creditor at the official bank rate applying to the currency of this contract, plus 2% per annum.

30 days after this date, the rate of interest chargeable shall be increased by half, but not above the maximum legal rate of interest.

8° / FORCE MAJEURE

If shipment is prevented for reasons of unforeseeable and insurmountable events, the shipment period shall be automatically extended by one month.

If, at the end of such extension, shipment is still impossible for the reasons indicated above, the buyer shall have the option:

– either of terminating this contract in respect of any quantity not shipped,
– or of continuing to perform this contract; in this case, the freight booked shall be the first available after the day when the buyer is informed by the seller that shipment is now possible; the shipment period shall be extended, such extension, however, being limited to five months; when this period has elapsed, this contract shall be automatically cancelled for any quantity not shipped.

The above-mentioned option shall be declared in writing by the buyer to the seller as soon as the latter has notified his inability to ship during the extended period, but not later than seven days from the end of the month following the shipment period stipulated in this contract.

This contract shall be deemed void if the buyer does not declare the above-mentioned option in the manner set out above.

In all cases the seller shall give prompt notice to the buyer and supply proof of Force Majeure.

9° / ARBITRATION CLAIMS

(*a*) *Quality claims:* Any claim relating to inferior quality shall reach the counter-party and the A.F.C.C. within a maximum period of 21 days after the final day of landing of the vessel.

(*b*) *Technical claims:* Any claim shall reach the counter-party and the A.F.C.C. within a maximum period of one year after the final day of landing of the vessel, or after the last scheduled date for shipment if such has not taken place.

(c) *Arbitration procedure and appeal:* The parties shall refer to the rules of the "Chambre Arbitrale" of the A.F.C.C.

10° / ARBITRATION CLAUSE

By express agreement, any dispute arising between the seller and the buyer for any reason whatsoever relating to this contract shall be settled by arbitration by the "Chambre Arbitrale" of the A.F.C.C. in accordance with its rules which both parties declare they are familiar with and accept. The arbitration award shall be final and not subject to appeal.

11° / APPLICABLE LAW

This contract and its consequences shall be subject to French law.

ASSOCIATION FRANÇAISE DU COMMERCE DES CACAOS

1st July 1991 — **FORM N 4**

Company/trading name of seller

OFFICIAL CONTRACT FOR TRANSACTIONS
IN COCOA BEANS ON C.I.F. NET LANDED WEIGHT
WITH " ARRIVAL " AND/OR " TENDER IN STORE " OPTIONS

Date

N°

Company/trading name of buyer

We confirm the verbal sale which we made with you	1
through	2
by order and on behalf of	3
subject to the Market Rules of the ASSOCIATION FRANÇAISE DU COMMERCE DES	4
CACAOS and the conditions set out on both sides of this contract, which the parties declare they	5
are familiar with and accept.	6

Quantity

(tonnes of 1,000 kg).   7

With a tolerance of plus or minus 2% in relation to the quantity sold.   8

Cocoa

9

10

Quality

Fair merchantable. Determined on arrival of the vessel at the port of destination, or in store in case   11
of tender in store. Mandatory acceptance of the goods in all cases.   12

13

Price

14

15

16

Conditions

At seller's option: 17
(a) SHIPMENT   from origin during   18
(b) ARRIVAL at   during   19
   by shipment either from origin or from any other port.   20
(c) TENDER IN STORE at   during   21
   with/without (1) reimbursement clause (cf. lines 57/58 on the reverse of this contract).   22
   Any exercise of an option which complies with the conditions of this sale shall be irrevocable.   23

Packing

In new, exportable, woven, non-returnable bags; actual tare.   24

Payment

At first presentation and in exchange for shipping documents or, in the case of tender in store, for   25
delivery documents specified on the reverse of this contract.   26

Special conditions (2)

27

28

29

30

BUYER'S STAMP AND SIGNATURE   SELLER'S STAMP AND SIGNATURE

(1) Delete as appropriate ; failing which the word "with" shall be deemed to be deleted   (2) Insert "None" if there are no special conditions.

SPECIAL CONDITIONS RELATING TO "OPTIONS"

1. – FULFILMENT BY "SHIPMENT". — The seller who chooses to fulfil this contract by this option shall send the declaration to his buyer not later than by midnight on the 14th day following the shipment period; in this case all the terms and conditions of the A.F.C.C. contract form n° 1 (C.I.F.) shall apply.

2. – FULFILMENT BY "ARRIVAL". — All the terms and conditions of the A.F.C.C. contract form n° 1 shall apply to transactions executed under this option, as long as they do not conflict with the following terms and conditions.

The present option may only be exercised by the seller if, at the time of the advice of shipment (declaration), the cocoa is afloat and scheduled to arrive at the port of destination specified on the bill of lading during the arrival period stipulated in this contract.

The declaration shall, in addition to what is specifically mentioned in the A.F.C.C. contract form n° 1, include the estimated time of arrival of the vessel at the port specified on the bill of lading, as indicated to the seller by the shipping company on the day of the said declaration.

The seller shall only be able to claim Force Majeure if he has declared in writing, not later than 15 days before the commencement of the arrival period stipulated in this contract, his intention to load at a port other than the port of origin. Such a declaration shall be forwarded promptly along the string of buyers and sellers.

3. – FULFILMENT BY "TENDER IN STORE". — Only sound cocoa, after reconditioning, may be delivered under this option.

All terms and conditions of the A.F.C.C. contract form n° 1 shall apply to transactions executed under this option, as long as they do not conflict with the following terms and conditions.

— *Advice of tender (declaration):* All advices of tender shall specify: the location of the goods, the warrant number or reference of the irrevocable delivery order issued by the warehousekeeper, the date of storage, the origin, the tonnage involved, the number of bags, the shipping marks, the date of the last weighing made in the warehouse, the expiry date of the rent and insurance and, if any, the name of the supervisor appointed by the seller.

All declarations shall specify whether the parcel is in complete or partial fulfilment of the quantity sold. Each declaration shall be considered to be the execution of a separate contract.

Each declaration shall be for a minimum of 10 tonnes, except for the balance of the quantity sold.

— *Delivery documents:* List:
  - Invoice based on the last weight certified in the warehouse;
  - Warrant or irrevocable delivery order issued by the warehousekeeper, mentioning the origin, the tonnage, the number of bags and their marks;
  - Any certificates and documents required under international agreements relating to transactions between the country of origin of the cocoa and the country of destination.

— *Weighing:* The weight from the last certified weighing shall be binding on the parties. However, if the last weighing took place more than 6 months before the declaration, the buyer shall be entitled:

- to a contractual rebate of 0.5% if the goods are not removed from the warehouse within 15 days after the date of presentation of documents.
- either to the 0.5% rebate indicated above or to the reweighing, if the goods are removed from the warehouse within 15 days after the date of presentation of documents. This reweighing shall take place in the presence of the buyer's and the seller's supervisors without interruption at the time of delivery from the warehouse; it shall give rise to an "adjustment invoice".

The seller shall bear the cost of unstowing, placing on the scales and reweighing.

In the event of the tolerance of minus 2% of the quantity sold being exceeded, the total shortfall shall give rise to compensation calculated on the basis of the difference between the selling price and the market value on the last day of reweighing.

In the event of the tolerance of plus 2% of the quantity sold being exceeded, the total excess shall remain for the account of the seller if the buyer refuses to take delivery of the total excess at the market value on the last day of reweighing.

— **Sampling:** Sealed samples shall be randomly drawn in the presence of the buyer's and the seller's supervisors within 15 days after the date of presentation of documents or, in the case of reweighing in this period, at the time and under the conditions of the reweighing.
The seller shall take all necessary measures to facilitate the access to the parcel for sampling.

— **Storage and insurance costs:** The goods shall be stored and insured at the contract price by the seller at his own expense up to at least the 15th day inclusive following the date of presentation of documents.
The goods shall remain at seller's risk until the declaration is issued.

— **Reimbursement clause:** The buyer shall reimburse the seller the costs from C.I.F. to warehouse and the cost of weighing of the parcel.

— **Payment:** The amount of the full invoice shall be paid 4 business days after the date of the declaration, in exchange for delivery documents complying with the conditions of this sale.

— **Arbitration claims:**
   (a) Quality claims: Any claim shall reach the counter-party and the A.F.C.C. within a maximum period of 21 days after the date of presentation of documents.
   (b) Technical claims: Any claim shall reach the counter-party and the A.F.C.C. within a maximum period of one year after the date of presentation of documents.
   (c) Arbitration procedure and appeal: The parties shall refer to the rules of the "Chambre Arbitrale" of the A.F.C.C.

   4. – **ARBITRATION CLAUSE.** — By express agreement, and dispute arising between the seller and the buyer for any reason whatsoever relating to this contract shall be settled by arbitration by the "Chambre Arbitrale" of the A.F.C.C. in accordance with its rules which both parties declare they are familiar with and accept. The arbitration award shall be final and not subject to appeal.
   5. – **APPLICABLE LAW.** — This contract and its consequences shall be subject to French law.

ASSOCIATION FRANCAISE DU COMMERCE DES CACAOS

ADDENDUM FOR PRICE FIXING TO CONTRACT

NO._____ of_____

PRICE:

I. It will be fixed by premium/discount of _____ in relation to the price of _____ of the position _____ of the cocoa terminal market of_____. Price will be expressed in _____ by _____.

II. The price of this contract shall be fixed by the buyers/sellers at the earliest on _____ and the latest on _____ at the market quotation of _____ of the cocoa terminal market of _____, in relation to the official buyer/seller price of the call concerned and/or at any other agreed price. In order that the price be properly fixed during a call, instructions must be received at the latest _____ before the said call. The price of this contract can be fixed at any other time by agreement between the parties.

III. The buyers/sellers reserve the right to fix the price of any quantity not yet fixed during the call of _____ (indicated in the above paragraph). If the terminal market is closed on that particular day, such quantity will be fixed according to the closing price established by the competent authorities of the terminal market of _____. If no closing price is fixed, the price of the said quantity will be fixed during the opening call of the next market day.

IV. The buyers/sellers can fix the price of only a part of this contract on the following conditions:

- that this part be equal to _____ tonnes (or multiple of the latter quantity), except for balance of contract;

- that this part fixed in one single operation be equal to a maximum of _____.

V Each fixing will be considered as a separate contract, unless agreed otherwise by the parties.

PAYMENT

I. It will be made at first presentation of documents, as indicated in the payment clause of the main contract.

II. The invoicing will be established in relation to the individual prices or their weighed average, at the option of the seller.

III. For any tonnage the price of which has not been fixed on the day of the invoicing, a provisional price will be taken into account, equal to the official seller's price of the position _____ of the cocoa terminal market of _____ at the opening call on the day of sending of the declaration or, in the case of delivery in warehouse, of the day of tendering of the goods.

IV. If necessary, buyers/sellers can claim margin calls in proportion to the price of the provisional invoice.

V.   The settlement of any balance resulting from price fixing will be made on presentation of documents establishing the existence of the said balance.

STAMP AND SIGNATURE OF BUYER   STAMP AND SIGNATURE OF SELLER

APPENDIX I

MARKET RULES

Rule 1 - Quality standards for fair merchantable cocoa:

(A) General characteristics:

To comply with the terms of the contract, the cocoa delivered must be reasonably free of beans with off-flavours, live insects, foreign matter, broken beans, fragments of beans and pieces of cocoa bean shell; the goods must not contain an excessive percentage of violet or germinated beans.

N.B.: The words "reasonably" and "excessive" are intended to give the arbitration panel a certain latitude in assessing the delivery in dispute.

(B) Bean count:

Unless otherwise stipulated in the contract, the term "main crop" shall mean the following:

- not subject to an allowance up to approximately 100 beans per 100 grams,
- subject to an allowance from approximately 100 beans per 100 grams up to approximately 120 beans per 100 grams,
- refusable above that (if the buyer requests rejection), with seller's obligation to replace the parcel in dispute at his own expense within a period to be set by the arbitration panel.

N.B. The word "approximately" is intended to give the arbitration panel a certain latitude in assessing criteria such as, inter alia, the dryness and homogeneity of the parcel in dispute.

(C) Definitions of quality:

Unless otherwise stipulated, the definitions of quality shall mean the following:

- "GOOD FERMENTED":   maximum 5% of defective beans and/or 5% of slaty beans;
- "FAIR FERMENTED":   maximum 10% of defective beans and/or 10% of slaty beans;
- "F.A.Q." (Fair Average Quality) :

maximum 12% of defective beans and/or 12% of slaty beans.

The goods shall be subject to an allowance if the quality is inferior to the specifications above; however, an arbitration panel may consider - if the buyer has so requested - that the goods no longer comply with the terms of the contract if they contain, in excess of the percentages above, such a number of defective and/or slaty beans that the panel deems the parcel to be no longer of fair merchantable quality.

(D)   Definitions:

The following meanings shall apply:

(a)   Defective beans:

- mouldy bean: a cocoa bean on the internal parts of which traces of mould are visible to the naked eye;

- flat bean: a cocoa bean the two cotyledons of which are so thin that it is not possible to cut it so as to obtain an entire surface of the cotyledon;

- insect-damaged bean: a cocoa bean the internal parts of which contain insects at any stage of development or show signs of damage caused thereby which are visible to the naked eye.

(b)   Slaty bean : a cocoa bean which shows a slaty colour on half or more of the internal surface of the cotyledon.

(c)   Violet bean: a cocoa bean which shows a violet colour on half or more of the internal surface of the cotyledon.

(d)   Germinated bean: a cocoa bean the shell of which has been pierced, split or broken by the growth of the seed germ.

In any event, the allowance or rejection of the parcel - if so requested by the buyer - can be ordered only by the duly constituted arbitration panel, which is the only body competent to decide on the claim.

Rule 2 - Shipment:

"Immediate" shipment means shipment within 15 calendar days of the date of the contract.

"Prompt" shipment means shipment within 30 calendar days of the date of the contract.

Rule 3 - Delivery:

"Immediate" delivery means delivery within 15 calendar days of the date of the contract.

"Prompt" delivery means delivery within 30 calendar days of the date of the contract.

Rule 4 - Transmission periods:

Any transmission must be prompt.

In the case of a string, a delay in the periods specified in the contract cannot be invoked as a reason for non-performance of contract if each member of the string can prove that he was not responsible for any delay.

Rule 5 - Prompt transmission:

Prompt transmission means a transmission without delay by the speediest channels, and at the latest on the next business day.

Rule 6 - Deferment of execution:

Unless expressly stipulated otherwise, any period shall expire on the last day at 24.00 hours.

Any period which normally expires on a Saturday, Sunday, or a non-business day in the country where the obligation is to be fulfilled shall be extended to the next business day.

Rule 7 - Interest

Unless expressly stipulated otherwise, debit interest shall be calculated at the official rate, increased by 2% per annum, of the Bank issuing the currency in which the contract has been written.

Rule 8 - Quality arbitration in string:

Quality arbitration shall be effected between the first seller and the last buyer, as if they were the only contracting parties, when the quantity in dispute is the subject of the same bill of lading and the same exporter's mark and when the contracts are identical except for date, price and the terms which would, in the event of dispute, be subject to a technical arbitration.

Each member claiming to be in the string shall remain guarantor of the execution of the award vis-à-vis his own counterparty.

When several contracts stipulate different shipment periods, the string may be maintained if the shipment has taken place within the period common to the whole.

Rule 9 - In a case where, before the execution of a contract, one of the parties becomes bankrupt, his counterparty may formally request the receiver to declare within one month whether he will execute the contract.

Failing a positive answer received within the stipulated period, the counterparty may freely dispose of the goods and ask that the "wash out" of the contract be fixed by arbitration against the defaulting party (with price deferential, any additional costs, penalty and all damages and interest at the expense of the latter).

Rule 10 - Quality arbitration:

When a bill of lading mentions several exporter's marks, each of those marks shall be the subject of separate sampling provided that each of those marks represents at least 75 bags.

When the bill of lading mentions several marks each representing fewer than 75 bags, the buyer may have the said marks sampled proportionately as if one single mark were involved; the samples thus drawn shall be accepted as the basis for a claim.

Rule 11 - No arbitration claim may be examined by the Arbitration Chamber of the A.F.C.C. if it has been lodged by a party which has not paid the Association the whole of the arbitration costs relating to an earlier claim.

Rule 12 - The following shall not apply to A.F.C.C. contracts:

- the Uniform Law on International Sales (signed in The Hague on 1 July 1964),

- the United Nations Convention on Contracts for the International Sale of Goods (the 1980 Vienna Convention or C.I.S.G.).

Updated 1.7.1992

DEFINITIONS

Unless otherwise stipulated, the following meanings shall apply:

Hour: the official time in the country where the obligation is to be fulfilled.

Twenty-four hours, forty-eight hours: a period of twenty-four or forty-eight consecutive hours, the hours corresponding to business days.

Day, calendar day: period of 24 hours, midnight to midnight.

Business day: any day other than a non-business day.

Non business day:

(a) Saturdays and Sundays.

(b) Public holiday: day on which work ceases in order to celebrate a religious or civic holiday (this concept relates to the official regulations and to the practices of the country in which the obligation is to be fulfilled).

(c) Non-working day: day falling between two public holidays justifying the possible making of a "bridge" (this concept relates to the official regulations and to the practices of the country in which the obligation is to be fulfilled).

Week: period of 7 days, whatever the first day.

Calendar week: period of 7 days commencing Monday.

Period of 10 days: period of 10 consecutive days
        (first 10 days: from 1 to 10 of the month
        second 10 days: from 11 to 20 of the month
        third 10 days: from 21 to the end of the month).

Fortnight: period of two consecutive weeks
   (first fortnight: from 1 to 15 of the month
   second fortnight: from 16 to the end of the month)

Month: period falling between any day of one month and the corresponding day of the following month.

Calendar month: each of the 12 divisions of the year.

Year: period falling between any date of one year and the corresponding date of the following year.

Calendar year: period of 12 months running from 1 January to 31 December.

N.B. Unless otherwise stipulated, the periods are counted without interruption. The day on which the event occurred initiating a period shall not be taken into account in calculating the period.

II

CAL cocoa contracts

Physical cocoa contracts rules and regulations issued by

The Cocoa Association of London Ltd[†] (CAL)

Rules and Regulations

Price Fixation addenda

[†] Readers intending to trade on CAL terms are strongly recommended to obtain a copy of the Association's Handbook. They will be advised of any changes that the Association may make. The address of the Association is:

The Cocoa Association of London Ltd
1 Commodity Quay
St Katharine Docks
London E1 9AX

Tel 071-481 2080   Tlx 884370   Fax 071-702 9924

THE COCOA ASSOCIATION OF LONDON LTD. MARKET RULES

DEFINITIONS	a.	These rules refer to raw cocoa beans and to cocoa products as applicable.
	b.	The word "party" means a Buyer or a Seller on a contract made subject to these rules or a broker or a person acting as a broker signing such contract on behalf of or as a broker or agent for the Buyer and Seller or either of them. The words "party" and "person" include persons, firms, companies and corporations.
	c.	In these rules unless the context otherwise requires, words implying the singular number only shall include the plural number, and words implying the plural number only shall include the singular number, and words implying persons shall include forms, companies and corporations.
	d.	All Notices to be given under these Rules shall be given by letter, telex, telegram or by other method of rapid written communication excluding transmissions by facsimile. Any notice to be given under these Rules may be delivered personally or addressed to the last known place of business of the party concerned.
	e.	Unless otherwise stated "a day" means a business day in London.
	f.	"A business day" means any day other than: Bank Holidays, Christmas Day, Good Friday, Saturdays, Sundays, any day appointed by Royal Proclamation as a Public Holiday and any day declared to be a non-business day by the Association (all which days are called "non-business days").
	g.	Where an act has to be done on or before a given day and such day shall happen to be a non-business day such act must be done on the next following business day, unless otherwise specified in the contract.
	h.	The hours of a business day are from 0900 hours to 1700 hours or such hours as may be determined from time to time by the Council.
	j.	The cash hours shall be 14.30 hours up to which time Town cheques and/or telegraphic transfers must be received for payment of documents. In respect of any payment received by cheque after such hours shall date from the next business day and a day's interest will be debited. In respect of any payment by cheques drawn on non clearing banks or for less than the current Town Clearing Threshold, interest shall be charged from due date until cheques have been cleared (interest at Barclays Bank base rate plus 2%).
	k.	For the purpose of conversion, 1 tonne (one thousand kilogrammes) equal 2,204.6 lbs.
	l.	"ICCO" means the "International Cocoa Organization".
	m.	The masculine gender shall include the feminine gender.
	n.	"the Association" means "The Cocoa Association of London Limited".
GENERAL	aa.	Forms of contract issued by members shall bear the seal of the Association approved for this purpose. Such seals shall be supplied only to members at such prices and on such terms as the Council may from time to time determine.
	bb.	Unless otherwise agreed between buyer and seller price fixation of contracts shall be based upon the terms and conditions contained within the Association's price fixation forms In Section 29.
	cc.	Brokers and/or others buying or selling shall be responsible as principals, before the time of concluding the contract, and insert their principals' name in the contract.
	dd.	No party to any contract shall be at liberty to assign his interest therein without the consent in writing of other party thereto.
	ee.	Cocoa Beans shall be packed in clean, sound new jute bags of sufficient strength, or in bags of such other material as may be approved by the Association from time to time.
		Cocoa products shall be packed in new hygienic cartons and/or packages, suitably lined and in wrappings of sufficient strength.
	ff.	'Sound' when applicable to cocoa products shall mean full and undamaged cartons and/or packages.
QUANTITY	1.1	About tonnes
		(The tonnage agreed between the seller and buyer)
	1.2	The words "about" or "more or less" when used to define quantities contracted for, refers merely to the tolerance; that is an accidental and/or unavoidable excess or deficiency beyond Sellers control, and not to the deliberate short or over delivery at the option of the Seller. The excess/deficiency shall in no case exceed 1.5 per cent on cocoa beans or 0.25 per cent on cocoa products. This margin shall be void whenever a contract is liquidated by payment of difference between purchase and sales prices in lieu of shipment or tender.
		Weight of products shall be that as printed on the package in accordance with Statutory Instrument 1988 Weights and Measures No 2040 [The Weights and measures (Misc Foods) Order 1988].
COCOA BEANS DESCRIPTIONS	2.1	Cocoa beans are the seed of the cocoa tree (Theobroma Cacao Linnaeus) which, unless otherwise specified, will be fermented, dry and free from smoky, hammy or other abnormal odours.
	2.2	Parcels are to be reasonably free from flat beans, germinated beans, fragments and pieces of shell and virtually free from foreign matter and adulteration. The beans are to be reasonably uniform in size.

The overall condition of a parcel is to conform to the generally accepted standards of international cocoa trade and be externally and internally sound and reasonably free from any insect, rodent or any other type of infestation.

SPECIAL CONDITIONS	3.1	Special Conditions must be mutually agreed between buyer and seller.

3.2 Sellers may relinquish their option as to which type(s)/grade(s)/brand(s) will be delivered against this contract or part thereof provided they advise buyers in writing prior to commencement of shipment period the name(s) and quantity(ies) of the type(s)/grade(s)/brand(s) they will deliver.

3.3 The price of this contract is based on the freight rate to U.K. basis ports agreed by the Cocoa Marketing Co. (Ghana) Ltd., with United Kingdom West Africa Lines for the season, excluding any bunker surcharge. Any bunker surcharge or subsequent variation in the basis freight during the said season will be for buyers account, as will any premiun charge or discount allowed by Cocoa Marketing Co. (Ghana) Ltd, for ports other than U.K. basis ports.

TERMS AND DESTINATION

4.1 Contracts can be issued on any terms to/at any destination/location all of which are mutually agreed by Sellers and Buyers:

As an example:　　Cost, Insurance and Freight (Amsterdam)
　　　　　　　　　　Cost and Freight (London)
　　　　　　　　　　Free on Board (Tema)
　　　　　　　　　　In/Ex Store (Hamburg)

CLASSIFICATION OF VESSLES CHARTERPARTIES, SHIPMENT AND DISCHARGE

5.1　(a)　The word "shipment" in these rules includes a shipment by sea, road, rail and/or air.

　　　(b)　"Shipment from Origin" shall mean shipment of cocoa beans and/or cocoa products from country of origin or otherwise mutually agreed.

　　　(c)

　　　　　(i)　**"Shipment on CIF terms"** when shipment is made direct from origin and the goods would normally be imported free of duty and Sellers are unable to supply such supporting documents, then the duty shall be for Seller's account.

　　　　　(ii)　**"Arrival on CIF terms"** when shipment is made from anywhere Sellers shall provide Buyers with an EUR1 certificate or any other document required for a duty free entry of the goods. If Sellers are unable to provide such documents duty to be for sellers account.

5.2 "Immediate" shipment shall mean shipment within fifteen calendar days from the date of contract.

5.3 "Prompt" shipment shall mean shipment within thirty calendar days from the date of contract.

5.4 "Afloat" shall mean a parcel which at the time of contract had already been shipped on board the vessel but had not broken bulk and/or commenced discharge at the final port of destination.

5.5 In cases of shipment by sea the word "vessels" shall mean any first class vessels and/or power engined ships (excluding tankers) classed not lower than 100 A1 or British Corporation BS or top classification in American, French, Italian, Norwegian, or other equal register or ships not inferior to these classifications (liner terms Bills of Lading). (Any vessels and/or power engined ships which have been chartered by conference owned line shall not be acceptable unless conference owner line guarantees that the vessel and/or ship is on a time charter).

5.6 In the event of a shipment by charter vessel or any other vessel below the laid down standard sellers shall give a full guarantee indemnifying buyers against:

　　　(a)　inability to obtain prompt delivery

　　　(b)　irregularities in the documents

　　　(c)　extra and/or unknown charges arising out of the terms of the charter party when these differ from recognised liner terms

AND

in the event of a vessel and/or ship as a result of a charter party dispute discharging its cargo in a port other than the port shown on the Bills of Lading, all costs of re-shipping the cargo to the original port of discharge will be for Sellers' account. Buyers to claim from Sellers any additional/extra insurance premium as a result of vessel/ship's age.

5.7 Shipments by sea shall be by vessel direct or indirect with or without transhipment at Seller's option.

Shipments by sea under charter party terms will be direct only.

5.8 Shipment in containers is not allowed without mutual consent.

5.9 A shipment shall consist of not less than five metric tonnes or 25 per cent of the contract quantity whichever is the lesser, except when necessary to complete the contract.

5.10 Where a shipowner, in exercise of his rights under the terms of the Bill of Lading, finally discharges the cargo at a port other than that named in the Bill of Lading, that port becomes the port of destination for all settlements under the contract.

5.11 Clean, Shipped on Board through Bills of Lading shall be considered proof of shipment in the absence of evidence to the contrary.

5.12 Each Bill of Lading/Ships Delivery Order or any other instrument of title shall be treated as a separate contract.

FOB TERMS 5.13 (a) **Sellers booking Freight**
Freight to be booked by Sellers' for Buyers' account. Port of Destination to be declared by the Buyer not later than twenty one days before the first day of the contract period, and provided this advice is passed on immediately by intervening Buyers and Sellers it shall be considered to be in time. Should Sellers then fail to load within the contractual shipment period they shall be deemed to be in default.

(b) **Buyers booking Freight**
Port of Destination to be declared by Buyers not later than 21 days before the first day of the shipment period.

Buyers to nominate vessel/s and tonnage required for loading and give minimum of 21 days' notice of the estimated time of arrival of the vessel/s at port of loading. Buyers to advise Sellers of any change/s in the estimated time of arrival.

Providing all intervening Buyers and Sellers have passed on the Port of Destination and estimated time of arrival of the vessel/s immediately it shall be considered to be in time.

Should Sellers fail to load on the duly nominated vessel/s they shall be deemed to be in default.

If the Buyers have not made freight available for loading by the end of the shipment period they shall be deemed to be in default.

5.14 **Transhipment**
In the case of transhipment(s) the name of the main carrier to the port of final destination shall be communicated to the Buyer by the Seller at least 7 days prior to arrival.

5.15 Vessels to discharge according to the conditions of the Bills of Lading in force with regular lines to the port of discharge, or in accordance with the custom of the port of discharge where the vessel must be presented by the Owner or Established Authorised Agent whose name shall be mentioned in the advice of shipment.

INSURANCE 6.1 Marine Insurance shall be covered by Seller/Buyer at the price of the contract with Lloyd's and/or first class Underwriter, and/or first class Insurance Companies for whose solvency Sellers are not to be responsible on the terms of and according to the Institute Commodity Trades Clauses (A), Institute War Clauses (Commodity Trades) and Institute Strike Clauses (Commodity Trades) all dated 5 September 1983 current and available at the time of shipment. Should the War Risks Insurance Premiums exceed 0.5 per cent the excess shall be for account of the Buyer.

6.2 In case of cost and freight and/or FOB contracts only, satisfactory Letter of Guarantee (or Policy of Insurance if required) to be deposited with Sellers for their security.

6.3 Cocoa beans tendered in/ex store shall be at risk of Sellers (to the amount of contract value only) to time of payment or 15.00 hours on the prompt date, whichever is earlier.

6.4 Marine Insurance on all Cocoa butter and Cocoa liquor contracts must include cover for melting from any cause whatsoever.

DECLARATION OF SHIPMENT/ TENDER 7.1 Declaration of shipment and tender shall only be made in writing, excluding facsimile transmissions.

7.2 Declarations made by cable shall be subject to errors of cable companies only.

7.3 Declarations made by telex shall contain evidence of the date and time of transmission and the receiver's call sign which shall be accepted as evidence of receipt of the declaration unless queried immediately. Sellers shall accept responsibility for any errors or faults in transmission of declarations made by telex.

7.4 Declarations made by letter shall be accompanied by a counterfoil stating the date sent out. Buyers must acknowledge receipt of such declarations by a valid and binding signature. For the purpose of this rule a rubber stamp of the firm, together with the full signature of the individual receiver of a declaration shall be considered sufficient. Buyers must state the date and time of receipt.

7.5 After shipment has been effected Sellers shall declare to Buyers with due despatch the following:

(a) Contract Number and Date of Contract
(b) Quantity of goods shipped (tonnes, bags and/or packages).
(c) Description of goods shipped.
(d) name of vessel.
(e) Bill of Lading, date and number, Container Number and Container Seal Number (if shipped in containers.)
(f) port of shipment.
(g) port of destination.
(h) Marks.
(j) serial number of original ICCO certificate when applicable.
(k) in the case of charter name of the owner or established authorised agent at the port of destination named in the Bill of Lading

7.6   Sellers shall be entitled to declare a shipment against contract for shipment, ship lost or not lost.

7.7   A declaration of tender in/ex store to buyers shall include the following:

    (a)   Contract number and date of contract
    (b)   quantity of goods (tonnes, bags and/or packages)
    (c)   description of goods
    (d)   name of warehouse and warehousekeeper
    (e)   warrant number (where applicable)
    (f)   marks
    (g)   gross and net weights
    (h)   rent and warehouse insurance paid by Sellers up to prompt date
    (J)   prompt date
    (k)   final day of landing
    (l)   last day of weighing
    (m)   serial number of original or split ICCO certificate when applicable
    (n)   EUR1 certificate original or split when applicable

Each warehouse warrant or any other instrument of title shall be treated as a separate contract.

7.8   (a)   Where there is a string of contracts the subject matter and terms of which are materially the same, except as to date or price, each Seller shall declare a shipment or tender within the time stipulated in the contract following his receipt of the declaration made to him. This stipulation cannot of course apply to the first Seller who has only the obligation to declare within the time stipulated in the contract.

       (b)   However, a declaration shall be deemed as proper even if it is beyond the time specified in the contract provided the first Seller shall have made his declaration within the time allowed by the contract and provided each intermediate Seller shall have made his declaration with due despatch.

       (c)   Buyers, except under circumstances laid down in **Market Rule 16**, may not refuse a declaration of shipment or tender because of lateness or minor omission from such declaration but any Seller whose delay or omission in declaring thereby causes the Buyer unavoidable extra expenses shall re-imburse the Buyer for such extra expenses.

       (d)   Buyers shall accept declaration under the arrival option providing that at the time of declaration by their Seller the cocoa beans were afloat on a vessel scheduled to arrive during the contract period. Should the vessel fail to arrive in time, Buyers shall accept the cocoa beans at a fair allowance in case of need to be settled by arbitration in London. No claim shall be made against Sellers if vessel becomes a casualty thereby delaying the arrival of the cocoa beans or causing their loss.

TENDERS IN/EX STORE

7.9   Tenders shall be of not less than about 5 tonnes of one mark in one store except when it is necessary to tender less in order to complete the contract, in which case the balance tendered may be of more than one mark provided it is in one store.

7.10   Unless otherwise stated cocoa beans sold in/ex store can be tendered "in bond" if dutiable.

7.11   The "prompt date" is the day by which the goods must be paid for except for spot cocoa (See Market Rule 7.12). The prompt date shall be the fifth business day after date of tender.

Buyers wishing to take up documents before the prompt date must give notice to Sellers not later than 11.45 hours on the day on which they wish to make payment.

7.12   All cocoa beans sold as "spot" shall be ready for tender in/ex store at date of contract and tendered with due despatch. Prompt date shall be the fifth business day after the date of the contract.

7.13   All cocoa beans sold for "immediate" tender shall be made ready for tender ex store and declared within fifteen calendar days of the date of contract.

7.14   All cocoa beans sold for "prompt" tender shall be made ready for tender in/ex store and declared within thirty calendar days of the date of contract.

7.15   Cocoa beans tendered in/ex store shall normally be invoiced on nett official warehouse weights.

Seller shall pay all port, quay and warehouse charges until the prompt date and warehouse re-delivery charges where applicable.

7.16   In the event of cocoa beans being damaged or destroyed while in warehouse at Sellers risk, Sellers shall have the option of:
    (a)   replacing original tender with Buyer's consent notwithstanding **Market Rule 7.18.**
    (b)   replacing damaged/destroyed portion
    (c)   buying back the damaged/destroyed portion at a price mutually agreed with the Buyer with immediate settlement of any difference or, failing mutual agreement, at a price to be decided by arbitration.

7.17   In the case of contracts where the Sellers have the option to either declare shipment or tender in/ex store, and elect to tender in/ex store the following shall apply:
    (a)   only sound bags of cocoa beans may be tendered
    and
    (b)   Buyers shall reimburse Sellers with the cost of landing on and delivery ex-quay and weighing

7.18   A declaration of tender shall not be withdrawn nor substitution allowed except with the consent of the Buyer or in case of dispute unless the reasons adduced shall in the the opinion of the arbitrators warrant such withdrawal and substitution within the contract period, or shipment or delivery.

PROCEDURE FOR SHIPMENT CONTRACTS	8.1	Break bulk cocoa beans and/or Cocoa Products shall be officially weighed and tared at port of destination named in the bill of lading promptly by buyers in accordance with the custom of the port.

8.2   Containerised cocoa beans and/or cocoa products shall be officially weighed and tared either at port of destination named in the bill of lading if facilities are available or at a location outside the port of destination by mutual agreement between contracting parties.

8.3   Where no direct weighing and taring facilities are available in the port area, official weighing and taring shall take place at a suitable location near the port of destination.

8.4   Sellers may appoint a representative to supervise weighing and must inform Buyers of the name of such representative before arrival of vessel at port of destination. Buyers must give due notice to Seller's representative at the time and place of weighing. Should Sellers not name their representative or should their representative fail to present after having received due notice of time and place of weighing, weights certified by sworn weighers and provided by Buyers shall be accepted by Sellers. Should Buyers fail to notify Seller's representative in accordance with this clause, shipping weights shall be accepted.

8.5   Outturn weights shall be established on the sound and full bags and/or package delivered but applied proportionally to the whole parcel.

Any settlements due under the terms of the contract to be established on the basis of the landed weights as soon as these are ascertained.

In the event of the whole Bill of Lading quantity being damaged, original shipping weights shall apply.

8.6   Where a Bill of Lading consists of more than one main mark, each main mark on that Bill of Lading shall be weighed separately, provided that the quantity of each main mark is 25 bags or more of cocoa beans or 10 packages or more of cocoa products.

In cases where there is more than one main mark of less than 25 bags of cocoa beans or 10 packages of cocoa products Buyers shall have the option of having these main marks weighed and samples proportionally bulked as though they were one and such weights and samples shall be accepted as basis of settlement and claims.

8.7   Final Buyers shall provide Sellers with certified official weights and tares not later than twenty-eight calendar days after the final day of landing of the vessel and/or date of tender and/or final day of unstuffing of the last container, provided those are passed on immediately by intervening buyers and sellers they shall be considered to be in time for the purpose of any claim or settlement.

Should Buyers fail to provide certified weights and tares in time, shipping weights shall be accepted.

In the event of total loss the parcel shall be invoiced on shipping weights.

8.8   For contracts for cocoa beans on 'shipping weight' terms, the Seller shall compensate the Buyers for any loss in weight in excess of an agreed percentage level. The level or "Franchise" represents the weight loss which could be expected due to natural shrinkage during the voyage.

Any loss in weight exceeding the franchise calculated on the net weight of the sound and full bags delivered, but applied to the whole parcel, shall be borne by Sellers at contract price. If tendered in/ex store any loss in weight on slack bags calculated at contract price on the net weight of the sound and full bags shall be for Seller's account.

8.9   For contracts for cocoa beans on 'delivered weight' terms where the quantity landed exceeds the quantity shipped by 1.5 per cent or more for West African cocoa beans and 2.0 per cent or more for all other origins, Buyers shall have the option to refuse the total excess or accept it at the market value at 13.00 hours on the final day of landing of the vessel.

In the case where the quantity landed is less than the quantity shipped by 1.5 per cent or more for West African cocoa beans and 2.0 per cent or more for all other origins, the total shortage shall be the subject of a settlement based on the difference between the contract price and the market value at 13.00 hours on the final day of landing of the vessel.

PROCEDURE FOR DELIVERIES IN/EX STORE	8.10	Buyers shall accept invoicing either on official warehouse warrant nett weights or if on the day of tender 12 months have expired from the last date of weighing, Buyers shall be entitled to reweighing within 28 days of date of tender at Seller's expense. If delivery from warehouse is due to take place within 28 days from date of tender, reweighing shall take place on delivery if required. If delivery is not due to take place within 28 days from date of tender, Buyers shall be entitled to reweighing and rehousing at Sellers expense. In the event of reweighing, invoices shall be established on the new weight. For contracts on shipping weight terms **Market Rule 8.8** applies.

QUALITY	9.1	Quality on arrival, or on date of tender if cocoa beans are tendered in/ex store, to be

If inferior thereto a fair allowance to be made in case of need to be settled by arbitration under the Association's Rules for Arbitration and Appeal.

QUALITY STANDARDS FOR RAW COCOA BEANS	9.2	Good Fermented:	To be not more than 5 per cent mouldy and/or insect damaged or 5 per cent slaty beans by count.
		Fair Fermented:	To be not more than 10 per cent mouldy and/or insect damaged or 10 per cent slaty beans by count.

Superior Bahia	Bahia cocoa beans conforming to the Memorandum dated 29 April 1970 covering quality on arrival issued by the Bahia Cocoa Trade Commission and any subsequent Memoranda.
Standard Malaysian Cocoa (SMC):	Malaysian cocoa beans conforming to the Standard Cocoa grades as established by the Standards and Industrial Research Institute of Malaysia (SIRIM)
Ecuador European Standard	Ecuadorean cocoa beans conforming to the European Standard of qualities for Ecuadorean Cocoa issued by Association Nacional De Exportadores De Cacao y Cafe Del Ecuador.
Indonesian Standard	Indonesian cocoa beans conforming to Indonesian Department of Trade Standard for Cocoa Beans SP-45-1976 (Revised February 1985) and any subsequent revisions.

9.3 Cocoa beans sold under the description "all faults" whether samples are shown or not shall be taken without guarantee of quality or condition.

DEFINITIONS OF COCOA BEAN DEFECTS

9.4 **Defective Bean:** A cocoa bean which is internally mouldy and/or insect damaged to the naked eye.

(a) Mouldy Bean: A cocoa bean on the internal parts of which mould is visible to the naked eye.

(b) Insect Damaged Bean: A cocoa bean the internal parts of which are found to contain insects at any stage of development, or to show signs of damage caused thereby, which are visible to the naked eye.

(c) Slaty Bean: A cocoa bean which shows a slaty colour on half or more of the surface exposed by a cut made lengthwise through the centre.

Smoky or Hammy Bean: A cocoa bean which has smoky or hammy smell or taste.

Flat Bean: A cocoa bean which is too thin to be cut to give a surface of the cotyledon.

Adulteration: Alteration of the composition of a parcel of cocoa beans by any means whatsoever so that the resulting mixture or combination does not conform to the contractual description.

Foreign matter: Any substance other than cocoa beans, broken cocoa beans, fragments of cocoa beans and pieces of cocoa bean shell.

Bean size: Bean size is normally defined by the bean count, i.e. the number of beans per 100 grammes.
To ascertain bean count, a sample of not less than 300 grammes of whole beans, irrespective of size but not including flat beans, will be counted to obtain the number of beans per 100 grammes.

DESCRIPTION OF COCOA PRODUCTS

9.5 Cocoa Nib: The cotyledon of roasted or unroasted cocoa beans containing a residue of shell or germ not exceeding 5 per cent calculated on the dry defatted matter and an ash content not exceeding 10 per cent calculated on the dry defatted matter.

Cocoa Mass: Cocoa nib, mechanically processed to a paste, which retains the natural fat content of cocoa nib.

Press Cocoa Butter: Fat obtained by pressure, from cocoa nib, cocoa mass, cocoa press cake, fat-reduced cocoa press cake or any combination of two or more thereof:

(a) having been treated by no process other than degumming by filtering, centrifuging and other physical processes used for this purpose and deodorisation by super-heated steam under vacuum and other physical processes used for this purpose: and

(b) containing not more than 0.35 per cent unsaponifiable matter determined using petroleum ether and not more than 1.75 per cent acidity expressed as oleic acid (FFA).

Expeller Cocoa Butter: Fat obtained by the expeller process from cocoa beans or from cocoa beans combined with cocoa nib, cocoa mass, cocoa press cake, fat-reduced cocoa press cake or any combination of two or more thereof:

(a) having been treated by no process other than degumming by filtering, centrifuging and other physical processes used for this purpose and deodorisation by super-heated steam under vacuum and other physical processes used for this purpose: and

(b) containing not more than 0.5 per cent unsaponifiable matter determined using petroleum ether and not more than 1.75 per cent acidity expressed as oleic acid (FFA).

Refined Cocoa
Butter:

Fat obtained by pressure, the expeller process, solvent extraction or any combination of those processes from cocoa beans, cocoa nib, cocoa dust, cocoa mass, cocoa press cake, fat-reduced cocoa press cake, expeller cocoa press cake or any combination of two or more thereof with or without the addition of cocoa fat from one or more of these cocoa products:

(a) having been refined through neutralisation by an alkaline solution or similar substance used for this purpose and decolourisation with one or more of the following substance namely, bentonite, active carbons or similar substances used for this purpose;

(b) having been treated by no additional process other than those specified for press cocoa butter and

(c) containing not more than 0.5 per cent unsaponifiable matter determined using petroleum ether and not more than 1.75 per cent acidity expressed as oleic acid (FFA) and shell and germ fat in a ratio to fat from the cotyledon not exceeding that existing naturally in cocoa beans.

Cocoa Press Cake

Cocoa nib or cocoa mass has been converted by pressure by a mechanical process to a solid compressed mass.

Expeller Cocoa
Press Cake:

Cocoa beans or cocoa dust or both with or without cocoa nib, cocoa mass, cocoa press cake, fat-reduced cocoa press cake or any combination of two or more thereof which has been converted by the expeller process to a solid compressed mass.

Cocoa Powder

The finely ground particles obtained from the mechanical disintegration of cocoa press cake.

QUALITY CLAIMS FOR RAW COCOA BEANS AND COCOA PRODUCTS

9.6   The quality of cocoa beans and/or cocoa products is to be determined using a sample taken in accordance with **Section 11** unless otherwise agreed between Sellers and Buyers.

9.7   In the event of quality being inferior to contract warranty Sellers are to make buyers a fair allowance.

9.8   Failure to reach amicable settlement of quality claims is to be resolved by arbitration in London.

9.9   Final buyers shall notify sellers of any claim for inferiority of quality not later than twenty eight calendar days after the final day of landing of the vessel and/or unstuffing of the container and/or tender in/ex store and provided the claim is passed on immediately by intervening Buyers and Sellers the claim shall be considered to be in time. Arbitration shall be held not later than fifty-six calendar days after the final day of landing and/or unstuffing of the contain and/or tender in/ex store.

At the time of making the claim in respect of cocoa beans, Buyers shall send one sealed sample with full particulars to:

> The Cocoa Association of London Ltd.
> Hermitage Court
> Sampson Street
> Wapping
> London E1

and a duplicate of the sealed sample to the Sellers.

In the event of a claim in respect of cocoa products a sealed sample shall be sent to an independent analyst by mutual consent of both Buyer and Seller.

SUPERVISION

10.1   Sellers may appoint a representative to supervise weighing and sampling on cocoa beans and or cocoa products or on stored cocoa beans and/or cocoa products sampling only, and must inform Buyers the name of such representative before arrival of vessel at port of destination or at time of tender. Should Sellers not name their representative or should their representative fail to be present after having received due notice of time and place of weighing and sampling, weights certified and samples sealed by sworn weighers and samplers and provided by Buyers, shall be accepted by Sellers. Should Buyers fail to notify Sellers' representative in accordance with this clause, shipping weights shall be accepted and no quality claim shall be admitted.

SAMPLING FOR COCOA BEANS

11.1   At least two sealed samples of cocoa beans shall be drawn by contracting parties from not less than 30 per cent of the sound bags only weighing not less than 2 kilos nett for each Bill of Lading/Warrant quantity or main mark in accordance with **Market Rule 11.4** and sealed promptly at the time of discharge or tender in/ex store in accordance with **Market Rule 11.3.**

11.2   Samples of cocoa beans shall be marked or labelled to show that they are drawn from not less than 30 per cent of the sound bags only and shall state:

Name of vessel (with Rotation Number, if any)
Country of Origin
Port of shipment
Port of destination

Mark(s)
Number of bags
Date of Sampling
Final day of discharge of the vessel and/or unstuffing of the final container
Bill of Lading Number/Delivery Order Number/Warrant Number as applicable

11.3   Sellers may appoint a representative to supervise sampling and must inform Buyers of the name of such representative before arrival at port of discharge or prior to tender in/ex store. Buyers must give due notice to Seller's representative of the time and place of sampling. Should the Sellers not name their representative or should their representative fail to be present after having received due notice of time and place of sampling, samples sealed by sworn weighers and samplers and provided by Buyers shall be accepted by Sellers. Should Buyers fail to notify Sellers' representative in accordance with this clause, no quality claim shall be admitted.

11.4   Where a Bill of Lading/Warrant consists of more than one main mark, each main mark on the Bill of Lading/Warrant shall be sampled separately, provided that the quantity of each main mark is 25 bags or more of cocoa beans.

In cases where there is more than one main mark of less than 25 bags of cocoa beans Buyers shall have the option of having these main marks' samples proportionally bulked as though they were one and such samples shall be accepted as basis of settlement and claims.

11.5   In the case of ports where no direct sampling facilities are available in the port area, then sampling shall take place at a suitable location near the port of destination promptly after last day of discharge.

11.6   All charges incurred in sampling shall be paid by Buyers unless otherwise agreed.

11.7   Sampling for cocoa beans sold on sample shall be on one of the following basis for arbitration purposes unless mutually agreed otherwise:

   (a)   Sellers shall give Buyers a sampling order on the warehouse, allowing them to draw one sample of not more than 2 kilos from at least 30 per cent of sound bags of each main mark or parcel with all charges for Sellers' account. If Buyers accept the quality and buy on this sample then the quality shall be considered as final with no claim for inferiority.

   (b)   Sellers shall supply to Buyers a sample of not less than 1 kilo, after approval of which, one of the following procedures shall be adopted:

      (i)   buyers and sellers shall agree the number of defective and/or slaty beans and/or other characteristics and make this the contractual basis of quality after which Buyers shall draw two sealed samples each weighing not less than 2 kilos nett from at least 30 per cent of each main mark or parcel tendered. Samples shall be marked or labelled in accordance with **Market Rule 11.2**. Any quality claim shall be based upon the difference between the agreed quality and the arbitrator's findings from the said sealed sample.

         OR

      (ii)   the balance of this sample shall be sealed either by two parties concerned or by an independent party and shall be retained for arbitration purposes. Buyers shall draw two sealed samples each weighing not less than 2 kilos nett from at least 30 per cent of each main mark or parcel tendered. Samples shall be marked or labelled in accordance with **Market Rule 11.2.** Any quality claim shall be based on the difference between the arbitrator's findings from the original sample, and the sealed arbitration sample.

11.8   Any principal to a contract is entitled to draw sealed samples as laid down in **Market Rule 11.1 or 11.9** but by doing so he shall relinquish his claim to be in a string for Quality arbitration purposes as laid down in **Arbitration and Appeal Rule 24.16.**

If one Superintendent is nominated as laid down in **Market Rule 11.3 and 11.11** to draw sealed samples by more than one principal of a contract where one Bill of Lading/Ship's Delivery Order/Warrant and vessel are the same, his seal and/or counter-seal shall be identifiable by the Superintendent's marking the sealed sample by number to indicate which principal in the chain is represented.

SAMPLING FOR
COCOA
PRODUCTS-
SHIPMENT

11.9   By mutual consent of the contracting parties at least one sound carton and/or sound bag shall be drawn at random by Buyer from each bill of Lading/Warrant quantity and/or main mark and sealed promptly at time of discharge or tender.

11.10   Samples of cocoa products shall be marked or labelled to show:

Name of vessel (with Rotation Number, if any)
Country of Origin
Port of shipment
Port of destination
Main mark(s)
Number of cartons/bags
Date of Sampling
Final day of discharge of the vessel and/or unstuffing of the final container
Bill of Lading Number/Delivery Order Number/Warrant Number as applicable.

11.11   Sellers may appoint a representative to supervise sampling and must inform Buyers of the name of such representative before arrival at port of destination or prior to tender in/ex store. Buyers must give due notice to Seller's representative of the time and place of sampling. Should the Sellers not name their representative or should their representative fail to be present after having received due notice of time and place of sampling, samples sealed by sworn weighers and samplers and provided by Buyers shall be accepted by Sellers. Should Buyers fail to notify Sellers' representative in accordance with this clause, no quality claim shall be admitted.

11.12 In the case of ports where no direct sampling facilities are available in the port area, then sampling shall take place at a suitable location near the port of destination promptly after last day of discharge.

11.13 All charges incurred in sampling shall be paid by Buyers unless otherwise agreed.

SAMPLING FOR COCOA PRODUCTS SOLD IN/EX STORE

11.14 Sampling for cocoa products sold on sample shall be on the following basis for arbitration purposes unless mutually agreed otherwise:

Sellers shall give Buyers a sampling order on the warehouse, allowing them to draw one sound carton and/or sound bag at random from each Warrant or main mark or parcel with all charges for Sellers' account. If Buyers accept the quality and buy on the basis of this sample then the quality shall be considered as final with no claim for inferiority.

11.15 Any principal to a contract is entitled to draw sealed samples as laid down in **Market Rule 11.1 or 11.9** but by doing so he shall relinquish his claim to be in a string for Quality arbitration purposes as laid down in **Arbitration and Appeal Rule 24.16.**

If one Superintendent is nominated as laid down in **Market Rule 11.3 and 11.11** to draw sealed samples by more than one principal of a contract where one Bill of Lading/Ship's Delivery Order/Warrant and vessel are the same, his seal and/or counter-seal shall be identifiable by the Superintendent's marking the sealed sample by number to indicate which principal in the chain is represented.

CHARGES

12.1 **CIF/WITH ARRIVAL, DELIVERY OR TENDER IN/EX STORE OPTION**
If cost, insurance and freight documents are presented all charges incurred for landing, weighing and sampling shall be paid by Buyers. If cocoa beans are tendered in/ex store against cost, insurance and freight contracts with a delivery option Buyers shall reimburse Sellers with the charges for landing and delivery ex quay and weighing.

12.2 All extra charges incurred due to late presentation of shipping documents shall be for Seller's account.

FUMIGATION

13.1 (a) If it is necessary for a parcel to be fumigated on arrival at port of destination, then all additional costs resulting from fumigation, over and above those normally incurred in taking delivery (but excluding interest charges) shall be for Seller's account.

(b) If a Buyer believes that a parcel needs fumigation, he must advise the Seller immediately and request agreement that fumigation is necessary. This contact may be, and would normally be, made through the intermediary of the contracting parties' appointed representatives at the port of destination. In this case, to support a claim, Buyers must receive telex or telegram confirmation from Sellers' and/or their appointed representative that fumigation is necessary.

(c) Should the Buyer fail to obtain Seller's agreement that fumigation is necessary, then, in order to establish the need for fumigation he must provide either:

(i) an order from a local official body (eg. Port Health Authority) that fumigation must be carried out.
or

(ii) a survey report from a competent independent authority confirming that fumigation is necessary.

In each case there must be evidence that the infestation could have originated in the country of origin

(d) Buyers shall take all reasonable actions to keep the additional costs, as in 13.1 (a) above, to a minimum in accordance with the custom of the port.

(e) If the Port Health Authority or the competent independent authority should deem it unnecessary for the cocoa to be fumigated all charges and fees of the inspection shall be for Buyers' account.

PAYMENT

14.1 Payment for shipments of cocoa beans and/or cocoa products shall be made in the place named in the contract against presentation and in exchange for documents as designated in **Market Rule 14.7.**

14.2 Payment for shipments made under contract on 'shipping weights' terms shall be for 100 per cent of the invoice amount established on shipping weights.

Payments for shipments made under contracts on 'delivery weights' terms shall be for 98 per cent of the invoice amount established on shipping weights.

Balance to be settled within 10 days after final invoice has been established in accordance with **Market Rule 8.7.**

14.3 In the event of the vessel becoming a casualty payment shall be made by Buyers against presentation of the proper documents in accordance with market Rule 14.7. In the case of delivery weights contract, shipping weights as shown on the Bill of Lading shall be used for payment purposes.

14.4 Payments for parcels of cocoa beans and/or cocoa products tendered under contract on in/ex store terms or, where Sellers exercise an 'in/ex store' option under a shipment contract, shall be made for 100 per cent of the invoice amount established on shipping weights or warehouse warrant weights as applicable against presentation and in exchange for proper documents in accordance with **Market Rule 7.17 and Market Rule 14.9.**

Payment shall be made before the prompt date only if proper documents have been presented early at the Buyers request in accordance with **Market Rule 7.11.**

14.5 Interest shall be payable on any sums which become due in respect of all contracts written under the rules and regulations of the Association, whether by debt or damages from the date on which such sums fall due to the date of payment, whether such payment is made before or after the commencement of proceedings.

Claims or allowances for interest shall be calculated at 2 per cent over the base rate of interest (or equivalent) published by Barclays Bank plc, London or such other appropriate interest rate as decided by the Council from time to time.

14.6   Documents may not be presented for payment earlier than the following business day after receipt of declaration.

DOCUMENTARY 14.7   For the purpose of fulfilling shipment contracts proper documents shall consist of:
REQUIREMENTS

(a)   complete set clean shipped on Board Bills of Lading and/or Ship's delivery Order showing date and place of shipment.

(b)   invoice

(c)   such documents as may be required by **Market Rule 14.9**

(d)   in the case of CIF contract, Policy or Certificate of Insurance as may be requested in **Market Rule 6.**

(e)   such documents as may be required under **Market Rule 14.10**

Sellers shall provide Buyers with an acceptable letter of guarantee for any documents which may be missing at time of presentation with the exception of those documents required by **Market Rule 14.9**, such acceptance by Buyers not to be unreasonably withheld.

14.8   For the purpose of fulfilling in/ex store contracts proper documents shall consist of:

(a)   warehouse warrants
(b)   invoice
(c)   such documents as may be required by **Market Rules 14.9 and 14.10**.

As an alternative to warehouse warrants Sellers may, with Buyers consent, present a delivery order or arrange a release to the Buyers by the warehousekeeper. Such release to be binding on the Seller. If Buyers require a warehouse warrant prior notice must be given to Seller in sufficient time to enable the warrant to be prepared.

14.9   On shipments of cocoa beans from a country which is a member state of the International Cocoa Agreement and on shipments of cocoa beans exported from a country which is not a member but which is to be imported into a member state, and where the Seller is responsible for payment of the levy, Sellers shall provide such documents as may be required by the International Cocoa Agreement and specified in the Economic and Control Rules of the International Cocoa Council whenever in force.

14.10   Sellers shall provide any appropriate certificates and/or documents required by the respective authorities in the country of destination named in the Bill of Lading to enable Buyers to claim any preferential rate of duty where applicable.

If the Seller lodges the required certificate or other documents at destination he shall provide the Buyer with all relevant details. Sellers to be responsible for extra duty incurred if this is not provided.

INSOLVENCY   15.1   If before the fulfilment of any contract either party shall suspend payment or become bankrupt or commit any act of a bankruptcy or being a company go into liquidation, whether voluntary or otherwise, except for the purpose of reconstruction, the other party may by notice in writing, call for the contract to be closed and the contract shall at the expiration of 24 hours from the receipt in the normal course of cable, telex or postal communication of such notice by the party to whom the notice is sent, be deemed to be closed on terms to be fixed by arbitration.

15.2   Subject to the provisions of **Market Rule 15.6** of this rule a party (hereinafter referred to as "the answerable party") shall for the purpose of this rule, be considered to have suspended payment, who, in relation to any other contract, has failed within the stipulated time, as defined in **Market Rule 15.3** to pay such sum, or any part thereof as may be due from his as damages and/or costs under an award duly made and published according to the rules of the Association, or any other association or body which may be declared at any time by the Council of the Association to be included in this paragraph (the association concerned being hereinafter referred to as "the appropriate association"), and on the happenings of that event the answerable party may accordingly be served by the other party with a twenty-four hours' notice stating that it is being served under this present paragraph and calling for the contract between the parties to be closed on the terms stated in **Market Rule 15.1** of this rule.

15.3   The 'stipulated time' for the purpose of **Market Rule 15.2** if no appeal from the award is claimed and proceeded with, shall mean the time, if any, specified in the award wherein payment is directed to be made by the answerable party and, when no time is specified in the award, shall mean the time specified in the Arbitration Rules of the appropriate association, and in the case of an appeal resulting in the award being upheld or varied only as to amount, shall mean the time specified therein or if no time specified, then the time specified in the Arbitration Rules.

15.4   If the answerable party claims that his failure to pay is due to currency restrictions or to some other circumstance beyond the control of a solvent debtor, he shall have the right to bring the matter before and be heard by the Council of the Association or a committee appointed for the purpose (hereinafter referred to as "the tribunal") provided in the case of a party residing in the United Kingdom he gives notice to that effect to the Secretary of the Association and to the other party not later than 12 noon on the day and in the case of a party resident overseas, not later than 12 noon on the third day, after the date of the twenty-four hours' notice with which he has been served under the provisions of

Market Rule 15.2. In either such case the twenty-four hours' notice shall remain in abeyance pending the determination of the matter by the Tribunal, unless in the meantime the answerable party does or suffers any new act or thing specified in **Market Rule 15.1** of this rule except suspension of payment if dependent for its interpretation upon the provisions of **Market Rule 15.2.** In the event of the answerable party doing or suffering any such new act or thing no further notice shall be required and the twenty-four hours' notice already served shall be deemed a good notice for all purposes and to expire on the happening of such last mentioned event, on which date the contract shall be deemed closed if not fulfilled or already closed under the provisions of the next paragraph.

15.5 If the answerable party does not, within the time specified in **Market Rule 15.4**, give notice of his desire to bring the matter before the Tribunal or if, having given notice, he fails to establish his claim before the Tribunal, then the contract between the parties shall if not fulfilled, be deemed closed on the day following the service upon the answerable party of the twenty-four hours' notice.

15.6 Should the Tribunal, after hearing both parties decide that the answerable party's failure to pay is due to one of the causes stated in **Market Rule 15.4** then he shall not, by reason of such failure be considered as having suspended payment and the twenty-four hours' notice mentioned in **Market Rule 15.2** shall, for the purpose of that Rule, be void.

15.7 In the event of there being more than one contract existing between the same parties which shall be closed in pursuance of **Market Rules 15.1 to 15.6** an account shall be taken of what is due from one party to the other in respect of such contracts, and the sum due from the one party, shall be set off against the sum due from the other party, and the balance of the accounts and no more shall be claimed or paid on either side respectively.

15.8 Where a broker or person acting as a broker, who is a party to a contract made under these rules, and who has disclosed the name of this principal on such contract, shall suspend payment or be a defaulter or issue a notice convening a meeting of his creditors or become bankrupt or insolvent, such principal shall complete the contract and in that event neither the broker or person acting as a broker nor his Trustee nor creditors shall have any right or interest in such contract beyond the brokerage.

DEFAULT

16.1 If it becomes apparent that either party to a contract will not fulfil his contractual obligations within the specified period, the counter party may declare him to be in default in respect of the contract, or any part thereof which has not been fulfilled.

16.2 The date of default will normally be the first business day after the end of the relevant delivery or shipping period, except when a contract provides for the Seller to make all arrangements for booking of the freight, shipment of the goods and to make a declaration of shipment to the Buyer. Then in the absence of a proper declaration the date of default will normally be noon on the 21st calendar day or the first business day thereafter after the end of the contractual shipment period.

No Seller subsequent to the original shippers may be declared to be in default if he is able to show that a declaration of shipment delivered to him has been passed on to the Buyer with due despatch.

(Arbitration/Appeal Rules 25.10 refers)

FORCE MAJEURE

17.1 Failure of performance can be attributable to force Majeure if, without any fault of the party seeking to be excused, an event occurs which is:

(a) irresistible — the event must render performance impossible not merely more onerous.

(b) unforeseeable — if the event is reasonably foreseeable, steps must be taken to prevent or avoid it, and

(c) external — the event must be outside the claimants sphere of responsibility.

17.2 The following events are examples of Force Majeure if they satisfy **Market Rule 17.1** : prohibition of exports or other legislative interference, fire, strikes, lock-outs, riots or war.

17.3 Should shipment and/or delivery of cocoa beans and/or cocoa products be prevented or delayed by a case of Force Majeure as defined in **Market Rule 17.1,** the time of shipment and/or delivery shall be extended by one calendar month, as long as the claimant notifies his contracting party promptly of the occurrence and cause of such Force Majeure.

If required the claimant must produce conclusive evidence to establish his claim of Force Majeure.

17.4 If shipment and/or delivery is still prevented at the end of the extended period, the parties shall agree a price, based on the market price at the end of the extended period, to close out the contract. Irrespective of which party claimed Force Majeure the following procedure shall be adopted:

(a) If the close-out price is higher than the contract price of the goods, the Seller shall pay the Buyer the difference between the close out price and the contract price.

(b) If the close-out price is lower than the contract price of the goods, the Buyer shall pay the Seller the difference between the close-out price and the contract price.

17.5 Failing an amicable agreement on the existence of Force Majeure or the close-out price the matter will be referred to Arbitration.

17.6 Where a contract gives the Seller an option to ship from origin and/or from anywhere to arrive at destination named in the contract during a certain period, **Market Rule 17.3** can only be applied if Sellers have declared, in writing, their option as follows:

(a) by the first day of the shipping period their intention to fulfil by shipment from origin.

(b) by at least fifteen calendar days before commencement of the arrival period named in the contract, their intention to fulfil by shipment from a specified port, other than at origin, in which case **Market Rule 16** shall apply.

Such declaration to be passed on immediately by intervening buyers and sellers.

ARBITRATION   18.1   Any dispute arising out of this contract shall be settled by Arbitration in London in accordance with the law of England where this contract is deemed to be made as provided for by the Rules, Regulations and Bye-laws of the Association which are deemed to be incorporated in this contract and both parties hereto shall be deemed to contract with full knowledge of the said Rules, Regulations and Bye-laws.

UNIFORM LAW   19.1   The following statutes shall not apply to contracts written and made subject to the Rules and Regulations of the Association:

(a) the Uniform Law on Sales and the Uniform Law on Formation to which effect is given by the Uniform Law on International Sales Act 1967.

(b) the United Nations Convention on Contracts for the International Sale of Goods of 1980.

(c) the United Nations Convention on Prescription (Limitation) in the International Sale of Goods of 1974 and the amending Protocol of 1980.

FIXATION ADDENDUM NO.1 FOR CAL CONTRACT FORM A   BUYERS
OPTION TO FIX

CONTRACT NO. .... DATED ....

Price **1.** (a) (i) ....

Premium/Discount to Sellers price of the London Cocoa Terminal Market
Delivery Position.

   (ii) at a Ratio of ....

to Sellers price of the London Cocoa Terminal Market .... Delivery Position

The resultant price to be expressed in: .... per metric ton (1000 Kilos)

  (b) The price of this contract to be fixed by BUYERS on any business day &/or days from .... to .... both dates inclusive at a stated London Cocoa Terminal Market price during trading hours. The price of this contract may also be fixed at any time by mutual agreement.

  (c) BUYERS have the option to fix the price of any part of this contract provided that the quantity fixed shall be 10 metric tons (5 metric tons in the case of Cocoa butter) or multiples thereof, except when necessary to complete the contract.

However, not more than .... metric tons may be fixed at any one time except by mutual agreement.

  (d) SELLERS reserve the right to fix the price of any unfixed quantity during the London Cocoa Terminal

Market .... call on .... If for unseen circumstances the Market be closed on that date, the unfixed quantity shall be fixed on the basis of the closing out price established by London Cocoa Terminal Market. If a closing out price is not established the price of any unfixed quantity shall be fixed during the opening call of the next business day.

  (e) Each individual fixation shall be a separate contract unless otherwise mutually agreed.

Insurance **2.** In respect of any unfixed portion the Insurance Cover, as defined in the Insurance Clause of the main contract, is limited to the amount of the provisional invoice as established in clause 3 of the addendum.

Payment **3.** To be made against documents in accordance with the payments clause of the main contract:

  (a) When the tonnage shipped has all been price-fixed, the invoice(s) to be established at each individual price of fixation unless otherwise mutually agreed.

  (b) When the tonnage shipped is greater than the tonnage already price-fixed the invoice(s) to be established at the fixed price(s) for the quantity already fixed as defined under clause 3(a) above but for any unfixed balance the invoice(s) to be established provisionally and based upon the official Sellers price

of the .... delivery position of the London Cocoa Terminal Market at the opening call on either

   (i) the date of the official tender and/or declaration,

  or (ii) ....

  (c) Settlement of any balance(s) arising on price fixation to be made immediately upon presentation of the Difference Account.

Closure of the **4.** In the event of closure of the London Cocoa Terminal Market in accordance with London Fox General
London Cocoa   Contract Provisions, Rule 5.1.3 (or as amended) the price for any unfixed portion of this contract shall
Terminal Market in be fixed on the basis of the official closing out price established by The London Cocoa Terminal Market.
accordance with
London Fox General
Contract Provisions
Rule 5.1.3

Special Conditions **5.** ....

| 70 |

FIXATION ADDENDUM NO.2 FOR CAL CONTRACT FORM A .... SELLERS OPTION TO FIX

CONTRACT NO. .... DATED ....

Price   1.   (a) (i) ....

Premium/Discount to Buyers price of the London Cocoa Terminal Market ....
Delivery Position.

(ii) at a Ratio of ....

to Buyers price of the London Cocoa Terminal Market .... Delivery Position.

The resultant price to be expressed in: .... per metric ton (1000 Kilos)

(b) The price of this contract to be fixed by SELLERS on any business day &/or days from .... to .... both dates inclusive at a stated London Cocoa Terminal Market price during trading hours. The price of this contract may also be fixed at any time by mutual agreement.

(c) SELLERS have the option to fix the price of any part of this contract provided that the quantity fixed shall be 10 metric tons (5 metric tons in the case of Cocoa butter) or multiples thereof, except when necessary to complete the contract.

However, not more than .... metric tons may be fixed at any one time except by mutual agreement.

(d) SELLERS reserve the right to fix the price of any unfixed quantity during the London Cocoa Terminal Market .... call on .... If for unseen circumstances the Market be closed on that date, the unfixed quantity shall be fixed on the basis of the closing out price established by London Cocoa Terminal Market. If a closing out price is not established the price of any unfixed quantity shall be fixed during the opening call of the next business day.

(e) Each individual fixation shall be a separate contract unless otherwise mutually agreed.

Insurance   2.   In respect of any unfixed portion the Insurance Cover, as defined in the Insurance Clause of the main contract, is limited to the amount of the provisional invoice as established in clause 3 of the addendum.

Payment   3.   To be made against documents in accordance with the payments clause of the main contract:

(a) When the tonnage shipped has all been price-fixed, the invoice(s) to be established at each individual price of fixation unless otherwise mutually agreed.

(b) When the tonnage shipped is greater than the tonnage already price-fixed the invoice(s) to be established at the fixed price(s) for the quantity already fixed as defined under clause 3(a) above but for any unfixed balance the invoice(s) to be established provisionally and based upon the official Sellers price

of the .... delivery position of the London Cocoa Terminal Market at the opening call on either

(i) the date of the official tender and/or declaration,

or (ii) ....

(c) Settlement of any balance(s) arising on price fixation to be made immediately upon presentation of the Difference Account.

Closure of the London Cocoa Terminal Market in accordance with London Fox General Contract Provisions Rule 5.1.3   4.   In the event of closure of the London Cocoa Terminal Market in accordance with London Fox General Contract Provisions, Rule 5.1.3 (or as amended) the price for any unfixed portion of this contract shall be fixed on the basis of the official closing out price established by The London Cocoa Terminal Market.

Special Conditions   5.   ....

71

CMAA cocoa contracts

Physical cocoa contracts issued by

The Cocoa Merchants' Association of America, Inc† (CMAA)

CMAA I-A

CMAA 2-A

CMAA 3-A

†   Contract forms are available from the CMAA, their address is:

The Cocoa Merchants' Association of America, Inc
26 Broadway
Suite 707
New York
New York 10004

Tel 212-363 7334   Tlx 256610   Fax 212-363 7678

STANDARD CONTRACT 1-A
GOVERNING SALES OF COCOA FOR DELIVERY AND/OR
SHIPMENT BASIS EX DOCK
OR EX WAREHOUSE

(REVISED EDITION JANUARY 5, 1990)

Any cocoa contract containing the clause:

"Subject to terms of Standard Contract 1-A of The Cocoa
Merchants' Association of America, Inc."

or a clause, phrase or sentence of equal or similar import, shall
be understood to incorporate the full terms of Contract 1-A as
hereinafter set forth as though said Contract 1-A were fully
written into the contract. Where, however, a contract contains
terms in addition to, or in conflict with any of the terms of
Contract 1-A, such terms shall supersede the terms of Contract
1-A.

SECTION 1:

Any export-duty or bounty in the country of production is
for account of seller.

SECTION 2:

Should shipment be prevented or delayed owing to prohibition
of exports, fire, strikes, lockouts, riots, war, revolution or
any other case of "Force Majeure", the time of shipment shall be
extended by one month, but should the delay exceed one month the
buyer shall have the option of canceling the contract for any
quantity not shipped or of accepting the cocoa for shipment as
soon as the cause for prevention or delay of shipment shall have
been removed, provided that if such shipment is not effected
within five months following the expiration date of the first
month's extension, the contract shall be automatically canceled
for any quantity not shipped. Such option is to be exercised in
writing as soon as the seller announces his inability to ship
within the extended period, or, at the latest, seven days after
the extended period has expired. Contract is void if the buyer
fails to exercise such aforesaid option as hereinbefore provided.
If required, seller must produce conclusive evidence to establish
his claim for extension.

SECTION 3:

The word "Shipment" shall mean shipment by steamer and/or
steamers. Motor-ships shall be deemed steamers.

The word "Vessel" shall mean steamer or motor-ship.

"Immediate Shipment" shall mean shipment within 15 calendar
days from date of contract.

"Prompt Shipment" shall mean shipment within 30 calendar
days from date of contract.

"Direct Shipment" shall mean shipment not involving trans-shipment.

"Indirect Shipment" shall mean shipment involving transship-ment.

The date of the "on board" Bill-of-Lading shall be proof of date of shipment.

SECTION 4:

Seller shall have the option of declaring vessel to buyer, in writing, by telex, by facsimile transmission, or by cable:

1. In the case of direct shipments:

    After the cocoa is actually on board the vessel named in the declaration; provided nothing unfavorable about the vessel or her cargo has become known in the insurance market on or prior to the date of such declaration.

2. In the case of indirect shipments:

    (a)   After the cocoa is actually on board the initial vessel named in the declaration and within twelve calendar days after arrival of such vessel at port of transshipment; provided nothing unfavorable about the vessel or her cargo has become known in the insurance market on or prior to the date of such declaration. Such declaration will cease to be in effect twelve calendar days after arrival of such vessel at the port of transshipment.

    (b)   After the transshipped cocoa is actually on board the declared vessel which is carrying the same to its final destination in accordance with the contract, and before entry of such vessel in the Customs House at destination; provided nothing unfavorable about the vessel or her cargo has become known in the insurance market on or prior to the date of such declaration.

        The term "insurance market" shall mean the daily casualty list published by the Maritime Associa-tion Of The Port Of New York, or, if this list ceases to become available, as the Board of Directors of the Association shall determine promptly upon cessation of the availability of said list.

SECTION 5:

This contract shall be void for any portion of the cocoa lost, seized or destroyed after shipment, provided seller shall have declared vessel to buyer in accordance with Section 4 here-inbefore. Buyer shall have the option to take the number of bags damaged after shipment and landed at port of destination at a fair allowance, such option to be exercised promptly. Seller failing to declare vessel in accordance with Section 4 hereinbe-fore guarantees delivery, but shall be entitled to a reasonable extension of shipping period for all cocoa lost, seized or destroyed after shipment, also for the number of bags damaged; such cocoa shall be replaced by seller on dock, or at seller's option, in warehouse at port of arrival designated in the contract; and such replacement shall be accepted by the buyer.

SECTION 6:

Any import duty or internal revenue or other tax imposed by the United States of America or a political subdivision therein is assumed and shall be paid by the buyer.

SECTION 7:   Quantities and Weights.

Where a contract calls for specific quantity by weight, seller may deliver 3% more or less than the quantity called for in the contract, without variation in price.

The word "about", referring to weight or number of bags shall mean 5% more or less, seller's option.

The aforesaid leeway of 3% or, respectively, 5%, shall be deemed void whenever a contract is liquidated by payment of difference between purchase and sale, in lieu of delivery.

A ton of cocoa shall be a metric ton.

Weights are to be ascertained on seller's dock, or in seller's warehouse by Public Weighers appointed by seller; such weights are to be incontestable. Cost of weighing shall be for seller's account.

Buyer shall have option, declarable on receipt of seller's delivery order, to appoint an agent, at buyer's expense, to be present when the cocoa is weighed.

In the event of a weighers' strike, some other form of determining weights by mutual agreement shall be agreed upon between the buyer and seller.

SECTION 7A:

If this contract covers a sale of cocoa beans, beans to be packed in clean, sound, new gunny bags of sufficient strength, or in bags of such other material as is typical for their origin. Bags fabricated from ribbon-weave polypropylene or other plastic material not permitted without buyer's consent.

SECTION 8:

Seller shall allow actual tare on all grades.

SECTION 9:

Each shipment and/or delivery-order constitutes a separate contract.

If seller tenders delivery from a dock or a warehouse at a port not designated in the contract, buyers shall nevertheless be obligated to accept such delivery. Seller, however, is to reim-

burse buyer for any bona fide expense incurred to make such
delivery equal to a delivery in the designated port. Minimum
quantity tenderable is to be 18 metric tons, unless otherwise
specified in the contract.

Tenders of cocoa in warehouse against contracts calling for
shipment and/or equivalent delivery from warehouse at seller's
option, shall be made not earlier than the number of days specified below from the commencement of the contract shipping period,
nor later than the number of days specified below from the expiration of contract shipping period.

FOR SHIPMENTS FROM	TO EAST COAST	TO WEST COAST
Brazil............................	15 days	25 days
Ecuador...........................	10 "	20 "
Trinidad..........................	10 "	20 "
Venezuela.........................	10 "	20 "
Central America and West Indies...	10 "	20 "
Santo Domingo.....................	10 "	20 "
Africa............................	21 "	45 "
Asia and Oceania..................	45 "	30 "
Others............................	21 "	45 "

SECTION 10:

Parts 1-13 to govern cocoa on dock as follows:

Part 1:

Cocoa sold for delivery on dock shall be tendered by
delivery order stating name of public weigher, and a sampling order.

Part 2:

A tender will be valid only if and when released by the
U.S.A. Food & Drug Administration and/or other Governmental
Agency.

Incorrect tender or tenders shall not invalidate the
seller's right and obligation to make correct tender or
tenders.

Tenders presented to buyers after 3 p.m. on any day,
Monday to Friday both inclusive, shall be timed as of 9 a.m.
of the day following. No tenders may be made on Saturday,
Sunday, or on a legal holiday.

Part 3:

Except as to insurance, which is governed by Part 5
hereinafter, the title to the cocoa passes to the buyer on
payment of seller's proforma invoice or when the dock accepts lodging of seller's delivery order, or by noon of the
first business day after expiration of the three business
days from presentation of tender as specified in Part 6
hereunder, whichever shall first occur.

Risk of condemnation or restriction by the U.S.A. Food
& Drug Administration and/or other Governmental Agency shall
be for seller's account while the cocoa is on the dock at
port of entry.

Part 4:

Lodging of delivery order with the dock by buyer or
buyer's endorsee shall be deemed approval of quality binding
upon all endorsements prior to and including lodger of such
delivery order, provided tender is valid in accordance with
Part 2 above, except as to the number of bags damaged by
seawater or other irregularities unknown or indeterminable
before weighing.

Part 5:

Seller is to keep the cocoa on the dock insured at his
contractual sales price until noon of the first business day
after expiration of the three business days from presentation of tender as specified in Part 6 hereunder or until
noon of the fourteenth calendar day after completion of
discharge of the vessel's cargo, whichever period shall last
expire.

Whenever the buyer shall have paid all or part of the
seller's invoice or proforma invoice, seller's insurance
shall be deemed held in trust by the seller for the buyer
until the removal of the cocoa from the dock shall have been
consummated provided so removed from the dock before expiration of seller's insurance as above set forth.

If the cocoa tendered by the seller should be wholly or
partly destroyed or lost or damaged before expiration of
seller's insurance as above set forth, seller shall forthwith return the buyer's payment for the number of bags
destroyed or lost or damaged, failing which seller's insurance shall be deemed held in trust by the seller for the
buyer until the buyer shall have received such reimbursement.

Failing such reimbursement after buyer's written demand
seller shall be deemed in default and subject to the default
penalties provided in Section 12 hereinafter.

Part 6:

Seller guarantees buyer three business days from presentation of tender, within which to weigh and remove the
cocoa from the dock; thereafter, failing such weighing and
removal, seller shall hold the cocoa on the dock as long as
vessel's agent permits; buyer is to refund seller for all
bona fide expenses actually incurred as a result of buyer's
failure to remove a correct tender of the cocoa from the
dock within such aforesaid time limit (3 business days).
Insurance, however, beyond time limit as provided in Section
10, Part 5, shall be covered by buyer who shall pay to
seller on demand the unpaid value of the number of bags
destroyed or lost or damaged at contract price on the basis

of net shipping weights. Such insurance shall be deemed
held in trust by the buyer for the seller without prejudice,
however, to any other of the seller's rights until the buyer
shall have paid the seller in full.

Part 7:

The number of bags destroyed or damaged before weighing
on dock, if all or part of a sale made after entry of vessel
in Custom House, shall be deducted from the contract, but
buyer shall have the option to take the damaged bags at a
fair allowance.

Part 8:

The number of bags destroyed or marine damaged before
expiration of seller's insurance, if tendered against a sale
made before entry of vessel in Custom House, shall be deducted from the contract whenever shipment shall have been
declared in accordance with Section 4 hereinbefore, but
buyer shall have option to take the damaged bags at a fair
allowance, subject to any restriction placed thereon by the
U.S.A. Food & Drug Administration and/or other Governmental
Agency; provided the undamaged portion (if any) of any
specific lot so marine damaged is not restricted by any
Governmental Agency.

Part 9:

The number of bags destroyed or damaged before expiration of seller's insurance, if tendered against a sale made
before entry of the respective vessel in Custom House, shall
be properly replaced by the seller in accordance with Section 5 hereinbefore, unless shipment shall have been declared in accordance with Section 4 hereinbefore and buyer
shall accept such replacement or replacements.

Part 10:

The number of bags restricted by the U.S.A. Food & Drug
Administration and/or other Governmental Agency (before the
risk of such restriction shall have passed to the buyer) and
tendered against a sale made after entry of the respective
vessel in Custom House, shall be properly replaced by the
seller in accordance with Part 11 hereinafter and buyer
shall accept such replacement or replacements; but if the
cocoa shall have been sold as a "specific lot", the number
of bags so restricted shall be deducted from contract.

Part 11:

Except as provided in Part 8 hereinbefore the number of
bags restricted by the U.S.A. Food & Drug Administration
and/or other Governmental Agency (before the risk of such
restriction shall have passed to the buyer) and tendered
against a sale made before entry of the respective vessel in
the Custom House, shall be properly replaced by the seller
by further tender and/or tenders in accordance with the

contract, or at seller's option, by tender or tenders,
irrespective of ocean Bill-of-Lading and declaration, if
any, on dock or from warehouse not later than 30 calendar
days after such restriction and buyer shall accept such re
placement or replacements. If no suitable cocoa of the
description contracted for is available for replacement
within 30 days, replacement shall be made by the earliest
available shipment and/or shipments at a differential to be
agreed upon amicably, or by arbitration.

Part 12:

Whenever vessel shall have discharged into a warehouse
in "general order" or otherwise, or whenever vessel or
vessel's agent shall have removed the cocoa from the dock
into warehouse, after tender and before expiration of the
time limit of 3 business days specified in Part 6 hereinbefore, such warehouse shall be deemed the dock.

Part 13:

Claims on account of quality shall be inadmissible as
provided in Part 4 hereinbefore. Where, however, such
cocoa, within 20 calendar days after weighing on dock,
discloses latent damage by seawater or otherwise, arbitration shall determine the extent of seller's liability, if
any, but in such arbitration the seller shall have the
benefit of any reasonable doubt. Latent damage is defined
as damage which could not have been determined by due diligence under the provisions of Part 4 hereinbefore.

Part 14: (intentionally omitted)

Parts 15-25 to govern cocoa in warehouse as follows:

Part 15:

Cocoa sold for delivery from warehouse shall be tendered by delivery order stating name of public weigher and
date of expiration of storage and fire insurance for full
contract value, coterminating with storage. The date of
expiration of storage and fire insurance shall not be prior
to three (3) business days from presentation of such delivery order to buyer.

Seller receiving payment against proforma invoice
shall, upon request, attach thereto a negotiable fire insurance certificate.

Part 16:

Incorrect tender or tenders shall not invalidate the
seller's right and obligation to make correct tender or
tenders.

Tenders presented to buyers after 3 p.m. on any business day, Monday to Friday both inclusive, shall be timed as
of 9 a.m. of the business day following.

Part 17:

Title passes to the buyer when payment is made against
seller's proforma invoice or when the warehouse accepts
lodging of seller's delivery order, or by noon of the first
business day after expiration of the three business days
from presentation of tender, whichever shall first occur.
Risk of condemnation or restriction by the U.S.A. Food &
Drug Administration and/or other Governmental Agency passes
to the buyer with title.

Part 18:

Lodging of delivery order, with the warehouse, by buyer
or buyer's endorsee, shall be deemed approval of quality
binding upon all endorsements prior to and including lodger
of such delivery order except as to the number of bags
damaged by seawater or other irregularities unknown or
indeterminable before weighing.

Part 19:

Seller, on expiration of storage stated in delivery
order, may order the cocoa weighed up for the buyer's account; repiling in warehouse is to be paid by the buyer.

Part 20:

The number of bags destroyed or damaged after sale and
before weighing, if part of a sale of spot warehouse cocoa,
shall be deducted from the contract.

Part 21:

The number of bags destroyed or damaged before weighing
in warehouse shall be properly replaced by the seller in
accordance with Section 5 hereinbefore, whenever such cocoa
shall have been tendered against a sale calling for shipment
or equivalent delivery from warehouse and buyer shall accept
such replacement or replacements.

Part 22:

The number of bags condemned or restricted by the
U.S.A. Food & Drug Administration and/or other Governmental
Agency, after sale and before rsk of condemnation or restriction has passed to buyer, shall be deducted from the
contract, provided such cocoa was all or part of a sale of a
specific lot; otherwise seller shall properly replace and
buyer shall accept such replacement or replacements.

Part 23:

The number of bags tendered against a contract calling
for shipment and/or equivalent delivery from warehouse but
condemned or restricted by the U.S.A. Food & Drug Administration and/or other Governmental Agency, after tender and
before risk of condemnation or restriction has passed to
buyer, shall be properly replaced by the seller within

contract period, or 30 days from date of condemnation or restriction, whichever is later, and buyer shall accept such replacement or replacements.

Part 24:

Claims on account of quality shall be inadmissible as provided in Part 18 hereinbefore. Where, however, such cocoa, within 20 days after weighing in warehouse discloses latent damage by seawater or otherwise, arbitration shall determine the extent of seller's liability, if any, but in such arbitration the seller shall have the benefit of any reasonable doubt.

Part 25 to govern both dock and warehouse cocoa as follows:

Part 25:

All payments against proforma invoice shall be held in trust and seller shall immediately, upon demand, refund buyer to the extent of that portion of the cocoa so invoiced which shall have failed to pass into buyer's possession, on dock or in warehouse, unless such failure be due to unjustifiable obstruction on buyer's part.

SECTION 11:

Part 1:

Any dispute under this contract shall be settled by arbitration in accordance with the rules of the Cocoa Merchants' Association of America, Inc., whose award shall be final and binding upon buyer and seller, and judgment upon the award may be entered in any court having competent jurisdiction.

Part 2:

Quality is to be equal to contract description.

However, bona fide tenders inferior thereto, provided within the requirements of the U.S.A. Food & Drug Administration and/or other Governmental Agency shall be accepted by the buyer subject to an allowance to be fixed, if necessary, by arbitration.

In the event however, that a shipment is detained by a Governmental Agency solely on account of infestation, seller shall promptly arrange for fumigation, all costs being for his account. If the Governmental Agency releases the shipment such fumigation, the buyer shall accept the cocoa. Cocoa not released after fumigation shall be properly replaced by seller as hereinbefore provided in Part 11 of Section 10.

If the contract calls for "shipment" or for "shipment and/or equivalent delivery", and bona fide tender is rejected by mutual written agreement or at arbitration, it must be properly replaced by the seller by further tender or tenders, in accordance with the contract, and/or at seller's option, with shipment from origin or any intermediate point, within 30 days from date of rejection, irrespective of ocean Bill-of-Lading and declaration, if any, on dock and/or ex warehouse not later than 30 calendar days after such aforesaid rejection and buyer shall accept such replacement or replacements. Unless specifically permitted by mutual agreement or by arbitration, any such replacement shipment, tender or tenders shall be made not later than aforesaid 30 days after aforesaid rejection of the first bona fide tender, failing which the seller shall be deemed in default.

If the contract calls for "delivery", and a bona fide tender is rejected by mutual agreement or at arbitration, tender must be replaced by the seller with further tender or tenders, in accordance with the contract, not later than the last business day of the delivery periods originally called for in the contract, unless an extension has been mutually agreed or decided at arbitration, failing which the seller shall be deemed in default. In any event, however, seller shall have not less than five (5) working days from the date of the first rejection of the initial tender in which to make such replacement.

In case of a rejection of the first bona fide tender, either by mutual agreement or at arbitration, seller shall declare his ability to replace the tender, unless such declaration is waived by mutual agreement or at arbitration. Such declaration shall be in writing, and shall reach the buyer not later than at the close of business on the third business day following the date of such rejection or, after fumigation, of refusal of entry by any Governmental Agency, failing which the seller shall be deemed in default.

Part 3:

A tender of cocoa rejected at arbitration may be accepted by the buyer, in writing, within 1 business day (Saturdays excluded) from receipt of arbitration award; such award is to specify the allowance which the buyer shall receive should he thus elect to take delivery.

SECTION 11-A:

Any import or internal freight charges resulting from diversion of ocean carrier from original port of destination as stated on issued Bill-of-Lading shall be shared equitably between the buyer and seller of this contract provided written declaration has been made prior to the date information of such diversion is made known by the carrier.

SECTION 12:

When either party to a contract claims that a default has occurred, then failing an amicable settlement, the dispute shall be referred to arbitration pursuant to the arbitration rules of The Cocoa Merchants' Association of America, Inc. If it is decided that a default has occurred, the contract shall be closed out at a price and weight, which price shall be the estimated market value of the cocoa contracted for on the day the default occurred or is established, within the discretion of the arbitrators. The arbitrators shall have full discretion to fashion an award as they deem appropriate under the circumstances, including, but without limitation, an award of damages consisting of (i) the difference between the contract price and the closing out price; (ii) ordinary, special and/or consequential damages, and (iii) reasonable legal, professional and other costs incurred in connection with the default and/or arbitration and/or enforcement of an award. The award rendered shall be paid in cash or by certified funds within fifteen (15) working days, and payment shall constitute a final and complete settlement of all claims by either party in respect of said contract.

SECTION 13:

If before the completion of any contract either party thereto shall suspend payment or become bankrupt or insolvent or die without leaving executors or others willing and able to take over his liabilities under the contract, such contract shall be forthwith closed at the market price then current for similar goods for delivery at the time named in the contract. Such market price shall be ascertained either by repurchase or resale or by arbitration at the option of the other party to the contract and the difference between the contract price and the price ascertained shall be the measure of damage payable by or to either party under such contract.

If ascertained by repurchase or resale or arbitration, such damages shall be payable within 10 days after determination thereof.

SECTION 14:

Where a buyer is otherwise in default the contract shall be forthwith closed and damages determined in accordance with Section 13.

SECTION 15:

All invoices are payable in New York City Funds.

STANDARD CONTRACT 2-A

Amended 12/1/90

THE COCOA MERCHANTS' ASSOCIATION OF AMERICA, Inc.

of

Covering F.O.B. Terms for Shipments to the United States

NEW YORK, N.Y.

CONTRACT NO.

Messrs.

We confirm having bought from you (through the Intermediary of)
sold to

(Effective 2/1/90)   SUBJECT TO THE F.O.B. TERMS OF THE INTERNATIONAL CHAMBER OF COMMERCE ("INCOTERMS") AS AMENDED FROM TIME TO TIME AND THE RULES AND CONDITIONS HEREIN AND ON THE REVERSE SIDE, UNLESS NEGATED BY SPECIFIC AGREEMENT HEREIN.

1—Quantity:

2—Description: cocoa beans, usual good quality of the season at time of shipment.

3—Quality: Quality on arrival to be Crop Cocoa, usual good quality.

4—Destination:

5—Price: , F.O.B. ocean carrying steamer at

6—Shipment: per direct steamer and/or steamers during
indirect

from

Partial shipments permitted (in lots of not less than
not permitted

The word Shipment shall mean shipment by steamer and/or steamers, motor ship and/or motor ships.
Immediate Shipment shall mean shipment within 15 calendar days from date of contract.
Prompt Shipment shall mean shipment within 30 calendar days from date of contract.
Direct Shipment shall mean shipment not involving transshipment.
Indirect Shipment shall mean shipment involving transshipment.
The date of on board Bill of Lading shall be proof of shipment.

6A—Containers: If this Contract covers a sale of cocoa beans, shipment in containers shall not be allowed without Buyer's consent. If such consent is given, shipment shall be effected under
(Effective 12/1/90) observance of the 'Standard Guidelines for Shipment of Cocoa Beans In Containers,' dated December 9, 1987, as amended from time to time by the Board of Directors.

7—Declaration: Each Bill of Lading from origin and/or Ship's Delivery Order shall be treated as a separate contract.
(Effective 12/1/90) To be communicated to Buyer, as soon as known by Seller, direct or through Seller's Agent, by cable, by telex or facsimile transmission, or by telephone and confirmed
in writing, with name of steamer, quantity, grade, contract date, port of shipment and destination.
Seller shall be entitled to declare a shipment against this contract, ship lost or not lost.
Declarations shall be binding upon Seller and Buyer and cannot be changed except by mutual consent.

If the Buyer has not received a declaration by midnight of the fourteenth calendar day after the shipping period, he may refuse any subsequent declaration and declare the Seller to be in default.

In the case of indirect shipments Seller must communicate to the Buyer the name of the vessel carrying the cocoa to its final bill of lading destination not later then seven calendar days prior to the scheduled arrival of said vessel.

8—Insurance: Buyer to effect Marine and War Risk Insurance for his account.

9—Weights and Franchise: Net   weights

If contract on basis of net shipping weights, any loss in weight exceeding   % of the net shipping weight is for account of Seller.

Claims for excess loss in weight accompanied by certified official weights and tares shall be submitted and settled promptly.

If contract on basis of net delivered weights, any variation from net invoice weight to be adjusted at contract price.

Provisional invoices, if any, shall be on the basis of   % of shipping weights.

Final invoice shall be established promptly upon determination of final outturn weights.

Claims and final invoices to be established on the basis of the landed net weights of full, sound bags but applied to the whole parcel.

Cocoa to be weighed within 15 working days after completion of discharge of the vessel or release by U.S. Government, whichever occurs latest.

In case Buyer has consented to shipment of this cocoa in containers, cocoa to be weighed within 15 working days after completion of discharge of the vessel, or 15 working days after release by U.S. Government, or 10 working days after completion of stripping of the container, whichever occurs latest.

9A—Packaging: If this contract covers a sale of cocoa beans, beans to be packed in clean, sound, new gunny bags of sufficient strength, or in bags of such other material as is typical for their origin. Bags fabricated from ribbon weave polypropylene or other plastic material not permitted without Buyer's consent.

10—Payment: In the event of the steamer becoming a casualty, payment shall be made by Buyer for full invoice value, net shipping weights, against usual shipping documents on presentation.

11—Special and Other Conditions:

ACCEPTED:

(Please sign and return)

SELLER   BUYER

_____   _____

Signature   Signature

12—Quality:

Cocoa to be equal to contract description; however, bona fide shipments inferior thereto, provided within the standards of the U.S. Government, shall be accepted by the Buyer subject to an allowance to be fixed, if necessary, by arbitration in New York as herein specified.

Claims for inferior quality must be made and arbitration samples, if required, drawn within fifteen working days after the cocoa is discharged from vessel or released by the U.S. Government, whichever occurs latest, and in any event prior to removal of cocoa from dock. Failing amicable adjustment, demand for arbitration—which may be submitted by cable—must be made not later than one month after such removal or release.

Cocoa shipped against this contract is guaranteed by Seller to pass inspection by and comply with the standards of the U.S. Government.

In the event, however, that a shipment is detained by the Government solely on account of infestation, Buyer shall promptly arrange for fumigation.

If the Government releases the shipment after such fumigation, the Buyer shall accept the cocoa, Seller paying all costs incurred in connection with fumigation. If the Government refuses release, Buyer may reject the cocoa and all costs incurred in connection with fumigation shall be paid by the Seller.

Where a shipment of cocoa against this contract is rejected by Buyer because

  (a) entry or release has been refused by U.S. Government, or

  (b) by mutual agreement or at arbitration

Seller shall, upon Buyer's demand, replace such cocoa within the contract period by delivery at destination specified herein, and/or by shipment from origin or any intermediate point, within 30 days after either of the contingencies enumerated under (a) or (b) has been established, whichever is the later period. Buyer shall hold in custody such unacceptable cocoa for the account of Seller until replacement and/or reimbursement for payment made against such cocoa, plus freight, insurance, labor, cartage, storage, interest and other bona fide expenses incurred by Buyer, have been paid; and Seller agrees to effect reimbursement of the principal amount of these expenses immediately upon Buyer's demand.

In the event that Seller cannot make replacement, the contract shall be closed out as provided for under the heading "DEFAULTS".

13—Defaults:
(effective 8/14/89)

When either party to a contract claims that a default has occurred, then failing an amicable settlement, the dispute shall be referred to arbitration pursuant to the arbitration rules of The Cocoa Merchants' Association of America, Inc. If it is decided that a default has occurred, the contract shall be closed out at a price and weight, which price shall be the estimated market value of the cocoa contracted for on the day the default occurred or is established, within the discretion of the arbitrators. The arbitrators shall have full discretion to fashion an award as they deem appropriate under the circumstances, including, but without limitation, an award of damages consisting of (i) the difference between the contract price and the closing out price; (ii) ordinary, special and/or consequential damages, and (iii) reasonable legal, professional and other costs incurred in connection with the default and/or arbitration and/or enforcement of an award. The award rendered shall be paid in cash or by certified funds within fifteen (15) working days, and payment shall constitute a final and complete settlement of all claims by either party in respect to said contract.

14—Quantities and/or Weights:

The words "about" or "more or less" when used to define quantities and/or weights contracted for, shall mean the nearest amount which Seller can fairly and reasonably deliver, but no excess or deficiency shall be greater than three percent. This leeway shall be void whenever a contract is liquidated by payment of difference between purchase and sale prices, in lieu of shipment or tender.

Unless otherwise stipulated, a ton shall be 2,240 lbs. net. If metric tons are specified, a ton shall be 2,204.6 lbs. net.

15—Supervision:

Seller may appoint a representative to supervise weighing and sampling and must state the name of such representative in the advice of shipment, but should Seller not name his representative or should his representative fail to be present, after having received due notice of time and place of weighing and sampling, weights certified and samples sealed by sworn weighers and samplers provided by the Buyer shall be accepted by Seller.

Should Buyer fail to notify Seller's representative in accordance with this clause, shipping weights shall be accepted and no quality claim shall be admitted.

16—Duties, Taxes, Etc.: Any export duty or other tax imposed by the Government of the exporting country or political subdivision thereof or any levy imposed under the International Cocoa Agreement is assumed and shall be paid by the Seller. Any import duty or other tax imposed by the U.S. Government or political subdivision thereof is assumed and shall be paid by the Buyer.

Unless otherwise stipulated, any charges incurred in landing, weighing and sampling shall be for account of Buyer.

17—Marking: Bags to be branded in English with the name of country of origin and otherwise to comply with laws and regulations of U.S. Government, in effect at time of shipment, governing marking of import merchandise. Any expense incurred by failure to comply with these regulations is to be borne by Seller.

17A—Shipping Documents: Unless mutually agreed otherwise by Seller and Buyer, usual shipping documents shall consist of a full set of clean on board ocean Bills of Lading and a shipper's invoice.

18—Force Majeure: Should shipment be prevented or delayed owing to prohibition of exports, fire, strikes, lockouts, riots, war, revolution or other cases of "Force Majeure" the time of shipment shall be extended by one month, but should the delay exceed one month the Buyer shall have the option of cancelling the contract for any quantity not shipped or of accepting the cocoa for shipment as soon as the cause for prevention or delay of shipment shall have been removed provided if such shipment not effected within five months following the expiration date of the first month's extension the contract shall be automatically cancelled for any quantity not shipped; such option to be declared in writing as soon as the Seller announces his inability to ship within the extended period, or, at latest, seven days after the extended period has expired, as reasonable time being allowed for passing on such announcements. Contract void if the Buyer fails to declare such aforesaid option as hereinbefore provided. If required, Seller must produce conclusive evidence to establish his claim for extension.

19—Insolvency or Other Failure to Meet Engagements: In the event that

(a) Buyer shall fail to make any payment required hereunder within three (3) business days after its due date, or

(b) at any time prior to the completion of this contract, there shall be filed by or against either party hereto, in any court, a petition in bankruptcy or insolvency or for reorganization or for appointment of a receiver or trustee of all or a portion of such party's property, or

(c) At any time prior to completion of this contract, either party shall make an assignment for the benefit of creditors, then and in any one of such events, this contract shall be forthwith closed at the market price then current for similar goods for delivery at the time or times, or for shipment during the period or periods, provided for in this contract. Such market price shall be ascertained, at the option of the aggrieved party, by repurchase or resale or by arbitration, and the loss, if any, suffered by such aggrieved party shall be the measure of damages to which such party shall be entitled and which shall be payable within fifteen (15) days after such determination. Such aggrieved party shall not be required to reimburse the other party for any profit derived from any repurchase or resale made pursuant to this provision.

20—Assignment: This contract may not be assigned by either party within the prior written consent of the other party.

21—Successors: The covenants, conditions and agreements contained in this contract shall bind and inure to the benefit of the parties and their respective heirs, distributees, executors, administrators, successors and, except as otherwise provided herein, their assigns.

22—Arbitration: Any question, controversy, claim or dispute whatever arising out of, or under this contract, not adjusted by mutual agreement, shall be settled by arbitration in the City of New York, State of New York, under the auspices of and in accordance with rules of THE COCOA MERCHANTS' ASSOCIATION OF AMERICA, INC. and judgment upon the award rendered may be entered in the Supreme Court of the State of New York in accordance with the provisions of the laws of the State of New York.

The parties to this contract do hereby waive personal service of any papers, notices or process necessary or proper in connection with the foregoing. Such papers, notices or process may be served in accordance with the rules of THE COCOA MERCHANTS' ASSOCIATION OF AMERICA, INC. This contract is deemed made in New York and shall be construed pursuant to the laws of the State of New York.

STANDARD CONTRACT 3-A

Amended 2/26/92

of

THE COCOA MERCHANTS' ASSOCIATION OF AMERICA, Inc.

for

COCOA ON { COST, INSURANCE, FREIGHT
COST AND FREIGHT } **TERMS TO UNITED STATES PORTS**

NEW YORK, N.Y.

CONTRACT NO.

SOLD BY

BOUGHT BY

THROUGH THE INTERMEDIARY (IF ANY) OF

SUBJECT TO THE RULES AND CONDITIONS HEREIN AND ON THE REVERSE SIDE, UNLESS NEGATED BY SPECIFIC AGREEMENT HEREIN.

1—Quantity:

2—Description:

3—Quality: Quality on arrival to be

4—Price:

Crop Cocoa, usual good quality.

{ cents per lb.
U.S. Currency
payable in
New York funds

5—Destination: Cost, Insurance, Freight
Cost and Freight { to landed
(Delete one)

6—Weights and Franchise:

Net weights

If contract on basis of net shipping weights, any loss in weight exceeding _____ % of the net shipping weight is for account of Seller.

Claims for excess loss in weight accompanied by certified official weights and tares shall be submitted and settled promptly.

If contract on basis of net delivered weights, any variation from net invoice weight to be adjusted at contract price.

Provisional invoices, if any, shall be on the basis of _____ % of shipping weights.

Final invoice shall be established promptly upon determination of final outturn weights.

Claims and final invoices to be established on the basis of the landed net weights of full, sound bags but applied to the whole parcel.

Cocoa to be weighed within 15 working days after completion of discharge of the vessel or release by U.S. Government, whichever occurs latest.

In case Buyer has consented to shipment of this cocoa in containers, cocoa to be weighed within 15 working days after completion of discharge of the vessel, or 15 working days after release by U.S. Government, or 10 working days after completion of stripping of the container, whichever occurs latest.

306

from

by first class steamer and/or steamers (in all cases the word "steamer" is understood to include any fully powered primarily engine driven vessel), direct and/or indirect with or without transshipment at other ports at Seller's option, on through Bill of Lading to destination.

Each Bill of Lading from origin and/or Ship's Delivery Order shall be treated as a separate contract.

Received on board Bills of Lading shall be proof and evidence of time of shipment.

Partial shipments permitted _____ NOT permitted (delete one)

7A—Containers:
Amended 12/1/90

If this contract covers a sale of cocoa beans, shipment in containers shall not be allowed without Buyer's consent. If such consent is given, shipment shall be effected under observance of the 'Standard Guidelines for Shipment of Cocoa Beans In Containers,' dated December 9, 1987, as amended from time to time by the Board of Directors.

7B—Packaging:

If this contract covers a sale of cocoa beans, beans to be packed in clean, sound, new gunny bags of sufficient strength, or in bags of such other material as is typical for their origin. Bags fabricated from ribbon weave polypropylene or other plastic material not permitted without Buyer's consent.

8—Insurance:

If contract on a COST, INSURANCE, FREIGHT basis:

Marine insurance shall be covered by Seller at the price of this contract with Lloyds and/or first class British or United States underwriters or insurance companies, for whose solvency Seller is not to be responsible, on the terms of and according to the Institute of London Underwriters' Cargo Clauses (extended cover) with particular average (warehouse to warehouse), including theft, pilferage, short and non-delivery, shipowners' liability, and loss or damage by freshwater, oil, other cargo, sweat, hookhole and other loss or damage however arising, whether by perils of the sea or otherwise all irrespective of percentage; including war, riots, strikes and civil commotions as per Institute War Clauses and Strike Clauses (extended cover) current and available at time of shipment.

All claims after adjustment payable in United States currency in New York.

If contract on a COST AND FREIGHT basis:

In the case of cost and freight contracts only, satisfactory letter of guarantee (or policy of insurance) if required, to be promptly deposited with Seller for his security.

9—Declaration:
(Effective 12/1/90)

To be communicated to Buyer, as soon as known by Seller, direct or through Seller's Agent, by cable, by telex or facsimile transmission, or by telephone and confirmed in writing, with name of steamer, quantity, grade, contract date, port of shipment and destination.

Seller shall be entitled to declare a shipment against this contract, ship lost or not lost.

Declarations are subject to cable error.

If the Buyer has not received a declaration by midnight of the fourteenth calendar day after the shipping period, he may refuse any subsequent declaration and declare the Seller to be in default.

In the case of indirect shipments Seller must communicate to the Buyer the name of the vessel carrying the cocoa to its final bill of lading destination not later then seven calendar days prior to the scheduled arrival of said vessel.

10—Payment:

In the event of the steamer becoming a casualty, payment shall be made by Buyer for full invoice value, net shipping weights, against usual shipping documents on presentation.

11—Special and Other Conditions:

ACCEPTED:

SELLER   BUYER

_____   _____
Signature   Signature

(Please sign and return)

12—Quality: Cocoa to be equal to contract description; however, bona fide shipments inferior thereto, provided within the standards of the U.S. Government, shall be accepted by the Buyer subject to an allowance to be fixed, if necessary, by arbitration in New York as herein specified.

Claims for inferior quality must be made and arbitration samples, if required, drawn within fifteen working days after the cocoa is discharged from vessel or released by the U.S. Government, whichever occurs latest, and in any event prior to removal of cocoa from dock. Failing amicable adjustment, demand for arbitration—which may be submitted by cable—must be made not later than one month after such removal or release.

Cocoa shipped against this contract is guaranteed by Seller to pass inspection by and comply with the standards of the U.S. Government.

In the event, however, that a shipment is detained by the Government solely on account of infestation, Buyer shall promptly arrange for fumigation.

If the Government releases the shipment after such fumigation, the Buyer shall accept the cocoa, Seller paying all costs incurred in connection with fumigation. If the Government refuses release, Buyer may reject the cocoa and all costs incurred in connection with fumigation shall be paid by the Seller.

Where a shipment of cocoa against this contract is rejected by Buyer because

   (a) entry or release has been refused by U.S. Government, or

   (b) by mutual agreement or at arbitration

Seller shall, upon Buyer's demand, replace such cocoa within the contract period by delivery at destination specified herein, and/or by shipment from origin or any intermediate point, within 30 days after either of the contingencies enumerated under (a) or (b) has been established, whichever is the later period. Buyer shall hold in custody such unacceptable cocoa for the account of Seller until replacement and/or reimbursement for payment made against such cocoa, plus freight, insurance, labor, cartage, storage, interest and other bona fide expenses incurred by Buyer, have been paid; and Seller agrees to effect reimbursement of the principal amount of these expenses immediately upon Buyer's demand.

In the event that Seller cannot make replacement, the contract shall be closed out as provided for under the heading "DEFAULTS".

13—Defaults:
(effective 8/14/89)

When either party to a contract claims that a default has occurred, then failing an amicable settlement, the dispute shall be referred to arbitration pursuant to the arbitration rules of The Cocoa Merchants' Association of America, Inc. If it is decided that a default has occurred, the contract shall be closed out at a price and weight, which price shall be the estimated market value of the cocoa contracted for on the day the default occurred or is established, within the discretion of the arbitrators. The arbitrators shall have full discretion to fashion an award as they deem appropriate under the circumstances, including, but without limitation, an award of damages consisting of (i) the difference between the contract price and the closing out price; (ii) ordinary, special and/or consequential damages, and (iii) reasonable legal, professional and other costs incurred in connection with the default and/or arbitration and/or enforcement of an award. The award rendered shall be paid in cash or by certified funds within fifteen (15) working days, and payment shall constitute a final and complete settlement of all claims by either party in respect to said contract.

14—Quantities and/or Weights:

The words "about" or "more or less" when used to define quantities and/or weights contracted for, shall mean the nearest amount which Seller can fairly and reasonably deliver, but no excess or deficiency shall be greater than three percent. This leeway shall be void whenever a contract is liquidated by payment of difference between purchase and sale prices, in lieu of shipment or tender.

Unless otherwise stipulated, a ton shall be 2,240 lbs. net. If metric tons are specified, a ton shall be 2,204.6 lbs. net.

15—Supervision: Seller may appoint a representative to supervise weighing and sampling and must state the name of such representative in the advice of shipment, but should Seller not name his representative or should his representative fail to be present, after having received due notice of time and place of weighing and sampling, weights certified and samples sealed by sworn weighers and samplers provided by the Buyer shall be accepted by Seller.

Should Buyer fail to notify Seller's representative in accordance with this clause, shipping weights shall be accepted and no quality claim shall be admitted.

16—Shipment:

Immediate shipment shall mean shipment within 15 calendar days from date of contract.

Prompt shipment shall mean shipment within 30 calendar days from date of contract.

Direct shipment shall mean shipment not involving transshipment.

Indirect shipment shall mean shipment involving transshipment.

16A—Shipping Documents:

Unless mutually agreed otherwise by Seller and Buyer, usual shipping documents shall consist of a full set of clean on board ocean Bills of Lading, shipper's invoice, and, in the case of a c.i.f. contract, a valid insurance certificate for not less than the invoice value of the shipment.

17—Duties, Taxes, Etc.:
(amended 2/26/92)

Any export duty or other tax imposed by the Government of the exporting country or political subdivision thereof or any levy imposed under the International Cocoa Agreement is assumed and shall be paid by the Seller. Any import duty or other tax imposed by the U.S. Government or political subdivision thereof is assumed and shall be paid by the Buyer.

Unless otherwise stipulated, any charges incurred in weighing and sampling shall be for account of Buyer.

18—Marking:

Bags to be brands in English with the name of country of origin and otherwise to comply with laws and regulations of U.S. Government, in effect at time of shipment, governing marking of import merchandise. Any expense incurred by failure to comply with these regulations is to be borne by Seller.

19—Force Majeure:

Should shipment be prevented or delayed owing to prohibition of exports, fire, strikes, lockouts, riots, war, revolution or other cases of "Force Majeure" the time of shipment shall be extended by one month, but should the delay exceed one month the Buyer shall have the option of cancelling the contract for any quantity not shipped or of accepting the cocoa for shipment as soon as the cause for prevention or delay of shipment shall have been removed provided if such shipment not effected within five months following the expiration date of the first month's extension the contract shall be automatically cancelled for any quantity not shipped; such option to be declared in writing as soon as the Seller announces his inability to ship within the extended period, or, at latest, seven days after the extended period has expired, as reasonable time being allowed for passing on such announcements. Contract void if the Buyer fails to declare such aforesaid option as hereinbefore provided. If required, Seller must produce conclusive evidence to establish his claim for extension.

20—Insolvency or Other Failure to Meet Engagements:

In the event that

(a) Buyer shall fail to make any payment required hereunder within three (3) business days after its due date, or

(b) at any time prior to the completion of this contract, there shall be filed by or against either party hereto, in any court, a petition in bankruptcy or insolvency or for reorganization or for appointment of a receiver or trustee of all or a portion of such party's property, or

(c) at any time prior to completion of this contract, either party shall make an assignment for the benefit of creditors, then and in any one of such events, this contract shall be forthwith closed at the market price then current for similar goods for delivery at the time or times, or for shipment during the period or periods, provided for in this contract. Such market price shall be ascertained, at the option of the aggrieved party, by repurchase or resale or by arbitration, and the loss, if any, suffered by such aggrieved party shall be the measure of damages to which such party shall be entitled and which shall be payable within fifteen (15) days after such determination. Such aggrieved party shall not be required to reimburse the other party for any profit derived from any repurchase or resale made pursuant to this provision.

21—Assignment:

This contract may not be assigned by either party without the prior written consent of the other party.

22—Successors:

The covenants, conditions and agreements contained in this contract shall bind and inure to the benefit of the parties and their respective heirs, distributees, executors, administrators, successors and, except as otherwise provided herein, their assigns.

23—Arbitration:

Any question, controversy, claim or dispute whatever arising out of, or under this contract, not adjusted by mutual agreement, shall be settled by arbitration in the City of New York, State of New York, under the auspices of and in accordance with rules of THE COCOA MERCHANTS' ASSOCIATION OF AMERICA, INC. and judgment upon the award rendered may be entered in the Supreme Court of the State of New York in accordance with the provisions of the laws of the State of New York.

The parties to this contract do hereby waive personal service of any papers, notices or process necessary or proper in connection with the foregoing. Such papers, notices or process may be served in accordance with the rules of THE COCOA MERCHANTS' ASSOCIATION OF AMERICA, INC. This contract is deemed made in New York and shall be construed pursuant to the laws of the State of New York.

Cocoa trade rules of the CSCE

Contract specifications are those which were in effect as of January 27, 1995.
Current specifications may be different and are subject to change. Up to date
information is available from:

The Coffee, Sugar & Cocoa Exchange, Inc
Four World Trade Centre
New York
New York 10048

Tel 212-938 2800   Tlx 127066   Fax 212-524 9863

COCOA RULES

¶ 5101

Rule 9.00. Definitions

As used in the Cocoa Rules:

Bulk storage means storage in an Exchange-licensed warehouse in a manner other than in Exchange-segregated lots.

Certificate of Grade means the Certificate of Growth, Description, Condition, Grade and Count described and authorized in the Cocoa Rules, and for the sake of brevity and convenience shall, throughout the Cocoa Rules, be called and referred to as the Certificate of Grade.

Condition, of cocoa, shall be understood to mean whether or not the cocoa is hammy or smoky.

Count, shall be understood to mean the number of cocoa beans per kilogram as determined by the licensed grader in accordance with the Cocoa Rules.

Deliverer, as used in connection with grading procedures, includes a party submitting cocoa for grading in advance of tender.

Delivery order means a written order to deliver goods directed to a warehouseman, carrier or other person who in the ordinary course of business issues warehouse receipts, bills of lading or other documents of title to goods.

Description is the adjective accompanying growth to indicate the season in which the cocoa was grown, a method of selection or curing or a commercial classification.

Exchange-segregated lot means a lot of ten (10) metric tons net of cocoa beans (in original shipping bags of average weight(s) customary for the growth) which has been identified for delivery under an Exchange contract by marking and separating it from other lots of cocoa and which is stored in a portion of an Exchange-licensed warehouse designated as a store for delivery purposes.

Growth is the common commercial name of a variety of cocoa to indicate the country in which it was produced or the district in such country or the port from which it was shipped.

Grade, as a noun, refers to the percentage of defective and/or slatey beans as provided in the Cocoa Rules.

Grade, as a verb, means the examination and/or certification of cocoa as to its growth, description, condition, grade and/or count.

Renumbered April 14, 1988.

¶ 5102

Rule 9.01. Hours of Trading

(a) Unless otherwise directed by the Board from time to time, trading hours of the Exchange in the case of Cocoa, shall be from 9:00 A.M. to 2:00 P.M. (9:00 A.M. to 12:00 P.M. on a half day). A warning signal shall be given five minutes before the close of Cocoa trading, and an additional signal at the close of Cocoa trading on each business day.

(b) Cocoa contracts shall not be recognized by the Exchange extending beyond a period of 24 months, including the current month. Trading in Cocoa contracts shall be conducted for delivery in March, May, July, September and December and shall at all times be conducted in any such month contained in an 24-month cycle. Trading in a new delivery month shall be initiated at the opening of trading on the first Exchange business day of the twenty-third month preceding any delivery month.

Adopted by the Board October 8, 1980, effective April 27, 1981.

Amended by the Board July 8, 1981; effective April 6, 1982.

Amended by the Board July 9, 1986; effective July 28, 1986.

Amended by the Board December 17, 1986; effective January 5, 1987.

Renumbered April 14, 1988.

Amended by the Board February 13, 1991; effective June 10, 1991.

Amended by the Board March 10, 1993; effective May 10, 1993.

¶ 5104

Rule 9.02. Delivery Points

The delivery of cocoa on Exchange contracts shall be made only from warehouses licensed by the Exchange located in the Port of New York District, the Delaware River Port District or the Port of Hampton Roads.

For purposes of this Rule, the Port of New York District shall mean the district defined from time to time by the laws of New York and New Jersey; the Delaware River Port District shall mean the district defined from time to time by the laws of New Jersey and Pennsylvania; and the Port of Hampton Roads shall mean the twenty-five square mile harbor formed by the confluence of the James, Nansemond and Elizabeth Rivers, and the Chesapeake Bay eastward into the Atlantic Ocean, and including on its perimeter the port facilities located in the cities of Chesapeake, Newport News, Norfolk and Portsmouth, Virginia; provided, however, the Port of Hampton Roads shall also be deemed to include the city of Suffolk, Virginia.

The seller may choose the delivery point. There shall be no differential in price based on the delivery point.

Amended by the Board July 9, 1980; effective with respect to the September 1982 contract month and contract months traded thereafter.

Renumbered April 14, 1988.

Amended by the Board April 8, 1992; effective May 18, 1992 commencing with the July, 1992 contract.

¶ 5108

Rule 9.03. Form of Contracts

No Contract for the future delivery of merchandise shall be noticed in any report, or in any manner recognized by the Exchange, unless both parties thereto shall be members of the Exchange excepting that members may offer their contracts for clearance to the Clearing Association, which may become by substitution a party thereto in place of a member, and thereupon such association shall become subject to the obligations thereof and entitled to all the rights and privileges of a member in holding, fulfilling or disposing thereof.

(a) Contracts for the future delivery of cocoa in contract months of September 1982 and thereafter shall be in the following form:

FORM OF CONTRACT FOR DELIVERY OF COCOA CONTRACT

OFFICE OF ....

NEW YORK...19 . . .

SOLD FOR

TO

. . . .

ten (10 metric tons net of cocoa beans (in original shipping bags of average weight(s) customary for the growth) the growth of any country or clime, including new or yet unknown growths, deliverable, from warehouses licensed by Exchange, at the seller's option, at one of the delivery points provided in Cocoa 9.02, between the first and last days of _____, inclusive; the delivery within such time is to be at seller's option, upon notice to the buyer of ten full business days, as may be prescribed by the Rules; the cocoa is to be of any grade and count permitted by the Rules; at the price of _____, dollars per ton for the standard grades, growths, condition and counts, with additions or deductions for other grades, growths and counts according to the rate of the Exchange, existing on the afternoon of the day previous to the date of the notice of delivery.

Seller has the option to tender cocoa in Exchange-licensed warehouses at one of the delivery points provided in Cocoa Rule 9.02, at an allowance and under such terms as may be prescribed in the Rules of the Exchange.

Either party is to have the right to call for margins as the variations of the market for like deliveries may warrant, which margins shall be kept good.

This contract is made in view of, and in all respects subject to the Rules and all differences and/or disputes that may arise hereunder shall be settled by arbitration pursuant to such Rules.

For, and in consideration of one dollar to the undersigned, in hand paid, receipt whereof is hereby acknowledged, the undersigned accepts this contract with all its obligations and conditions.

(b) Oral contracts (which shall always be presumed to have been made in the foregoing form) shall have the same force as written ones, if acknowledged in writing by both of the contracting parties before the close of the business day on which made.

(c)(i) All contracts for the future delivery of Cocoa shall be binding upon members and of full force and effect until the quantity and quality of the Cocoa specified in such contract shall have been delivered, and the price specified in said contract shall have been paid. No contract shall be entered into with any stipulation or understanding between the parties at the time of making such contract that the terms of said contract as specified above are not to be fulfilled, or that the Cocoa is not to be delivered and received in accordance with said Sections.

(ii) Subject to the prohibition in paragraph (i), the Deliverer and Receiver may enter into a mutually acceptable written agreement to deliver and receive under conditions other than those stipulated in the Rules. A delivery so made shall be considered complete upon written notification by the Deliverer and the Receiver to the Exchange and to the Clearing Association. The making of any such agreement shall relieve the Clearing Corporation of any further obligations with respect to any Exchange contract involved, and the Deliverer and Receiver shall indemnify the Exchange and the Clearing Corporation against any liability, cost or expense either may incur for any reason as a result of the execution, delivery or performance of such contract or such agreement, or any breach thereof or default thereunder.

Amended by the Board July 9, 1980; effective with respect to the September 1982 contract month and contract months traded thereafter.

Amended by the Board November 10, 1982; effective February 1, 1983.

Renumbered April 14, 1988.

¶ 5109

Rule 9.04. Minimum Variations

No member shall offer to buy or sell cocoa at variations of less than $1.00 per ton.

Renumbered April 4, 1988.

¶ 5180

Rule 9.05. Notice of Delivery or Demand for Cocoa Issuance of Notice

When notice of delivery on the part of the seller or of demand of cocoa by a buyer is required by contract it shall be given by the party furnishing the cocoa in one case, and the buyer in the other case, to the party requiring said notice, ten full business days prior to the date of delivery; said notice shall be given before 10:00 A.M. of the day of issuance (excepting as hereinafter provided). The issuer of a delivery notice shall have it registered and stamped at the office of the Clearing Association before 5:00 P.M. on full business days and 1:00 P.M. on partial business days. No notice shall be issued, or call for delivery, on a day other than a full business day.

Every delivery notice shall be issued ten full business days in advance of the business day designated for delivery.

Should the office of the party to whom notice is to be given be closed, it shall be good service to give notice to the Exchange. It shall endorse thereon the day and time of its receipt, and post notice thereof on the bulletin board of the Exchange.

Cessation of Trading

(a) All trading in the current months shall cease at 12 o'clock noon or 30 minutes after the completion of the opening call, whichever is the later, on the business day prior to the last business day upon which Delivery Notices may be issued in that month.

Formal Requisites of Delivery Notice

All notices must be for ten (10) metric tons of cocoa.

Delivery notices must state the growth of cocoa and the description of such growth, and the delivery must consist of cocoa of one growth and description of such growth only. Delivery notices must also state where the cocoa will be delivered.

If a notice is tendered by the deliverer before the prescribed hours, on the tenth business day before the delivery of cocoa is due, the notice shall be accepted by any member of the Exchange to whom cocoa is due under contract; and the price shall be made equal to the price of the contract on which it shall be tendered, provided that it is otherwise in accordance with such contract; and the cocoa delivered on such notice shall be accepted in settlement of the contracts specified in the notice.

Each acceptor of a notice shall continue his (or their) liability to each other for the fulfillment of the contract under the Rules until the contract has been fulfilled.

A holder of a notice may at the option of the issuer thereof arrange to have such notice taken back by such issuer upon such terms as are mutually agreed to by such issuer and such holder.

The hours for the presentation of bill and delivery of negotiable warehouse receipts, weighmaster's return, certificate of grade and payment for cocoa shall be between 12:00 noon and 2:01 P.M.

Delivery notices may be issued only against contracts cleared through the Clearing Association, and may only be issued by said Association or a member thereof and the Clearing Association, shall retain all original margins held against contracts against which delivery notices may be issued or demanded until all such contracts have been completed in the last detail, or if notified of a default, shall retain the original margins on the contract in default until the default has been remedied or until the injured party to the defaulted contract has been reimbursed for the loss suffered and, if so ordered by the Arbitration Committee or any Special Arbitration Committee of the Exchange, the Clearing Association, shall make available such original margins to pay the loss on a defaulted contract and make good to defaulted party any loss in excess of such margins held for account and risk of the defaulting party.

The issuer of a delivery notice shall, on demand deliver to the holder thereof a sampling order (or orders), giving the name of the vessel and month of arrival thereof, and the marks and chop numbers of the cocoa therein named.

(b) Notwithstanding the provisions of paragraph (a) above, if a member transfers any contracts after the close of trading in accordance with Rule 3.06(f) the failure of such member to issue a Delivery Notice with respect to such contracts shall not be deemed a violation of this Rule.

FORMS

DELIVERY NOTICE

New York,

A.M. o'clock

To CSC CLEARING CORPORATION.

Take notice that on .... we shall deliver to you at .... ten (10) metric tons in about .... bags of .... cocoa, in Exchange-segregated lots in accordance with the terms of the contract of sale to you at .... dollars per ton. We pledge ourselves to deliver a Sampling Order to the holder of this notice. We further pledge ourselves to deliver on the delivery date between the hours of 12:00 Noon and 2:01 P.M., to the holder of this notice, the negotiable warehouse receipt(s) for this cocoa against payment for said cocoa, in accordance with the Rules of the Coffee, Sugar & Cocoa Exchange, Inc.

....

Per...

CONDITIONS

In consideration of one ($1.00) dollar paid to the acceptor, receipt of which is hereby acknowledged, it is agreed that the holder hereof will, between the hours of 12:00 Noon and 2:01 P.M. on the delivery date, receive the negotiable warehouse receipt(s) and pay for the cocoa at the above rate per pound for standard grades and growths, with additions or deductions for other grades, according to the rate of the Coffee, Sugar & Cocoa Exchange, Inc. existing on the afternoon of the day previous to the date of this notice. It is further agreed that each acceptor hereof shall continue his (or their) liability to each other for the fulfillment of the contract until this notice shall have been returned to the issuer thereof, and negotiable warehouse receipt(s) shall have been delivered, at which time all responsibility of intermediate parties shall cease.

CSC Clearing Corporation

Per...

.... o'clock: ....

New York, ... 19....

Messrs. T. & Co.:

We accept the above, with all its conditions and obligations, and you will please take a notice that, in accordance therewith, we shall deliver you ten (10) metric tons (in about .... bags) of cocoa, on account of our contract of sale to you, dated .... the cocoa to be paid for at the price indicated on the delivery notice.

Amended by the Board July 9, 1980; effective with respect to the September 1982 contract month and contract months traded thereafter.

Amended by the Board May 10, 1983; effective October 17, 1983 with respect to delivery months commencing with the December 1983 delivery month.

Amended by the Board March 12, 1986; effective October 29, 1986, commencing with the July 1987 delivery month.

Amended by the Board November 11, 1987; effective December 17, 1987 with respect to delivery months commencing with the March 1988 delivery month.

Renumbered April 14, 1988.

Amended by the Board February 13, 1991; effective September 20, 1991.

¶ 5184

Rule 9.06. Penalty for Fraudulent or Fictitious Use of Names in the Issue of Notices for Cocoa

No member of the Exchange shall make a fraudulent or fictitious use of any name or names in the issue of any notice for the delivery of any commodity pursuant to an Exchange contract.

Amended by the Board March 12, 1986; effective October 29, 1986, commencing with the July 1987 delivery month.

Renumbered April 14, 1988.

¶ 5192

Rule 9.07. Good Delivery

A tender of Cocoa shall be considered a good delivery when all requirements of the Rules pertaining thereto shall have been performed by both parties or a settlement made consistent therewith. A tender, conforming to the Rules, must be accepted and paid for by the receiver before 2:01 P.M. on the specified day of delivery. Unless otherwise mutually agreed upon, such payment shall be made in the form of a certified check drawn by the receiver to the order of the deliverer on a New York City bank or trust company, or a cashier's check or official check drawn by a New York City bank or trust company to the order of the deliverer.

Cocoa tendered against a contract and found to be not a good delivery may be replaced by the tenderer provided that the replacement meets all of the requirements of the Rules of the Exchange and also all of the requirements of the delivery notice to which it is applicable.

Where cocoa tendered is found to be not a good delivery (for failed grade or for any other reason) the declaration of submission and sampling order for the replacement(s) must be presented to the Exchange at least five business days prior to the delivery date specified in the Delivery Notice. If the deliverer elects to submit the declaration of submission and sampling order after the time limits prescribed herein, the Exchange shall not be responsible in the event the results of such declaration and order cannot be issued by the delivery date in which case the deliverer would be in default unless a mutually acceptable written agreement has been entered into as provided under Cocoa Rule 9.03.

All merchandise delivered pursuant to any Exchange futures contract shall be of grades conforming to United States standards, if such standards shall have been officially promulgated and adopted by the Commodity Futures Trading Commission.

DEFAULTS—COCOA

Except as otherwise provided for in the Rules, a member shall be in default who shall fail to issue or to tender a notice, as required in Cocoa Rule 9.05 or other section of the Rules, in fulfillment of any sale contracts outstanding in his name after trading in the current month has ceased: or when the deliverer fails to tender to the receiver before 2:01 P.M. on the specified day of delivery warehouse receipts, Certificate of Grade issued by the Exchange, weighmaster's return and invoice (except as provided in last paragraph of Cocoa Rule 9.11 and in Cocoa Rule 9.12) or such data as prescribed by the Exchange which evidences these documents, or otherwise fails to comply with the Rules relating to delivery of cocoa.

The delivery weight of a contract shall be ten metric tons (10% metric tons) (1% more or less). Any variation from ten metric tons of more thsn 1% but not in excess of 5% shall constitute a default by the deliverer on part of a contract; any variation in excess of 5% of ten metric tons shall constitute a default by the deliverer on an entire contract. Such default, partial or entire, shall not be excused or modified whether the weight variation be due to excessive or insufficient tender or failure to replace cocoa rejected by duly approved graders because of grade or growth.

Deficiency of weight due to allowances made in accordance with the Rules on cocoa retendered on weighmaster's return in force is excepted from the provisions of this section.

A receiver shall be in default on an entire contract who, upon receipt of a tender of cocoa in completion of an outstanding contract in conformity with the Rules shall fail to pay in full the amount of the deliverer's invoice in accordance with the Rules.

Defaults, unless mutually adjusted, shall be reported to the Arbitration Committee by the member who has failed to receive satisfaction on the contract, and he shall also make formal application for arbitration of the matter pursuant to the Exchange Arbitration Rules then in effect.

DAMAGES—COCOA

Damages of $5.50 per ton, plus any proven loss because of the default, shall be paid by the defaulting member to the injured member as follows:

On ten (10) metric tons when an entire cocoa contract is in default;

On any variation from ten (10) metric tons of not more than 5% when part of a cocoa contract is in default.

The proven loss hereinabove referred to shall be the loss established before the Arbitration Committee as evidenced by the decision and award of said Committee and the award of said Committee shall be final and binding upon every corporation, including the Clearing Corporation, firm or person who may have a financial responsibility for or interest in the related defaulted contract.

It shall be a violation of the Rules to default intentionally on any Exchange contract. If in the course of any arbitration there shall appear evidence of an intentional default, the Arbitration Committee shall report such evidence to the Exchange.

Settlements, however, consistent with the Rules may be made between parties at issue by mutual consent.

Amended by the Board July 9, 1980; effective with respect to the September 1982 contract month and contract months traded thereafter.

Amended by the Board March 12, 1986; effective October 29, 1986, commencing with the July 1987 delivery month.

Amended by the Board April 13, 1988; effective commencing with the December 1988 delivery period.

Renumbered April 14, 1988.

Amended by the Board February 13, 1991; effective September 20, 1991.

Amended by the Board of November 13, 1991; effective June 5, 1992 with the implementation of COPS for cocoa.

¶ 5196

Rule 9.08. Settlement of Contracts of Deceased or Bankrupt Members After Trading in Current Month Has Ceased

If the death of a member is posted or announced after trading in the current month has ceased, so that a contract with him for future delivery of merchandise in the current month cannot be closed in the open market as provided in the Rules, then the other party to such contract shall, within six Exchange business hours after such death is announced or posted, close it as follows:

(a) If it is a contract in which such deceased member was the seller, the other party to such contract shall buy an amount of spot merchandise or delivery notices evidencing the same; in all cases in an amount equal to that called for in the contract.

(b) If it is a contract in which such deceased member was the buyer, the other party to such contract shall sell an amount of spot merchandise equal to that called for in such contract, or, at his option, shall sell such an amount for future delivery in the subsequent month, delivering against such sale the merchandise which would have been delivered against the contract with the deceased member.

Notice of the time, manner and price at which such deceased member's contracts were thus closed shall be given promptly to his estate, and such price shall be the basis of settlement between the parties to the contract.

Amended by the Board March 12, 1986; effective October 29, 1986, commencing with the July 1987 delivery month.

Renumbered April 14, 1988.

¶ 5200

Rule 9.09. When Tender of Cocoa Deemed Accepted

All bags of Cocoa tendered shall be regarded as accepted unless protest in writing be made by the receiver upon the deliverer as is hereinafter provided.

The protest herein referred to shall specify the faults that are found with the tender and shall be accompanied by a demand that such faults be corrected before the time set for delivery. Copy of said protest shall be served on the Exchange for possible reference to the Arbitration Committee. If, at the time of delivery, the holder of the notice shall refuse to accept the cocoa tendered because the conditions complained of have not been corrected, the Arbitration Committee shall decide whether or not the faults which were the subject of the protest justified refusal to accept the delivery. If the Arbitration Committee finds that the refusal to accept delivery was justified, the deliverer shall be in default. If the Arbitration Committee finds that the refusal to accept delivery was unjustified, the receiver shall be in default.

Renumbered April 14, 1988.

Amended by the Board April 13, 1988; effective May 16, 1988.

¶ 5204

Rule 9.10. Settlement of Contract, Issuance of Notices and Deliveries on Exchange Holidays—Cocoa

All Cocoa contracts falling due on Exchange holidays shall be settled on the preceding day; but where two holidays occur on consecutive days, contracts falling due upon the first of such holidays shall be settled upon the business day immediately preceding, and those maturing upon the second of such holidays shall be settled upon the business day next following the same.

Delivery notices in fulfillment of contracts for future delivery shall not be issued on Saturdays and such holidays as are prescribed by the By-Laws, or ordered by the Exchange or by the Board of Managers, except as hereinafter provided.

When the last day on which a delivery notice may be issued for delivery in the current month is declared a holiday too late for the issuance thereof on the preceding notice day, such notice may be given in the usual manner on such holiday.

When the last delivery day of the current month is declared a holiday too late for a delivery notice to be issued requiring delivery on the preceding business day, the delivery shall be completed on said holiday.

Members having Cocoa contracts open in the current month must keep their offices open for the purpose of receiving such notices or of completing such deliveries.

Amended by the Board March 12, 1986; effective October 29, 1986, commencing with the July 1987 delivery month.

Renumbered April 14, 1988.

¶ 5216

Rule 9.11. Delivery and Payment of Cocoa

1. Sound cocoa must be delivered from one store in a warehouse licensed by the Exchange, located at one of the delivery points specified in Cocoa Rule 9.02, in an Exchange-segregated lot, as that term is defined in Cocoa Rule 9.00, having no more than five chops, except when a chop is added to make a deficiency in weight, but in no case shall the number of chops exceed six. For the purposes of this rule sound cocoa shall mean cocoa for which no external condition has been noted by the Exchange sampler and which is packaged in bags made of sisal, henequen, jute, burlap or woven material having similar properties (any other material not permitted), without inner lining or outer covering of any other material; provided, however, cocoa packaged in bags of polypropylene or other plastic material which has a United States Customs entry date prior to February 1, 1992 shall be considered sound.

(a) The party who is the holder of a delivery notice shall notify the issuer thereof and upon request shall show it to the issuer, but such party shall retain the delivery notice until the delivery is completed.

(b) Should the Certificate of Grade be ready for presentation, the issuer of the notice shall on the day of delivery, between the hours of 12:00 Noon and 2:01 P.M., present at the office of the party holding the delivery notice a bill, weigher's return, Certificate of Grade, and negotiable warehouse receipt duly endorsed or such data prescribed by the Exchange which evidences for foregoing documents, for each delivery of about ten (10) metric tons of cocoa, whereupon the delivery and payment shall be simultaneously made.

(c) Upon delivery of a negotiable warehouse receipt, it shall be the option of the deliverer to add to the invoice charges for unexpired storage charges from date of delivery evidenced as paid on the warehouse receipt or to allow the charges of the warehouse, in which the cocoa is stored from the date to which the storage has been paid and so stamped on the warehouse receipt to the date of delivery.

(d) Should the Certificate of Grade not be ready for presentation, the delivery shall take place as outlined above, but the estimated value of the cocoa tendered must be stated upon the bill; the receiver in making payment of the bill presented may retain $11.00 per ton on the net weights delivered until the Certificate of Grade is furnished. Any deliverer of cocoa who shall present a bill showing a grade and growth greater than the equivalent of $11.00 per ton, shall be subject to a complaint under the

Disciplinary Rules of the Exchange. The difference between the amount stated upon the bill and that paid shall be, if demanded, deposited in a designated depository of the Exchange in the same manner as required in the deposit of margins, until the certificate of grade is furnished. On such deposits the party shall be entitled to interest at the rate allowed by the depository on the amount ascertained in final settlement to be due to each; but all such deposits are at the risk of the parties depositing them.

Amended by the Board July 9, 1980; effective with respect to the September 1982 contract month and contract months traded thereafter.

Amended by the Board November 10, 1982; effective February 1, 1983.

Amended by the Board March 12, 1986; effective October 29, 1986, commencing with the July 1987 delivery month.

Amended by the Board April 8, 1987; effective July 15, 1987 applicable to all sampling orders submitted to the Exchange for delivery on the December '87 cocoa contract.

Renumbered April 14, 1988.

Amended by the Board March 20, 1991; effective August 1, 1991.

Amended by the Board November 13, 1991; effective June 5, 1992 with the implementation for COPS for cocoa.

Amended by the Board October 14, 1992; effective February 8, 1993.

¶ 5220

Rule 9.12. Special Relief at Arbitration

In addition to the authority elsewhere vested in the Arbitration Committee by the Arbitration Rules of the Exchange, the Committee is hereby given explicit authority to grant measures of relief to a member of the Exchange under the circumstances and in the manner hereinafter provided.

If a member shall issue a Delivery Notice against cocoa beans stored in a warehouse licensed by the Exchange and, because of contingencies beyond his control that affect a substantial number of warehouses licensed by the Exchange, he is unable to have the cocoa weighed into an Exchange lot and to have the cocoa sampled and graded in accordance with the Rules of the Exchange, but is able to obtain a Negotiable Warehouse Receipt covering the number of bags to make approximately ten (10) metric tons net, the Arbitration Committee may, after investigating the matter, authorize the deliverer to proceed with the fulfillment of his contract by presenting to the receiver such Negotiable Warehouse Receipt together with a pro forma invoice for the cocoa covered by the same, which invoice the receiver shall pay after deducting two percent for any subsequent adjustment in weights and $11.00 per ton for any subsequent adjustment in grade.

Any required adjustments in payments made as hereinabove provided shall be made immediately after the impediments that necessitated the pro forma payments are removed and the requirements of the Rules affecting the merchandise so tendered in fulfillment of a contract must be conformed with promptly when the interference is removed.

If a member, seeking relief under the provisions of this Rule, shall claim that his difficulties are due to contingencies beyond his control, he may present supporting evidence to the Arbitration Committee and that Committee shall be the sole and final judge as to whether or not such was the case or whether the contingencies cited would justify the relief sought by the member.

Any apparently false or fraudulent statement of fact or circumstances made to the Arbitration Committee by a member of the Exchange to obtain the benefit of any relief that may be granted by the Committee pursuant to this rule may be reported to the Board of Managers by the Committee, or any member thereof, or by any member of the Exchange who may have knowledge of the matter, whereupon the Board shall report the matter to the President who shall proceed under the Disciplinary Rules. If found guilty, the offending member may be penalized as provided in the Disciplinary Rules of the Exchange.

Amended by the Board March 12, 1986; effective October 29, 1986, commencing with the July 1987 delivery month.

Renumbered April 14, 1988.

¶ 5224

Rule 9.13. Duties and Taxes to be Paid by Buyer of Cocoa

Whenever an Import Duty, or Internal Tax is levied upon Cocoa, such duty or tax, shall, unless otherwise explicitly provided in the contract, be assumed and be payable by the buyer.

Renumbered April 14, 1988.

¶ 5228

Rule 9.14. Sampling Cocoa

(a) All cocoa to be delivered in Exchange-segregated lots which must be graded pursuant to the rules of the Exchange shall be sampled in accordance with the provision of this rule:

(i) Each lot of cocoa to be sampled shall be sampled by two (2) duly licensed master samplers.

(1) The master samplers shall be selected at random from a list of duly licensed master samplers by the Exchange and shall not have acted in any capacity as an importer with respect to such cocoa. Any master sampler which has also been granted a warehouse license shall be excluded from this selection process. Upon receipt of an order to draw new samplers from a particular lot of cocoa, the President shall designate two (2) licensed master samplers other than those who drew the original samples.

(2) The total charge for such sampling shall be payable by the deliverer to the master sampler. In the case of an initial delivery under a Certificate of Grade or an initial delivery under a recertification of grade, the deliverer shall include one half of the charge for sampling in the bill which shall be presented to the receiver and paid by the receiver on the day of delivery as required by Cocoa Rule 9.11.

(ii) For sound cocoa to be sampled hereunder, no external condition may appear on the bags. In the event an external condition of the bags does exist, it shall be noted by the sampler who shall record such condition on the sampling label and the Exchange shall promptly notify the owner of such condition. The existence of any external conditions on the bags noted by the sampler shall automatically cancel the Declaration of Submission.

(iii) For every lot of cocoa to be sampled hereunder, a sampling order, in such form as prescribed by the Exchange, shall be sent by the deliverer to the Exchange at least five business days prior to the delivery date specified on the Delivery Notice accompanied by a declaration of submission which shall contain such information as required by the Exchange. If a deliverer elects to submit a sampling order after the time limit prescribed herein, the Exchange shall not be responsible in the event the results have not been determined by the delivery date in which case the deliverer would be in default unless a mutually acceptable written agreement has been entered into as provided under Cocoa Rule 9.03.

(1) Form of Declaration of Submission

DECLARATION OF SUBMISSION

PURSUANT TO THE RULES OF THE

COFFEE, SUGAR & COCOA EXCHANGE, INC.

DATE _____

COFFEE, SUGAR & COCOA EXCHANGE, INC.

I/WE HEREWITH ENCLOSE SAMPLING ORDER

FOR THE FOLLOWING COCOA TENDERED OR TO BE

TENDERED ON THE EXCHANGE:

(Strike out LOT NO _____ MARK _____
portion not GROWTH _____ DESCRIPTION _____
applicable) NO. OF BAGS _____ EX SS _____
DATE OF CUSTOMS ENTRY _____

(A) This Cocoa has been previously delivered on the Exchange under D.N. No. _____, Lot No. _____, Dated _____

(B) This Cocoa has not been previously tendered by Me/Us and rejected or delivered on the Exchange; it is contained in original bags in original condition and was discharged in the U.S. Port of _____

(2) Form of Sampling Order

(3) Form of Grading Request

[A] *GRADING ON TENDER*

I/We request that this cocoa be graded by three licensed graders pursuant to the Rules of the Exchange as follows:

Complete grading   [   ]   Partial Grading:
                                          For condition   [   ]
                                          For grade   [   ]
                                          For count   [   ]

[B] *GRADING BEFORE TENDER*

I/We request that this Cocoa be graded by three licensed graders pursuant to the Rules of the Exchange as follows:

Complete grading   [   ]   Partial Grading:
                                          For condition   [   ]
                                          For grade   [   ]
                                          For count   [   ]

(b) All sampling orders for cocoa delivered on delivery notices shall be for about two and one-half $(2^1\!/_2)$ kilograms per chop of 100 bags or less and about five (5) kilograms per chop for chops of more than 100 bags and all samples shall belong to the receiver in lieu of a chop allowance.

(c) When the cocoa is sampled for grading purposes by the deliverer, after being weighed for delivery, the weight of the samples drawn from each chop shall be deducted from the invoice by the deliverer and from the warehouse receipt by the warehouseman.

(d) The minimum number of bags of cocoa to be sampled by samplers on sampling orders as above described shall be as follows:

Chops of	On Original Sampling	On Re-sampling
5 bags or less	Every Bag	Every Bag
6 to 25 bags	5 bags	5 bags
26 to 50 bags	10 bags	25% of total bags
51 to 75 bags	15 bags	25% of total bags
76 to 100 bags	20 bags	25% of total bags
101 and more	20% of total bags	25% of total bags

Each sample shall consist of cocoa drawn from at least two sides of every pile, at least one of which must be drawn from the long side of the tier or aisle.

(e) All cocoa sampled on orders as herein provided shall be sampled into bags furnished by the Exchange bearing a label approved by the Exchange providing for information to be furnished by the Exchange showing delivery notice number, date of import, name of deliverer and name of receiver. The sampler shall fill in the following further information, viz, lot number, number of bags, mark, steamer, location, name of warehouseman, floor number, number of bags sampled, weight of sample, and date of sampling and a brief description of the External Condition of the original shipping bags, which information shall be in the form of a certificate which shall be signed by the sampler. The bags shall then be sealed and the certificate signed jointly by the samplers.

(f) Once the sample has been drawn, the master sampler shall scrape the bag surface area of the tier hole to re-close the bag weaving to minimize spillage.

Amended by the Board November 11, 1981; effective December 1, 1981.

Amended by the Board November 10, 1982; effective December 1, 1982.

Amended by the Board June 8, 1983; effective June 30, 1983.

Amended by the Board March 12, 1986; effective October 29, 1986, commencing with the July 1987 delivery month.

Amended by the Board April 8, 1987; effective July 15, 1987, applicable to all sampling orders submitted to the Exchange for delivery on the December '87 cocoa contract.

Renumbered April 14, 1988.

Amended by the Board April 13, 1988; effective May 16, 1988.

Amended by the Board April 13, 1988; commencing with the December 1988 delivery period.

Amended by the Board November 13, 1991; effective June 5, 1992 with the implementation of COPS for cocoa.

Amended by the Board October 14, 1992; effective November 9, 1992.

Amended by the Board July 13, 1994; effective September 13, 1994.

¶ 5232

Rule 9.15. Fraudulently Packed Cocoa

Fraudulently packed cocoa shall be rejectable.

The receiver of cocoa can require any package to be opened and the actual quality shall be ascertained, in which event all expense and loss shall be paid by the party whose sampler is shown to be in error.

False or fraudulently packed cocoa shall include bags containing a foreign substance, bags containing damaged cocoa in the interior without indication of such damage upon the exterior of the bags, bags composed of good cocoa immediately next to the bag and decidedly inferior cocoa in the interior of the bags in such manner as not to be readily detected by the trier, bags the marks on which indicate a specific growth or grade, but which contain cocoa of a decidedly inferior or different growth or grade.

Renumbered April 14, 1988.

¶ 5236

Rule 9.16. Original Shipping Bags

Any claim by an receiver that Cocoa beans tendered under an Exchange contract are not in original shipping bags of average weight(s) customary for the growth shall be submitted to the Arbitration Committee.

Renumbered April 14, 1988.

¶ 5240

Rule 9.17. Claims for Fraudulent Packing of Cocoa

After cocoa has been examined, received and passed by the broker or agent of the buyer, no claim may be made against the seller except for fraudulent packing. Claims for fraudulent packing must be made by the buyer within eight days of discovery thereof, and the date of the discovery shall be incorporated in the sworn statement of the claimant; in no case, however, shall any claim for fraudulent packing be valid after ninety days from the date of the delivery.

Claims for fraudulent packing shall be made in writing, and shall state the particulars of the fraudulent packing, the marks by which the Cocoa was sold, and all other legible marks and numbers upon the bags. It shall also state the loss sustained by the buyer; such loss shall be the difference in market value on the day the claim is dated between the fraudulent bag and a bag of Cocoa of the grade and growth bought in proper condition.

Any claim made in accordance with the above, and verified by oath or affirmation, shall be deemed prima facie valid in favor of the claimant, subject to reference to the Arbitration Committee.

In all cases of claims for fraudulent packing, the party making the claim shall have the right to return or the seller to demand the return of such bag or bags; in this event, the seller shall pay the cost of transportation both from and returning to the delivery point, and shall deliver other bags of the grade and growth sold, if demanded by the buyer.

Renumbered April 14, 1988.

¶ 5244

Rule 9.18. Grading Cocoa

(a) All cocoa to be delivered in Exchange-segregated lots must be certified as deliverable with respect to growth, description, condition, count and grade in accordance with the provisions of this rule.

(b) The growth, description, condition, count and grade of cocoa which may be delivered on an Exchange contract are as follows:

(i) *Growth and Description*

The following growths and descriptions of cocoa, as such growths and descriptions may from time to time be known in the trade, may be delivered at the premiums or at par as indicated below;

Group A—Addition of $160—per metric ton

Ghana—Main Crop	Nigeria—Main Crop
Ivory Coast—Main Crop	Sierra Leone—Main Corp
Lome—Main Crop	

Group B—Addition of $80—per metric ton

Arriba (Ecuador)	Jamaica	Samoa
Bahai (Brazil)	Java	San Thorme
Cameroon	Liberia—Main Crop	Surinam
Sri Lanka	Masie Nguema	Tabasco (Mexico)
Chiapas (Mexico)	(Fernando Poo)	
Costa Rican	New Guinea	Trinidad
Ghana—Mid-Crop	New Hebrides	Venezuela
Grenada	Nicaragua	Victoria (Brazil)
Guatemala	Nigeria—Light Crop	Zaire
Hispaniolas (Dominican Republic)		
Honduras	Panama	
Ivory Coast	Salvador	

Group C—At Par

Bolivia

Haiti

Malaysia

Para (Brazil)

Peru

Sanchez (Dominican Republic) and all other growths not presently specified above.

(ii) Condition

Cocoa which is smoky or hammy is not deliverable.

(iii) Count

(1) The standard count and the maximum count of each group of cocoa shall be as follows:

Class	STANDARD COUNT	MAXIMUM COUNT
A	1000 per kg.	1200
B	1100	1300
C	1200	1600

Cocoa exceeding the maximum of its class to be deliverable at the next lower class premium and count requirement.

Cocoa exceeding 1600 beans per kilo shall not be deliverable.

(2) The following variations of count may be delivered at the discounts noted below:

Discount for excess Bean count above standard

		Total Discount
For 1st. 25 beans or part thereof	$ 2.00 per ton	$ 2.00 per ton
For 2nd 25 beans or part thereof	4.00 per ton	6.00 per ton
For 3rd 25 beans or part thereof	6.00 per ton	12.00 per ton
For 4th 25 beans or part thereof	8.00 per ton	20.00 per ton
For 5th 25 beans or part thereof	10.00 per ton	30.00 per ton
For 6th 25 beans or part thereof	12.00 per ton	42.00 per ton
For 7th 25 beans or part thereof	14.00 per ton	56.00 per ton
For 8th 25 beans or part thereof	16.00 per ton	72.00 per ton
For 9th 25 beans or part thereof	18.00 per ton	90.00 per ton
For 10th 25 beans or part thereof	20.00 per ton	110.00 per ton
For 11th 25 beans or part thereof	22.00 per ton	132.00 per ton
For 12th 25 beans or part thereof	24.00 per ton	156.00 per ton
For 13th 25 beans or part thereof	26.00 per ton	182.00 per ton
For 14th 25 beans or part thereof	28.00 per ton	210.00 per ton
For 15th 25 beans or part thereof	30.00 per ton	240.00 per ton
For 16th 25 beans or part thereof	32.00 per ton	272.00 per ton

(iv) *Grade*

(1) The standard grade is cocoa, otherwise sound, defective to a maximum extent of: 4% by count show mold or 4% by count are insect infested or damaged; or a total of 6% by count show mold and are insect infested or damaged (or such other standards or lesser percentages as may from time to time be prescribed by the Food and Drug Administration or similar Federal Agency) and slatey to a maximum extent of ten percentum by count. Except as provided in subparagraph (2)[A] of this paragraph, cocoa which exceeds any of the percentages prescribed in this rule shall not be delivered on an Exchange contract.

(2) The following variations from standard grade may be delivered at the premiums or discounts indicated below:

[A] For each one percentum slatey more than ten percentum, a deduction of $2.20 per metric ton; but in the case of Sanchez and Haiti cocoa beans, no deduction shall be made for excess slate.

(c) The growth, description, condition, count and grade of cocoa to be delivered on an Exchange contract must be established by duly licensed graders in accordance with the following rules:

(i) All cocoa to be delivered on an Exchange contract must be graded between the fifteenth business day prior to the first business day of a delivery period and the last delivery day of such delivery period inclusive, as evidenced by the Certificate of Grade except as otherwise provided on redeliveries.

(1) Any person who plans to deliver cocoa or replace cocoa tendered for delivery which has not previously been graded must send a declaration of submission in the form prescribed by Cocoa Rule 9.14 and a sampling order to the Exchange at least five days prior to the delivery date specified on the Delivery Notice. If a deliverer elects to submit a declaration of submission after the time limit prescribed herein, the Exchange shall not be responsible in the event the results cannot be issued by the delivery date in which case the delivery would be in default unless a mutually acceptable written agreement has been entered into as provided under Cocoa Rule 9.03.

[A] The deliverer may elect to have the cocoa graded either (a) before the Delivery Notice is tendered, provided that it is in Exchange-segregated lots, or (b) when the Delivery Notice is tendered for delivery. The deliverer shall indicate such election on the declaration of submission.

[B] The cocoa will be graded by a panel of three licensed graders in accordance with both the instructions on that form and with such procedures as from time to time may be promulgated by the Board of Cocoa Graders.

⤐→Effective with respect to all delivery months through and including September 1994.

(2) If the cocoa which is to be delivered has been graded previously, but not in this delivery period, the deliverer may elect to have the cocoa completely regraded or partially regraded, in accordance with the procedures outlined above in subparagraph (c)(i)(l) of this rule.

⤐→Effective with respect to the December 1994 delivery month and all delivery months thereafter.

(2) If the cocoa which is to be delivered has been graded previously, but no valid Certificate of Grade is in effect with respect to the grade of cocoa, the deliverer may elect to have the cocoa completely regarded or partially regarded, in accordance with the procedures outlined above in subparagraph (c)(i)(1) of this rule.

(ii) The sample of cocoa, which will be taken by two duly licensed master samplers as provided in Cocoa Rule 9.14(a)(i), shall be promptly submitted for examination to the licensed graders.

(l) The graders shall be selected by the Exchange from the entire list of licensed graders, and the Exchange, in a practical and equitable manner, shall rotate the service of graders.

(2) The graders selected shall have no direct interest, beneficial or prejudicial, in the cocoa to be graded.

(3) All grading of cocoa, except as may be provided in Cocoa Rule 9.19 and 9.20, shall be conducted in the City of New York.

(4) Samples of cocoa shall be submitted to the graders bearing only an identification number; the Exchange shall supply the other information required on the Certificate of Grade under Cocoa Rule 9.18(d)(i)(l) after the cocoa has been graded.

(iii) The graders shall promptly meet to grade the cocoa and each grader shall use every effort within his knowledge and experience to determine the true growth, description, condition, count and grade of the cocoa and shall not knowingly grade a parcel of cocoa in which he has a direct interest, beneficial or prejudicial. The graders shall forward their decision as to the grade of the cocoa within three business days following, but excluding, the day of their appointment.

(iv) Each grader shall grade the cocoa as follows:

(1) If the graders agree that the cocoa (a) is of the growth and description tendered and (b) is not hammy or smoky, then:

[A] Each of the graders shall grade the cocoa and specify his determination of grade on a grading memorandum.

[B] If the panel of graders determines that the cocoa satisfies the requirements for delivery set forth hereunder, the panel shall so indicate on the grading memorandum and a Certificate of Grade, setting forth the growth, description, count, condition and grade of the cocoa, as provided in Cocoa Rule 9.18(d) shall be authenticated.

(2) If the panel of graders determines that the cocoa (1) is not the growth and description tendered or (2) is hammy or smoky or (3) does not satisfy the grade requirements for delivery set forth hereunder, no Certificate of Grade shall be issued, and the panel of graders shall file a written report with the Exchange which sets forth the reasons for its determination and the deliverer shall be promptly notified that the cocoa cannot be delivered on an Exchange contract.

(3) If any grader determines that the cocoa is of the growth and description tendered, but is hammy or smoky or, conversely, if any grader determines that the cocoa is not hammy or smoky but is not of the growth and description tendered, then

[A] each grader shall report his determination to the the Exchange, and

[B] the cocoa shall be promptly submitted for examination to a new panel of three licensed graders, to be graded in accordance with the same procedure as outlined in paragraphs (c)(ii) and (c)(iii) above; provided, however, that before the cocoa is submitted to the panel for grading, the deliverer shall be notified and he may request that new samples be taken for reexamination by the original graders or withdraw the lot of cocoa under examination and substitute therefor another lot of cocoa of the same growth and description, which shall be graded in accordance with the procedure outlined in paragraphs (c)(ii) and (c)(iii) above; and

[C] each grader on the panel shall grade the cocoa by voting, in accordance with the procedures outlined in paragraph (c)(iv).

(v) The graders shall determine the count of cocoa by multiplying by four the number of beans in 250 grams, fairly taken from the sample under examination and jointly weighed and counted.

(1) At the request of either grader, the test may be repeated a second and third time, but if more than one test is made, the results shall be averaged.

(2) The count, so established shall be final and binding and shall be recorded on the grading memorandum.

(vi) The fees for grading shall be such amounts as may from time to time be established by the Board. All grading fees shall be payable by the deliverer to the Exchange within ten days of receipt of an invoice from the Exchange. This fee shall be distributed by the Exchange to the graders selected hereunder in the amounts established by the Board. In the case of an initial delivery under a Certificate of Grade or an initial delivery under a recertification of grade, the deliverer shall include one half of the grading fees paid to the Exchange in the bill which shall be presented to the receiver and paid by the receiver on the day of delivery as required by Cocoa Rule 9.11, unless it shall be determined that the cocoa is not good delivery, in which case the entire grading fee shall be for the account of the deliverer, unless such fees are otherwise apportioned by the Board.

(d) The growth, description, condition, count and grade of cocoa finally established by the graders under the foregoing procedure shall be recorded in a Certificate of Growth, Description, Condition, Count and Grade (the "Certificate of Grade").

(i) The Certificate of Grade shall be in such form as prescribed by the Exchange. The Certificate of Grade shall include the following information:

(1) The certificate of grade shall bear upon its face a declaration that the cocoa is good delivery, that it is of the growth and description named therein and that the condition and grade are within Exchange requirements and also shall state the quantity, mark and date of customs entry of each chop, with the grade thereof, shall bear upon its face the Exchange number and the lot numbers, the date of each and every delivery notice issued for the cocoa graded and to be graded under said certificate and state the percentage of moldly and of insect-infested, including insect-damaged, beans as determined by each grader or by the panel.

[A] The Certificate of Grade shall state on its face the date of the determination of grade.

[B] When the date of the Certificate of Grade falls in the month prior to the month of delivery, such certificate of grade shall be redated as of the first delivery date of the month of delivery, and the date so placed thereon by the Exchange shall be deemed the true date of the Certificate of Grade for all purposes.

(2) The receiver and the deliverer shall be entitled to a copy of the Certificate of Grade.

[A] A fractional Certificate of Grade shall be issued for any part or parts of a certificate in force. Such fractional certificates shall bear the date and the identification marks and numbers of the original certificate, and shall be issued by the Exchange, upon the payment of such fees as may from time to time be established by the Board, after being verified by comparison with the original certificate (which shall then be cancelled), and can be used together with a similar certificate or certificates in force or as a part of a new delivery

(ii) The growth, description, condition, count and grade of a particular lot of cocoa indicated on the Certificate of Grade shall be deemed the true growth, description, condition, count and grade of such cocoa and

⋙→*Effective with respect to all delivery months through and including September 1994.*

(1) for purposes of delivery, the Certificate of Grade shall be valid, as regards growth, description, condition, count and grade of a lot of cocoa for the entire delivery period, and

(2) For purposes of redelivery, the Certificates of Grade shall be valid indefinitely, as regards growth, description, condition and count, of a lot of cocoa, or any chop thereof, as long as the lot or chops to which it is applicable can be identified. The Certificate of Grade shall be valid as to grade during the entire month of the initial delivery (provided the bags are in good external condition).

⋙→*Effective with respect to the December 1994 delivery month and all delivery months thereafter.*

(1) for purposes of delivery, the Certificate of Grade shall be valid, as regards growth, description, condition, count and grade of a lot of cocoa for the entire delivery period in or for which the Certificate of Grade was issued and the next subsequent period, and

(2) for purposes of redelivery, the Certificate of Grade shall be valid indefinitely, as regards growth, description, condition and count, of a lot of cocoa, or any chop thereof, as long as the lot or chops to which it is applicable can be identified. The Certificate of Grade shall be valid as to grade during the entire month of the initial delivery period in or for which the Certificate of Grade was issued and the next subsequent delivery period (provided the bags are in good condition).

(iii) The Exchange shall not issue a Certificate of Grade if:

(1) The graders certifying to the grade have not been licensed by the Exchange;

(2) Any two graders certifying to the grade are members of the same firm;

(3) The same party acts as a deliverer and receiver of the cocoa, except upon proof that such party is acting for two principals and that the actual deliverer and receiver are in fact separate and distinct; or

(4) The cocoa is not to be delivered pursuant to a contract sold on the Exchange.

Amended by the Board November 11, 1981; effective December 1, 1981.

Amended by the Board November 10, 1982; effective December 1, 1982.

Amended by the Board April 13, 1983; effective May 5, 1983 with respect to delivery months commencing with the July 1983 delivery month.

Amended by the Board May 16, 1984; effective December 6, 1984 with respect to delivery months commencing with the May 1986 delivery month.

Amended by the Board September 10, 1986; effective October 20, 1986.

Amended by the Board March 12, 1986; effective October 29, 1986, commencing with the July 1987 delivery month.

Renumbered April 14, 1988.

Amended by the Board April 13, 1988; effective May 16, 1988.

Amended by the Board April 13, 1988; effective commencing with the December 1988 delivery period.

Amended by the Board November 13, 1991; effective June 5, 1992 with the implementation of COPS for cocoa.

Amended by the Board October 14, 1992; effective February 8, 1993, commencing with the December 1994 contract. (2 delivery period certificates)

¶ 5248

Rule 9.19. Grading Cocoa not Exchange Delivery; Informal Examination

(a) Any Person who has been licensed by the Exchange as a cocoa grader, may examine any parcel of cocoa beans upon the request of any member of non-member of the Exchange to determine the quality and condition of such cocoa and may sign, as a grader licensed by the Exchange, a letter reporting his findings and opinion (hereinafter referred to as the letter) providing the provisions of this Rule are observed:

(b) The party requesting the examination of the cocoa shall inform the grader as to the owner of the cocoa and of the names of any other parties who may have an actual or potential interest therein and provide evidence of the agreement of the owners to the examination.

(c) The grader shall have no direct interest, beneficial or prejudicial, in the parcel of cocoa to be examined, and upon request shall produce a letter confirming that he is an Exchange-licensed grader, which letter must be acknowledged by the Secretary of the Exchange.

(d) The cocoa to be examined shall be sampled by a master sampler licensed by the Exchange, under the direction of the grader by whom he shall be selected, to whom he shall make a written report identifying the parcel of cocoa sampled and the number of bags sampled, with any other particulars that may be requested by the grader, and the sampler shall seal the sample where drawn and deliver the sealed sample to the grader. The grader shall pay the master sampler and collect the master sampler's fee from the party requesting the examination of the cocoa. The fee for sampling shall be the regular fee for sampling plus any additional amount that may be agreed upon to cover any extra work involved in sampling the parcel of cocoa to be examined.

(e) The grader shall use every effort within his knowledge and experience to determine the true quality and condition of the parcel of cocoa and the letter which he shall sign as a grader licensed by the Exchange shall accurately set forth his findings as to the quality and condition of the cocoa for which such letter is issued.

(f) The grader shall collect from the party requesting the examination of the cocoa such fees as the Board may from time to time prescribe.

(g) The grader shall deliver his letter, duly signed, and the sampler's report to the party requesting the examination; and to the Secretary of the Exchange a copy of each, sealed in an envelope, properly marked and dated for identification, and such envelope shall not be opened except by order of the Board. Such envelopes shall be retained for a period of not less than six years from the date thereon.

(h) The grader shall pay to the Exchange one fifth ($1/5$) of the fee collected for examining cocoa pursuant to this rule.

(i) Any complaint against a master sampler or grader for violation of this rule, or for misconduct thereunder, shall be made to the Warehouse and License Committee who shall hear the complaint and the defense and if the complaint shall appear to that Committee to be justified it shall report the matter, with its recommendations, to the Board for action by it.

(j) The penalty for violation of this rule may be the suspension of revocation of the license of the licensee found guilty and/or such other penalty as the Board, within the Rules, may determine.

Amended by the Board November 10, 1982; effective December 1, 1982.

Renumbered April 14, 1988.

¶ 5252

Rule 9.20. Grading Cocoa not Exchange Delivery; Formal Examination

(a) Any person holding cocoa beans stored in a public warehouse, whether or not licensed by the Exchange, may submit such cocoa for examination by persons who have been licensed by the Exchange as cocoa graders, providing the conditions in this Rule are observed.

(b) The holder of the cocoa shall send to the Secretary of the Exchange a sampling order for the cocoa involved, accompanied by a request for such an examination and an agreement to pay the costs pertaining thereto.

(c) The Exchange shall appoint a licensed master sampler to sample the cocoa. The cocoa shall be graded by three graders licensed by the Exchange to be selected by the Secretary of the Exchange. The sampling and grading shall be done in accordance with Exchange rules and practice.

(d) The graders shall have no direct interest, beneficial or prejudicial, in the parcel of cocoa to be examined.

(e) The graders shall use every effort within their knowledge and experience to determine the true quality and condition of the parcel of cocoa and the certificate which they shall sign as graders licensed by the Exchange shall accurately set forth their findings as to the quality and condition of the cocoa for which such certificate is issued.

(f) Each of the graders shall collect from the party requesting the examination a fee corresponding to the regular grading fees of the Exchange.

(g) The graders shall report their grades to the Exchange, who shall cause them to be recorded on a proper form, and after the same has been duly signed by the licensed graders the certificate shall be signed and dated by the Exchange who shall affix thereto the corporate seal of the Exchange, but such certificate shall not be valid for a delivery of cocoa against an Exchange contract.

(h) Modification of the above Rule may be made, if necessary, to conform to any arrangement which might be made by an individual member or a non-member with the U.S. Government in the event cocoa has been seized or detained by a Governmental authority in which case the fee for examination shall be $5 for each grader to each sample examined.

Amended by the Board November 10, 1982; effective December 1, 1982.

Renumbered April 14, 1988.

Amended by the Board April 13, 1988; effective May 16, 1988.

¶ 5256

Rule 9.21. Statement of Open Contracts

After the close of trading on the last business day preceding first notice day, and throughout the period of the current month, every member of the Exchange, who is also a member of the Clearing Association, and who also shall have on his books open long and short contracts in any given current month, which have been cleared with the Clearing Association, shall file with the Association a statement of his gross open long contracts in said current month and a statement of his gross open short contracts in said current month and thereafter he shall be qualified to receive delivery notices against his gross long position and may deliver to the Clearing Association delivery notices against his gross short position. The member receiving from the Clearing Association delivery notices shall automatically assume a sales position with the Association to the amount that the contracts represented by the delivery notices received by him from the Association are in excess of his net long position with the Clearing Association. The member delivering delivery notices to the Clearing Association shall automatically assume a purchase position with the Association equal to the amount that the contracts represented by the delivery notices delivered by him to the Clearing Association are in excess of his net open short position with the Clearing Association.

Amended by the Board March 12, 1986; effective October 29, 1986, commencing with the July 1987 delivery month.

Renumbered April 14, 1988.

¶ 5260

Rule 9.22. Application of Notices

Every member of the Exchange who shall carry long Exchange contracts for account of customers, shall, for his own use as herein specified, list such contracts for delivery in the current month, together with all contracts in the current month carried for his own account, in chronological sequence—contracts of the same date following the sequence shown in the records of the carrying member—and any delivery notices received by the carrying member shall be applied to the outstanding long contracts in the sequence shown on the above mentioned list in the sequence of time notices are received, and if more than one notice should be received simultaneously the delivery notices bearing the smallest number shall be applied successively.

Amended by the Board March 12, 1986; effective October 29, 1986, commencing with the July 1987 delivery month.

Renumbered April 14, 1988.

Rule 9.23. Weighing Cocoa

1. Cocoa to be delivered in an Exchange-segregated lot must weigh ten (10) metric

tons, one percent (1%) more or less, (in original shipping bags of average weight(s) customary for the growth) and must be weighed in accordance with the following rules.

(a) All cocoa to be delivered hereunder must be weighed (unless a Weighmaster's return is in force as hereinafter provided) within thirteen full business days preceding the delivery and must be weighed by a duly licensed Weighmaster (or a weigher employed by such Weighmaster).

(b) Before the cocoa is weighed, (i) all unnecessary bagging must be removed from the cocoa (or a fair deduction for the weight thereof shall be made) and for this purpose all bagging in excess of that which is customary, and not essential to cover and protect the cocoa in a proper manner shall be deemed unnecessary (the tare allowance on Exchange deliveries of cocoa shall be actual tare, as established by the weighers in the customary manner); (ii) any bags of cocoa having an accumulation of dust or other foreign matter must be brushed clean (or replaced by other bags not having such an accumulation); and (iii) the scales must be tested by the weigher; provided however, that unless otherwise ordered by the Board, scales that have been tested within ten working days need not be tested again until the expiration of that time, but the owner of the scales must produce evidence of the last test by showing a card of identification upon which is recorded the number and make of the scales, the date when tested and the signature of the Weighmaster (or his substitute) who was present at the time the test was made.

(c) All cocoa for Exchange delivery shall be weighed as follows:

(1) If weighed in pounds:

(i) Drafts of bags totaling 750 pounds or less shall be weighed to a one pound notch.

(ii) Drafts of bags totaling from 751 pounds to 1,500 pounds shall be weighed to a two pound notch.

(iii) Drafts of bags totaling from 1,501 to 3,000 pounds shall be weighed to a four pound notch.

(2) If weighed in kilos:

(i) Drafts of bags totaling 375 kilograms or less shall be weighed to a $1/2$ kilogram notch.

(ii) Drafts of bags totaling 376 to 750 kilograms shall be weighed to a one kilogram notch.

(iii) Drafts of bags totaling from 751 to 1,500 kilograms shall be weighed to a 2 kilogram notch.

(3) If cocoa is weighed in pounds the Weighmaster's return must be converted the metric equivalent by the Weighmaster.

(d) The Weighmaster who weighs any cocoa into Exchange-segregated lots shall:

(1) Not have acted in any capacity as an importer with respect to cocoa;

(2) Securely fix to one of the visible bags in each chop a durable tag, approved by the Exchange, identifying the chop of cocoa as to steamer, date of import, mark, number of bags in chop, lot number, chop number and date of weighing. In addition, the weigher shall mark with marking ink on a prominent bag in each lot the lot number and the number of bags in the lot;

(3) Execute a Weighmaster's return, which shall include the following:

(i) The Weighmaster's return shall state the weight, identification and exact location of the cocoa and the date the cocoa was weighed.

The identification and location of the cocoa may be given by including the information specified in paragraph 1(d)(1) herein and the following further information: name and location of the warehouse, the floor number and store in which the cocoa was weighed.

(ii) The Weighmaster's return will be deemed to include the following certification:

"I hereby certify that the cocoa specified in this return was weighed in accordance with every provision of the By-Laws and Rules of the Coffee, Sugar & Cocoa Exchange, Inc., and that the weights stated herein were carefully determined and checked and, to the best of my knowledge and belief, are the true weights of the cocoa embraced in this return; also, that the date of this return is the date on which the weighing of said cocoa was completed."

2. The weight of the cocoa determined in accordance with the rules set forth in paragraph 1 of this rule, as evidenced of the Weighmaster's return, shall be deemed the true weight of the cocoa for the following purposes:

(a) For delivery of cocoa, provided the cocoa has been weighed within thirteen full business days;

(b) For redelivery of cocoa and for delivery of cocoa which has not been weighed within thirteen full days, in whole or for any complete chop or chops, provided such chop or chops have at no time been moved from the exact location specified in the Weighmaster's return (except that, with the approval of the Warehouse & License Committee, and on such terms and conditions as said committee may prescribe, such bags may, when necessary, be moved at the same location under the supervision of a licensed Weighmaster in order to put such bags in good external condition) and provided further that the following allowances are made for loss of weight.

(1) In the case of Sanchez, Haiti or Jamaica cocoa, the allowances for loss in weight shall be as follows:

(i) On lots comprised of cocoa which arrived at a port in the continental United States on a date less than forty days prior to the date on which the actual weighing was completed, as shown by the Weighmaster's return on which the delivery is invoiced, hereinafter the Weight Return Date; both dates exclusive, when redelivered or delivered within 30 days of the Weight Return Date, one percent; when redelivered or delivered within 31 and 60 calendar days of the Weight Return Date, two percent; thereafter an additional one-fourth of one percent for each additional 30 calendar day period or fractional part thereof following the Weight Return Date.

(ii) On lots comprised of cocoa which arrived at a port in the continental United States on a date more than forty days, but less than seventy days, prior to the Weight Return Date, both dates exclusive, when redelivered or delivered within 30 calendar days of the Weight Return Date, one percent; thereafter an additional one-fourth of one percent for each additional 30 calendar day period or fractional part thereof following the Weight Return Date.

(iii) On lots comprised of cocoa which arrived at a port in the continental United States on a date seventy days or more prior to the Weight Return Date, both dates exclusive, when redelivered or delivered within 30 calendar days of the Weight Return Date, one-fourth of one percent; thereafter an additional one-fourth of one percent for each additional 30 calendar day period or fractional part thereof following the Weight Return Date.

(iv) For the purpose of this rule, the date of arrival of cocoa shall be the date on which the vessel in which the cocoa was imported was entered at the United States Custom House at the port in the continental United States at which the cocoa was discharged. The name of the vessel and date of entry shall be plainly stated on every invoice for Sanchez, Haiti or Jamaica cocoa delivered on the Exchange.

(a) Omission of such information shall invalidate the invoice and the deliverer shall be in default in respect to the contract to which the invoice was applicable.

(b) In case of falsification of such information the deliverer may be proceeded against before the Arbitration Committee by any member who has thereby been caused loss or damage and shall, in addition, be subject to discipline as provided in the Disciplinary Rules of the Exchange.

(2) In the case of other growths and descriptions of cocoa the allowance for loss of weight shall be one-quarter of one percent for each 30 calendar day period or fractional part thereof from the Weight Return Date.

3. Any Cocoa to be delivered in Exchange-segregated lots may, at the option of the holder, be reweighed and may be delivered and redelivered on such reweights (subject to the allowances hereinabove provided) but the reweighing of such cocoa shall invalidate the original weights for the purposes of delivery or redelivery.

4. Any bag of cocoa shall be deemed unmerchantable, and may be rejected, unless it is the approximate standard weight of a bag of the particular growth of cocoa, or an approximate weight not exceeding the customary maximum or not less than the customary minimum of weights of a particular growth, shipments of which are made from the country of origin in bags of varying capacities: provided, however, and anything herein to the contrary notwithstanding, bags originally of standard or average weight that have become slack through the usual process of handling and the contents of which are the original contents of such bags shall be deemed to be the original bags of standard or average weight for all Exchange purposes.

Amended by the Board July 8, 1981; effective August 21, 1981.

Amended by the Board November 11, 1981; effective December 1, 1981.

Amended by the Board September 8, 1982; effective September 27, 1982.

Amended by the Board February 16, 1983; effective September 8, 1983 with respect to delivery months commencing with the December 1983 delivery month.

Amended by the Board September 10, 1986, effective January 5, 1987 (eliminate checkweighing).

Renumbered April 14, 1988.

Amended by the Board November 13, 1991; effective June 5, 1992 with the implementation of COPS for cocoa.

Amended by the Board October 14, 1992; effective November 9, 1992.

¶ 5284

Rule 9.24. Rebagging of Cocoa

When to protect the contents of an original bag(s) of cocoa stored in a warehouse licensed by the Exchange, it shall be necessary to rebag such cocoa, such rebagging may be done, within the discretion of the Committee on Warehouse Licenses, and upon the following conditions:

1. The owner of the cocoa shall make a written request to the Exchange reciting the circumstances requiring the rebagging, the name and address of the warehouse, steamer, date of arrival, mark, growth and number of bags in lot of cocoa and approximate number of such bags requiring rebagging: also, name of weigher licensed by the Exchange who is to do such rebagging, and the owner shall agree to assume all expenses involved.

2. The Exchange shall refer such request to the Committee on Warehouse Licenses who may, within their discretion, permit such rebagging to be done under the supervision of a second licensed weigher who shall be appointed by the Exchange.

3. The new bag(s) shall be marked with the mark or marks of the original bag(s) and a record of such rebagging shall be made by the warehouse company upon the warehouse receipt covering the cocoa. A record of such rebagging shall also be made by the weighmaster, certified to by the weighmaster appointed by the Exchange and reported to the Exchange. Such bag(s) shall be deemed original bags for Exchange purposes.

4. All expenses incurred in connection with such rebagging shall be borne by the owner of the cocoa.

Renumbered April 14, 1988.

Amended by the Board April 13, 1988; effective May 16, 1988.

¶ 5340

Rule 9.25. Minimum and Maximum Variation in Offers

All offers to buy or sell merchandise for future delivery shall be in dollars and no transactions in cocoa shall be permitted wherein the difference in price shall consist of a smaller fraction than one dollar per ton for each ton of cocoa represented by such contract or contracts; additional money considerations are prohibited.

To avoid abnormal fluctuations of price and injurious speculation incident thereto, trades in cocoa for future delivery in any month, during any one day, shall not be made at prices varying more than $88.00 per ton above or below the settlement price of such month for the preceding business session of the Exchange, as fixed by the Clearing

Association, or if no settlement price has been established from the price of the first transaction.

If a settlement price for all of the first two delivery months subsequent to the two nearby delivery months shall move by the maximum permissible amount in the same direction for two successive business days, the maximum permissible fluctuation referred to in above paragraph shall be increased to $132.00 per ton commencing the next business day. Such increase shall remain in effect until there shall have been two successive business days in which the settling price for all of the first two delivery months subsequent to the two nearby delivery months shall not have moved (in either direction) by the original maximum permissible amount, (i.e. $88.00 per ton) in which event the maximum permissible fluctuation shall be reinstated at $88.00 per ton on the following business day.

For the purpose of this Rule, the closing price shall not be less than the minimum price nor more than the maximum price prescribed herein.

Switches may only be offered, bid for, traded in and reported at prices for the respective months that are within the day's trading range as hereinabove determined. If there have been no trades in either or both months involved in the switch at the time such switch is consummated, prices must be established at a reasonable relationship to the trading range of the more actively traded futures month. When the market is either limit up bid or limit down offered, and when there have been no trades recorded in any of the permissible trading months, switches may be consummated provided prices are fixed with one end of the switch at the limit up from the previous close or one end of the switch at the limit down from the previous close, whichever situation applies. Provided, however, that nothing contained herein shall prohibit any straddle executed pursuant to Rule 502(b) of the Clearing Association from being priced in accordance with that Rule.

The limits on price fluctuations hereinabove provided shall not apply to trading in contracts for the two nearby delivery months on and after the first business day immediately succeeding the last trading day of the preceding delivery month.

At the discretion of the Board of Managers, any limit of trading herein provided for may, from time to time, and without previous notice, be changed or suspended, or temporarily modified.

Amended by the Board February 16, 1983; effective August 17, 1983 with respect to delivery months commencing with the December 1983 delivery month.

Amended by the Board July 9, 1986; effective September 4, 1986.

Amended by the Board December 17, 1986; effective March 31, 1987.

Renumbered April 14, 1988.

Amended by the Board March 16, 1988; effective July 5, 1988.

¶ 5348

Rule 9.26. Statement of Open Contracts

(A) Statement of Open Contracts. All members of the Exchange who are members of the Clearing Association shall report each day, on "Statement of Open Contracts" forms for Cocoa, approved from time to time by the Board, to the Clearing Association the number of purchases (longs) and sales (shorts) which are open on the members' books for each delivery month.

Each clearing member shall file a Statement of Open Contracts form not later than forty-five minutes before the opening of trading on the Exchange business day following the day for which the report of open positions is made.

Only the net position of a customer in each delivery month will be reported by the clearing member to the Clearing Association as open interest, unless stipulated by such customer that longs and shorts in the same month are for two or more clients, in which case the position will be reported to the Clearing Association as longs and shorts.

Where a clearing member transfers contracts to or from another clearing member each of the members involved in the transfer shall file a statement on the day of the transfer on a form prescribed by the Exchange addressed to the Clearing Association advising it of the transfer.

Contracts against which delivery notices have been issued or stopped, are not to be included in the total of the open contracts of the current month.

If a clearing member is carrying contracts for another clearing member, only the carrying clearing member shall report such contracts.

(B) Corrections.

The filing of an erroneous position report by a clearing member shall constitute a violation of this Rule, unless such clearing member shall report any errors before 11:00 A.M. of the Exchange business day following the day for which the report is made. Any error in an open position report must be corrected when discovered.

Clearing Members making corrections in their report of open positions after 11:00 A.M. of the Exchange business day following the day for which the report of open positions is made shall promptly file with the Exchange as well as with the Clearing Association a statement of the details of such correction, the manner in which the error occurred and, if a carrying clearing member be the cause of the error, the name of such carrying clearing member.

Amended by the Board April 9, 1986; effective May 7, 1986.

Amended by the Board March 12, 1986; effective October 29, 1986, commencing with the July 1987 delivery month.

Renumbered April 14, 1988.

Amended by the Board April 13, 1988; effective May 16, 1988.

¶ 5352

Rule 9.27. Breaks

In the event that any clearing member or person placing an order directly with a floor broker shall claim a "break" with respect to any trade, or shall claim that a floor broker shall have failed to execute an order on a day when in the exercise of due diligence he could have done so, such clearing member or such person shall have waived any claims against the floor broker responsible unless such clearing member or such person shall have advised such floor broker thereof not later than 15 minutes prior to the opening on the business day following the day on which such "break" is claimed to have occurred or such order should have been executed; provided that no such claim shall be waived if the floor broker became aware of the failure so to execute such order by 15 minutes prior to the opening on such following business day and failed to report the same to such clearing member or such person. The term "break" with respect to any trade shall mean the failure of such trade to clear, correctly (either because of failure to clear, duplication of clearance or discrepancy in month, price or quantity).

Renumbered April 14, 1988.

¶ 5356

Rule 9.28. Arbitration Of Disputes

(1)(a) Any dispute between members, except as to grade or external condition, in which one member claims that the other member has failed to meet his obligations as Deliverer or Receiver under a Cocoa contract traded on this Exchange shall be settled by arbitration in accordance with the provisions of this rule; provided that, if the claimant does not notify the Exchange of such failure within three Exchange business days of the date on which such member becomes aware of such failure, said member shall be deemed to have waived his rights under this Rule, without prejudice to any other rights or remedies at law or under any other provisions of the Rules.

(b) Each notice filed pursuant to subparagraph (a) hereof shall be accompanied by a nonrefundable check payable to the Exchange in the amount of $375.

(2) Upon receipt by the Exchange of the notice and payment required by paragraph (1) hereof, the Exchange shall forward one copy of said notice to the member against whom the claim is being asserted and one copy of said notice to any other member joined in the arbitration pursuant to subparagraph (3)(h) hereof.

(3) A Special Arbitration Committee of three disinterested members of the Cocoa Committee shall be appointed by the Chairman of the Board within one business day of the Exchange's receipt of the notice and payment required by paragraph (1) hereof. The Special Arbitration Committee shall establish the date, time and place for a

hearing. Each Special Arbitration Committee shall determine the procedures to be followed in any hearing before it, except that the following shall apply in every case:

(a) A member who is a party to the arbitration ("party") shall be entitled to appear personally at the hearing(s).

(b) Each party, at his own expense, shall have the right to be represented by counsel in any aspect of the proceedings.

(c) Each party shall be entitled to (i) prepare and present all relevant facts in support of the claims and grievances, defenses or counterclaims which arise out of the transaction or occurrence that is the subject matter of the proceeding and to present rebuttal evidence to such claims or grievances, defenses or counterclaims made by other parties, (ii) examine other parties, (iii) examine any witnesses appearing at the hearing(s), and (iv) examine all relevant documents presented in connection with the claim or grievance, or any defense or counterclaim applicable thereto.

(d) The formal rules of evidence shall not apply.

(e) No verbatim record shall be made of the proceedings, unless requested by a party who shall bear the cost of such record. If such a request is made, a stenographic transcript shall be taken, but not transcribed unless requested by a party who shall bear the cost of such transcription.

(f) Ex parte contacts by any party with members of the Special Arbitration Committee shall not be permitted.

(g) The Special Arbitration Committee shall have the power, on the request of any party or on its own motion, to require any person to testify and/or produce documentary evidence in the proceedings as and to the extent provided for in Section 516 of the By-Laws.

(h) Any party to the dispute may apply to the Special Arbitration Committee for permission to join as a party any other member (i) who is or may be liable to such party for all or part of the claim being asserted against him or (ii) who claims an interest in the subject of the dispute. The Special Arbitration Committee shall have complete and absolute discretion to grant or deny any such application, in whole or in part.

(i) The rights and duties set forth in this Rule with respect to parties shall apply to any member joined as a party pursuant to subparagraph (3)(h) hereof.

(4) To compensate the aggrieved party for the necessary adjustments in his position, the party adjudged in default shall pay five percent of the settlement price determined by the Special Arbitration Committee, or $11.00 per metric ton, whichever shall be greater, to the aggrieved party in addition to the settlements outlined below.

(5) In the case where a Deliverer is determined to be in default by the Special Arbitration Committee for failure to meet delivery obligations then:

(a) where the settlement price determined by the Special Arbitration Committee is higher than the price stated on the Delivery Notice, the Deliverer shall be required to pay to the Receiver the difference between such settlement price and the price stated on the Delivery Notice; or

(b) where the settlement price determined by the Special Arbitration Committee is lower than the price stated on the Delivery Notice, the Receiver shall be required to pay to the Deliverer the difference between such settlement price and the price stated on the Delivery Notice.

(6) In the case where a Receiver is determined to be in default by the Special Arbitration Committee for failing to meet receiving obligations then:

(a) where the settlement price determined by the Special Arbitration Committee is higher than the price stated on the Delivery Notice, the Deliverer shall be required to pay to the Receiver the difference between such settlement price and the price stated on the Delivery Notice; or

(b) where the settlement price determined by the Special Arbitration Committee is lower than the price stated in the Delivery Notice, the Receiver shall be required to pay to the Deliverer the difference between such settlement price and the price stated on the Delivery Notice.

(7) Notwithstanding paragraphs (4), (5) and (6) hereof, any party shall be entitled to offset his obligations under this Rule to any other party to the extent of net variation

margin payments made to or received from such other party through the Clearing Association from the date of issuance of the Delivery Notice to the date of payment of the arbitration award, provided that notification of settlement or variation margins in this manner shall be given in writing by the parties to the Clearing Association upon payment of the arbitration award as provided in paragraph (9) of this Rule.

(8)(a) The Special Arbitration Committee shall render its award in writing adjudging which, if any, party is in default, declaring the settlement price, awarding the amount of money, if any, to be paid by the party in default, and granting any further remedy or relief which it deems just and equitable.

(b) The Special Arbitration Committee may, in its sole and absolute discretion, order that the amounts payable pursuant to paragraphs (5) or (6), as the case may be, be paid directly to the aggrieved part, in whole or in part, by a party other than the Deliverer or Receiver, as the case may be; provided that, the aggrieved party's rights shall not be prejudiced by any such order.

(c) The award of the Special Arbitration Committee shall be final and binding upon each of the parties to the arbitration, and judgment upon such award may be entered by any court having jurisdiction. In addition, any award, if not complied with within the time specified in the award, shall be enforceable by disciplinary proceedings pursuant to the Rules.

(9) The payments prescribed above shall be made by the close of business on the second Exchange business day after notification in writing of the Special Arbitration Committee's award. Payment and settlement of any default as determined above shall be effected through the Exchange. Such payment shall be accepted as final payment.

Adopted by the Board July 8, 1981; effective April 13, 1982.

Amended by the Board March 12, 1986; effective October 29, 1986 commencing with the July 1987 delivery month.

Renumbered April 14, 1988.

Amended by the Board April 13, 1988; effective May 16, 1988.

Amended by the Board July 13, 1994; effective August 22, 1994 (external conditions).

¶ 5360

Rule 9.29. External Condition Procedure

(a) Any claim by a member that cocoa tendered for delivery or delivered under an Exchange contract has an external condition on the bag which renders it unsound shall be in accordance with the provisions of this rule.

(1) The receiver shall notify the Exchange of any claim hereunder within three (3) business days of the Date of Delivery. Failure to notify the Exchange within the specific time shall be deemed a waiver of the receiver's rights to assert a claim that cocoa tendered for delivery or delivered under an Exchange contract has an external condition on the bag.

(2) The receiver's notice to the Exchange shall identify the location of the cocoa involved, together with the basis for the receiver's claim that an external condition on the cocoa bag exists. Upon receipt of such notice the receiver shall be billed and immediately thereafter pay to the Exchange a non-refundable fee in the amount of $375. A copy of such notice shall also be served upon the deliverer by the receiver.

(b) The Exchange will cause the cocoa to be surveyed by an Exchange licensed master sampler ("sampler") selected randomly by the Exchange from the panel of licensed samplers. The sampler selected shall not include any sampler who previously sampled the cocoa either in the current delivery period or a prior delivery period for which a valid Certificate of Grade with respect to grade exists or any sampler who, in the Exchange's sole discretion, might not be impartial.

(c) The sampler will survey the cocoa which is the subject of the dispute and determine whether any external condition exists on the bags. The determination of the sampler shall be final and binding, and there shall be no appeals therefrom.

(d) If the sampler determines that no external condition exists on the bags of cocoa which are the subject of the dispute, the receiver, in addition to the fee paid to the Exchange to initiate this procedure, shall pay the sampler's fee.

(e) If the sampler determines that the bags of cocoa which are the subject of the dispute have an external condition, the deliverer shall be required to correct the external condition existing on the bags or substitute other cocoa within five business days after receipt of written notification of the decision of the sampler. The deliverer shall also be responsible for payment of the sampler's fee.

(f) The filing of a notice in accordance with this rule shall not affect the obligation of a receiver to pay for cocoa delivered against a cocoa contract, provided that all documents necessary for such delivery have been duly presented to the receiver by the deliverer.

Adopted by the Board July 13, 1994; effective August 22, 1994.

Resolutions

¶ 5444

No. 1. Prearranged Trade—Interpretation

Resolved, that

"A prearranged trade is one arranged (before its announced execution) between two or more members in a manner designed to prevent other members from having a fair and reasonable opportunity of sharing in it, or otherwise conceived in violation of the spirit of fair, free and open trading.

This interpretation, however, shall not extend to such trades as may by special circumstances attaching to them require preliminary negotiations, when such preliminary negotiations can be justified as reasonably necessary to the accomplishment of fair and orderly marketing, and provided such trades are executed at the ring in compliance with the By-Laws and Rules.

¶ 5448

No. 2. Resolution Pursuant to Trading Rule 3.13—Cross Trades

WHEREAS, a member has requested an interpretation as to whether the following transaction is subject to the requirements of the Cross Trade Rule:

A floor broker directly or indirectly related to a principal executes an order for an unaffiliated customer by trading at open outcry with another floor broker who is not directly or indirectly related to such principal, but is executing an order for a proprietary account of that principal.

NOW THEREFORE BE IT RESOLVED that it is the interpretation of this Board that the above transaction is not subject to the requirements of the Cross Trade Rule, provided, that the following conditions are met: that there is no prearrangement, that neither broker knows the nature or identity of the account for which the other is trading, and that the first floor broker neither knows nor through a previous course of conduct or otherwise, should have any reason to know that the unaffiliated broker is or could be expected to be acting for a proprietary account of the principal.

¶ 5450

No. 3. Resolution Re Publication of Open Position (Rule 9.26)

RESOLVED, that the Exchange shall publish each business day the number of contracts for the future delivery of cocoa open as of the close of trading on the preceding business day, in accordance with the following procedure:

(i) As soon as reasonably possible after 11:00 A. M., the Exchange shall publish a report of the open positions as of the close on the previous trading day, reflecting any corrections in reports submitted to the Clearing Association before that time pursuant to Cocoa Rule 9.26.

Amended by the Board April 13, 1988; effective May 16, 1988.

¶ 5452

No. 4. Cocoa Grading Fees

WHEREAS, Cocoa Rule 9.18 authorizes the Board to establish fees, payable by the deliverer to the Exchange, for grading cocoa in accordance with the Rules;

NOW, THEREFORE, BE IT RESOLVED, that with respect to each lot graded by Exchange licensed graders, deliverers shall pay the Exchange the following fees, which shall be distributed by the Exchange to such graders as indicated below:

(i) $90 per lot of one or two chops, of which each such grader shall receive $15;

(ii) $102 per lot of three chops, of which each such grader shall receive $18;

(iii) $114 per lot of four chops, of which each such grader shall receive $21; and

(iv) $126 per lot of five or six chops, of which each such grader shall receive $24;

RESOLVED, that the term "lot" as used in this resolution shall mean the entire quantity of cocoa beans tendered in fulfillment of an Exchange contract; provided, however, that if only a portion of a lot shall be graded the fee to be paid to the Exchange shall be the corresponding portion of the fee adjusted to the next higher even dollar amount (the "adjusted fee") and that portion of the fee to be distributed to each appropriate licensed grader shall be one-third of:

(i) 50% of the adjusted per lot fee in the case of one or two chops;

(ii) 53% of the adjusted per lot fee in the case of three chops;

(iii) 55% of the adjusted per lot fee in the case of four chops;

(iv) 57% of the adjusted per lot fee in the case of five or six chops; and

BE IT FURTHER RESOLVED, that where a Declaration of Submission is filed with the Exchange and cocoa is received for grading and where the Exchange is then requested to cancel the Submission for Grading, the Exchange shall retain

(i) 50% of the per lot fee in the case of one or two chops;

(ii) 47% of the per lot fee in the case of three chops;

(iii) 45% of the per lot fee in the case of four chops; and

(iv) 43% of the per lot fee in the case of five or six chops.

The remainder of the fee(s) shall be returned to the deliverer. Where the Exchange receives a request to cancel the Submission for Grading and the grading has already occurred, no portion of the fee(s) shall be returned to the deliverer.

Adopted by the Board July 8, 1981; effective August 27, 1981.

Amended by the Board June 12, 1985; effective July 29, 1985.

Amended by the Board December 18, 1991; effective April 1, 1992.

¶ 5454

No. 5. Warehouse Procedures and Recordkeeping Requirements for the Storage of Exchange Cocoa

RESOLVED, THAT the minimum acceptable standards and procedures to be followed by Exchange licensed cocoa warehousemen in connection with the storage of Exchange cocoa.

I. *LOCATION AND PHYSICAL STRUCTURE OF WAREHOUSE*

Any location for the storage of Exchange cocoa must be maintained on a continuing basis in accordance with the following standards:

1. It must be weather tight as to roof, walls, doors and windows.

2. It must comply with pertinent local fire regulations and have sufficient floor load limits.

3. It must have light sufficient to permit cleaning crews to work, and weighing and sampling to be performed efficiently, but it need not have natural light.

4. It must have sufficient ventilation to the outside.

5. It must not be artificially heated.

6. It shall have (and the warehouseman shall maintain) a sufficient number of material handling devices (e.g., fork lift trucks, elevators, etc.) which are operable and available to perform the warehouseman's duties in an orderly and efficient fashion.

II. *HOUSEKEEPING PRACTICES*

1. The floor shall be maintained broom clean at all times.

2. The walls, ceiling, overhead pipes, and beams shall be maintained reasonably free of cobwebs, accumulated dirt, dust, excreta, or loose foreign matter.

III. *BASIC STORAGE PRACTICES*

In order to ensure adequate space for sampling, inspection and effective fire protection, assist ventilation, aid in circulation and generally provide ample space for appropriate pest control programs:

1. Cocoa should be stored on pallets which provide a minimum of 4 inches distance from the floor.

2. The pallets must be kept clean and in good repair. They must be cleaned of all foreign matter, including, but not limited to, dirt, dead insects, pupal cases, webbing, etc., before each use.

3. Cocoa should not be stored nearer than 2 feet from the ceiling, nor closer than 18 inches below any sprinkler head.

4. Cocoa should not be stored less than 24 inches from any wall.

5. Piles of cocoa shall be stored in such a manner as to permit at least two faces (front or back and one long side) to be available for inspection and/or sampling. Cocoa shall not be stored higher than 5 pallets high. The aisles should have sufficient space for equipment to operate without contacting bags of cocoa.

6. Slack bags must be placed on a separate pallet in front of the pile.

IV. *STORED COCOA*

1. All cocoa bags entering a licensed store must be kept clean and free from any and all foreign matter which could be detrimental to the delivery of the cocoa contained therein on the Exchange. The owner of the cocoa shall be responsible for the cleaning of cocoa bags entering a licensed store.

2. The warehouse shall be responsible to the owner for maintaining cocoa bags in a licensed store in accordance with Exchange standards. The warehouse shall conduct a weekly inspection of each lot of Exchange cocoa to determine its condition and conformity with Exchange standards.

3. Torn bags, bags from which beans are sifting, or bags which are in peril of having cocoa beans spilled therefrom must be promptly repaired. The floor of the licensed store must be kept free of spilled beans.

4. Except with respect to the prompt repair of torn bags, bags from which beans are sifting or bags which are in peril of cocoa beans being spilled therefrom, prior to undertaking any other maintenance of cocoa bags in a licensed store, including the rebagging of cocoa, the warehouse shall notify the owner, in writing, of the maintenance to be performed and provide the owner five business days from receipt of the notice within which to respond.

If no response is received by the warehouse within such time, the owner shall be deemed to have authorized the maintenance and all costs associated with said maintenance.

5. It shall be the responsibility of the warehouseman to ensure that each chop of Exchange cocoa is properly identified, both in the storage area and in the warehouseman's office records.

V. *PEST CONTROL*

1. Warehousemen who store Exchange cocoa shall cause recognized pest control

companies to conduct periodic inspections of their facilities and implement effective pest control programs so that there shall be no birds, rodents or other animals (including dogs and cats) in a licensed store.

2. No ingredient used for pest or rodent control shall be used in such a manner or in such places as to contaminate the cocoa.

3. The warehouseman shall remove from the area in or around the storage facility such known bird attractions as grains, foods and similar materials.

VI. *CONTROL OF OTHER PRODUCTS STORED IN COCOA AREAS*

No odorous products or things may be stored in such manner or place as to enable the odor to be imparted to the cocoa. The odor from any odorous product or thing must not be discernible within the cocoa storage area. No cocoa should be stored in any area where such foreign odors prevail.

VII. *RECORD RETENTION*

The following records relating to Exchange cocoa shall be kept and maintained by the warehouseman for at least the indicated periods of time after the cocoa has been removed from the warehouse, or otherwise no longer identified as Exchange cocoa:

Category of Document	Time Period
Delivery Orders	1 year
Sampling Orders	2 years
Receiving Reports	2 years
Stock Record Cards	2 years
Negotiable Warehouse Receipts	2 years
Non-Negotiable Warehouse Receipts	2 years
Documents reflecting any movement of Exchange cocoa into or from a licensed store	2 years
Weight Returns	2 years

VIII. *REQUIREMENTS*

All records must be kept neat, tidy, orderly and current so that independent auditors can verify warehouse records against physical stocks.

1. Before cocoa may be placed in a licensed store, the warehouseman must be in possession of a copy of the delivery order (or equivalent document or information) and the following identifying information for such cocoa, which shall be reflected in the warehouseman's records relating to such cocoa:

  a. Growth

  b. Number of bags

  c. Shipper's brand (if on the bags)

  d. Crop year (if on the bags)

  e. Marks and chop numbers (or letters) *in their entirety*

  f. Carrier (*i.e.,* vessel, railroad or truck transport); location (pier, etc.); and date of arrival of vessel (where appropriate)

2. When cocoa is physically placed in the store, the warehouseman shall record the identifying information for the cocoa on the warehouse receiving report (or equivalent record). The warehouseman shall also record thereon all exceptions—*i.e.,* the number of stained, torn, mended, slack, short or improperly marked bags. A written record of any exception noted by the warehouseman shall be made, and the warehouseman shall send a written report describing such exception immediately to the storer of the cocoa. If no exception is noted, a written report to that effect shall be sent to the storer as soon as practicable. If improperly marked bags arrive at the warehouse, the storer shall be notified of such fact immediately by telephone before the delivering carrier leaves the warehouse.

3. The warehouseman shall compare the identifying information for the cocoa set forth on the delivery order with the information on the cocoa bags. If there is a material difference between the information supplied on the delivery order (or equivalent record) and the information on the bags, the warehouseman shall note such difference on the warehouseman's receiving form (or equivalent record) and shall notify the storer of the cocoa immediately of the discrepancy.

4. The warehouseman shall record the identifying information for the cocoa, as set forth on the cocoa bags, on warehouse tags, which shall be affixed at all times to at least two sides of each pile of cocoa bags.

5. The warehouseman shall maintain stock record cards (or equivalent records) for each chop of Exchange cocoa on which shall be recorded all pertinent details necessary to fulfillment of an efficient warehouseman's responsibilities, including all movements of the cocoa, changes in its ownership and when the cocoa has been weighed.

6. When cocoa is sampled for the purpose of grading by Exchange licensed graders, a copy of the sampling order shall be left with the warehouseman and shall be maintained by the warehouseman as part of the permanent files for the cocoa covered by the sampling order.

    a. When a sample is drawn, the warehouseman shall sign three copies of the sampling order in the space provided.

    b. By signing the sampling order, the warehouseman shall be deemed to certify that on the date he signed the sampling order the sampler appeared at the licensed store indicated on the sampling order and left the premises with samples in his possession.

    c. The warehouseman shall retain a copy of the sampling order which shall be retained in accordance with this resolution.

7. Once an Exchange lot number has been assigned to cocoa, it shall become part of the permanent record of that cocoa and shall be noted on the warehouse record cards, warehouse tags, etc.

8. Any physical deliveries of bags of cocoa from the warehouse should be reflected on the Record Cards by deducting the number of bags delivered from the total number of bags in storage.

9. When bags of cocoa are to be weighed into Exchange lots, orders should be received from the owner of the cocoa with complete identification and instructions as to:

    a. Exchange lot number

    b. Warehouse receipt (if previously issued) or other appropriate chop identification

    c. The approximate number of bags in each chop, together with identifying marks and chops (The exact number of bags will be given to the warehouseman by the weigher.)

    d. Carrier (*i.e.,* vessel, railroad or truck transport; location (pier, store, etc.); and arrival date of vessel (where appropriate))

    e. Cargo number

    f. Weighing instructions and name of the weighmaster

10. The warehouseman should receive from the weighmaster a complete report of the weight of bags that are torn, mended and slack; the weight of the sound bags; the Exchange lot number for the bags; the location of the bags; any exceptions, including improperly marked bags; and whether any bags were lost in levelling off.

11. The warehouseman shall separate Exchange cocoa from cocoa which has not been certificated so that at any time the total number of bags of Exchange cocoa can be determined.

12. It is a violation of Exchange Rules for a warehouseman to provide any weighmaster or weigher with any information pertaining to any previous weighing of cocoa without the prior permission of the Exchange.

IX. *VIOLATIONS*

Violations of the standards and procedures set forth in this resolution shall not be grounds for a receiver to reject a delivery or to hold a deliverer in default, provided, however, that nothing in this section shall alter or abridge the rights of a receiver under any other provision of the Rules to reject a delivery or to hold a deliverer in default.

Adopted by the Board July 8, 1981; effective August 1, 1981.

Amended by the Board February 15, 1989; effective April 3, 1989.

Amended by the Board November 13, 1991; effective December 26, 1991.

Amended by the Board November 13, 1991; effective June 5, 1992 with the implementation of COPS for cocoa.

¶ 5456

No. 6. Rebagging of Cocoa—Interpretation

WHEREAS, Cocoa Rule 9.24 permits rebagging of cocoa to protect the contents of an original bag of cocoa (stored in a warehouse licensed by the Exchange) which original bag has become soiled, torn, or otherwise damaged; and

WHEREAS, Cocoa Rule 9.11 requires that "sound cocoa must be delivered", and

WHEREAS, questions have arisen as to whether rebagging permits/includes "reconditioning" so as to yield sound cocoa:

NOW, THEREFORE, BE IT RESOLVED that the Board hereby interprets rebagging to refer to the transfer of the entire, sound contents of a damaged bag into new, clean, whole bags, which transfer was effected by a licensed weighmaster and a checking weighmaster. Rebagging is neither applicable nor available to bags where any portion of the contents has been damaged, wet or in any other circumstances has become not sound. Proper rebagging is tantamount to original bagging.

BE IT FURTHER RESOLVED that "reconditioning", a process wherein damaged cocoa beans are purged and the remaining are repackaged, is absolutely prohibited. Reconditioned cocoa beans are considered not sound for purposes of delivery against any Exchange contract. This prohibition is universal and pertains whether the cocoa was "reconditioned" on the dock or in a licensed warehouse or in any other location.

Adopted by the Board February 13, 1985; effective April 28, 1986.

¶ 5458

No. 7 Grading Procedure When Cocoa Does Not Meet Count Requirement (Rule 9.18)

WHEREAS, Cocoa Rule 9.18 states that cocoa exceeding the maximum count of its class is deliverable at the next lower class and count requirement; and

WHEREAS, the Board of Managers wishes to clarify Exchange grading procedures when a lot of cocoa does not meet the count requirement for the class stated in the Declaration of Submission;

NOW, THEREFORE BE IT RESOLVED; when a lot of cocoa does not meet the count requirement for the class set forth in its Declaration of Submission the lot shall be rejected, the grading process stopped, and the submitter advised of the rejection and the reason for such rejection. Thereafter, the submitter may present another Declaration of Submission to the Exchange noting the next lower (or higher) class and payment of the appropriate fee, whereupon the cocoa shall be graded in accordance with the Rules.

Adopted by the Board May 15, 1991; effective August 1, 1991.

V

▨ ▨ ▨

Cocoa contract rules and trading procedure rules of the London Commodity Exchange

Contract specifications are those which were in effect as of Feb 1, 1995. Current specifications may be different and are subject to change. Up to date information is available from:

The London Commodity Exchange
1 Commodity Quay
St Katharine Docks
London E1 9AX

Tel 0171-481 2080   Tlx 884370   Fax 0171-702 9923

5.2 Contract rules: cocoa

5.2.1 Interpretation

In rules 5.2.2 to 5.2.10 and the administrative procedures in force thereunder "the Committee" means the Cocoa Terminal Market Committee. Expressions defined in rule 1.1.1 bear the meanings there assigned to them.

5.2.2 Quantity, description, price and delivery

(a) The cocoa contract shall be for one or more lots of cocoa beans of a growth and quality conforming to these contract rules.

see Note 1
(b) Each lot shall be of 10 tonnes net weight, or 1½ per cent more or less, but any such excess or deficit over or under 10 tonnes shall be settled at the official quotation of the morning of the date of tender or, in the case of an unquoted month, at the market value at 10.00 hours on the date of tender.

see Note 2
(b) Each lot shall be of 10 tonnes net weight, or 1½ per cent more or less, but any such excess or deficit over or under 10 tonnes shall be settled at the official quotation of the market day last preceding the date of tender.

(c) The price shall be expressed in sterling per tonne in nominated warehouse in the United Kingdom, or in nominated warehouse in or in the Committee's opinion sufficiently close to Amsterdam, Antwerp, Bremen, Hamburg or Rotterdam, with minimum fluctuations of £1.

Note 1: 5.2.2 (b) (effective up to but not including September 1994 delivery)

Note 2: 5.2.2 (b) (effective for September 1994 delivery onwards)

5.2.3 Packing and weights

(a) Cocoa shall be packed in original sound bags in external good order. Each bag of cocoa shall have a net weight not exceeding 75 kilogrammes.

(b) Cocoa shall be invoiced on landed weights or on reweights in conformity with the administrative procedures. Actual tare shall be allowed, to the nearest 25 grammes.

5.2.4 Import duty

(a) Cocoa qualifying on account of its origin for a preferential rate of import duty must be tendered either

(i) subject to paragraph (e) below, with such documents as are required to enable the buyer to take delivery at the preferential rate (or with such proof as to the same as is mentioned at (c) below), or

(ii) duty paid by the seller.

(b) Cocoa not so qualifying may be tendered either

(i) duty unpaid, whereupon duty shall be paid by the buyer, or

(ii) duty paid, the amount thereof to be borne by the seller.

(c) The proof mentioned in paragraph (a) (i) above is proof that such documents as will enable the buyer to take delivery at the preferential rate of duty have been lodged with the appropriate authorities, or irrefutable proof of the availability of such documents, such in either case as to satisfy the customs authorities in the country where the cocoa is stored for importation at the preferential rate. Where such storage is in the United Kingdom the lotting account must state that the certificate of origin is lodged with and accepted by HM Customs and Excise.

(d) No deduction shall be made from the contract price on account of any difference between preferential and non-preferential rates of duty.

(e) Where the importation of cocoa from a particular origin at a preferential rate of duty is subject to a quota, any parcel in excess of the quota shall be tendered duty paid.

5.2.5 Quality and condition

(a) Cocoa which is smoky or hammy shall not be tenderable.

(b) Save as otherwise provided in or under these contract rules, only cocoa of the following growths shall be tenderable. In the case of growths in groups 2, 3, 4 or 5 the discount shown against that group shall be allowed by the seller. In respect of Contract No. 7, the cocoa must in every case be fermented cocoa.

Contract No. 7

	basis % slaty	% defective
Group 1 (at Contract Price)		
Ghana	5	5
Cote d'Ivoire	5	5
Nigeria	5	5
Sierra Leone	5	5
Togo	5	5
Cameroon	5	5
Equatorial Guinea (Bioko)	5	5
Zaire	5	5
Western Samoa	3	3
Granada Fine Estates	2	2
Trinidad & Tobago Plantation	2	2
Jamaica	2	2
Group 2 (at a discount of £25 per tonne)		
Sao Tome and Principe	3	3
Sri Lanka	5	5
Papua New Guinea	5	5
Group 3 (at a discount of £50 per tonne)		
Brazil Bahia Superior	4	4
Brazil Vitoria Superior	4	4
Ecuador	12	5
Group 4 (at a discount of £75 per tonne)		
Malaysia	5	5
Group 5 (at a discount of £100 per tonne)		
All other growths	5	5

(c) Cocoa of a growth listed at (b) above may be tendered notwithstanding that its quality is inferior to that specified, provided the inferiority does not in the graders' opinion amount to more than a further 5% slaty and 5% defective and such quality allowance as is determined by the graders is allowed by the seller.

(d) Cocoa with a bean count not exceeding 110 beans per 100g shall be tenderable without a bean count allowance. Cocoa with a bean count exceeding 110 beans but not exceeding 120 beans per 100g shall be tenderable subject to a bean count allowance to be determined by the graders. Cocoa with a bean count exceeding 120 beans per 100g shall not be tenderable.

(e) A tender may be subject to discount or allowance under more than one provision of this rule.

(f) In the event of an origin changing its name or the description of growths of cocoa the Committee may give directions as to the style under which an affected growth is to be tendered.

5.2.6 Levy

Cocoa which is subject to a levy imposed under an international cocoa agreement may be tendered, provided the levy is borne by the seller.

5.2.7 Charges
see note 1

The seller shall pay all port and quay charges, and all rent up to and including the fourteenth day from the date of tender. Where delivery is made in the United Kingdom, the seller shall pay the charges for delivery ex warehouse.

5.2.7 Charges
see note 2

The seller shall pay all port and quay charges, and all rent up to and including the fourteenth day from the date of tender.

Note 1: 5.2.7 *(effective up to but not including July 1994 delivery)*

Note 2: 5.2.7 *(effective for July 1994 delivery onwards)*

5.2.8 Parcels

Each tender shall comprise not more than two parcels of sound cocoa each of no fewer than five bags, both parcels the product of one country and lying in the same warehouse. Each parcel shall be of one mark ex one vessel.

5.2.9 Administrative procedures

(a) The contract shall (without prejudice to any other provision herein) be subject to such administrative procedures as may from time to time be announced by the Committee, provided always that if there be any conflict between the administrative procedures and these contract rules the provisions of these rules shall prevail.

(b) The Committee may at its discretion at any time revoke, alter or add to the administrative procedures. Any such amendment shall be circulated to the members of the London Cocoa Terminal Market and shall have such effect on existing as well as new contracts as the Committee may direct.

5.2.10 General contract provisions

The general contract provisions set out in rules 5.1.2 (execution on market floor), 5.1.3 (war or government intervention), 5.1.4 (trade emergency), 5.1.5 (force majeure), 5.1.6 (new legislation), 5.1.7 (default), 5.1.8 (arbitration), 5.1.9 (Articles and Rules), 5.1.10 (law and jurisdiction) and 5.1.11 (powers of directors and committees) shall apply to the contract. For this purpose the futures market committee referred to in those provisions shall be the Committee.

[The Schedule of Months Quoted at Calls is to be found at the end of this section as Table A.]

5.2 Administrative procedures: cocoa

5.2.11 Tender documents

A tender shall state the price and the date of contract and, in respect of each parcel, shall be accompanied by

(i) in the case of an original tender, a written undertaking to the Clearing House that a clean warrant of entitlement to the parcel is immediately available in London and will be presented to the Clearing House on demand in accordance with these administrative procedures;

(ii) a valid certificate of quality;

(iii) a lotting account conforming to the requirements of procedure 5.2.22; and

(iv) such documentary evidence as may from time to time be required by the Committee that any levy payable under an international cocoa agreement has been paid by the seller.

5.2.12 No withdrawal or substitution

A tender shall not be withdrawn nor substitution allowed except with the consent of the buyer or, in case of dispute, unless so ordered by the Committee.

5.2.13 Clerical errors

Obvious clerical errors in a tender, which can be readily rectified by reference to the other party, shall not be treated as constituting a default.

5.2.14 Timing of tenders

(a) The seller may make a tender to the Clearing House by 09.30 hours on any market day in the delivery month as herein provided. Notwithstanding the foregoing on the last date for tendering the seller may make a tender to the Clearing House by 16.00 hours. No tender shall be made on a day which is not a market day or on a day on which dealings on the London Cocoa Terminal Market are suspended.

(b) Upon receipt by the Clearing House a tender shall be passed to the buyer without delay. It shall be endorsed with the date and time of receipt and despatch by the Clearing House.

(c) A tender which has been received by the Clearing House in time shall, subject to the foregoing, be accepted by the buyer as a valid tender for the date of receipt.

(d) Should a tender not be duly made to the Clearing House by 16.00 hours on the last date for tendering the seller shall, subject to the contract rules, be deemed in default.

(e) The last date for tendering shall be the last market day of the delivery month; provided that where on that market day dealings on the London Cocoa Terminal Market are suspended the last date for tendering shall be the next following market day on which dealings are not suspended.

5.2.15 Tender fee

A seller or buyer who makes or receives a tender on behalf of another party shall be entitled to recover from such party any tender fee payable to the Clearing House.

5.2.16 Weights

(a) Cocoa shall be invoiced on landed weights, or if reweighed under paragraph (b), (c) or (d) below on reweights, as recorded in the warrant, less the weight of samples drawn up to and including the date of payment and the actual tare.

(b) If the tender is made more than six months after the last day of the month in which the cocoa was last weighed, the seller shall either

(i) at his expense have the cocoa reweighed before tender or

see Note 1

(ii) allow from the contract price a sum equal to ¼ per cent of the official quotation of the morning on the date of tender (or, if there be no official quotation, of the market value at 10.00 hours on the date of tender) per tonne net weight for every additional period of six months or part thereof, subject to a maximum of 1¼ per cent.

see Note 2

(ii) allow from the contract price a sum equal to ¼ per cent of the official quotation of the market day last preceding the date of tender per tonne net weight for every additional period of six months or part thereof, subject to a maximum of 1¼ per cent.

(c) Cocoa may not be tendered more than 36 months after the last day of the month in which it was last weighed. After that time it must be reweighed before tendering.

(d) If Cocoa is moved by a nominated warehousekeeper from one nominated warehouse of his to another, it may not thereafter be tendered until it is reweighed and a new lotting account prepared. If cocoa is moved out of the control of a nominated warehousekeeper it may not thereafter be tendered until it is regraded and reweighed at the nominated warehouse of another warehousekeeper and a new lotting account prepared.

Note 1   5.2.16 (b)(ii)   (effective up to but not including September 1994 delivery)

Note 2   5.2.16 (b)(ii)   (effective for September 1994 delivery onwards)

5.2.17 Payment, risk

(a) Payment shall be effected on a net basis through the "Clearing House's Protected Payment

System" on the prompt date or where a notice is given under procedure 5.2.18 (d), on the market day following that on which notice is given. The cocoa is at seller's risk until payment is made or until midnight on the day payment is due whichever is the sooner.

(b) The prompt date shall be the fourteenth day after the date of tender; provided that if the fourteenth day is not a market day, or if on that day dealings on the London Cocoa Terminal Market are suspended, the next following market day on which dealings are not suspended shall be the prompt date.

5.2.18 Taking up of documents

(a) Warrants for each lot of cocoa tendered shall be lodged with the Clearing House not later than 12.00 hours on the prompt date.

(b) Payment is to be made and documents are to be taken up by the buyer without prejudice to the reference of any claim or dispute to arbitration.

(c) If payment is not made and documents taken up by 14.00 hours on the prompt date (or any earlier date for which notice has been given under procedure 5.2.18 (d)), the Clearing House may sell the cocoa for the account of whom it may concern. Any surplus or deficit resulting from such sale, with an account for interest and the costs of sale, shall be settled with the Clearing House forthwith.

(d) A buyer desiring to take up documents before the prompt date shall give notice to the Clearing House by 16.00 hours on the market day prior to that on which he wishes to take them up. Documents must be presented to the Clearing House by 12.00 hours on the market day following that on which notice is given and taken up by the buyer by 14.00 hours.

(e) If in any case the invoice is not ready by the time payment is to be made, payment shall be made and received on account.

5.2.19 Writing up of rent

(a) A warrant will not be accepted unless rent is written up (that is to say, the warrant is endorsed by the warehousekeeper with the words "Rent Paid") in respect of the period to at least the last day of the month immediately preceding the delivery month. Subject to paragraph (b) below, the seller shall make an allowance for any rent short of the prompt date at the daily rate per lot for the time being determined by the Committee. Subject as aforesaid, the buyer shall make an allowance at the same rate for any rent written up beyond the prompt date.

(b) In the last two sentences of paragraph (a) above, concerning allowance for rent, the references to the prompt date are to be construed as references to the fourteenth day after the date of tender, whether or not it is a market day or a day on which dealings are suspended.

5.2.20 Acceptance of tenders

A buyer shall be deemed to have accepted a tender for all purposes by 17.00 hours on the seventh marketday after payment for documents unless he has

(i) within such period notified the Clearing House, which will in turn immediately notify the seller, of his intention to refer a dispute to arbitration and

(ii) referred such dispute to arbitration not later than the next market day in accordance with the relevant arbitration rules.

5.2.21 Grading

(a) Before a parcel of cocoa may be tendered for the first time application must be made to the Exchange for the parcel to be graded and a certificate of quality issued showing the parcel to be tenderable subject to such allowance as may be specified.

(b) Application shall be made by an authorised floor member trading in the London Cocoa Terminal Market in a form for the time being approved by the Committee. It shall be accompanied by a sealed dock sample of not less than 2kg in respect of each parcel. The sample shall have been drawn from not less than 30 per cent of the number of sound bags in the parcel not more than 56 days before its submission to the Exchange. It shall be contained in a recognised sample bag or package having a tare not exceeding 100g. The recognised sample bag shall be marked with the following information as a condition of acceptance for grading:

(i) Country of origin and Growth Description

(ii) The sample was drawn from not less than 30% of the sound bags

(iii) Number of bags of Cocoa Beans

(iv) Mark(s)

(v) Warrant Number

(vi) Port of Landing

(vii) Date of sampling and weighing

(viii) Final day of Landing

(ix) Warehouse where stored

(x) Lotting account number

(xi) In a case falling within paragraph (bb) below, the name or identifying mark of the independent nominated warehousekeeper.

(bb) Where the Authorised Floor Member applying for grading has an interest of 5 percent or more in the capital of the nominated warehousekeeper in whose warehouse the parcel is stored, he shall inform the warehousekeeper of that fact and the Member shall notify the fact to the Exchange before a sample is drawn. The Exchange shall then instruct an independent nominated warehousekeeper to supervise, at the Authorised Floor Member's expense, the drawing and sealing of the sample for conformity to paragraph (b) above. Neither the Exchange nor the directors shall have any liability whatsoever for the performance by such an independent nominated warehousekeeper of his supervisory duties.

(c) The Exchange may weigh the sample before it is graded. During the course of such weighing the seal of the sample shall not be broken by the Exchange and the tare shall be assumed to be 100g. A sample found on such weighing to be of less than 2kg net weight shall not be graded. The Exchange shall notify the authorised floor member of the deficiency and shall retain the sample for 5 market days for collection. If not collected by or on behalf of the authorised floor member the sample may be disposed of as the Exchange shall think fit. Subject to paragraph (d) below the net weight ascertained under this paragraph shall be conclusive for the purposes of these administrative procedures.

(d) If in the course of grading a sample the graders find that it was submitted in a bag or package having a tare exceeding 100g they may decline to grade it.

(e) The application for grading shall be accompanied by a lotting account conforming to the requirements of procedure 5.2.22. Where the application is for regrading it shall also be accompanied by the last certificate of quality.

(f) Where a certificate of quality states that the parcel is not tenderable no second application for grading may be made.

(g) The certificate of quality shall be valid for six months and any unexpired part of the last month.

(h) Subject to paragraph (f) above, an application for regrading of a parcel may be made no earlier than one month before the time for expiry of the current certificate of quality. Upon regrading a current certificate shall cease to be valid.

(i) If a current certificate of quality shall be defaced, lost, destroyed or not received by the owner of the parcel to which it relates, the owner or his agent may apply in writing to the Secretary advising him of the circumstances and requesting the issue of a duplicate certificate. If the Secretary is satisfied with such application he may issue a duplicate at a price for the time being fixed by the Committee. Such a duplicate shall be as effective for all purposes of these contract rules and administrative procedures as the original certificate of quality.

5.2.22 Lotting account

(a) Each lotting account shall be dated no later than two working days after the date of the sample submitted for grading of the parcel to which it relates. It shall show that on that date not less than 30 per cent of the number of bags in the parcel were sampled within the warehouse and that all bags in the parcel were original, sound and externally in good order.

(b) In paragraph (a) above "working days" means days which are working days at the nominated warehouse where the parcel is stored.

(c) Each lotting account shall also state

   (i) the mark on the bags,

   (ii) name of vessel or flight number or identity of land carnage,

   (iii) country of origin, growth and quality,

   (iv) number of bags,

   (v) nominated warehouse in which stored,

   (vi) final day of landing,

   (vii) date when delivery into warehouse was completed,

   (viii) final day of original weighing,

   (ix) gross weight, tare and date when last weighed (stating whether reweighed pursuant to procedure 5.2.16(b), (c) or (d)),

   (x) warrant number,

   (xi) date when sample (or last sample, where more than one) drawn,

   (xii) weight of sample, or samples, drawn,

   (xiii) whether the parcel is subject to preferential or non-preferential rate of duty,

   (xiv) where the parcel is subject to preferential duty, that the documents mentioned in rule 5.2.4 (a) and (c) are available in accordance with that rule, and

   (xv) in a case falling within rule 5.2.21 (bb), the name or identifying mark of the independent nominated warehousekeeper.

(d) The lotting account shall be issued by the nominated keeper of the nominated warehouse mentioned at (c) (v) above.

5.2.23 Force majeure

(a) For the purposes of this rule "force majeure" shall mean any occurrence outside the control of either party to a contract which hinders or prevents the performance in whole or in part by a party of his obligations under the contract (other than an obligation to make a payment), including but not limited to fire, storm, flood, earthquake, explosion, accident howsoever caused, strike, lockout, work to rule or other industrial action, act of God, act of government or other national or local authority or any agency thereof and delay in transportation or communication.

(b) Neither party to the contract shall be deemed in default of his obligations nor shall any penalty or damages be payable if and to the extent that performance of any obligation is hindered or prevented by force majeure.

(c) If force majeure hinders or prevents a party from performing any obligation for a period of five days beyond the time limit fixed in or under the contract, the commodity if not already delivered to the buyer shall be invoiced back at a price to be determined by the futures market committee at its absolute discretion. Such price shall be binding on the parties. No dispute as to the price may be referred to arbitration but the completion of invoicing back shall be without prejudice to the right of either party to refer any dispute arising out of the contract to arbitration under the Rules.

5.2.24 Default

(a) ----

(b) ----

(c) ----

(d) ----

6.12.00   Trading Rules: Cocoa

6.12.01   Opening and Closing (Trading at Calls).

(a)   The call chairman shall note the identity of the lowest seller and the highest buyer in respect of each delivery month. These sellers and buyers shall become the registered seller and buyer. The registered seller and buyer shall be obliged respectively to sell or buy the minimum quantity if an acceptance of their offer or bid is made while the delivery month is still being called by the call chairman. Where, in the call chairman's opinion, two or more traders call the same price simultaneously the call chairman will nominate a "first seller" or "first buyer" and note any further seller or buyer.

(b)   The challenge of "How Many?", meaning 5 lots, if not accepted in full, shall establish the challenger as the registered seller or buyer for the balance of the 5 lots while the delivery month concerned is still being called. Likewise, if a seller or buyer names any quantity, he will be liable for any unfulfilled balance of the quantity until the delivery month or price changes (except with regard to crosses). If a registered seller or buyer names a quantity but is only filled in part, and if he then crosses the balance, having done so, and if there is no other buyer or seller before him, he may become the registered buyer or seller respectively.

(c)   The challenge of "How Many?", if answered by a further challenge of "How Many?", shall commit the second challenger to 10 lots.

Thus,   Seller:-   "How Many?" = 5 lots
         Buyer:-   "How Many?" = 10 lots
         Seller:-   "How Many?" = 15 lots
         Buyer:-   "How Many?" = 20 lots

(d)   A seller or buyer having traded in a delivery month may declare himself as a seller or buyer "over". This entitles him to be noted by the call chairman as the registered seller or buyer in respect of the particular delivery month.

(e)   A seller or buyer having traded a delivery month, and having fulfilled his order, may register himself as "Seller In" at a higher level, or "Buyer In" at a lower level, provided there is no other seller or buyer at the traded level in the same delivery month. If he does not do so and no other trader wishes to trade at that level, the call chairman will establish a new registered seller and buyer in respect of that delivery month.

(f)   Any bid higher than the last offered price or offer lower than the last bid price shall be ruled invalid.

(g)   The call chairman will conduct business in one delivery month at a time. Therefore, offers and bids for any month other than the delivery month being called will be invalid.

(h)   The procedure adopted by the call chairman for conducting calls shall be as follows:

The call chairman shall ask for a seller in respect of the first quoted delivery month. If there is no immediate acceptance of this offer, he shall ask for a buyer in respect of the same delivery month. When the chairman considers interest in this first delivery month has ceased he will announce the next delivery month and move on to the second quoted delivery month adopting the same procedure.

This procedure will continue until all quoted delivery months are closed.

(i)   Delivery months, the named member trading, bids, offers and acceptances shall be decided by the call chairman whose decision shall in every case be final.

6.12.02   Open Trading

(a)   All offers, bids and trades shall be by loud, clear, open outcry. Offers and bids shall be accepted by the cry of "RIGHT", except where several traders are offering or bidding the same price for the same delivery month. In this case to ensure that traders are not able to select a particular seller or buyer, it is required that to trade at that price, prospective sellers or buyers must offer or bid that price. When a bid or offer is accepted by more than one trader, the registered seller or buyer shall take precedence provided he accepts promptly. Should the registered seller or buyer not accept, the first acceptance shall take precedence.

(b)   In the event of a seller or buyer offering or bidding "over" at the price at which he has just traded, he will become the registered seller or buyer until that same delivery month trades at a different level, provided he accepts any further offers or bids promptly. It is the duty of the first seller or buyer to reply to any formal request for a quote (eg "How now?") in respect of the delivery month in which he is registered in order to maintain his position.

(c)   It shall be the seller's duty to name his quantity first during any trade.

(d)   Straddles

When trading straddles the first seller and buyer rules shall apply, when practicable. Traders shall ensure that the differential between the delivery months traded reflects the current market value of both delivery months.

6.12.03   Self Trades/Crossing

(a)   A floor trader may execute a transaction in which he acts as both Buyer and Seller in respect of a contract month or a straddle for which he is the registered buyer or seller at the price of the transaction and for which there is a minimum fluctuation Market. Such a transaction will only be treated as executed once it has been announced to the market clearly and audibly stating the quantity, price and contract month or straddle involved.

(b) Save as set out in (c) below, he may only execute such a transaction once he is the registered buyer/seller at that price through;

(i) being the registered buyer/seller prior to having orders or instructions for both sides of the transaction;

(ii) fully satisfying the registered buyer /seller at that price; or

(iii) if there is no registered buyer /seller at that price, creating a minimum fluctuation market and announcing the quotation clearly and audibly in order to allow the market a reasonable opportunity to accept the quotation and not through offering or bidding over.

(c) The floor trader may execute such a transaction at either the bid or offer price where there is a minimum fluctuation market, subject only to being liable to be picked up by the market for a minimum quantity, if it is executed to fill the order of a client who has instructed the member that his order should be executed in one transaction and the size of the order is or exceeds 50 lots.

(d) Such a transaction may only be executed for a client, other than another Authorised Floor Member of the Exchange, if the member has previously notified the client of the potential conflict of interests which may exist in executing such a transaction and the client has not objected to his orders being executed in that way.

6.12.04 Against Actuals

Subject to rules 6.07.03 (d) and 6.10.10, Against Actuals shall be transacted at or between the prevailing bid and offer prices when the market floor is open.

6.12.05 Maintenance of an orderly Market.

(a) If, in the opinion of the Market Manager, having consulted the Floor Committee Chairman and the Compliance Director, trading upon the Market ceases to be orderly open trading shall be suspended and a special call shall be commenced immediately.

(b) In the event that a special call should progress through the official commencement time of the closing call the special call shall be completed before commencing the closing call.

VI

Comparison of various cocoa bean quality standards

This table is reproduced by courtesy of the International Trade Centre
UNCTAD/GATT, Geneva.

Table VI.1 Comparison of various grading standards

Country	Standard authority	Description	Bran count per 100 grams	Faults (by percentage)						% Moisture	% Foreign matter	Other specifications and comments
				Mould	Slate	Inf	Germ	Flat	Violet			
	AFCC	Good Fermented	100	5	5	(d)	NS	NS	NS	NS	NS	Rejection possible if bean count above 120.
		Fair Fermented	100	10	10	(d)	NS	NS	NS	NS	NS	
		Fair Average Quality	100	12	12	(d)	NS	NS	NS	NS	NS	
	CAL	Good Fermented	100 (h)	5	5	(d)	NS	NS	NS	NS	NS	For West African cocoa only.
		Fair Fermented	100 (h)	10	10	(d)	NS	NS	NS	NS	NS	
(a)	FAO Model Ordinance	Grade I	(b)	3	3	3	(c)	(c)	NS	7.5	0	To be of merchantable quality, all cocoa must be free of foreign odours, and must not be adulterated.
		Grade II	(b)	4	8	6	(c)	(c)	NS	7.5	0	Can only be marketed under special contract.
		Sub-standard (SS)	NS	Cocoa which exceeds Grade II limits								
Brazil	National Foreign Trade Council	Superior	NS	4	2	(d)	2	(e)	NS	8.0	NS	Max. of each individual defect 2%, sum not to exceed 4%.
		Good Fair	NS	6	4	(d)	4	(e)	NS	8.0	NS	Max. of each individual defect 4%, sum not to exceed 6%.
		Subgrade	NS	8	8	5	10	(e)	NS	8.0	1	Slight smoke odour admissible.
Cameroon		Grade I	(b)	3	3	3	(c)	(c)	NS	7.5	0	FAO standards. To be of merchantable quality, all cocoa must be free of foreign odours, and must not be adulterated.
		Grade II	(b)	4	8	6	(c)	(c)	NS	7.5	0	Can only be marketed under special contract.
		Sub-standard (SS)	NS	Cocoa which exceeds Grade II limits								
Congo	OCC	Supérieure	NS	3	3	3	3	3	NS	NS	NS	Max. of 3% of infested, germinated or flat.
		Courante	NS	4	8	6	6	6	NS	NS	NS	Max. of 6% of infested, germinated or flat.
		Limite	NS	NS	20	12	12	12	NS	NS	NS	Bags of Supérieure marked with 1 disk, Courante with 2 and Limite with 3.
Papua New Guinea	Cocoa Board	Export Quality	100	5	1	(d)	(i)	(i)	NS	5.5–7.5	1	Board approved fermenting and drying process free from foul or foreign odours.

Table VI.1 Continued

Country	Standard authority	Description	Bran count per 100 grams	Faults (by percentage)						% Moisture	% Foreign matter	Other specifications and comments
				Mould	Slate	Inf	Germ	Flat	Violet			
Papua New Guinea	Cocoa Board	Export Quality	100	5	1	(d)	(i)	(i)	NS	5.5–7.5	1	Board approved fermenting and drying process tree itom loul or foreign odours.
Côte d'Ivoire	Ministry of Agriculture	Grade 1	uniform	3	3	3	(c)	(c)	(c)	8.0	0	Lots must be of uniform colour and flavour – free of musty or smoky flavour – max. 10% in excess of or below average of 1/3 of the average weight of the beans (Grade 1 only).
		Grade 2	NS	4	8	6	(c)	(c)	(c)	8.0	0	Any cocoa which does not meet Grade 2 specs. Export prohibited.
		Sous-grade	NS	Cocoa which exceeds Grade II limits								
Dominican Republic	Cocoa Department	Sanchez	159	4	NS	3	3	(e)	NS	9.5	1	Smoky beans not permitted – maximum defect count on exportable cocoa 6%.
	Ministry of Agriculture	Hispaniola, Gr. I	120	3	1	3	3	(e)	10	7.5	0	Cocoa which does not meet grading standards must be marked 'stocklot' on the bags and documents and may be sold on special contract against sample only.
		Hispaniola, Gr. II	130	1	3	3	3	(e)	15	7.5	0	
Ecuador	Ministry of Industry, Commerce, etc	ASSPS	71–74	0	5	0	0	0	10	NS	0	
		ASSS	75–77	1	9	(d)	(d)	(d)	15	NS	0	
		ASS	81–83	3	12	(d)	(d)	(d)	20	NS	0	
		ASNS	81–83	2	13	(d)	(d)	(d)	25	NS	0	
		ASW	80–91	5	18	(d)	(d)	(d)	25	NS	0	
		ASES	80–83	2	18	(d)	(d)	(d)	30	NS	0	
		ASE	91–95	6	30	(d)	(d)	(d)	25	NS	0	
		Natural	80–83	4	19	(d)	(d)	(d)	30	NS	0	Natural may include 1% that 1% Monilia damaged, 1% insect damaged and 1% black beans.
Gabon		Supérieure	NS	3	3	3	3	3	NS	NS	NS	Max. of 3% of infested, germinated or flat.
		Courante	NS	4	8	6	6	6	NS	NS	NS	Max. of 6% of infested, germinated or flat.
		Limite	NS	NS	20	12	12	12	NS	NS	NS	
Ghana	Ministry of Agriculture	Grade I	NS	3	3	3	(c)	(c)	NS	7.5	0	
		Grade II	NS	4	8	6	(c)	(c)	NS	7.5	0	

Country	Authority	Grade	Bean count								Remarks
Indonesia	INCA	Grade AA I	≤85	3	3	3	(c)	NS	7.5	0	To be of merchantable quality, all cocoa must be free of foreign odours, and must not be adulterated.
		Grade AA II	≤85	4	8	6	(c)	NS	7.5	0	
		Grade A I	≤100	3	3	3	(c)	NS	7.5	0	Live insects – none
		Grade A II	≤100	4	8	6	(c)	NS	7.5	0	
		Grade B I	101–110	3	3	3	(c)	NS	7.5	0	Broken beans/nib or shell ≤3%
		Grade B II	101–110	4	8	6	(c)	NS	7.5	0	
		Grade C I	111–120	3	3	3	(c)	NS	7.5	0	'F' in the description denotes fine flavour
		Grade C II	111–120	4	8	6	(c)	NS	7.5	0	
		Subgrade	Cocoa which exceeds Grade II limits								
Malaysia	Federal Agricultural Marketing Authority (FAMA)	SMC I-A	≤100	3	3	2.5	(c)	NS	7.5	0	Cocoa showing live infestation (more than 10 live insects per bag) is rejected unless fumigated at owner's request
		SMC I-B	>100 ≤110	3	3	2.5	(c)	NS	7.5	0	
		SMC I-C	>100 ≤120	3	3	2.5	(c)	NS	7.5	0	
		SMC II-A	≤100	4	8	5	(c)	NS	7.5	0	Export of ungraded cocoa from the mainland is prohibited.
	Applies voluntarily to both Sabah and Peninsula	SMC II-B	>100 ≤110	4	8	5	(c)	NS	7.5	0	The Sabah Cocoa Grading Council, a trade association, has pledged that its membership will adhere voluntarily to the FAMA scheme and has appointed three independent superintendence firms to do the sampling for it.
		SMC II-C	>110 ≤120	4	8	5	(c)	NS	7.5	0	
		Sub-standard	>120	>4	>8	>5	(c)	NS	NS	NS	
Nigeria	Federal Produce Inspection Service (FPIS)	Grade I	(b)	3	3	3	(c)	NS	7.5	0	To be of merchantable quality, all cocoa must be free of foreign odours and must not be adulterated. Can only be marketed under special contract.
		Grade II	(b)	4	8	6	(c)	NS	7.5	0	Since the cocoa trade has been privatized these FAO standards have not been rigorously applied to exports.
		Sub-standard (SS)	NS	Cocoa which exceeds Grade II limits							
Sierra Leone	SLPMB	Grade I	96	3	3	3	3	NS	NS	NS	Max. of 15% of mould, slaty, infested, germinated or flat.
		Grade II	96	4	8	6	6	NS	NS	NS	Max. of 30% of mould, slaty, infested, germinated or flat.
		Subgrade	Cocoa which exceeds Grade II limits								Cocoa to be free of smoky or hammy flavour.
Solomon Islands	Commodities Export Marketing Authority	Grade I	NS	3	3	3	(c)	NS	NS	0	Cocoa for export must be fermented, thoroughly dry, free from abnormal or foreign odours and free from adulteration, reasonably free from live insects, broken beans, fragments and pieces of shell.
		Grade II	NS	4	8	6	(c)	NS	NS	0	

Table VI.1 Continued

Country	Standard authority	Description	Bran count per 100 grams	Mould	Slate	Inf	Germ	Flat	Violet	% Moisture	% Foreign matter	Other specifications and comments
Togo		Grade I	(b)	3	3	3	(c)	(c)	NS	7.5	0	FAO standards.
		Grade II	(b)	4	8	6	(c)	(c)	NS	7.5	0	To be of merchantable quality, all cocoa must be free of foreign odours, and must not be adulterated. Can only be marketed under special contract.
		Sub-standard (SS)	NS	Cocoa which exceeds Grade II limits								
Vanuatu	Dept. of Agriculture Livestock & Forestry	I-A	<100	3	3	3	(c)	(c)	NS	7.0	NS	These standards were proposed in 1986 and were in the process of being implemented in 1987. Their current application has not yet been confirmed, however. Before adoption of this system the Papua New Guinea grading practice was followed with 8% maximum moisture contents.
		I-B	101-120	3	3	3	(c)	(c)	NS	7.0	NS	
		II	>120	4	<8	<6	(c)	(c)	NS	7.0	NS	
		Sub-standard	122-200	5-10	>8	6-20	(c)	(c)	NS	7.0	NS	
		Inferior	>200	>10	>50	>20	(c)	(c)	NS	7.0	NS	
United States	21 Code of Fed. Reg.	FDA Defect Action Levels (DALS)	NS	4	NS	4	NS	NS	NS	NS	0	Cocoa must be sound, reasonably free of foreign matter, foreign odour. Free of live insect infestation and other adulteration. Total detect count may not exceed 6%
Western Samoa	1989 Cocoa Act	Export Standard	100	5	5	(c)	5	(e)	NS	5.5-7.5	1	<5% in total of slaty, flat, broken, fragments, germinated or defective beans. Free from foul and foreign odours
Zaire		Bonne Qualité	80	5	5	5	NS	NS	NS	NS	NS	Max. 10% mould and infested
		Courante	81-85	5	5	5	NS	NS	NS	NS	NS	Max. 10% mould and infested

Key:

NS Not specified

(a) This ordinance has been adopted by several countries, in some cases with modifications, but it has no force of law per se.
(b) Not more than 12 per cent of the beams should be outside the range of +/− one-third of the average weight.
(c) Included in insect infested.
(d) Included in mould.
(e) Included in germinated.
(f) Included in foreign matter.
(g) Detailed schedule of discounts according to bean size.
(h) If description includes Main Crop.

The above table has been updated from that in Cocoa: A Shipper's Manual published by the International Trade Centre.

356

VII

ICCO statistics of the world summary, production and grindings

Table VII.1 World cocoa bean production, grindings, stocks and prices. Annual summary data, 1960/61–1993/94

Cocoa year a/	Gross crop	Grindings b/	Surplus/ deficit c/	Total end-of-season stocks d/	ICCO buffer stocks e/	End-of-season stocks as a percentage of grindings:		ICCO daily price (annual average)	
						Total stocks f/	Free stocks g/	US$ tonne h/	SDRs/tonne i/
		(thousand tonnes)				Percent			
1960/61	1172	1002	158	481	—	48.0	48.0	493	493
1961/62	1149	1095	43	524	—	47.9	47.9	477	477
1962/63	1172	1141	19	543	—	47.6	47.6	522	522
1963/64	1210	1188	10	553	—	46.5	46.5	522	522
1964/65	1505	1307	178 j/	731 j/	—	55.9	55.9	389	389
1965/66	1221	1379	−170	561	—	40.7	40.7	491	491
1966/67	1363	1382	−33	528	—	38.2	38.2	569	569
1967/68	1370	1410	−54	474	—	33.6	33.6	644	644
1968/69	1260	1378	−131	343	—	24.9	24.9	913	913
1969/70	1417	1357	46	389	—	28.7	28.7	730	730
1970/71	1554	1420	118	507	—	35.7	35.7	586	586
1971/72	1581	1528	37	544	—	35.6	35.6	583	545
1972/73	1409	1546	−151	393	—	25.4	25.4	1014	865
1973/74	1446	1500	−68	325	—	21.7	21.7	1455	1209
1974/75	1532	1476	41	366	—	24.8	24.8	1331	1091
1975/76	1489	1495	−24	345	—	23.1	23.1	1655	1429
1976/77	1344	1423	−92	253	—	17.8	17.8	3632	3130
1977/78	1505	1378	112	365	—	26.5	26.5	3283	2683

Cocoa year a/	Net world crop c/	Grindings b/	Surplus/deficit c/	Total end-of-season stocks d/	ICCO buffer stock e/	Total stocks % f/	Free stocks % g/	ICCO price h/i/	ICCO price h/i/
1978/79	1510	1470	25	390	—	26.5	26.5	3504	2714
1979/80	1671	1487	167	557	—	37.5	37.5	2825	2166
1980/81	1695	1556	122	679	100	43.6	43.6	2098	1735
1981/82	1732	1598	117	796	100	49.8	43.6	1868	1656
1982/83	1531	1629	−113	683	100	41.9	35.8	1949	1815
1983/84	1512	1703	−206	477	100	28.0	22.1	2413	2320
1984/85	1952	1859	73	550	100	29.6	24.2	2222	2234
1985/86	1974	1847	107	657	100	35.6	30.2	2149	1890
1986/87	2011	1910	81	738	175	38.6	29.5	2023	1607
1987/88	2197	1985	190	928	250	46.8	34.2	1707	1269
1988/89	2466	2130	311	1239	248	58.2	46.5	1344	1035
1989/90	2408	2203	181	1420	245	64.5	53.3	1193	902
1990/91	2507	2331	151	1571	242	67.4	57.0	1193	863
1991/92	2282	2313	−54	1517	233	65.6	55.5	1166	831
1992/93	2376	2395	−43	1474	230	61.5	51.9	1051	751
Estimate 1993/94	2429	2480	−75	1399	178	56.4	49.2	1370	968

Notes:
a/ Cocoa year: 1 October to 30 September.
b/ Grindings: Estimates for the cocoa years 1960/61 to 1971/72 are derived from calendar year estimates.
c/ Surplus/deficit: Current net world crop (gross crop adjusted by subtracting 1% for loss in weight) minus grindings.
d/ Total end-of-season stocks: Computed on the basis of yearly surplus/deficit and assuming that world stocks of cocoa beans, at the end of the 1973/74 cocoa year, amounted to 325 000 tonnes.
e/ ICCO buffer stock: The 1986/87 value includes 48.4 thousand tonnes purchased on a forward basis, but not delivered to ICCO warehouses as at 30 September 1987.
f/ Total end-of-season stocks as a percentage of grindings.
g/ Free stocks (total end-of-season stocks excluding ICCO buffer stock) as a percentage of grindings.
h/i/ ICCO daily price is the average of the quotations of the nearest three active futures trading months on the London Cocoa Terminal Market and on the New York Coffee, Sugar and Cocoa Exchange.
j/ Adjusted by 5000 tonnes to account for sales for non-traditional uses.

Table VII.2 Production of cocoa beans by country. Five-year averages: 1960/61–1964/65 to 1985/86–1989/90; annual data 1990/91 to 1993/94

Country	Five-year average						Annual			
	1960/61–1964/65	1965/66–1969/70	1970/71–1974/75	1975/76–1979/80	1980/81–1984/85	1985/86–1989/90	1990/91	1991/92	1992/93	1993/94 (estimate)
	(thousand tonnes)									
AFRICA										
Angola	0.3	0.4	0.5	0.2	0.2	0.1	–	–	–	–
Cameroon	81.7	93.3	113.6	103.9	114.6	125.8	115.0	105.0	90.0	95.0
Congo	6.5	1.2	2.0	2.6	1.8	1.2	0.5	0.7	0.3	0.3
Côte d'Ivoire	104.7	147.0	208.0	294.5	443.7	689.5	804.4	747.0	697.0	850.0
Equatorial Guinea	30.1	32.7	17.2	6.9	7.8	6.7	5.2	3.5	5.7	5.5
Gabon	3.4	3.9	4.9	3.6	2.3	1.7	1.4	1.4	2.0	1.8
Ghana	451.0	392.3	403.9	309.4	199.0	246.3	293.4	242.8	312.1	245.0
Guinea	–	–	–	0.6	3.0	2.8	2.2	3.4	2.2	3.0
Liberia	1.0	1.7	2.8	3.3	5.2	3.4	2.0	0.5	0.3	0.3
Madagascar	0.5	0.6	0.9	1.6	1.9	2.4	2.5	3.3	4.0	3.5
Nigeria	218.1	226.8	248.9	178.4	153.9	137.0	160.0	110.0	145.0	135.0
Sao Tome and Principe	9.3	9.8	10.1	6.2	4.7	3.5	2.6	2.6	3.0	3.0
Sierra Leone	3.6	3.6	5.9	7.5	9.3	8.5	13.0	7.5	2.8	2.8
Tanzania	–	0.2	0.7	1.0	1.3	1.5	2.5	2.0	2.0	2.0
Togo	13.4	18.6	21.1	15.1	12.9	10.4	9.3	8.0	6.0	6.0
Uganda	–	–	0.2	0.1	0.2	0.3	0.6	0.6	0.8	0.8
Zaïre	–	4.8	5.4	3.8	4.5	4.9	3.4	3.2	4.0	4.0
Other Africa	–	2.8	10.1	3.0	6.3	7.0	–	–	0.4	0.4
Total	923.6	939.6	1056.2	941.9	972.6	1252.9	1418.0	1241.5	1277.6	1358.4

NORTH, CENTRAL AND SOUTH AMERICA

Bolivia	2.1	1.5	1.4	2.2	2.5	2.7	3.5	3.5	3.5	3.5
Brazil	121.7	171.5	202.7	272.2	340.1	355.7	368.1	306.2	308.6	270.0
Colombia	16.2	18.1	21.8	31.2	40.4	51.1	52.0	50.0	50.0	50.0
Costa Rica	11.1	7.5	6.0	8.1	5.2	5.4	4.0	3.0	3.0	3.0
Cuba	2.2	1.6	1.9	1.7	1.7	2.3	2.2	2.2	2.2	2.2
Dominica	0.2	0.1	0.1	—	—	—	—	—	—	—
Dominican Republic	34.5	30.0	35.8	31.3	38.5	47.1	42.0	47.5	52.0	50.0
Ecuador	43.6	58.9	67.4	81.3	76.2	90.0	111.1	85.0	67.4	80.0
Grenada	2.6	2.6	2.6	2.2	2.3	1.4	1.2	0.8	0.9	1.0
Guatemala	0.5	0.5	0.7	2.2	1.6	1.3	0.5	1.0	0.8	0.8
Haiti	2.3	3.2	3.4	2.7	3.1	2.9	1.9	3.2	2.1	2.5
Honduras	0.2	0.2	0.3	0.5	0.7	2.1	3.3	2.7	3.9	3.5
Jamaica	2.1	1.8	2.1	1.6	2.2	2.2	1.8	2.3	2.2	2.2
Mexico	22.3	25.4	28.9	32.4	35.1	42.2	43.0	45.0	50.0	45.0
Nicaragua	0.4	0.6	0.4	0.1	0.1	0.2	0.3	0.3	0.3	0.3
Panama	1.2	0.6	0.6	0.9	1.0	1.0	1.0	1.0	1.0	1.0
Peru	2.5	2.1	2.0	5.4	9.2	10.9	11.0	11.0	11.0	11.0
Saint Lucia	0.2	0.1	0.1	0.1	0.1	0.1	0.1	0.1	0.1	0.1
Trinidad & Tobago	5.7	5.2	4.4	3.0	2.1	1.7	1.8	1.5	1.7	1.8
Venezuela	19.9	19.4	17.9	15.2	13.9	11.8	15.9	15.0	15.5	15.5
Other Americas	0.4	0.1	0.5	0.5	0.6	0.5	0.2	0.2	0.2	0.2
Total	292.0	350.9	401.0	494.7	576.4	632.5	664.9	581.5	576.4	543.6

Table VII.2 Continued

Country	Five-year average						Annual			
	1960/61–1964/65	1965/66–1969/70	1970/71–1974/75	1975/76–1979/80	1980/81–1984/85	1985/86–1989/90	1990/91	1991/92	1992/93	1993/94 (estimate)
	(thousand tonnes)									
ASIA AND OCEANIA										
Fiji	—	0.1	0.1	0.1	0.2	0.3	0.3	0.4	0.3	0.3
India	—	—	—	0.4	2.9	6.0	6.0	6.0	6.0	6.0
Indonesia	0.8	1.4	2.3	6.2	21.3	70.8	150.0	180.0	240.0	260.0
Malaysia	0.4	1.7	7.5	23.5	71.7	198.6	221.0	220.0	225.0	210.0
Papua New Guinea	14.1	22.4	29.1	29.1	28.9	37.1	33.4	40.9	38.8	38.0
Philippines	3.6	4.1	3.6	3.4	4.8	6.2	5.0	5.0	6.0	6.0
Samoa	4.0	2.8	1.8	1.4	1.0	0.6	—	—	—	—
Solomon Islands	—	0.1	0.2	0.2	0.9	2.3	4.1	3.5	2.6	3.0
Sri Lanka	2.4	2.3	1.9	1.9	2.6	2.2	1.4	1.4	1.4	1.4
Thailand	—	—	—	0.1	0.1	0.3	0.4	0.4	0.4	0.4
Vanuatu	0.6	0.7	0.6	0.7	0.9	1.3	2.2	1.5	1.6	1.8
Other Asia and Oceania	—	—	0.2	0.1	0.1	0.1	0.1	0.1	0.1	0.1
Total	25.9	35.5	47.3	67.1	135.4	325.9	423.9	459.2	522.2	527.0
World total	1241.5	1326.0	1504.5	1503.7	1684.4	2211.3	2506.8	2282.2	2376.2	2429.0

Note: Totals may differ from sum of constituents due to rounding.

Table VII.3 Grindings of cocoa beans by country. Five-year averages: 1961–1965 to 1985/86–1989/90; annual data 1990/91 to 1993/94

(thousand tonnes)

Country	Five-year average						Annual			
	1961–1965	1966–1970	1971–1974/75	1975/76–1979/80	1980/81–1984/85	1985/86–1989/90	1990/91	1991/92	1992/93	1993/94 (estimate)
WESTERN EUROPE										
European Community:										
Belgium/Luxembourg	15.3	17.9	19.0	17.0	31.1	38.2	44.9	46.4	47.3	48.0
Denmark	4.3	4.3	3.9	2.9	2.6	2.4	2.9	2.6	2.7	2.7
France	63.5	49.4	43.0	42.7	49.1	44.5	70.5	66.8	81.9	90.0
Germany	n.a.	n.a.	n.a.	n.a.	n.a.	n.a.	294.2	306.0	304.6	296.7
Germany, Fed. Rep. of ...	132.6	137.9	144.9	152.6	179.5	229.5	n.a.	n.a.	n.a.	n.a.
Greece	3.3	4.6	5.0	5.0	4.8	5.3	4.2	1.6	2.4	2.2
Ireland	8.6	10.4	9.3	5.9	6.8	9.7	7.8	8.5	8.7	9.0
Italy	37.6	42.1	38.0	31.7	38.0	46.1	55.7	62.0	57.9	62.0
Netherlands	105.3	113.2	120.3	127.0	153.5	211.0	267.7	294.2	308.9	328.8
Portugal	1.8	2.5	3.3	0.9	0.2	0.2	0.2	0.2	0.2	0.2
Spain	26.7	32.5	32.6	30.8	33.7	37.3	45.4	45.8	43.1	46.0
United Kingdom	91.5	92.9	90.9	71.4	85.7	101.7	144.7	152.3	168.5	168.9
Austria	11.4	12.7	13.2	9.8	11.2	11.9	14.6	14.1	13.9	14.0
Finland	0.3	1.9	2.7	1.7	1.0	0.2	0.1	0.1	0.2	0.1
Norway	5.3	9.2	5.2	4.8	4.9	3.8	2.2	3.3	2.0	2.6
Sweden	7.9	7.0	5.8	5.7	3.5	3.9	0.8	0.4	0.1	–
Switzerland	13.3	15.6	17.4	15.4	18.6	20.6	21.7	22.7	21.3	23.0
Yugoslavia*	7.4	11.2	14.6	13.0	11.2	12.4	12.0	12.0	5.0	8.0
Total	536.2	565.2	569.0	538.4	635.5	778.7	989.6	1038.9	1068.6	1102.2

Table VII.3 Continued

Country	Five-year average (thousand tonnes)						Annual			
	1961–1965	1966–1970	1971–1974/75	1975/76–1979/80	1980/81–1984/85	1985/86–1989/90	1990/91	1991/92	1992/93	1993/94 (estimate)
EASTERN EUROPE										
Bulgaria	3.8	7.7	9.6	7.3	5.8	5.4	4.0	4.0	4.0	4.0
Czechoslovakia*	13.4	17.2	19.0	16.7	16.9	18.2	20.0	20.0	2.0	n.a.
Czech Republic	n.a.	n.a.	n.a.	n.a.	n.a.	n.a.	n.a.	n.a.	12.0	16.0
Slovak Republic	n.a.	n.a.	n.a.	n.a.	n.a.	n.a.	n.a.	n.a.	4.1	7.0
German Democratic Rep.	14.2	17.8	20.0	20.5	16.8	18.3	n.a.	n.a.	n.a.	n.a.
Hungary	7.3	9.5	11.8	13.1	11.2	11.8	9.8	7.3	5.6	6.0
Poland	12.7	18.0	29.2	23.3	13.1	22.3	24.5	25.0	25.0	30.0
Romania	3.5	5.4	9.5	10.9	6.7	5.0	6.0	6.0	3.6	4.0
USSR*	54.2	91.7	134.2	107.8	140.8	149.3	83.3	11.5	n.a.	n.a.
Russian Federation	n.a.	n.a.	n.a.	n.a.	n.a.	n.a.	n.a.	14.6	70.0	75.0
Other former USSR	n.a.	n.a.	n.a.	n.a.	n.a.	n.a.	n.a.	5.9	25.0	25.0
Total	109.3	167.4	233.1	199.6	211.2	230.4	147.6	94.3	151.3	167.0
AFRICA										
Algeria	—	—	0.2	0.3	0.1	0.1	—	—	—	—
Cameroon	11.2	22.2	30.0	30.8	18.0	25.1	20.0	17.0	12.3	15.0
Côte d'Ivoire	2.0	27.7	38.0	53.9	75.8	107.8	118.1	110.0	95.0	110.0
Egypt	0.8	1.1	0.7	0.9	1.6	1.3	1.0	1.7	0.3	1.0
Ghana	26.2	48.7	48.0	37.8	19.9	22.9	29.9	23.4	27.1	30.0
Nigeria	—	13.9	27.2	21.4	27.6	17.0	13.1	18.0	20.0	20.0
Sierra Leone	—	—	—	—	—	0.2	1.6	1.0	0.2	—
South Africa	3.5	4.2	5.2	3.7	3.7	3.0	5.3	3.0	3.5	3.5
Other Africa	1.4	1.6	1.1	0.6	1.1	1.4	0.6	1.2	1.8	1.5
Total	45.2	119.4	150.2	149.1	147.8	178.7	189.6	175.3	160.2	181.0

* Note: Data refer to former Czechoslovakia (up to December 1992), former USSR (up to December 1991) and former Socialist Federal Republic of Yugoslavia.

NORTH, CENTRAL AND SOUTH AMERICA

Argentina	7.6	8.1	8.0	2.2	2.1	2.1	4.3	3.5	3.5	3.5
Bolivia	2.1	1.5	1.5	2.2	2.5	2.4	2.4	2.4	2.4	2.4
Brazil	46.6	59.6	91.7	141.0	197.1	230.5	260.0	225.0	225.0	230.0
Canada	15.4	17.6	16.1	11.5	17.8	21.0	25.0	26.0	29.0	35.0
Chile	1.1	1.1	0.7	0.6	0.2	0.3	0.2	0.3	0.2	0.2
Colombia	29.5	37.4	35.4	31.9	38.6	46.2	47.0	44.0	45.0	42.0
Costa Rica	—	—	0.3	3.4	4.1	4.5	4.0	4.7	4.7	4.7
Cuba	2.2	1.6	2.0	2.1	1.7	4.1	3.0	2.5	2.2	2.2
Dominican Republic	15.7	3.5	6.6	6.0	5.8	5.1	5.5	5.5	5.5	5.5
Ecuador	6.0	10.0	16.4	64.4	38.4	37.3	48.4	45.0	38.0	34.0
Guatemala	0.4	0.3	0.3	0.2	0.3	0.3	0.4	0.4	0.4	0.4
Honduras	—	—	0.1	0.1	0.1	0.1	0.1	0.1	0.1	0.1
Jamaica	0.4	0.6	0.4	0.3	0.5	0.6	0.3	0.4	0.4	0.4
Mexico	12.5	19.2	21.1	28.7	31.0	40.2	43.0	35.0	30.0	28.0
Panama	—	—	—	0.1	0.7	0.9	0.8	0.8	1.0	0.9
Peru	2.9	3.2	4.0	3.7	8.3	11.2	13.5	11.0	11.0	11.0
Trinidad and Tobago	0.1	0.1	0.1	0.1	0.1	0.1	0.1	0.1	0.1	0.1
United States	263.2	282.5	258.3	177.4	197.8	236.0	267.9	302.6	324.2	314.0
Uruguay	0.5	0.6	0.6	0.5	0.3	0.2	0.3	0.3	0.3	0.3
Venezuela	8.1	7.4	6.8	6.8	6.9	6.0	7.0	8.0	8.5	8.5
Other Americas	3.3	4.3	4.3	2.6	0.5	0.5	0.6	0.4	0.4	0.4
Total	417.7	458.5	474.8	485.8	554.6	649.6	733.8	718.1	732.0	723.6

Table VII.3 Continued

Country	Five-year average						Annual			
	1961–1965	1966–1970	1971– 1974/75	1975/76– 1979/80	1980/81– 1984/85	1985/86– 1989/90	1990/91	1991/92	1992/93	1993/94 (estimate)
	(thousand tonnes)									
ASIA AND OCEANIA										
Australia	12.8	13.8	15.2	13.1	6.4	0.3	—	—	—	—
China	4.4	2.8	4.9	10.6	13.2	16.0	28.4	30.0	23.5	34.0
India	—	—	0.3	0.9	2.5	5.8	5.9	6.5	6.5	6.2
Indonesia	0.8	1.1	1.9	5.7	10.2	15.2	32.0	35.0	45.0	50.0
Israel	1.0	1.2	1.4	1.3	1.2	1.0	0.7	0.5	0.5	0.6
Japan	25.3	33.7	34.0	25.5	32.1	38.1	40.8	42.3	38.9	40.0
Korea, Republic of	—	—	0.3	0.9	1.6	2.1	3.7	2.9	3.0	3.0
Malaysia	—	—	—	2.8	14.6	43.0	78.0	95.0	98.0	100.0
New Zealand	3.4	3.9	4.1	4.0	4.6	1.6	0.1	0.2	0.2	0.2
Philippines	7.8	8.4	6.9	7.1	11.3	6.9	15.0	12.0	11.0	12.0
Singapore	—	—	1.0	3.2	17.1	40.9	54.5	50.0	45.0	48.0
Sri Lanka	—	—	0.2	1.0	1.9	1.8	1.2	1.4	1.4	1.4
Thailand	—	—	—	0.1	0.1	0.5	3.6	3.8	2.6	3.0
Turkey	1.1	1.1	1.5	1.1	2.9	4.2	5.9	6.5	7.5	8.0
Other Asia and Oceania	1.8	3.7	3.4	0.2	0.2	0.1	0.1	0.1	0.1	0.1
Total	58.3	69.8	75.0	77.6	119.8	177.6	269.9	286.2	283.2	306.5
World total	1166.8	1380.3	1502.0	1450.4	1669.0	2014.9	2330.5	2312.8	2395.2	2480.4
Origin grindings	177.8	271.1	343.7	454.2	518.9	636.6	754.6	708.9	694.5	718.8

Note: Totals may differ from sum of constituents due to rounding.

Index